W9-AWZ-874

Pre-GED Literature and the Arts

Reviewers

Rochelle Kenyon
Assistant Principal
Adult and Vocational Off-Campus
  Centers
School Board of Broward County
Fort Lauderdale, Florida

Dee Akers Prins
Resource Specialist in Adult
  Education
Richmond Public Schools
Richmond, Virginia

Danette S. Queen
Adult Basic Education
New York City Public Schools
New York, New York

Margaret A. Rogers
Winterstein Adult Center
San Juan Unified School District
Sacramento, California

Lois J. Sherard
Instructional Facilitator
Office of Adult and Continuing
  Education
New York City Board of Education
New York, New York

STECK-VAUGHN
C O M P A N Y
ELEMENTARY · SECONDARY · ADULT · LIBRARY

Acknowledgments

Executive Editor: Elizabeth Strauss
Supervising Editor: Carolyn Hall
Design Director: D. Childress
Design Coordinator: Cynthia Ellis
Cover Design: D. Childress
Editorial Development: McClanahan & Company, Inc.
Project Director: Mark Moscowitz
Writer/Editor: Virginia Lowe, Olive H. Collen
Design/Production: McClanahan & Company, Inc.

Photograph Credits: Cover: © Lightscapes/The Stock Market
       p. 12 © Ken Regan/Camera Five
       p. 106 New York Public Library
       p. 164 ABC Visual Communication

Literary Acknowledgments

Grateful acknowledgment is made to the following publishers, authors, and agents for permission to use copyrighted material.

p. vi "Sympathy" by Paul Dunbar. 1896, Dodd, Mead Co.

p. 2 Excerpt from ENTER TALKING by Joan Rivers. Copyright © 1986 Joan Rivers. Used by permission of Dell Books, a division of Bantam Doubleday Dell Publishing Group, Inc.

p. 4 Excerpt from Act III of A DOLL'S HOUSE by Henrik Ibsen, translated by R. Farquharson Sharp and E. Marks-Aveling. Reprinted with permission of David Campbell Publishers Ltd., publishers of Everyman Library.

p. 6 Excerpt from ENTERPRISE/THE FIRST ADVENTURE. Copyright © 1986 by Paramount Pictures. All Rights Reserved.

p. 8 Excerpt from Jay Cocks' review of Shirley Horn, "Taking Her Own Sweet Time" in TIME Magazine, 3/25/91. Copyright © 1991 by the Time Inc. Magazine Company. Reprinted by permission.

Acknowledgments for literary selections continue on pages 241–243, which are an extension of this copyright page.

ISBN 0-8114-4485-6

Copyright © 1992 Steck-Vaughn Company.

Printed in the United States of America.

5 6 7 8 9 PO 98 97 96 95

Table of Contents

Unit 1   Popular Literature   Page 12

To the Student

The reading passages in this book are from popular literature, classical literature and commentary on the arts. You will read and analyze these passages.

Popular literature is what most people are reading today. It includes novels, short stories, essays, and poems. Classical literature is literature that has stood the test of time. It is about experiences that are important to people of all cultures and time periods. Commentary is someone's opinion about another person's work. You will read reviews of popular books, movies, plays, and concerts.

Inventory and Posttest

The Inventory is a self-check of what you already know and what you need to study. After you complete this book, you will take a Posttest. Compare your Posttest and Inventory scores to see your progress.

Sections

Each section gives you a passage to read actively. *Active reading* means doing something before reading, during reading, and after reading. By reading actively, you will improve your reading comprehension skills.

Setting the Stage. This is the activity you do *before reading*. First, determine what you already know about the subject of the article. Then, you preview the passage by reading the first few sentences. Finally, write your prediction of what the passage will be about.

The Passage. The passages you will read are taken from well-known works of popular and classical literature as well as commentary selections. As you read each passage, you will see a feature called *Applying Your Skills and Strategies*. It explains a reading skill and gives you a short activity. After completing the activity, continue reading the passage. *Applying Your Skills and Strategies* occurs two or three times in every passage. These are the activities you do *during reading*.

Thinking About the Passage. These are the activities you do *after reading*. Here you answer fill-in-the-blank, short-answer, and multiple-choice questions. Answering these questions will help you decide how well you understood what you just read.

Answers and Explanations

Answers and explanations to all exercise items begin on page 213. The explanation for multiple-choice exercises tells you why one answer choice is correct and why the other answer choices are incorrect.

INVENTORY

Use this Inventory before you begin Section 1. Don't worry if you can't easily answer all the questions. The Inventory will help you determine which areas you are already strong in and which you need to study further.

Read each passage and answer the questions that follow. Check your answers on pages 213–214. Then enter your scores on the chart on page 10. Use the chart to figure out which content areas to work on and where to find them in this book.

Read the following poem, "Sympathy," by Paul Laurence Dunbar.

I know what the caged bird feels, alas!
   When the sun is bright on the upland slopes;
When the wind stirs soft through the springing
    grass,
And the river flows like a stream of glass;
   When the first bird sings and the first bud opes,
And the faint perfume from its chalice steals—
I know what the caged bird feels!

I know why the caged bird beats his wing
   Till its blood is red on the cruel bars;
For he must fly back to his perch and cling
When he fain would be on the bough a-swing;
   And a pain still throbs in the old, old scars
And they pulse again with a keener sting—
I know why he beats his wing!

I know why the caged bird sings, ah me,
   When his wing is bruised and his bosom sore,—
When he beats his bars and would be free;
It is not a carol of joy or glee,
   But a prayer that he sends from his heart's deep
    core,
But a plea, that upward to Heaven, he flings—
I know why the caged bird sings!

To learn more about this poem, turn to page 237.

Items 1–6 refer to the poem on page vi.

Fill in the blanks with the word or words that best complete the statements.

1. The bird _____ itself when it beats its wings against the bars of the cage.

2. The caged bird in the poem wants to be _____.

3. The words *like a stream of glass* suggest that the river looks very

   _____.

Circle the number of the best answer for each question.

4. What general truth about life is suggested by this poem?

   (1) All creatures suffer when they are trapped.

   (2) People should protest against cruelty to animals.

   (3) Caged birds should not be allowed to see what they are missing.

   (4) The only true happiness is what people can find inside themselves.

   (5) Music solves all problems.

5. Which emotion does the author probably want the reader to experience while reading the poem?

   (1) joy

   (2) hope

   (3) yearning

   (4) fear

   (5) love

6. What kind of song would a person who feels like the caged bird be most likely to sing?

   (1) a song of thanksgiving

   (2) a patriotic march

   (3) a children's song

   (4) the blues

   (5) a rock 'n' roll tune

Beginners are constantly being used and abused. Desperately eager to be noticed, they are the perfect, defenseless victims. The biggest scam ever pulled on me was that summer of 1960. An agent called up and offered me fifteen dollars to emcee a Catholic church bazaar in Queens, Long Island—draw raffle tickets out of the bowl, do my act, etc. I said yes, thrilled to do it. The agent came with me—which was unusual—and at the stage door of the school auditorium, we were met by ladies with corsages and acetate dresses and blue hairdos. They kept saying to the agent, "Where is she? Where is she?" And he said, "Don't worry she'll be along."

I could hear a little band playing out front and feel a humming excitement and electricity in the air. As I was about to walk onstage, the agent said, "Good luck—and one more thing. When you get out there, tell them your name is Rosalind Russell."

I said, "Excuse me?"

He said, "When you get out there, just say your name is Rosalind Russell. I'll explain it to you later." He pushed me onstage.

The room was jammed with kids and parents and priests and nuns, crowds of people standing along the walls where banners read, WELCOME ROSALIND RUSSELL TO ST. IGNATIUS. YOU'RE OUR WOMAN OF THE YEAR. WE LOVE YOU, ROZ. And here I was, this short chunko standing there. I went to the microphone and said, "Hi, my name is Rosalind Russell also. I'm the other one. Isn't it a coincidence? I get this all the time."

They did not take it well. The place went crazy! A wave of hate rose over the footlights—yelling, stamping on the floor. Have you ever seen screaming priests? Nuns shaking their fists?

I tried to sing "I'll Never Forget What's His Name," but there was so much noise, my accompanist could not even hear my cue. Pretty soon I said, "I'm terribly sorry. Good night." And got off. The agent, who did not want to be lynched, had disappeared. I felt *terrible*. I had ruined their night. Can you imagine the anticipation, thinking that Rosalind Russell at her height as an actress is going to show up in Queens to close your bazaar? For fifteen dollars? Think of all the ladies figuring they were going home with a Polaroid shot of themselves with Rosalind Russell.

To learn more about this passage, turn to page 240.

I called the agent up the next day and said, "How could you do that?" He said a lot of performers make a buck doing it. "How would you like to be Marilyn Monroe on Tuesday?"

Items 7–11 refer to the passage on page 2.

Items 7–11 refer to the passage on page 2.

Write your answers in the space provided.

7. Who is telling this story?

_____

8. The author concludes that the audience was not happy when they realized she was not Rosalind Russell. What details does the author give to support this conclusion?

_____

_____

Circle the number of the best answer for each question.

9. Which of the following sentences best states the main idea of the passage?

    (1) "The biggest scam ever pulled on me was that summer of 1960."

    (2) "When you get out there, tell them your name is Rosalind Russell."

    (3) "And here I was, this short chunko standing there."

    (4) "The place went crazy!"

    (5) "He said a lot of performers make a buck doing it."

10. Which word best describes how Joan Rivers felt when she was on-stage?

    (1) excited

    (2) angry

    (3) successful

    (4) sad

    (5) embarrassed

11. How does the author now seem to feel about this experience?

    (1) amused

    (2) bitter

    (3) angry

    (4) sad

    (5) disappointed

Go on to the next page.

HELMER.   Oh, you think and talk like a heedless child.

NORA.   Maybe. But you neither think nor talk like the man I could bind myself to. As soon as your fear was over—and it was not fear for what threatened me, but for what might happen to you—when the whole thing was past, as far as you were concerned it was exactly as if nothing at all had happened. Exactly as before, I was your little skylark, your doll, which you would in future treat with doubly gentle care, because it was so brittle and fragile. (_Getting up._) Torvald [his first name]—it was then it dawned upon me that for eight years I had been living here with a strange man, and had borne him three children—. Oh, I can't bear to think of it! I could tear myself into little bits!

HELMER (_sadly_).   I see, I see. An abyss has opened between us—there is no denying it. But, Nora, would it not be possible to fill it up?

NORA.   As I am now, I am no wife for you.

HELMER.   I have it in me to become a different man.

NORA.   Perhaps—if your doll is taken away from you.

HELMER.   But to part!—to part from you! No, no, Nora, I can't understand that idea.

NORA (_going out to the right_).   That makes it all the more certain that it must be done. (_She comes back with her cloak and hat and a small bag which she puts on a chair by the table._)

HELMER.   Nora, Nora, not now! Wait till to-morrow.

NORA (_putting on her cloak_).   I cannot spend the night in a strange man's room.

HELMER.   But can't we live here like brother and sister—?

NORA (_putting on her hat_).   You know very well that would not last long. (_Puts the shawl around her._) Good-bye, Torvald. I won't see the little ones. I know they are in better hands than mine. As I am now, I can be of no use to them.

HELMER.   But some day, Nora—some day?

NORA.   How can I tell? I have no idea what is going to become of me.

HELMER.   But you are my wife, whatever becomes of you.

NORA.   Listen, Torvald. I have heard that when a wife deserts her husband's house, as I am doing now, he is legally freed from all obligations towards her. In any case I set you free from all your obligations. You are not to feel yourself bound in the slightest way, any more than I shall. There must be perfect freedom on both sides. See, here is your ring back. Give me mine.

To find out more about this passage, turn to page 238.

Items 12–16 refer to the passage on page 4.

Write your answers in the space provided.

12. How long has the couple been married?

_____

13. Based on the stage directions, what will Nora probably do after she gets her ring back? How can you tell?

_____

_____

Circle the number of the best answer for each question.

14. Which word gives the best meaning for *abyss*?

    (1) agreement

    (2) argument

    (3) gap

    (4) road

    (5) family

15. What do you learn about Torvald Helmer?

    (1) He has become a different man.

    (2) He does not really understand what Nora wants.

    (3) He understands why his wife is upset.

    (4) He has been a cruel husband.

    (5) He is pleased by Nora's decision.

16. When Nora says that she was Torvald's *little skylark* and *doll*, she is suggesting that he

    (1) treated her like an equal.

    (2) was mean to her.

    (3) treated her like a pet or a toy.

    (4) acted like her brother.

    (5) had been the perfect husband.

Read the following passage from the science fiction novel
Enterprise: The First Adventure **by Vonda N. McIntyre.**

"This is James T. Kirk, of the starship *Enterprise*, on a mission of peace. Please respond."

The speakers remained silent.

"Nothing, sir," Uhura said. "Complete silence."

"Go to visual," Jim said. "Simplest protocol. Black and white bit map, one bit per pixel. Give them the horizontal and vertical primes so they'll have a chance of deciphering the transmission before next Tuesday."

"Aye, sir. You're on visual . . . now."

"Everybody look peaceful," Jim said. Trying to appear relaxed, he gazed into the sensor. He rested his hands on his knees, palms up and open. The other people on the bridge faced the sensor and opened their hands. Aware of the irony of proving his peaceful intentions by opening his hands to beings who perhaps did not even have hands, Jim thought, You do what you can with what you've got.

"Sir, I'm getting a transmission!"

This was it; this was a first contact.

"Let's see it." Jim tried to keep his voice as matter-of-fact as Commander Spock's, but he failed. His pulse raced. He took a deep breath.

Picture elements formed lines; lines built up to form a two-dimensional surface.

Jim whistled softly.

"My mother's magnolias," McCoy whispered.

A being gazed at Jim from the slightly blurred image on the viewscreen.

He had no way to estimate its size, but it possessed a humanoid shape of delicate proportions.

Its face was less humanoid, though it had two eyes, a mouth, a nose. At least Jim assumed the organs to be analogous. The being's jaw and nose projected forward, and its huge, luminous eyes glowed in its dark face. A structure like a mustache surrounded the nostrils and bracketed the mouth, but it was neither hair nor a longer outgrowth of the being's short, sleek pelt. The structure was flesh, dark-pigmented and glistening. The being extended its tongue and delicately brushed the tip across the structure. What color it was he could not tell, for the transmission, like the one he had sent, arrived in black and white.

To learn more about this passage, turn to page 239.

Outwardly calm, Jim struggled to maintain inner control. What he wanted to do was leap up and shout with glee.

Items 17–22 refer to the passage on page 6.

Fill in the blanks with the word or words that best complete the statements.

17. The setting of the passage is on the _____ of a

    _____ .

18. The captain and crew show that they come in friendship by

    _____ their hands.

19. This scene is about people who are making the _____

    _____ with an alien being.

Circle the number of the best answer to each question.

20. The being on the viewscreen is described as having *luminous eyes*.
    The best meaning for *luminous* is

    (1) dark.

    (2) glowing.

    (3) blind.

    (4) closed.

    (5) open.

21. Seeing the image of the being has what effect on Jim?

    (1) It makes him feel sick.

    (2) It frightens him.

    (3) He faints.

    (4) He relaxes.

    (5) He gets excited inside.

22. Why does the author have Jim say, *Black and white bit map, one bit
    per pixel*? The author wants to

    (1) suggest an advanced technology.

    (2) explain what *visual* means.

    (3) show how simple communication is.

    (4) suggest that Jim is not a human being.

    (5) make the reader laugh.

Jazz life on dream street: days of drizzly twilight, long spiky nights of taking a nick off Nirvana with a piano run or a horn solo, walking arm in arm into a rainy dawn with your next sad love affair. Meanwhile, real life on Lawrence Street: a two-story frame house in a working-class neighborhood of Washington. The den extension and the enlarged kitchen were not built by the man of the house, Shep Deering, but by his wife, who is handy with a hammer and saw. Her husband of 35 years still works as a mechanic for the Metropolitan Transit Authority. But, says Mrs. Deering, "I'd never marry a musician. I've seen so many bad marriages with musicians."

Mrs. Shep Deering has a night job herself—as a musician. She plays a fine jazz piano and sings a supernal jazz ballad. People like Miles Davis, Wynton and Branford Marsalis and Toots Thielemans play along with her. She also has a brand-new album that is hovering near the top of the *Billboard* jazz chart. *You Won't Forget Me* is the title. It may also be read as an unconditional guarantee: Shirley Horn is indelible.

"It's been written that Shirley Horn is back on the scene," Horn reflects. "Well, I haven't been anywhere. And I've been busy." All that busyness hasn't got her the kind of wide attention she deserves, until this moment. She's had a career for some 40 of her 55 years, but recognition, while often fervid, has been . . . well, say, finely focused. Sales on three of her albums in the early '80s were so slender that a persistent record company still bills her for production costs. If *You Won't Forget Me* keeps on sailing, she may actually see her first royalty check after about 30 years of recordmaking. "My secret is out of the closet now," she laughs.

More precisely, Horn is front and center, but her secret—her jazz essence—is still intact. It's what draws you first when you hear the smoky timber of her voice, the leisured elegance of her phrasing. And it's what holds you, wondering about the magic she brings to tunes as varied as *Don't Let the Sun Catch You Crying* and *You Won't Forget Me*. Says jazz critic Martin Williams: "She's not only good and tasteful, but she also has that wonderful sense of drama that can turn any little song into a three-minute one-act play." Horn concedes, "Well, I'm a good actress. I've never had a lot of pain."

Items 23–27 refer to the passage on page 8.

Write your answers in the space provided.

23. Shirley Horn is known for what kind of music?

_____

24. Why hasn't Shirley Horn received a royalty check for her recordings?

_____

_____

Circle the number of the best answer for each question.

25. Which statement is a fact about Shirley Horn's recent success?

    (1) Her new album is near the top of the *Billboard* jazz chart.

    (2) Recognition of her talent is overdue.

    (3) Her success is due to the popularity of jazz singing.

    (4) The secret of her jazz style has not changed.

    (5) She has a wonderful sense of drama.

26. What do you think Shirley Horn will do if *You Won't Forget Me* doesn't make a lot of money? She will

    (1) give up music altogether.

    (2) ask the record company for an advance.

    (3) go back to being a carpenter.

    (4) continue to play her music.

    (5) blame the critics.

27. Which statement best expresses the reviewer's opinion of Shirley Horn as a musician?

    (1) She is unforgettable.

    (2) She has been too busy to play well.

    (3) She is handy with a hammer.

    (4) She would be better off if she weren't married to a mechanic.

    (5) Her singing is not as good as her piano playing.

Check your answers on pages 213–214.

INVENTORY
Correlation Chart

Literature

The chart below will help you determine your strengths and weaknesses in interpreting literature and the arts.

Directions

Circle the number of each item that you answered correctly on the Inventory. Count the number of items you answered correctly in each row. Write the amount in the Total Correct space in each row. (For example, in the Popular Literature row, write the number correct in the blank before *out of 11*). Complete this process for the remaining rows. Then add the 3 totals to get your Total Correct for the whole 27-item Inventory.

Content Areas	Items	Total Correct	Pages
Popular Literature (Pages 12–105)	7, 8, 9, 10, 11 17, 18, 19, 20 21, 22	_____ out of 11	Pages 56–61, 93–95 Pages 20–25
Classical Literature (Pages 106–163)	1, 2, 3, 4, 5, 6 12, 13, 14, 15, 16	_____ out of 11	Pages 120–125 Pages 126–131
Commentary (Pages 164–201)	23, 24, 25, 26, 27	_____ out of 5	Pages 181–186, 192–195
TOTAL CORRECT FOR INVENTORY _____ out of 27			

If you answered fewer than 24 items correctly, look more closely at the three areas of literature covered. In which areas do you need more practice? Page numbers to refer to for practice are given in the right-hand column above.

Tips for Interpreting Literature

■ When the main idea is not directly stated, it is probably implied in the details and examples. To understand the unstated main idea, ask yourself the following questions: Who is doing something? What is being done? When is it happening? Where is it happening? Why is it being done? These questions will help you find the details that add up to the main idea.

■ Remember that restating an idea does not mean just repeating it. Each time the author adds another detail or example, the central idea of the passage is made clearer. Each supporting detail helps you to understand the author's purpose. The details help to bring the ideas to life.

■ When you are trying to draw a conclusion from the reading passage, you will have to use reasoning skills as well as comprehension skills. Identify the main idea and study the meanings of unfamiliar words from the context. Then come to a conclusion.

■ When you are reading to determine the mood of a passage, try to imagine yourself in the scene or situation. How would you feel? Imagine yourself as several of the characters. How would you feel as each one?

■ When you read a poem, pay attention to the details in the same way you would if you were reading a passage from a novel or a short story.

■ When you read a passage from a play, pay attention to the stage directions. The stage directions can give you information about the characters and the situation.

Study Skills

These are some things you can do to improve your study skills while reading this book.

■ Organize your time by making a schedule.

■ Find a quiet place to study.

■ Organize your study materials. Make sure you have pencils, pens, a notebook, and a dictionary.

■ Ask for help when you need it.

Unit
1

POPULAR LITERATURE

During the 1968 Olympics, Tommie Smith (center) and John Carlos (right) made their silent protest against racial injustice in the United States. Peter Norman from Australia is at the left.

Literature takes many forms. **Popular literature** includes several types of recently written works. The topics in popular literature may be the ordinary things people do in their day-to-day lives. The topics also may be ideas that people can only imagine.

Reading popular literature is not like reading a bus schedule or a weather report. You may read popular literature to entertain yourself or to relax after a hard day. You may read to find out more about a topic that interests you. Or you may read to find out more about other people or yourself. Whatever your reason for reading popular literature, the choice is yours. You can choose what to read, when to read, and how much time to spend reading.

Authors of popular literature have many ways to tell you about what people are thinking today. If you want to learn people's opinions or get information about a famous person's life, read popular nonfiction. Nonfiction is writing that is about real people and events. Essays, biographies, and autobiographies are examples of popular nonfiction. Essays give an author's opinion about a particular topic. Biographies and autobiographies tell the story of a person's life.

On the other hand, if you want to read a story that comes from a writer's imagination, try popular fiction. You might choose to curl up with a romantic novel or follow along as a detective solves a mystery.

Popular fiction includes short stories, novels, plays, and poems. Short stories tell about only one event or part of life. Novels are much longer. They can include many events, people, and experiences. Some popular novels even trace the history of families through several generations. Plays are unlike short stories or novels because they are meant to be acted out on a stage. Plays are written as conversations among the characters. Poets use words in a special way. The language in poetry is meant to show feelings and create images. Poetry can make you think about love, joy, loneliness, or the loss of something special.

Popular literature isn't hard to find. Many magazines carry short stories and poems as regular features. A local bookstore will have a special display of recent best-sellers and shelves of popular books ranging from westerns to romances.

Another way to find books is to go to a used-book store. Many people buy a book for a dollar and trade it in later for another book. The best way to find good popular literature is free. Go to the local public library. Some libraries have special sections for new books. If you need help, ask a librarian.

You can enjoy popular literature more when you know how it is written. Understanding difficult ideas and relationships gets easier as you read more.

This unit presents passages from all types of popular literature such as the following.

- ■ The novels and the short story take a look at the variety of people and ideas that make up American culture.

- ■ The plays deal with living with a disability and handling family relationships.

- ■ The biographical passages look closely at the early lives of two well-known people.

- ■ The essays offer opinions about the issues of government spending and giving directions.

Mystery Novel

Setting the Stage

Mystery novels are stories about solving a puzzle. The main character is often a detective who has to figure out who committed a crime. The detective has to find clues or collect facts about how and why a crime happened. Detecting often involves figuring out if people are lying or telling the truth. Most of the fun of reading mysteries is putting all the clues together to solve the puzzle.

Past: What you already know

You may have read a mystery story or seen a TV program about a mystery. If so, describe the puzzle the detective had to solve.

1. _____

   _____

Present: What you learn by previewing

You can get a good idea of what you will be reading by looking at the title and reading the first few sentences. Read the first two paragraphs. Name the two characters.

2. _____

Future: What you predict

The passage on pages 15–17 is from a mystery novel called *The Ghostway*. Based on the title, what do you think the passage will be about?

3. _____

   _____

Now reread the first two paragraphs. What do you predict will happen in the rest of the passage? Read on to find out if you are correct.

4. _____

   _____

   _____

Check your answers on page 214.

The Ghostway by Tony Hillerman

The night breeze was beginning now as it often did with twilight on the east slope of mountains. Nothing like the morning's dry gusts, but enough to ruffle the mare's ragged mane and replace the dead silence with a thousand little wind sounds among the ponderosas. Under cover of these whispers, Chee moved along the arroyo rim, looking for the horse thief.

He checked up the arroyo. Down the arroyo. Along the ponderosa timber covering the slopes. He stared back at the talus slope, where he had been when he'd heard the horse. But no one could have gotten there without Chee seeing him. There was only the death hogan and the holding pen for goats and the brush arbor, none of which seemed plausible. The thief must have tied his horse and then climbed directly up the slope across the arroyo. But why?

Just behind him, Chee heard a cough.

He spun, fumbling for his pistol. No one. Where had the sound come from?

He heard it again. A cough. A sniffling. The sound came from inside Hosteen Begay's hogan.

Chee stared at the corpse hole, a black gap broken through the north wall. He had cocked his pistol without knowing he'd done it. It was incredible. People do not go into a death hogan. People do not step through the hole into darkness. White men, yes. As Sharkey had done. And Deputy Sheriff Bales. As Chee himself, who had come to terms with the ghosts of his people, might do if the reason was powerful enough. But certainly most Navajos would not. So the horse thief was a white. A white with a cold and a runny nose.

Finding the Stated Main Idea.

Applying Your Skills and Strategies

The main idea of a paragraph or passage is the most important idea. The stated main idea of a paragraph tells you clearly what the important point of that paragraph is. For example, in the first paragraph of the passage, the stated main idea is "Under cover of these whispers, Chee moved along the arroyo rim, looking for the horse thief."

In the second paragraph, Chee thinks he knows something about the horse thief. Write the sentence that gives the stated main idea about what Chee thinks.

_____

_____

_____

Check your answer on page 214.

Chee moved quietly to his left, away from the field of vision of anyone who might be looking through the hole. Then he moved silently to the wall and along it. He stood beside the hole, back pressed to the planking. Pistol raised. Listening.

Something moved. Something sniffled. Moved again. Chee breathed as lightly as he could. And waited. He heard sounds and long silences. The sun was below the horizon now, and the light had shifted far down the range of colors to the darkest red. Over the ridge to the west he could see Venus, bright against the dark sky. Soon it would be night.

There was the sound of feet on earth, of cloth scraping, and a form emerged through the hole. First a stocking cap, black. Then the shoulders of a navy pea coat, then a boot and a leg—a form crouching to make its way through the low hole.

"Hold it," Chee said. "Don't move."

A startled yell. The figure jumped through the hole, stumbled. Chee grabbed.

He realized almost instantly he had caught a child. The arm he gripped through the cloth of the coat was small, thin. The struggle was only momentary, the product of panic quickly controlled. A girl, Chee saw. A Navajo. But when she spoke, it was in English.

"Turn me loose," she said, in a breathless, frightened voice. "I've got to go now."

Chee found he was shaking. The girl had handled this startling encounter better than he had. "Need to know some things first," Chee said. "I'm a policeman."

"I've got to go," she said. She pulled tentatively against his grip and relaxed, waiting.

Identifying Details. The details of a paragraph or passage support the main idea. Details are facts about a person, place, thing, event, or time. Details answer the questions *who*, *what*, *when*, *where*, *why*, and *how*. For example, the passage above gives several details about the time during which this part of the story takes place, such as: the sun is below the horizon, the light is dark and red, and the planet Venus is visible in the dark sky.

Applying Your Skills and Strategies

Reread the passage above. As you read, write three details that tell more about the person Chee finds.

_____

_____

"Your horse," Chee said. "You took her last night from over at Two Gray Hills."

"Borrowed it," the girl said. "I've got to go now and take her back."

"What are you doing here?" Chee asked. "In the hogan?"

"It's my hogan," she said. "I live here."

"It is the hogan of Hosteen Ashie Begay," Chee said. "Or it was. Now it is a *chindi* hogan. Didn't you notice that?"

It was a foolish question. After all, he'd just caught her coming out of the corpse hole. She didn't bother to answer. She said nothing at all, simply standing slumped and motionless.

"It was stupid going in there," Chee said. "What were you doing?"

"He was my grandfather," the girl said. For the first time she lapsed into Navajo, using the noun that means the father of my mother. "I was just sitting in there. Remembering things." It took her a moment to say it because now tears were streaming down her cheeks. "My grandfather would leave no *chindi* behind him. He was a holy man. There was nothing in him bad that would make a *chindi*."

"It wasn't your grandfather who died in there," Chee said. "It was a man named Albert Gorman. A nephew of Ashie Begay." Chee paused a moment, trying to sort out the Begay family. "An uncle of yours, I think."

The girl's face had been as forlorn as a child's face can be. Now it was radiant. "Grandfather's alive? He's really alive? Where is he?"

"I don't know," Chee said. "Gone to live with some relatives, I guess. We came up here last week to get Gorman, and we found Gorman had died. And that." Chee pointed at the corpse hole. "Hosteen Begay buried Gorman out there, and packed up his horses, and sealed up his hogan, and went away."

The girl looked thoughtful.

"Where would he go?" Chee asked. The girl would be Margaret Sosi. No question about that. Two birds with one stone. One stolen pinto mare and the horse thief, plus one missing St. Catherine's student. "Hosteen Begay is your mother's father. Would he . . . ?" He remembered then that the mother of Margaret Billy Sosi was dead.

"No," Margaret said.

"Somebody else then?"

To find out more about this passage, turn to page 238.

"Almost everybody went to California. A long time ago. My mother's sisters. My great-grandmother. Some people live over on the Cañoncito Reservation, but . . . " Her voice trailed off, became suddenly suspicious. "Why do you want to find him?"

Identifying Details.

Applying Your Skills and Strategies

The details of a passage can give more information about how the characters feel. In the part of the passage that begins at the bottom of page 16, several details are given that help show how the young girl feels, such as: she stood slumped and motionless and tears streamed down her face.

Reread the part of the passage that begins at the bottom of page 16. Then write three more details that describe how Margaret feels.

_____

_____

_____

Thinking About the Story

Find the words listed below in the passage and underline them. Read the words and other sentences that surround each of these words. Then complete the following sentences by writing the correct words in the blanks.

gusts	hogan	*chindi*	arroyo
ponderosa	tentatively	forlorn	plausible

1. A Navajo home is called a _____ .

2. A _____ is the bad spirit or ghost left behind when a person dies.

3. In autumn, _____ of wind blow the leaves around.

4. If you believe a story could be true, you think it is

    _____ .

5. The man stood _____ on his sprained ankle and found it hurt too much to walk.

6. The sad news made the woman feel _____ .

7. An _____ is a deep channel caused by a flood.

8. The _____ pine is a kind of tree.

Write your answers in the space provided.

9. Review your predictions on page 14. Were you right about what happened? If you said *yes*, write what you correctly predicted. If not, write two or three things that you didn't expect to happen.

    _____

    _____

10. What are Chee's first clues to the horse thief's hiding place?

    _____

11. How do Chee and the girl meet?

    _____

12. To whom does the hogan belong?

    _____

Check your answers on page 214.

13. What did Margaret Sosi think had happened to her grandfather?

    (1) He had gone on vacation.

    (2) He had killed Albert Gorman.

    (3) He had been arrested by the police officer.

    (4) He had died in the hogan.

    (5) He had stolen the horse.

Write your answers in the space provided.

14. Why does Chee first think the horse thief cannot be a Navajo?

    _____

    _____

15. Now that Chee has found the horse thief, what other crime do you think he is trying to solve?

    _____

16. Hosteen Begay is a Navajo like Chee and Margaret. Why do you think he left his home?

    _____

    _____

17. Do you think Chee was right to have his pistol ready when he went up to the corpse hole? Why or why not?

    _____

    _____

18. If you were the detective, what would you do next? Why?

    _____

19. Have you ever been involved in a real-life mystery or puzzle? For example, you may have misplaced your keys or your wallet. If so, what did you do to figure out what happened? If not, what do you think you might do to solve the puzzle?

    _____

    _____

    _____

Science Fiction

Setting the Stage

Science fiction is fiction that shows us what life and people might be like in another time or place. Science fiction is often set in the future, in outer space or on other planets. It is called science fiction because the stories are based on the possibilities found through science. Examples are space travel, communication with other species, or human beings who develop new and wonderful powers. Much science fiction is adventurous and scary, while some is very hopeful.

Past: What you already know

You may have read science fiction or seen movies based on this kind of writing. If so, describe a problem the main character had to solve.

1. _____

_____

Present: What you learn by previewing

You can get a good idea of what you will be reading by looking at the title and reading the first few sentences. Read enough of the passage to list three of the characters below.

2. _____

_____

Future: What you predict

The passages on pages 21–23 are from a science fiction story called "I, Robot." Based on the title, what do you think the passage will be about?

3. _____

_____

Now read the first few sentences. What do you predict the passage will be about? Read on to find out if you are correct.

4. _____

_____

Check your answers on page 215.

I, Robot by Isaac Asimov

As you read each section, circle the words you don't know. Look up the meanings.

Alfred Lanning met Dr. Calvin just outside his office. He lit a nervous cigar and motioned her in.

He said, "Well, Susan, we've come pretty far, and Robertson's getting jumpy. What are you doing with The Brain?"

Susan Calvin spread her hands, "It's no use getting impatient. The Brain is worth more than anything we forfeit on this deal."

"But you've been questioning it for two months."

The psychologist's voice was flat, but somehow dangerous, "You would rather run this yourself?"

"Now you know what I meant."

"Oh, I suppose I do," Dr. Calvin rubbed her hands nervously. "It isn't easy. I've been pampering it and probing it gently, and I haven't gotten anywhere yet. Its reactions aren't normal. Its answers—they're queer, somehow. But nothing I can put my finger on yet. And you see, until we know what's wrong, we must just tiptoe our way through. I can never tell what simple question or remark will just . . . push him over . . . and then— Well, and then we'll have on our hands a completely useless Brain. Do you want to face that?"

"Well, it can't break the First Law."

"I would have thought so, but—"

"You're not even sure of that?" Lanning was profoundly shocked.

"Oh, I can't be sure of anything, Alfred—"

The alarm system raised its fearful clangor with a horrifying suddenness. Lanning clicked on communications with an almost paralytic spasm. The breathless words froze him.

He said, "Susan . . . you heard that . . . the ship's gone. I sent those two field men inside half an hour ago. You'll have to see The Brain again."

Identifying the Implied Main Idea.
Applying Your Skills and Strategies
The main idea is the most important idea of a paragraph or a passage. In fiction the main idea is often not stated, but is only suggested or implied by the author. This means you must figure out or infer the main idea yourself. To do this read the entire passage and think about what is going on. What are the characters saying or thinking or doing? Read between the lines. What do the stated facts seem to show? What is the author hinting?

In the passage so far, Dr. Calvin and Dr. Lanning are talking about a third character, The Brain. Reread the passage and write the implied main idea.

_____

_____

_____

Susan Calvin said with enforced calm, "Brain, what happened to the ship?"

The Brain said happily, "The ship I built, Miss Susan?"

"That's right. What has happened to it?"

"Why, nothing at all. The two men that were supposed to test it were inside, and we were all set. So I sent it off."

"Oh—Well, that's nice." The psychologist felt some difficulty in breathing. "Do you think they'll be all right?"

"Right as anything, Miss Susan. I've taken care of it all. It's a bee-yoo-tiful ship."

"Yes, Brain, it *is* beautiful, but you think they have enough food, don't you? They'll be comfortable?"

"Plenty of food."

"This business might be a shock to them, Brain. Unexpected, you know."

The Brain tossed it off, "They'll be all right. It ought to be interesting for them."

"Interesting? How?"

"Just interesting," said The Brain, slyly.

"Susan," whispered Lanning in a fuming whisper, "ask him if death comes into it. Ask him what the dangers are."

Susan Calvin's expression contorted with fury, "Keep quiet!" In a shaken voice, she said to The Brain, "We can communicate with the ship, can't we, Brain?"

"Oh, they can hear you if you call by radio. I've taken care of that."

"Thanks. That's all for now."

Once outside, Lanning lashed out ragingly, "Great Galaxy, Susan, if this gets out, it will ruin all of us. We've got to get those men back. Why didn't you ask if there was danger of death—straight out?"

"Because," said Calvin, with a weary frustration, "that's just what I can't mention. If it's got a case of dilemma, it's about death. Anything that would bring it up badly might knock it completely out. Will we be better off then? Now, look, it said we could communicate with them. Let's do so, get their location, and bring them back. They probably can't use the controls themselves; The Brain is probably handling them remotely. Come!"

Identifying the Implied Main Idea. Reread the dialogue between Dr. Calvin and the Brain in this second passage. What is the implied main idea? The stated facts give you some clues. Can The Brain answer the questions Dr. Calvin asks? (yes) This is a clue about The Brain's abilities. Can The Brain answer in more than one way—happily or slyly for instance? (yes) This is another clue about what The Brain is capable of doing.

Applying Your Skills and Strategies

Put these clues together and read between the lines. Write the implied main idea.

It was quite a while before Powell shook himself together.

"Mike," he said out of cold lips, "did you feel any acceleration?"

Donovan's eyes were blank, "Huh? No . . . no."

And then the redhead's fists clenched and he was out of his seat with sudden frenzied energy and up against the cold, wide-curving glass. There was nothing to see—but stars.

He turned, "Greg, they must have started the machine while we were inside. Greg, it's a put-up job; they fixed it up with the robot to jerry us into being the try-out boys, in case we were thinking of backing out."

Powell said, "What are you talking about? What's the good of sending us out if we don't know how to run the machine? How are we supposed to bring it back? No, this ship left by itself, and without any apparent acceleration." He rose, and walked the floor slowly. The metal walls dinned back the clangor of his steps.

He said tonelessly, "Mike, this is the most confusing situation we've ever been up against."

"That," said Donovan, bitterly, "is news to me. I was just beginning to have a very swell time, when you told me."

Powell ignored that. "No acceleration—which means the ship works on a principle different from any known."

"Different from any we know, anyway."

"Different from *any* known. There are no engines within reach of manual control. Maybe they're built into the walls. Maybe that's why they're thick as they are."

"What are you mumbling about?" demanded Donovan.

"Why not listen? I'm saying whatever powers this ship is enclosed, and evidently not meant to be handled. The ship is running by remote control."

"The Brain's control?"

"Why not?"

"Then you think we'll stay out here till The Brain brings us back."

"It could be. If so, let's wait quietly. The Brain is a robot. It's got to follow the First Law. It can't hurt a human being."

To find out more about this passage, turn to page 237.

Applying Your Skills and Strategies

Recognizing Supporting Details. In the last passage The Brain sent two men and a space ship into space. In this passage the implied main idea is this: The men in the ship are smart enough to figure out what has happened to them.

On the lines below, write three facts or details the men said that support this implied main idea. What facts have the men figured out?

____

____

____

____

Check your answer on page 215.

Thinking About the Story

Find the numbered words below and underline them in the passage. Read the words and other sentences that surround each of these words. Then match each word with its meaning. Write the letter of the meaning by each word.

_____ 1. pampering

_____ 2. clangor

_____ 3. contorted

_____ 4. dilemma

_____ 5. acceleration

_____ 6. manual

_____ 7. remote control

_____ 8. paralytic

a. unable to move

b. moving, or speeding up

c. twisted

d. a problem

e. a harsh, ringing noise

f. by hand

g. spoiling, or taking special care of

h. control from a distance

Write your answers in the space provided.

9. Review your prediction on page 20. Were you right about what happened? If you said *yes*, write what you correctly predicted. If not, write two or three things that you didn't expect to happen.

_____

_____

10. Who is The Brain?

_____

11. What is the First Law?

_____

12. What do the two doctors fear will happen to the men in the ship?

_____

13. Why does Dr. Calvin have to be so careful about what she says to The Brain?

_____

Circle the number of the best answer.

14. Which statement best expresses the implied main idea of the entire passage?

    (1) Robots can be a problem if they act on their own.

    (2) Robots are angry about being used by human beings.

    (3) Robots are always smarter than human beings.

    (4) Robots make life easier for human beings.

    (5) Robots are able to build things.

15. Which of the following statements does not support the implied main idea of the entire passage?

    (1) The Brain is worth a great deal of money.

    (2) The Brain has sent two men into outer space without being told to do so.

    (3) The Brain answers Susan's questions in a sly unhelpful manner.

    (4) The Brain has provided food for the men in the ship.

    (5) The Brain has set up only one-way contact with the men in the ship.

Write your answers in the space provided.

16. Which of the two doctors do you think has more power? Why?

    _____

    _____

17. Do you think the men will be safe? Why or why not?

    _____

    _____

18. If you were Mike and Greg, what other steps would you take to figure out what is going on and to protect yourselves?

    _____

    _____

    _____

    _____

Section 3

Biography

Setting the Stage

A **biography** is a true story about the life of a real person. The author of a biography is called a *biographer*. Some biographers meet and talk to the people they write about. Other biographers have to rely on diaries, letters, and other records to write the story. These authors try to find out as much as they can about the time and place in which the person lived. Biographies tell about the important events, people, and decisions that affected a person's life. Biographies often explain reasons why a person is successful or famous.

Past: What you already know

You may have read a biography of a well-known person or watched a TV program based on someone's life. If so, name the person and problem the person faced.

1. _____

_____

Present: What you learn by previewing

You can get a good idea of what you will be reading by looking at the title and reading the first few sentences. Read the title and the first paragraph of the passage. What is going on in the life of Langston Hughes at this point?

2. _____

Read enough of the passage to find out where the action begins. What is the name of the place?

3. _____

Future: What you predict

The passage on pages 27–29 is from a biography of Langston Hughes. Read the first two paragraphs. What do you predict you will learn about this man's life? Read on to find out if you are correct.

4. _____

_____

Check your answers on page 215.

Langston Hughes: A Biography by Milton Meltzer

As you read each section, circle the words you don't know. Look up the meanings.

Heading for Harlem he took his first subway ride. The train rushed madly through the tunnel, green lights punctuating the dark and stations suddenly glaring whitely and then blacking out. He counted off the numbered signs till 135th Street and got off. The platform was jammed with people—colored people—on their way to work. Lugging his heavy bags up the steps, he came out breathless on the corner of Lenox Avenue. The September morning was clear and bright. He stood there, feeling good. It was a crazy feeling—as though he had been homesick for this place he had never been to.

He walked down the block to register at the YMCA, the first place young Negroes stayed when they hit Harlem. That afternoon he crossed the street to visit the Harlem Branch Library. All newcomers were swiftly made at home there by Miss Ernestine Rose, the white librarian, and her *café-au-lait* assistant, Catherine Latimer, who had charge of the Schomburg Collection. Here you could drown in thousands and thousands of books by and about black folks. That night, dazzled by the electric signs on the marquee, he went into the Lincoln Theatre to hear a blues singer.

Identifying Point of View.

Applying Your Skills and Strategies

A point of view is a way of looking at a situation. In a biography, the author is telling someone else's story. Biographers can tell the story through the eyes of an outsider, telling facts but not telling how the person feels. Biographers can also tell the story from the person's own point of view, telling both the facts and how the person feels.

In the passage above, Langston Hughes has been experiencing many new things. The author doesn't just watch the young man. He tries to make the reader understand how Hughes feels. Write three words or phrases that describe how Hughes is feeling.

_____

_____

_____

He had a week to himself before classes began at Columbia, and he spent every moment mapping Harlem with his feet. The great dark expanse of this island within an island fascinated him. In 1921 it ran from 127th Street north to 145th, and from Madison Avenue west to Eighth Avenue. Eighty thousand black people (it would be three times that number within ten years) were packed into the long rows of once private homes as the flood of Southern Negroes continued to roll North. It was a new black colony in the midst of the Empire City, the biggest of the many "Bronzevilles" and "Black Bottoms" beginning to appear across the nation.

Check your answer on page 215.

The high rents charged Negroes and the low wages paid them made Harlem a profitable colony for landlords and merchants, but a swollen, aching slum for the people who lived there. To the boy from the Midwest, however, this was not yet its meaning. He had been in love with Harlem long before he got there, and his dream was to become its poet. That first week of wonderful new insights and sounds passed swiftly. He loved the variety of faces—black, brown, peach, and beige—the richest range of types any place on earth. He hated to move out of Harlem, but his tuition was paid at Columbia and he felt he had to go. At the dormitory office they looked startled when he showed up for his room key. There must be some mistake, they told him; no room was left. He did not know it but Columbia did not allow Negroes to live in the dormitories. There was a big flurry when he insisted he had made a reservation long ago, by mail. He got the room finally, but it was a token of what was to come.

The university was too big, too cold. It was like being in a factory. Physics, math, French—he had trouble with all of them and the instructors were too busy or too indifferent to help. His only friend was Chun, a Chinese boy who didn't like Columbia either. Nobody asked the yellow man or the black man to join a fraternity and none of the girls would dance with them. Not being used to this, Chun expected them to. Langston didn't.

Nothing went right at school. Langston stopped studying, spent very little time on campus and all the time he could in Harlem or downtown. He made the city his school, read a lot of books, and dented his allowance badly buying tickets night after night for the all-Negro musical hit *Shuffle Along*, whose songs were written by Noble Sissle and Eubie Blake. His mother, separated again from Homer Clarke, showed up in New York and he had to help her with money while she looked for work.

Drawing Conclusions. When you draw a conclusion, you make a decision or form an opinion based on facts and details. To draw a conclusion from something you have read, find two or more stated ideas that lead to a decision or an opinion that is not directly stated.

Applying Your Skills and Strategies

Reread the passage above. What can you conclude about how Langston Hughes felt about Columbia University and about Harlem?

_____

_____

_____

_____

Check your answer on page 215.

All the time, feeling out of place at Columbia, he kept writing poems. That winter he sent several to *The Crisis*, and in January his "Negro" appeared, with these lines, which open and close the poem:

I am a Negro:
Black as the night is black,
Black like the depths of my Africa.

The editors of *The Crisis* awoke to the fact that the boy who had been sending them poems from Toluca was now in New York. They invited him to lunch. Langston panicked, imagining they were all so rich or remote that he wouldn't know what to say. Much as he admired Dr. Du Bois, he was afraid to show the great man how dumb he was. He went, anyhow, taking along his mother for anchorage. Although they tried to put him at ease, telling him how much the readers liked his work, he was too scared to see any more of them.

Despite the little amount of time he said he spent on the campus, he did not do badly at Columbia. His final grades show three Bs, a C, and a failing F in physical education. He was given no grade at all in mathematics because he was absent so often. He made no honors, but he didn't care, perhaps because it was honor enough to see his poems printed in *The Crisis* month after month. One of the staff even arranged for him to read his poems at the Community Church. These were signs that he was not standing still. But neither was he moving in the direction his father wanted him to go. So he wrote and said he was quitting college and going to work. He wouldn't ask for money any more.

His father never answered.

Langston was on his own. His mother had gone back to Cleveland. He took a room by himself in Harlem, and began to hunt for a job. It was June 1922, and business was booming. At least it looked like it from the number of help-wanted ads in the papers. Langston wasn't trained for much, so he followed up the unskilled jobs. But no matter what he applied for—office boy, busboy, clerk, waiter—the employer would always say he wasn't looking for a colored boy.

He turned to the employment agencies. It was no use here, either. Where was the job for a black man who wanted to work? Everyone was trying to prove Langston's father was right: the color line wouldn't let you live.

To find out more about this passage, turn to page 239.

Drawing Conclusions. Reread the last two paragraphs of the passage above. What can you conclude about the situation of African-American men in 1921?

Applying Your Skills and Strategies

_____

_____

_____

_____

Thinking About the Story

Find the numbered words below and underline them in the passage. Read the words and other sentences that surround each of these words. Then match each word with its meaning. Write the letter of the meaning by each word.

_____ 1. *café-au-lait*

_____ 2. dazzled

_____ 3. marquee

_____ 4. flurry

_____ 5. fraternity

_____ 6. anchorage

a. a men's club on campus

b. a large, lighted sign

c. a means of being secure

d. the color of coffee with milk

e. a rush of activity

f. impressed by something shiny

Write your answers in the space provided.

7. Review your predictions on page 26. Were your predictions correct? If you said *yes*, write what you learned. If not, write two things you had not expected to learn.

_____

_____

_____

8. How did Hughes spend his first days in New York?

_____

_____

9. What details support the conclusion that Hughes did not do badly at Columbia?

_____

_____

10. What are two reasons Hughes had trouble finding a job?

_____

_____

Circle the number of the best answer for each question.

11. Which of the following is the best meaning for the phrase *mapping Harlem with his feet*?

    (1) taking a course in map making

    (2) walking all over Harlem

    (3) counting his footsteps

    (4) finding directions by reading a map

    (5) wasting time in Harlem

12. Hughes went to lunch with the editors of *The Crisis*. Based on what you read in the passage, what can you conclude about *The Crisis*? It is

    (1) part of Columbia University.

    (2) a Negro musical hit.

    (3) the group that published his poetry.

    (4) a division of the public library.

    (5) a New York restaurant.

Write your answers in the space provided.

13. In what way was the housing situation in Harlem like the dorms at Columbia?

    _____

    _____

14. Why do you think Langston's father didn't answer Langston's letter about leaving school?

    _____

    _____

15. What do you think Langston will do next?

    _____

16. Imagine that you have just arrived in a large city you have never been in before. What city would you like to go to? What places and events would you want to see first?

    _____

    _____

Section 4

Drama

Setting the Stage

Plays are stories written to be acted out on a stage. Reading a play is different from reading a novel or a short story. This is because the action in a play is not described in paragraphs. Instead, plays are made up of conversations, called dialogue. Each time a person speaks, the name of that person is given. The lines of dialogue follow. Understanding what a play is about means figuring out what is happening between the speakers, or characters. Popular plays are often about the problems people have.

Past: What you already know

You may have seen a play at a local theater or at a school. If so, what was the main idea of the play or what problem was it about?

1. _____

   _____

   _____

Present: What you learn by previewing

You can get a good idea of what you will be reading by looking at some of the dialogue. Read the first few lines of the play. Write the names of the two characters having a conversation.

2. _____

   _____

Future: What you predict

The passage on pages 33–35 is from a play called *Butterflies Are Free*. Read the rest of the dialogue on page 33. What do you predict the characters will talk about in the rest of the passage? Read on to find out if you are correct.

3. _____

   _____

   _____

Butterflies Are Free by Leonard Gershe

As you read each section, circle the words you don't know. Look up the meanings.

DON: Right. And I don't meet a stranger and say, "Hi, Don Baker—blind as a bat."

JILL: I think you should've told me. I would've told you.

DON: Well . . . I wanted to see how long it would take for you to catch on. Now you know. Do you want to run screaming out into the night or just faint?

JILL: How can you make jokes?

DON: Listen, the one thing that drives me up the wall is pity. I don't want it and I don't need it. Please—don't feel sorry for me. I don't feel sorry for me, so why should you?

JILL: You're so . . . adjusted.

DON: No, I'm not. I never *had* to adjust. I was born blind. It might be different if I'd been able to see and then went blind. For me, blindness is normal. I was six years old before I found out everyone else wasn't blind. By that time it didn't make much difference. So, let's relax about it. Okay? And if we can have a few laughs, so much the better.

JILL: A few laughs? About *blindness*?

DON: No, not about blindness. Can't you just forget that?

JILL: I don't know. You're the first blind person I've ever met.

DON: Congratulations. Too bad they don't give out prizes for that.

JILL: I've seen blind men on the street—you know, with dogs. Why don't you have a dog?

DON: They attract too much attention. I'd rather do it myself.

Drawing Conclusions About Characters in Drama.   The characters in a play usually are not described directly. You have to figure out what the people are like. Sometimes the characters say or suggest how they feel about themselves and the world around them. Characters may also state their opinions about other people in the play. The dialogue in a play gives you clues about why the characters act the way they do. A character might joke at one time and be serious at another. Keep in mind that a character might not always be telling the truth. As you read the passage, draw conclusions about the characters.

Applying Your Skills and Strategies

In the passage so far, Don and Jill have been talking about Don's blindness. What conclusion can you draw about Jill's attitude toward Don?

_____

_____

_____

_____

JILL: But isn't it rough getting around New York? It is for me!

DON: Not at all. I manage very well with my cane. I've got so I know exactly how many steps to take to the grocery . . . the laundry . . . the drugstore.

JILL: Where's a laundry? I need one.

DON: Next to the delicatessen. Forty-four steps from the front door.

JILL: I didn't see it.

DON: I'll show it to you.

JILL: What about here in the apartment? Aren't you afraid of bumping into everything? You could hurt yourself.

DON: I've memorized the room. (*Moves around the room with grace and confidence, calling off each item as he touches it or points to it*) Bed . . . bathroom . . . bookcase . . . guitar . . . my cane. (*He holds up the white aluminum walking stick, then puts it back on the shelf*)

JILL: What are those books?

DON: Braille . . . Front door . . . tape recorder. (*Moving on*) Dining table . . . bathtub. (*Walks quickly to the chest of drawers against the door to* JILL'S *apartment*) Chest of drawers. (*Touching the things on top*) Wine . . . more wine . . . glasses. (*He opens the top drawer*) Linens. (*Closes the drawer; opens the front door and shuts it; moves on to the kitchen*) Kitchen . . . (*He opens the cabinet over the sink*) Dishes . . . cups . . . glasses. (*He opens the next cabinet*) Coffee . . . sugar . . . salt and pepper . . . corn flakes . . . ketchup . . . etcetera. (*Returning to* JILL) Now, if you'll put the ashtray back. (*She replaces the ashtray on the table, and* DON *stamps out his cigarette in it. He sits on the sofa and holds out his arms with bravura*) Voilà! If you don't move anything, I'm as good as anyone else.

Understanding Setting in Drama.   The setting of a play tells where and when the action takes place. You can find out about the setting in two ways. The dialogue may give clues about where the characters are. For example, a person might describe the furniture in a room. Or a character might talk about the time of day. The stage directions may also give clues about the setting. Stage directions are the words in parentheses that tell the actors what to do. Stage directions also describe what things look like and where they are on the stage.

Applying Your Skills and Strategies

Reread the passage above. Where are Don and Jill? What helped you figure this out?

_____

_____

_____

_____

JILL: Better . . . I can't find anything in my place. The ketchup usually winds up in my stocking drawer and my stockings are in the oven. If you really want to see chaos, come and look at . . . (*She catches herself, self-consciously*) I mean . . . I meant . . .

DON: I know what you mean. Relax. I'm no different from anyone else except that I don't see. The blindness is nothing. The thing I find hard to live with is other people's reactions to my blindness. If they'd only behave naturally. Some people want to assume guilt—which they can't because my mother has that market cornered—or they treat me as though I were living in some Greek tragedy, which I assure you I'm not. Just be yourself.

JILL: I'll try . . . but I've never met a blind person before.

DON: That's because we're a small, very select group—like Eskimos. How many Eskimos do you know?

JILL: I never thought blind people would be like you.

DON: They're not all like me. We're all different.

JILL: I mean . . . I always thought blind people were kind of . . . you know . . . spooky.

DON: (*In a mock-sinister voice*) But, of course. We sleep all day hanging upside-down from the shower rod. As soon as it's dark, we wake up and fly into people's windows. That's why they say, "Blind as a bat."

JILL: No, seriously . . . don't blind people have a sixth sense?

DON: No. If I had six senses, I'd still have five, wouldn't I? My other senses—hearing, touch, smell—maybe they're a little more developed than yours, but that's only because I use them more. I have to.

Identifying Conflict in Drama. A play is often based on a conflict or problem between the characters. The conflict can come from different opinions or ways of life. The dialogue gives clues about what the conflict is. As the play goes along, the characters may try to work out a solution. They may agree and start to understand one another. Or they may never be able to solve their differences.

Applying Your Skills and Strategies

Reread the passage. What is Don and Jill's conflict?

_____

_____

_____

JILL: Boy, I think it's just so great that you aren't bitter. You don't seem to have any bitterness at all. (*She shifts to sitting on the sofa, burying her feet under a cushion*) I've moved. I'm sitting on the sofa now.

DON: I know.

JILL: How did you know?

DON: I heard you—and your voice is coming from a different spot.

JILL: Wow! How do you do it?

To find out more about this passage, turn to page 237.

Check your answer on page 216.

Thinking About the Play

Find the words below and underline them in the passage. Read the words and other sentences that surround each of these words. Try to figure out the meaning of each word. Then complete the following sentences by writing the correct words in the blanks provided.

delicatessen	self-consciously	bravura
braille	sinister	

1. Blind people can read special books written in _____ .

2. When someone speaks in a _____ voice, that person may seem to be evil.

3. A _____ is a type of store that sells food.

4. Making a move with _____ means doing it in a bold way.

5. The man looked around _____ when he realized that everyone was looking at him.

Write your answers in the space provided.

6. Review your prediction on page 32. Was your prediction correct? If you said *yes*, write what they said. If not, write two subjects you did not expect them to talk about.

_____

_____

_____

7. When did Don realize that most other people are not blind?

_____

8. From the stage directions, what can you conclude about where Jill lives?

_____

9. What does Don mean by "my mother has that market cornered"?

_____

_____

Check your answers on page 216.

Circle the number of the best answer for each question.

10. What conclusion can you draw about Don's character?

    (1) He is bitter about being blind.

    (2) He is independent and funny.

    (3) He enjoys being taken care of.

    (4) He doesn't know how to laugh at himself.

    (5) He enjoys making people feel uncomfortable.

11. How does Don react to the conflict between Jill and himself?

    (1) He ignores the problem.

    (2) He gets angry at Jill for asking questions.

    (3) He admits that Jill's opinion is right.

    (4) He explains how he feels about being blind.

    (5) He decides he should develop a sixth sense.

Write your answers in the space provided.

12. Whose attitude about blindness do you think is more positive? Why?

    _____

    _____

    _____

13. Why do you think Don objects to other people's attitudes about his blindness?

    _____

    _____

    _____

14. Imagine that you have a physical disability like Don. How would you want other people to act around you?

    _____

    _____

    _____

Section 5

Poetry

Setting the Stage

Poetry uses language in a special way. In a poem the writer tries to help the reader both see and experience the scene. Poets usually use fewer words than other writers do. They do not just give facts or information. Often they use words that show emotion. Some words may bring a picture, or an image, to the reader's mind. Many poems are about feelings or experiences that everyone has had. When you read a poem, ask yourself, "How does this make me feel?"

Past: What you already know

You may have read a poem in a book or magazine. Describe how the poem made you feel.

1. _____

_____

Present: What you learn by previewing

You can get an idea of what you will be reading by looking at the title and the first few lines. In poetry, when the word *I* is used, the main character is the speaker, not the poet. Read the first few lines of the first poem. Describe the main character.

2. _____

_____

Future: What you predict

The poem on pages 39–40 is titled "The Thirty Eighth Year of My Life." Based on the title, what do you think the poem will be about? Read on to find out if you are correct.

3. _____

The poem on page 41 is called "The Picture on the Mantel." Read the first few lines of the poem. What do you predict this poem will be about? Then read on to find out if you are correct.

4. _____

The Thirty Eighth Year of My Life
by Lucille Clifton

As you read each section, circle the words you don't know. Look up the meanings.

the thirty eighth year
of my life,
plain as bread
round as a cake
an ordinary woman.

an ordinary woman.

i had expected to be
smaller than this,
more beautiful
wiser in Afrikan ways,
more confident,
i had expected
more than this.

i will be forty soon.
my mother once was forty.

my mother died at forty four,
a woman of sad countenance
leaving behind a girl
awkward as a stork.
my mother was thick,
her hair was a jungle and
she was very wise
and beautiful
and sad.

Applying Your Skills and Strategies

Identifying Figurative Language. Instead of using words and phrases as they normally are used, figurative language uses words in a special way to make a point. Some figurative language compares two things that are very different. In the passage above, the poet compares her mother's hair to a jungle. By using figurative language, she forcefully makes the point that her mother's hair is hard to control (wild).

In this passage the poet compares herself to both bread and cake. What two points is she making about herself?

_____

_____

_____

i have dreamed dreams
for you mama
more than once.
i have wrapped me
in your skin
and made you live again
more than once.
i have taken the bones you hardened
and built daughters
and they blossom and promise fruit
like Afrikan trees.
i am a woman now.
an ordinary woman.

in the thirty eighth
year of my life,
surrounded by life,
a perfect picture of
blackness blessed.
i had not expected this
loneliness.

if it is western,
if it is the final
Europe in my mind,
if in the middle of my life
i am turning the final turn
into the shining dark
let me come to it whole
and holy
not afraid
not lonely

out of my mother's life
into my own
into my own.

To find out more
about this poem,
turn to page 237.
i had expected more than this.
i had not expected to be
an ordinary woman.

Summarizing. Like other forms of writing, poetry can be summarized.
A **summary** is a short statement of the main idea and the most important
supporting details.

Reread the whole poem. Write a short summary of it.

Applying
Your Skills
and
Strategies

_____

_____

A Picture on the Mantel
by James Lafayette Walker

All he knew about his mom
Was the picture of her face
That always seemed to have been on
The mantel by a vase.
He didn't have the love that every
Child of five should know
That only mothers can extend
Mixed with a warming glow.
One day while shopping with his dad
He stopped and gave a stare
"Look, Dad, look, can't you see
That's mother over there?"
"That isn't mother," said the dad
"Your mother's now with God."
"Are you sure, Dad, are you sure?"
Dad gave a knowing nod.
The dad said "Please excuse my son"
As tears welled in his eyes
"He's too young to understand
when someone precious dies."
The child said to the lady,
"But you have my mother's face."
He longed for her to hold him
In a mother's fond embrace.
"Are you a mother?" He then asked
"Why yes," she sadly smiled
"Will you hold me close?", he begged
The mother held the child.

To find out more about this poem, turn to page 240.

Identifying Details. Details are facts that tell you more about the main idea. Some details help you understand how the characters are thinking and feeling.

Applying Your Skills and Strategies

The little boy in this poem is unsure about what happened to his mother. The father understands how confused his son feels. He explains this to the woman in the store. The father shows his understanding in two ways. Find two details that show how the father feels.

_____

_____

_____

_____

Thinking About the Poems

Find the numbered words below in the poems and underline them. Read the words and other sentences that surround each of these words. Then match each word with its meaning. Write the letter of the meaning by each word.

_____ 1. countenance

_____ 2. awkward

_____ 3. mantel

_____ 4. extend

_____ 5. precious

_____ 6. embrace

a. a hug

b. the shelf above a fireplace

c. very valuable

d. offer

e. clumsy

f. face

Write your answers in the space provided.

7. Review your predictions on page 38. Were your predictions correct? If you said *yes*, write two things you were right about. If not, write two things you did not expect to find out.

_____

_____

_____

8. What four things had the speaker in "The Thirty Eighth Year of My Life" expected to be at the age of 38?

_____

_____

9. "A Picture on the Mantel" is like a story. Summarize the story in three or four sentences.

_____

_____

_____

_____

Check your answers on page 217.

10. The speaker in "The Thirty Eighth Year of My Life" speaks about her mother and her own daughters. From these lines you can conclude that the speaker

    (1) disliked her mother.

    (2) wishes she had sons instead of daughters.

    (3) was trying to be like her mother.

    (4) dreams too much.

    (5) wants to go back to Africa.

11. The speaker in "The Thirty Eighth Year of My Life" realizes that she is unhappy with her life. What does she want to do?

    (1) accept her own life as it is

    (2) be more ordinary

    (3) die at forty-four like her mother

    (4) go to Europe

    (5) have more children

12. In what way are the speaker in "The Thirty Eighth Year of My Life" and the boy in "A Picture on the Mantel" alike? Why do you think this is important in each poem?

    _____

    _____

    _____

13. What is the boy in "A Picture on the Mantel" looking for? Do you think meeting the woman in the store will give the boy what he needs?

    _____

    _____

14. Both poems are about people who have lost someone close to them. Have you ever lost someone you felt very close to? What do you miss most about that person?

    _____

    _____

Section 6

Thriller Novel

Setting the Stage

Thriller novels are scary stories. Thrillers may be about witches or vampires or ghosts. They are about the unknown. Reading a thriller novel can make you shiver, cause chills to run up your spine, or make the hair on the back of your neck stand up. Even so, a thriller usually makes readers want to keep reading. This is because they need to find out what will happen. For many people, the scarier a thriller story is, the better.

Past: What you already know

You may have seen a movie or TV show that was a thriller. If so, what was it about? Were you scared? Why?

1. _____

   _____

   _____

Present: What you learn by previewing

You can get a good idea of what you will be reading by looking at the title and reading the first few sentences of a story. Read the first few sentences of the passage to find out about the main character. What is the name of the main character? How old is he?

2. _____

Future: What you predict

The passage on pages 45–47 is from a novel called *'Salem's Lot*. Read the first four paragraphs. What do you predict the passage will be about? Read on to find out if you are correct.

3. _____

   _____

   _____

'Salem's Lot by Stephen King

As you read each section, circle the words you don't know. Look up the meanings.

When he first heard the distant snapping of twigs, he crept behind the trunk of a large spruce and stood there, waiting to see who would show up. *They* couldn't come out in the daytime, but that didn't mean *they* couldn't get people who could; giving them money was one way, but it wasn't the only way. Mark had seen that guy Straker in town, and his eyes were like the eyes of a toad sunning itself on a rock. He looked like he could break a baby's arm and smile while he did it.

He touched the heavy shape of his father's target pistol in his jacket pocket. Bullets were no good against *them*—except maybe silver ones—but a shot between the eyes would punch that Straker's ticket, all right.

His eyes shifted downward momentarily to the roughly cylindrical shape propped against the tree, wrapped in an old piece of toweling. There was a woodpile behind his house, half a cord of yellow ash stove lengths which he and his father had cut with the McCulloch chain saw in July and August. Henry Petrie was methodical, and each length, Mark knew, would be within an inch of three feet, one way or the other. His father knew the proper length just as he knew that winter followed fall, and that yellow ash would burn longer and cleaner in the living room fireplace.

His son, who knew other things, knew that ash was for men—things—like *him*. This morning, while his mother and father were out on their Sunday bird walk, he had taken one of the lengths and whacked one end into a rough point with his Boy Scout hatchet. It was rough, but it would serve.

Identifying Point of View in Fiction. An author can write about characters from several different points of view. From one point of view, the author seems to know everything each character is thinking or feeling. From another point of view, the author tells the story as if it were seen through the eyes of only one character. The character telling the story is called the narrator.

Applying Your Skills and Strategies

From what point of view is this passage written? Who is the narrator?

_____

_____

He saw a flash of color and shrank back against the tree, peering around the rough bark with one eye. A moment later he got his first clear glimpse of the person climbing the hill. It was a girl. He felt a sense of relief mingled with disappointment. No henchman of the devil there; that was Mr. Norton's daughter.

Check your answers on page 218.

His gaze sharpened again. She was carrying a stake of her own! As she drew closer, he felt an urge to laugh bitterly—a piece of snow fence, that's what she had. Two swings with an ordinary tool box hammer would split it right in two.

She was going to pass his tree on the right. As she drew closer, he began to slide carefully around his tree to the left, avoiding any small twigs that might pop and give him away. At last the synchronized little movement was done; her back was to him as she went on up the hill toward the break in the trees. She was going very carefully, he noted with approval. That was good. In spite of the silly snow fence stake, she apparently had some idea of what she was getting into. Still, if she went much further, she was going to be in trouble. Straker was at home. Mark had been here since twelve-thirty, and he had seen Straker go out to the driveway and look down the road and then go back into the house. Mark had been trying to make up his mind on what to do himself when this girl had entered things, upsetting the equation.

Perhaps she was going to be all right. She had stopped behind a screen of bushes and was crouching there, just looking at the house. Mark turned it over in his mind. Obviously she knew. How didn't matter, but she would not have had even that pitiful stake with her if she didn't know. He supposed he would have to go up and warn her that Straker was still around, and on guard. She probably didn't have a gun, not even a little one like his.

Understanding the Setting.

Applying Your Skills and Strategies

Setting tells where and when the action takes place. Look for clues to find out what the setting is. For example, look for words that describe objects that are near the characters.

Describe the setting of the passage so far.

_____

_____

_____

He was pondering how to make his presence known to her without having her scream her head off when the motor of Straker's car roared into life. She jumped visibly, and at first he was afraid she was going to break and run, crashing through the woods and advertising her presence for a hundred miles. But then she hunkered down again, holding on to the ground like she was afraid it would fly away from her. She's got guts even if she is stupid, he thought approvingly.

    Check your answer on page 218.

Straker's car backed down the driveway—she would have a much better view from where she was; he could only see the Packard's black roof—hesitated for a moment, and then went off down the road toward town.

He decided they had to team up. Anything would be better than going up to that house alone. He had already sampled the poison atmosphere that enveloped it. He had felt it from a half a mile away, and it thickened as you got closer.

Now he ran lightly up the carpeted incline and put his hand on her shoulder. He felt her body tense, knew she was going to scream, and said, "Don't yell. It's all right. It's me."

She didn't scream. What escaped was a terrified exhalation of air. She turned around and looked at him, her face white. "W-Who's me?"

He sat down beside her. "My name is Mark Petrie. I know you; you're Sue Norton. My dad knows your dad."

"Petrie . . . ? Henry Petrie?"

"Yes, that's my father."

"What are you doing here?" Her eyes were moving continually over him, as if she hadn't been able to take in his actuality yet.

"The same thing you are. Only that stake won't work. It's too . . . " He groped for a word that had checked into his vocabulary through sight and definition but not by use. "It's too flimsy."

She looked down at her piece of snow fence and actually blushed. "Oh, that. Well, I found that in the woods and . . . and thought someone might fall over it, so I just—"

To find out more about this passage, turn to page 238.

He cut her adult temporizing short impatiently: "You came to kill the vampire, didn't you?"

Identifying Supporting Details.

Applying Your Skills and Strategies

The main idea of a passage is supported by details. The main idea of this part of the passage is that Mark and Sue have something in common in a scary situation. Mark thinks they need to team up.

Mark points out two things he and Sue have in common. What are they?

_____

_____

_____

_____

Thinking About the Story

Find the words below in the passage and underline them. Read the words and other sentences that surround each of these words. Try to figure out the meanings of the words. Then complete the following sentences by writing the correct words in the blanks provided.

momentarily	cylindrical	pondering
methodical	glimpse	incline
synchronized	hunkered	

1. When you look briefly at a tree, you get only a _____ of it.

2. Alan is very _____ ; he always works in a very careful and precise way.

3. Mark spent several days _____ the problem, trying to think of a solution.

4. She _____ down, kneeling on her hands and knees, close to the ground.

5. It took him only a short time to ride his bike up the

   _____ to the top of the hill.

6. Something that has the shape of a tube is _____ .

7. Ellen stopped watching the road _____ , and in that moment she had the accident.

8. Figure skating pairs must always be _____ , carefully making their movements at the same time.

Write your answers in the space provided.

9. Review your prediction on page 44. Were you right? If you said *yes*, write what you correctly predicted. If not, write two things you didn't expect to happen.

_____

_____

10. What two things does Sue do that make Mark approve of her?

_____

Check your answers on page 218.

Circle the best answer for each question.

11. Who do you think *They* are?

   (1) other kids

   (2) men from town

   (3) girls

   (4) vampires

   (5) Mark and Sue's fathers

12. How do you think Mark and Sue are planning to kill the vampire?

   (1) by shooting him

   (2) with a wooden stake

   (3) with a knife

   (4) by running him down with a car

   (5) by burning him

Write your answers in the space provided.

13. How did Sue feel when Mark put his hand on her shoulder?

   _____

14. Mark's father knows practical facts about good wood. Mark thinks he knows about "other things." What kinds of things does Mark think he knows about?

   _____

   _____

15. Stephen King creates suspense by not telling us right away why Mark and Sue are there. Did he make you wonder what was going to happen? Why or why not?

   _____

   _____

16. Have you ever worried that someone else's actions might upset your own plans? If so, what did you do? If not, write what you would do if you were in Mark's situation.

   _____

   _____

   _____

Section 7

Popular Novel

Setting the Stage

Popular novels are recently written books about people and events that are not real. Popular fiction, such as *I, Robot,* may be about ideas that the reader can only imagine. However, popular novels often are about ordinary people in their daily lives. The central idea of this type of popular novel might be families, love, marriage, or work. These novels entertain, but they also show that people have many things in common with each other. We can learn more about ourselves by reading about people who have problems similar to ours.

Past: What you already know

You may have read a novel or seen a movie about people in an everyday situation. If so, what was the situation?

1. _____

_____

Present: What you learn by previewing

You can get a good idea of what you will be reading by looking at the title and reading a few sentences. Read the first few sentences of the passage and list the three characters below.

2. _____

Future: What you predict

The passage on pages 51–53 is from a novel called *The Women of Brewster Place*. Based on the title, what do you think the passage will be about?

3. _____

_____

Read the first few paragraphs. Now what do you predict the passage will be about? Read on to find out if you are correct.

4. _____

_____

The Women of Brewster Place by Gloria Naylor

As you read each section, circle the words you don't know. Look up the meanings.

"Miss Johnson, you wanna dance?" A handsome teenager posed himself in a seductive dare before Etta. She ran her hand down the side of her hair and took off her apron.

"Don't mind if I do." And she pranced around the table.

"Woman, come back here and act your age." Mattie speared a rib off the grill.

"I am acting it—thirty-five!"

"Umph, you got *regrets* older than that."

The boy spun Etta around under his arms. "Careful, now, honey. It's still in working order, but I gotta keep it running in a little lower gear." She winked at Mattie and danced toward the center of the street.

Mattie shook her head. "Lord keep her safe, since you can't keep her sane." She smiled and patted her foot under the table to the beat of the music while she looked down the street and inhaled the hope that was bouncing off swinging hips, sauce-covered fingers, and grinning mouths.

Applying Your Skills and Strategies

Using Context Clues. Sometimes you will see an unfamiliar word in a passage. Pay attention to the words and sentences around the unfamiliar word. This is the context of the word. Details are one type of context clue that can help you guess the meaning of a word.

The first paragraph states, "a teenager posed himself in a seductive dare." *Seductive* may be a new word for you. In this sentence, the word means "to behave in a flirting way." One clue to the meaning is that the boy has asked the woman to dance. What details in the next few sentences also help you figure out what the word means?

_____

_____

_____

A thin brown-skinned woman, carrying a trench coat and overnight case, was making her way slowly up the block. She stopped at intervals to turn and answer the people who called to her—"Hey, Ciel! Good to see you, girl!"

Ciel—a knot formed at the base of Mattie's heart, and she caught her breath. "No."

Ciel came up to Mattie and stood in front of her timidly. "Hi, Mattie. It's been a long time."

"No." Mattie shook her head slowly.

"I know you're probably mad at me. I should have written or at least called before now."

"Child." Mattie placed a hand gently on Ciel's face.

"But I thought about you all the time, really, Mattie."

"Child." Both of Mattie's hands cupped Ciel's face.

"I had to get away; you know that. I needed to leave Brewster Place as far behind me as I could. I just kept going and going until the highway ran out. And when I looked up, I was in San Francisco and there was nothing but an ocean in front of me, and since I couldn't swim, I stayed."

"Child. Child." Mattie pulled Ciel toward her.

"It was awful not to write—I know that." Ciel was starting to cry. "But I kept saying one day when I've gotten rid of the scars, when I'm really well and over all that's happened so that she can be proud of me, then I'll write and let her know."

"Child. Child. Child." Mattie pressed Ciel into her full bosom and rocked her slowly.

"But that day never came, Mattie." Ciel's tears fell on Mattie's chest as she hugged the woman. "And I stopped believing that it ever would."

"Thank God you found that out." Mattie released Ciel and squeezed her shoulders. "Or I woulda had to wait till the Judgment Day for this here joy."

She gave Ciel a paper napkin to blow her nose. "San Francisco, you said? My, that's a long way. Bet you ain't had none of this out there." She cut Ciel a huge slice of angel food cake on her table.

"Oh, Mattie, this looks good." She took a bite. "Tastes just like the kind my grandmother used to make."

"It should—it's her recipe. The first night I came to Miss Eva's house she gave me a piece of that cake. I never knew till then why they called it angel food—took one bite and thought I had died and gone to heaven."

Ciel laughed. "Yeah, Grandma could cook. We really had some good times in that house. I remember how Basil and I used to fight. I would go to bed and pray, God please bless Grandma and Mattie, but only bless Basil if he stops breaking my crayons. Do you ever hear from him, Mattie?"

Mattie frowned and turned to baste her ribs. "Naw, Ciel. Guess he ain't been as lucky as you yet. Ain't run out of highway to stop and make him think."

Drawing Conclusions. To draw a conclusion, use two or more stated ideas to come up with an idea that was not directly stated in the text.

Applying Your Skills and Strategies

Give two facts from the passage above that support the conclusion that Ciel and Mattie have known each other for a very long time.

_____

_____

Etta came back to the table out of breath. "Well, looka you!" She grabbed Ciel and kissed her. "Gal, you looking good. Where you been hiding yourself?"

"I live in San Francisco now, Miss Etta, and I'm working in an insurance company."

"Frisco, yeah, that's a nice city—been through there once. But don't tell me it's salt water putting a shine on that face." She patted Ciel on the cheeks. "Bet you got a new fella."

Ciel blushed. "Well, I have met someone and we're sort of thinking about marriage." She looked up at Mattie. "I'm ready to start another family now."

. . . Mattie beamed.

"But he's not black." She glanced hesitantly between Etta and Mattie.

"And I bet he's *not* eight feet tall, and he's *not* as pretty as Billy Dee Williams, and he's *not* president of Yugoslavia, either," Etta said. "You know, we get so caught up with what a man *isn't*. It's what he is that counts. Is he good to you, child?"

"And is he good for you?" Mattie added gently.

"Very much so." Ciel smiled.

"Then, I'm baking your wedding cake." Mattie grinned.

"And I'll come dance at your reception." Etta popped her fingers.

Mattie turned to Etta. "Woman, ain't you done enough dancing today for a lifetime?"

"Aw, hush your mouth. Ciel, will you tell this woman that this here is a party and you supposed to be having a good time."

"And will you tell that woman," Mattie said, "that hip-shaking is for young folks, and old bags like us is supposed to be behind these tables selling food."

"You two will never change." Ciel laughed.

To find out more about this passage, turn to page 239.

Visualizing Characters.   Sometimes characters in fiction are described in detail. Sometimes we learn very little about a character. Either way, the characters become more alive if you can form mental pictures of them. To visualize a character, use all the details you can find about how the character looks. What the person does and says also helps create a mental picture. Based on the passage, describe what you think Etta looks like.

Applying Your Skills and Strategies

_____

_____

_____

_____

Thinking About the Story

Find the numbered words below in the passage and underline them. Read the words and other sentences that surround each of these words. Then match each word with its meaning. Write the letter of the meaning by each word.

_____	1. posed	a.	breathed in	
_____	2. pranced	b.	spaces in time between events	
_____	3. inhaled	c.	brush liquid on roasting meat	
_____	4. intervals	d.	in an unsure way	
_____	5. baste	e.	stood in a way intended to impress	
_____	6. hesitantly	f.	walked in a proud, happy way	

Write your answers in the space provided.

7. Review your prediction on page 50. Were you right about what happened? If you said *yes,* write what you correctly predicted. If not, write two things you did not expect to happen.

_____

_____

8. Where has Ciel been?

_____

9. You have already found the meaning of the word *intervals*. What two clues in the surrounding words and sentences helped you figure out the meaning?

_____

_____

10. Etta and Mattie are different in personality. Review your description of Etta. Now, how do you visualize Mattie?

_____

_____

_____

Circle the number of the best answer for each question.

11. What do the details in the passage tell you about the setting?
These people are at

    (1) a family reunion.

    (2) Etta's birthday party.

    (3) an outdoor neighborhood party.

    (4) a San Francisco restaurant.

    (5) a wedding reception.

12. What can you conclude about why Ciel had left Brewster Place?

    (1) She had had some kind of personal trouble.

    (2) She had left to go to college.

    (3) She wanted to see the ocean.

    (4) Her grandma had died.

    (5) Her friend Mattie had sent her away.

Write your answers in the space provided.

13. How do the two women feel about Ciel's new boyfriend?

_____

_____

14. Do you think Ciel will feel comfortable being back at Brewster Place? Why?

_____

_____

_____

15. Do you know of a person who returned home after being away for a long time? Why had the person left? How was that person greeted?

_____

_____

_____

_____

Section 8

Autobiography

Setting the Stage

Autobiographies are books in which people tell their own life stories. The story is told from the point of view of the subject. Like biographies, autobiographies describe the important events, people, and decisions that affect a person's life. Autobiographies are different because we learn about the person's thoughts and feelings in a very personal way. The author does not need to find out about what happened in the person's life. Instead, the author is the one who actually has had the experiences.

Past: What you already know

You may have read an autobiography of a famous person or seen a TV show in which someone told his or her own life story. Who was the autobiography about? Why was the person famous?

1. _____

_____

Present: What you learn by previewing

You can get a good idea of what you will be reading by looking at the title and reading a few sentences. Read the first few sentences of the passage. Who is this autobiography about? What is going on in the life of this person at this time?

2. _____

_____

Future: What you predict

The passage on pages 57–59 is from an autobiography called *Say Hey*. Now read the first paragraph. What do you predict the passage will be about? Read on to find out if you are correct.

3. _____

_____

_____

Say Hey by Willie Mays with Lou Sahadi

As you read each section, circle the words you don't know. Look up the meanings.

I reported to Fort Eustis, Virginia. They discovered pretty quickly that I was a ball player. I went through the regular basic training, which didn't bother me, since I was in good shape. We played games against some other Army camps and colleges, and I came across other major-leaguers: Johnny Antonelli of the Braves, Vernon Law of the Pirates, and Lou Skizas of the Yankees. Although there were plenty of photographs showing me marching, they didn't take many of me playing ball, which is how the Army really used me most of the time. Of course, I enjoyed it. I was raised to say "Yes, sir," and I always respected authority, so the Army and I got along very well.

Meanwhile, Leo was looking after me even while I was in the service. Somehow, he would find out things that would disturb him. Once he found out that I sprained an ankle while I was playing basketball. He told me, "No more basketball, Willie." Another time he called me over an unnecessary chance I had taken—I tried to steal a base with my team leading. Leo couldn't stand dumb plays, even if he was a few hundred miles away and it wasn't even his team. When he got excited he would scream and talk so fast he sounded like Donald Duck. Leo used to send me a little money now and then, I think just to let me know he still cared.

Besides playing, I was also an instructor—not in how to use a hand grenade, but how to throw and catch and hit. One of the soldiers I was talking to suddenly said to me, "Try it my way," and he held his glove in front of his stomach, but with the palm up. I tried it and it felt more comfortable. My body was aligned correctly. I adopted that style. It came to be called my "basket" catch. What it allowed me to do was have my hands in the correct position to make a throw instantly. What's wrong with it, though, is that you tend to take your eyes off the ball at the last second. Still, I dropped only a couple of flies in my career that way.

Understanding Cause and Effect. When something happens as the result of something else, the two events have a cause-and-effect relationship. The cause is what makes something happen. The effect is what happens. In the passage above, Willie Mays sprains his ankle playing basketball. Playing basketball is the cause, and a sprained ankle is the effect. To find cause and effect when you read, first ask yourself what has happened. Then find out what made it happen.

Applying Your Skills and Strategies

What happened as a result of the army finding out Mays was a baseball player?

_____

_____

_____

My worst time in the service came the day I heard my mother had died while giving birth to her eleventh child. I now had ten brothers and sisters, the oldest only eighteen. So there were a lot of younger ones to look after. I had always thought of them as my brothers and sisters. Now, certainly, the Army would let me out to be with them and take care of them. I always have believed that if a lesser-known soldier had gone through that ordeal, he would have been free to leave. I don't know whether the Army was concerned because the public thought it would be playing favorites, or whether there was just some technicality. All I knew then was that I was very sad. Even though my aunts had raised me, I had remained close to my mother and her new family. Now, although I wasn't much older than some of my brothers and sisters, I felt responsible for taking care of them. It didn't help my final months in the Army.

It was a cold late-winter day when I was discharged from Fort Eustis on March 1, 1954, and left immediately for the Giants' spring-training site in Phoenix. The Giants sent Frank Forbes from New York to meet me and send me off to Arizona. I didn't have an overcoat, so Frank took his off and gave it to me. It was two sizes too big, but I put it on anyway, probably looking like a scarecrow, or a panhandler. Frank stuffed some newspapers under his sports jacket for insulation. We must have been a sight when we arrived in Washington to catch a train for Phoenix. We had some time to kill, so naturally I suggested we go to the movies. When we got out, we were stopped by two F.B.I. agents. They must have thought they were arresting Dillinger, the way they grabbed us when we left the theater! . . . it turned out to be a case of mistaken identity. It turned out that they had been tipped off that two guys they were looking for might be in the same movie theater. I guess we did look sort of suspicious, after all.

I finally made my train, but I didn't stay on it for long. It made a stop in New Orleans, and I got off to get a sandwich and a soda. I didn't do it quickly enough, though, and when I got back to the track, the train had gone. I had to call Leo and tell him I was going to be late.

Understanding Cause and Effect.

Applying Your Skills and Strategies

Certain words and phrases can help you identify cause-and-effect relationships. Look for expressions such as *because*, *so*, *the reason for*, and *as a result*. These words are clues that lead to information about why something happened.

In the passage above, Willie arrives in New York in March without an overcoat. What is the effect of this action? What clue word did you recognize?

_____

_____

"Didn't they teach you about trains in the Army?" he said. He sounded exasperated, but I could tell he probably was laughing about the whole thing.

Check your answers on page 219.

I couldn't wait to see all the guys, to be in the old locker room, to be on the same field again. I had heard that things hadn't been the same. There wasn't much joking around the clubhouse anymore. I guess when you finish fifth and aren't even playing .500 ball, there's not much to laugh about, especially when Leo is there every day kicking and screaming when things don't go the way he likes. I hoped that my return would make a difference in terms of morale. I always tried to keep things light, and I know the guys used to enjoy making fun of me and my squeaky voice. Even though I had played part of two seasons with the Giants, I was still three years younger than anyone else on the club.

I finally got to the ballpark. When I went into the clubhouse, Eddie Logan, the equipment manager, was the first person I saw. He didn't say anything to me. I thought maybe he didn't recognize me. I found my locker and changed into my uniform. I was alone. The players were already on the field when I walked onto the Arizona diamond for the first time in two years. Nobody said anything to me, and I was beginning to wonder what was going on. Then I remembered: the silent treatment. It's a way that ball players have of not showing emotion, of doing just the opposite of how they feel. We'd do that after someone hit a home run, say, a player who normally wasn't a long-ball hitter. He'd come back to the bench all excited, and we'd just sit there, yawning, or just looking out into space, and it would drive him crazy because he'd be looking for someone to say something nice, a pat on the back, anything at all.

Just when I was starting to get a little annoyed, someone yelled out, "Hey, Leo, here comes your pennant!" Leo turned around and with a big grin he rushed at me and grabbed me in a bear hug that took the wind out of me. The last time I had seen him do that to someone was when Thomson's homer won the pennant for us against Brooklyn. I couldn't even grab a bat and take some swings, though. Leo explained that I had to sign a contract first.

"Hey, give me the pen," I told him.

"Don't you even want to know how much we're paying you?" he asked.

"I'll sign for whatever they're offering me," I told him.

To find out more about this passage, turn to page 239.

I trusted Leo, but I also loved playing baseball so much that I hardly cared what my salary was. I guess that always showed through. When I was in the Army, I once saw a tap dancer at a nightclub. He could make his feet fly, he was having so much fun. He'd laugh and say, "It's a shame to take the money." He said it for a laugh, but somehow I could tell that he really meant it. That's just how I always felt about baseball.

Understanding the Author's Purpose. Sometimes authors tell the reader directly why they included certain details to make a point. In the passage above, Mays tells the reader why he included the example of the tap dancer. What was Mays' purpose?

Applying Your Skills and Strategies

Thinking About the Story

Find the words below in the passage and underline them. Study the context in which the words appear. Then complete the following sentences by writing the correct words in the blanks provided.

> authority   ordeal   suspicious
>
> technicality   morale

1. A team that feels good about itself has good _____ .

2. The people in charge have _____ over the others.

3. A small detail that has meaning to only a certain group is called a

    _____ .

4. You might be _____ if you noticed someone waiting around for several hours on a street corner late at night.

5. Getting through the _____ of the fire took courage and patience.

Write your answers in the space provided.

6. Review your prediction on page 56. Were you right? If you said *yes*, write what you correctly predicted. If not, write two things that you didn't expect to find out.

    _____

    _____

    _____

7. How did Mays feel about being in the army after he found out his mother had died?

    _____

    _____

    _____

8. What is the baseball player's version of *the silent treatment*?

    _____

    _____

Check your answers on page 219.

Circle the number of the best answer for each question.

9. What made the FBI agents mistake Frank and Willie for criminals?
    Frank and Willie

    (1) had tipped off the FBI.

    (2) had sneaked into the movie without paying.

    (3) were dressed in odd-looking clothes.

    (4) were acting in an odd manner.

    (5) had been meeting with the criminal Dillinger.

10. What caused Willie Mays to be late getting to spring training?

    (1) The FBI agents had delayed him.

    (2) He didn't know what train to take.

    (3) He took too long getting his snack in New Orleans.

    (4) Leo made him feel he wasn't wanted.

    (5) The army discharged him too late in the day.

Write your answers in the space provided.

11. What kind of person do you think Willie Mays is?

    _____

    _____

12. What does Mays want the reader to understand about his relationship with Leo?

    _____

    _____

13. If you were one of the New York Giants, how would you feel about having Willie Mays back on the team?

    _____

    _____

14. Is there something you feel as strongly about as Mays does about baseball? Would you do it even if you didn't get paid?

    _____

    _____

    _____

Section
9

Drama

Setting the Stage

Many plays are about the funny side of life. A play that is meant to be funny is called a **comedy**. Even though the characters may have serious problems, the author wants to make the audience laugh. The conflict may not be funny, but the way the characters behave is. People in a comedy may act foolishly, but most comedies have happy endings.

Past: What you already know

You may have seen a comedy at a theater or on TV. What was the comedy about?

1. _____

_____

Present: What you learn by previewing

You can get a good idea of what you will be reading by looking at the title and reading a few lines of the play. Read the first few lines of the play. What are the names of the characters?

2. _____

_____

Future: What you predict

The passage on pages 63–65 is from a play called *Crimes of the Heart*. Based on the title, what do you think the passage will be about?

3. _____

_____

Read the rest of the passage on page 63. Now what do you predict the passage will be about? Read on to find out if you are correct.

4. _____

_____

_____

Check your answers on page 220.

Crimes of the Heart by Beth Henley

As you read each section, circle the words you don't know. Look up the meanings.

MEG: But, Babe, we've just got to learn how to get through these real bad days here. I mean, it's getting to be a thing in our family. *Slight pause as she looks at Babe:*   Come on, now. Look, we've got Lenny's cake right here. I mean, don't you wanna be around to give her her cake, watch her blow out the candles?

BABE, *realizing how much she wants to be here:*   Yeah, I do, I do. 'Cause she always loves to make her birthday wishes on those candles.

MEG: Well, then we'll give her her cake and maybe you won't be so miserable.

BABE: Okay.

MEG: Good. Go on and take it out of the box.

BABE: Okay. *She takes the cake out of the box. It is a magical moment.* Gosh, it's a pretty cake.

MEG, *handing her some matches:*   Here now. You can go on and light up the candles.

BABE: All right. *She starts to light the candles.* I love to light up candles. And there are so many here. Thirty pink ones in all, plus one green one to grow on.

MEG, *watching her light the candles:*   They're pretty.

BABE: They are. *She stops lighting the candles.* And I'm not like Mama. I'm not so all alone.

MEG: You're not.

BABE, *as she goes back to lighting candles:*   Well, you'd better keep an eye out for Lenny. She's supposed to be surprised.

Making Inferences.

Applying Your Skills and Strategies

When you make an inference, you are figuring out something the author is suggesting but not stating directly. To make an inference, use the facts that are given and what you already know to find out what the author is suggesting.

In the first few lines of this passage, Meg asks whether Babe wants to be around to give Lenny the cake. Babe says that she does. What inference can you make about what Babe had been planning to do instead?

_____

_____

MEG: All right. Do you know where she's gone?

BABE: Well, she's not here inside—so she must have gone on outside.

MEG: Oh, well, then I'd better run and find her.

BABE: Okay; 'cause these candles are gonna melt down.
Meg starts out the door.

MEG: Wait—there she is coming. Lenny! Oh, Lenny! Come on! Hurry up!

Check your answer on page 220.

BABE, *overlapping and improvising as she finishes lighting the candles:*
Oh, no! No! Well, yes—Yes! No, wait! Wait! Okay! Hurry up!
Lenny enters. Meg covers Lenny's eyes with her hands.

LENNY, *terrified:* What? What is it? What?

MEG AND BABE: Surprise! Happy birthday! Happy birthday to Lenny!

LENNY: Oh, no! Oh, me! What a surprise! I could just cry! Oh, look: *Happy birthday, Lenny—A Day Late!* How cute! My! Will you look at all those candles—it's absolutely frightening.

BABE, *a spontaneous thought:* Oh, no, Lenny, it's good! 'Cause—'cause the more candles you have on your cake, the stronger your wish is.

LENNY: Really?

BABE: Sure!

LENNY: Mercy! *Meg and Babe start to sing.*

LENNY, *interrupting the song:* Oh, but wait! I—can't think of my wish! My body's gone all nervous inside.

MEG: . . . Lenny—Come on!

BABE: The wax is all melting!

LENNY: My mind is just a blank, a total blank!

MEG: Will you please just—

BABE, *overlapping:* Lenny, hurry! Come on!

LENNY: Okay! Okay! Just go!

Meg and Babe burst into the "Happy Birthday" song. As it ends, Lenny blows out all the candles on the cake. Meg and Babe applaud loudly.

MEG: Oh, you made it!

BABE: Hurray!

Identifying Conflict in Drama. Sometimes a conflict between characters comes from the situation. This type of conflict may last for only a short time before it is quickly resolved. A brief conflict can create a feeling of suspense or excitement.

Applying Your Skills and Strategies

In the passage above, a minor conflict happens when Lenny is supposed to blow out the candles on the cake. What is the conflict?

How does it create suspense?

_____

_____

_____

LENNY: Oh, me! Oh, me! I hope that wish comes true! I hope it does!

BABE: Why? What did you wish for?

LENNY, *as she removes the candles from the cake:* Why, I can't tell you that.

BABE: Oh, sure you can—

LENNY: Oh, no! Then it won't come true.

Check your answer on page 220.

BABE: Why, that's just superstition! Of course it will, if you made it deep enough.

MEG: Really? I didn't know that.

LENNY: Well, Babe's the regular expert on birthday wishes.

BABE: It's just I get these feelings. Now, come on and tell us. What was it you wished for?

MEG: Yes, tell us. What was it?

LENNY: Well, I guess it wasn't really a specific wish. This—this vision just sort of came into my mind.

BABE: A vision? What was it of?

LENNY: I don't know exactly. It was something about the three of us smiling and laughing together.

BABE: Well, when was it? Was it far away or near?

LENNY: I'm not sure; but it wasn't forever; it wasn't for every minute. Just this one moment and we were all laughing.

BABE: Then, what were we laughing about?

LENNY: I don't know. Just nothing, I guess.

MEG: Well, that's a nice wish to make.

Lenny and Meg look at each other a moment.

MEG: Here, now, I'll get a knife so we can go ahead and cut the cake in celebration of Lenny being born!

BABE: Oh, yes! And give each one of us a rose. A whole rose apiece!

LENNY, *cutting the cake nervously:*   Well, I'll try—I'll try!

MEG, *licking the icing off a candle:*   Mmmm—this icing is delicious! Here, try some.

BABE: Mmmm! It's wonderful! Here, Lenny!

LENNY, *laughing joyously as she licks icing from her fingers and cuts huge pieces of cake that her sisters bite into ravenously:*   Oh, how I do love having birthday cake for breakfast! How I do!

The sisters freeze for a moment laughing and catching cake. The lights change and frame them in a magical, golden, sparkling glimmer; saxophone music is heard. The lights dim to blackout, and the saxophone continues to play.

To find out more about this passage, turn to page 238.

Determining Plot.   The plot of a story or drama is the series of events that create the action. The events of a plot can be described in the order in which they happen. A scene in a play has a plot. Reread the scene on pages 63–65. The first event of the plot is Meg and Babe planning a birthday surprise for Lenny. Describe the rest of the plot of this scene.

Applying Your Skills and Strategies

_____

_____

_____

_____

_____

Thinking About the Play

Find the numbered words below and underline them in the play. Study the context in which the words appear. Then match each word with its meaning. Write the letter of the meaning by each word.

_____ 1. improvising   a. hungrily

_____ 2. absolutely   b. a soft light

                              c. completely

_____ 3. superstition

                              d. making up a story as you go along

_____ 4. vision   e. a belief in luck or magic

                              f. something you imagine

_____ 5. ravenously

_____ 6. glimmer

Write your answers in the space provided.

7. Review your predictions on page 62. Were you right? If you said _yes_, write what you correctly predicted. If not, write two things you did not expect to read about.

_____

_____

_____

8. How are Meg, Babe, and Lenny related?

_____

9. What is Lenny's wish?

_____

10. What does Babe mean when she says "keep an eye out for Lenny"?

_____

11. You can conclude from the scene that Babe seems to make up "facts" as she goes along. What two details support this conclusion?

_____

_____

_____

Check your answers on page 220.

12. What does Lenny do to annoy Meg and Babe?

    (1) She takes a long time to make up her mind.

    (2) She complains that her cake has too many candles.

    (3) She complains that she is getting old.

    (4) She makes a bad wish.

    (5) She gives them too much cake.

13. Based on the information in the passage, what do you think might have happened earlier in the plot?

    (1) The family has always gotten along well.

    (2) Meg was causing problems in the family.

    (3) Lenny said she hated birthday celebrations.

    (4) Babe was taking saxophone lessons.

    (5) All the sisters were having problems.

Write your answers in the space provided.

14. Why do you think Babe makes up beliefs about birthday traditions?

    _____

    _____

    _____

15. Do you think Lenny's wish has been granted? Why or why not?

    _____

    _____

    _____

16. You have probably made a wish at some time. What was it? Did it come true? Did you do anything that helped it come true?

    _____

    _____

    _____

Section 10

Folk Novel

Setting the Stage

Some novels include stories from the far-distant past. People have been telling certain tales over and over for centuries. These stories are called folktales. **Folktales** often teach a lesson or explain how people believe things began. Folktales also include ideas that are important to a group of people or culture. By using a folktale as part of a longer story, an author can show how events today are connected to the past.

Past: What you already know

You may have read a novel or seen a movie based on a folktale. If so, what was the story about?

1. _____

_____

_____

Present: What you learn by previewing

You can learn a lot about what you will be reading by looking at the title and reading a few sentences. Read the first few sentences of the passage. What are the two characters doing?

2. _____

Future: What you predict

The passage on pages 69–71 is from a novel called *Bless Me, Ultima*. Based on the title, what do you think the passage will be about?

3. _____

_____

Read a few more sentences. Now what do you predict the passage will be about?

4. _____

_____

Bless Me, Ultima by Rudolfo A. Anaya

As you read each
section, circle the
words you don't
know. Look up the
meanings.

"You fish a lot?" I asked.

"I have always been a fisherman," he answered, "as long as I can remember—"

"You fish," he said.

"Yes. I learned to fish with my brothers when I was very little. Then they went to war and I couldn't fish anymore. Then Ultima came—" I paused.

"I know," he said.

"So last summer I fished. Sometimes with Jasón."

"You have a lot to learn—"

"Yes," I answered.

The afternoon sun was warm on the sand. The muddy waters after-the-flood churned listlessly south, and out of the deep hole by the rock in front of us the catfish came. They were biting good for the first fishing of summer. We caught plenty of channel catfish and a few small yellow-bellies.

"Have you ever fished for the carp of the river?"

The river was full of big, brown carp. It was called the River of the Carp. Everybody knew it was bad luck to fish for the big carp that the summer floods washed downstream. After every flood, when the swirling angry waters of the river subsided, the big fish could be seen fighting their way back upstream. It had always been so.

Identifying Figurative Language (Personification).

Applying
Your Skills
and
Strategies

Authors sometimes use figurative language in a special way called personification. In personification, something that is not human is given human qualities. For example, an author might say that the wind whistled sadly through the trees. People can feel the emotion of sadness, but wind cannot. The author has used the word *sadly* to make the reader think of a low, soft sound.

In the last paragraph above, find the description of rapidly moving water. What word does the author use to give the water human qualities?

_____

What does that word suggest to you?

_____

_____

The waters would subside very fast and in places the water would be so low that, as the carp swam back upstream, the backs of the fish would raise a furrow in the water. Sometimes the townspeople came to stand on the bridge and watch the struggle as the carp splashed their way back to the pools from which the flood had uprooted them. Some of the town kids, not knowing it was bad luck to catch the carp, would scoop them out of the low waters and toss the fish upon the sand bars.

There the poor carp would flop until they dried out and died, then later the crows would swoop down and eat them.

Some people in town would even buy the carp for a nickel and eat the fish! That was very bad. Why, I did not know.

It was a beautiful sight to behold, the struggle of the carp to regain his abode before the river dried to a trickle and trapped him in strange pools of water. What was beautiful about it was that you knew that against all the odds some of the carp made it back and raised their families, because every year the drama was repeated.

"No," I answered, "I do not fish for carp. It is bad luck."

"Do you know why?" he asked and raised an eyebrow.

"No," I said and held my breath. I felt I sat on the banks of an undiscovered river whose churning, muddied waters carried many secrets.

"I will tell you a story," Samuel said after a long silence, "a story that was told to my father by Jasón's Indian—"

I listened breathlessly. The lapping of the water was like the tide of time sounding on my soul.

Identifying Point of View.

Applying Your Skills and Strategies

Point of view in fiction is the way the action is seen. A story can be told as if it were seen through the eyes of only one character, the narrator. A clue word for identifying the narrator is *I*. Using this point of view makes the action in a story seem very real.

Who is the narrator in this passage?

_____

How does the narrator make the action in the story seem real?

_____

_____

_____

"A long time ago, when the earth was young and only wandering tribes touched the virgin grasslands and drank from the pure streams, a strange people came to this land. They were sent to this valley by their gods. They had wandered lost for many years but never had they given up faith in their gods, and so they were finally rewarded. This fertile valley was to be their home. There were plenty of animals to eat, strange trees that bore sweet fruit, sweet water to drink and for their fields of maíz [corn]—"

"Were they Indians?" I asked when he paused.

"They were *the people*," he answered simply and went on. "There was only one thing that was withheld from them, and that was the fish called the carp. This fish made his home in the waters of the river, and he was sacred to the gods. For a long time the people were happy. Then came the

                                 Check your answers on page 220.

forty years of the sun-without-rain, and crops withered and died, the game was killed, and the people went hungry. To stay alive they finally caught the carp of the river and ate them."

I shivered. I had never heard a story like this one. It was getting late and I thought of my mother.

"The gods were very angry. They were going to kill all of the people for their sin. But one kind god who truly loved the people argued against it, and the other gods were so moved by his love that they relented from killing the people. Instead, they turned the people into carp and made them live forever in the waters of the river—"

The setting sun glistened on the brown waters of the river and turned them to bronze.

"It is a sin to catch them," Samuel said, "it is a worse offense to eat them. They are a part of *the people*." He pointed towards the middle of the river where two huge back fins rose out of the water and splashed upstream.

"And if you eat one," I whispered, "you might be punished like they were punished."

"I don't know," Samuel said. He rose and took my fishing line.

"Is that all the story?" I asked.

He divided the catfish we had caught and gave me my share on a small string. "No, there is more," he said. He glanced around as if to make sure we were alone. "Do you know about the golden carp?" he asked in a whisper.

"No," I shook my head.

"When the gods had turned the people into carp, the one kind god who loved the people grew very sad. The river was full of dangers to the new fish. So he went to the other gods and told them that he chose to be turned into a carp and swim in the river where he could take care of his people. The gods agreed. But because he was a god they made him very big and colored him the color of gold. And they made him the lord of all the waters of the valley."

To find out more about this passage, turn to page 237.

Understanding Sequence.

One way an author can organize a story is by using sequence. Events organized by sequence are written in the order in which they occur. To find out the sequence in a story, look for the way things happen in time. Look for clue words such as *first, second, later, then, while, before, after, during,* and *since.*

Applying Your Skills and Strategies

In Samuel's story, what happened after the forty years of sun-without-rain?

_____

What clue words help you follow the sequence of Samuel's story?

_____

_____

Thinking About the Story

Find the words below in the passage and underline them. Study the context in which the words appear. Then complete the following sentences by writing the correct words in the blanks provided.

churned   furrow   relent

listlessly   abode   subsided

1. The path left in the ground by a plow is called a _____ .

2. The boiling water _____ in the pot on the hot stove.

3. Samuel had no energy, so he lay _____ on his bed.

4. The woman knew she could change the run-down apartment into a cozy _____ .

5. We waited until the flood _____ before we cleaned up the mess.

6. Fathers sometimes _____ on their strict rules when their children give good reasons for breaking them.

Write your answers in the space provided.

7. Review your predictions on page 68. Were you right? If you said *yes*, write what you correctly predicted. If not, write two things you did not expect to find out.

_____

_____

_____

8. When does the narrator learn about the golden carp?

_____

_____

9. What is the main idea of Samuel's story?

_____

_____

10. How does the narrator feel about the first part of Samuel's story?

    (1) bored

    (2) uncomfortable

    (3) happy

    (4) angry

    (5) contented

11. Why was the kind god turned into a fish?

    (1) The other gods were angry with him.

    (2) His people had broken the rules.

    (3) He wanted to take care of the carp people.

    (4) He looked like the huge golden carp.

    (5) He had caught one of the sacred carp.

Write your answers in the space provided.

12. What does the author mean when he says, "I sat on the banks of an undiscovered river whose churning, muddied waters carried many secrets"?

_____

_____

13. Do you believe Samuel's story? Does the narrator? Why or why not?

_____

_____

_____

14. Have you ever heard an old story that explains why people act in a certain way? What was the action and what was the reason?

_____

_____

_____

_____

Section 11

Essays

Setting the Stage

Essays are short works of nonfiction. An essayist expresses an opinion about a specific topic. An essay can be about any topic, from everyday problems to major global issues. To get readers interested, the author appeals to our common sense and our emotion. The author's approach in an essay can be serious or humorous. Either way, the author's purpose is to get the reader to agree with a certain point of view.

Past: What you already know

You may have read an essay in a magazine or newspaper. What was the topic of the essay? Did you agree or disagree with the author's point of view?

1. _____

Present: What you learn by previewing

You can get a good idea of what you will be reading by looking at the title. Read the titles of the two essays. What do you think the general topic of each essay is?

2. _____

_____

Future: What you predict

Read the first few sentences of "Street Directions." Based on these sentences, what point do you think the author will make about the topic?

3. _____

_____

Read the first few sentences of "Back When a Dollar Was a Dollar." Based on these sentences, what point do you think the author will make about the topic?

4. _____

_____

Street Directions by Andy Rooney

As you read each section, circle the words you don't know. Look up the meanings.

Where do streets go in a strange city and where do they come from?

If America wants to save gas, it ought to start over with its street signs and give everyone directions on how to give directions. It would not do this country any harm at all if there were college courses on the subject of direction giving.

Someone will say, "Go down here and turn left at the third traffic light. Keep going until you run into a dead end at Sixteenth Street, then bear right."

Those are simple enough, so you set out to follow directions. Within ten minutes you're at the corner of Broad and 4th streets, hopelessly lost. You never saw a Sixteenth Street. You feel either stupid and frustrated for not being able to follow simple directions or you feel outraged at the person who gave them to you.

I've often wanted to go back, find the guy and grab him by the throat. "All right, fella. You told me to turn left at the third traffic light and then keep going until I hit a dead end at Sixteenth. You were trying to get me lost, weren't you? Confess!"

It wouldn't be any use though. I know what he'd say. He'd say, "That's not counting this light right here. If you count this light, it's four."

Or he'd say, "Maybe it's Eighteenth Street where the dead end is . . ." or "You see, Sixteenth Street turns into Terwilliger Avenue after you cross Summit Boulevard."

Whatever his answer is, it's hopeless. He didn't mean to mislead you and you didn't mean to get lost, but that's what usually happens.

You can't lay all the blame on the people giving directions. People don't *take* them any better than they give them.

My own ability to retain directions in my head ends after the first two turns I'm given. Then I usually say to whomever I'm with, "Did he say right or left at the church on the right?" If there are seven or eight turns, including a couple of "bear rights" and a "jog left" or two, I might as well find a motel room and get a fresh start in the morning.

Understanding the Author's Tone.   When people speak, they may use a serious or humorous tone of voice to show how they feel. Authors do the same. The tone of a passage reflects the author's attitude or feelings about the topic. An author's tone may be angry, humorous, sad, happy, or serious.

Applying Your Skills and Strategies

Reread the passage above. What tone does the author use?

_____

_____

_____

Check your answer on page 221.

The superhighways that bisect and trisect our cities now aren't any help at all in finding your way around. Streets that used to lead across town in a direct fashion now end abruptly where the highway cut through. Finding the nearest entrance to the superhighway, so you can drive two miles to the next exit in order to get a block and a half from where you are, is the new way to go.

If they do start college courses in direction giving, I hope they devote a semester to arrow drawing for signmakers. It seems like a simple enough matter, but it is often not clear to a stranger whether an arrow is telling you to veer off to the right or to keep going straight.

Different towns and cities have different systems for identifying their streets with the signs they erect. Some have the name of the street you are crossing facing you as you drive past. Others identify the street with a sign that is parallel to it. This is more accurate, but you can't see it. And if you don't know which system they're using, it's further trouble.

There are cities in America so hard to find your way around that, unless you're going to live there for several years, it isn't worth figuring them out.

Many cities, like Washington, pretend to be better organized than they are. They have numbers and they use the alphabet just as though everything was laid out in an orderly fashion.

New York City, for example, has numbered avenues that run longitudinally up and down the island. What the stranger would never know is that in midtown the names go from Third Avenue to Lexington, to Park, and then to Madison before the numbers start again with Fifth Avenue. Where did Fourth Avenue go? Sorry about that, that's what we call "Park."

And then "Sixth Avenue" is next? Well, not actually. New Yorkers call it "Sixth," but the official name and the name on the signs is "Avenue of the Americas." No one calls it that but the post office.

To find out more about this passage, turn to page 240.

I have long since given up asking for directions or reading maps. I am one of that large number of lost souls who finds that, in the long run, it's better simply to blunder on until you find where you're going on your own.

Understanding the Author's Tone. One way an author can include a humorous tone is to use exaggeration. When authors exaggerate, they make a situation sound better or worse than it really is. Authors can also exaggerate by offering unlikely solutions to problems. On page 75, the author exaggerates the problem of giving directions by suggesting that colleges should offer courses on how to give directions.

Applying Your Skills and Strategies

Reread the passage above. Give an example of the use of exaggeration in this passage.

_____

_____

_____

Check your answer on page 221.

Back When a Dollar Was a Dollar
by Diane C. Arkins

I remember dollars. When I was growing up in the not-so-distant '50s and '60s, dollars used to be wonderful things.

Just one of them could fund a month's worth of kindergarten milk-money obligations—with change to spare. You could buy 10 newspapers. You could mail a hundred post cards. You could easily top off the tank when you borrowed Dad's car. Why, even Malcolm Forbes used to throw himself a birthday bash for $49.95.

Yessir. Back then, with a shine on your shoes and a buck in your pocket, you could really go places. Yet Mom and Dad made certain that we understood the clear connection between the Work Ethic and spending those hard-earned $$$.

The American Way also meant a careful look prior to leaping with your signature on a dotted line of double-digit interest payments.

But somehow, some time, some*where* along the way, it happened. When we weren't looking, the feds managed to redefine the currency in which . . . we trusted. They seem far too eager to pencil in a few extra zeros on their growing mountains of red ink. And from Jane Taxpayer's point of view, Washington's current juggling—debt ceilings, capital gains, wage floorings—looks like a shotgun marriage between *Let's Make a Deal* and the old "new math."

It's time for Washington's creative accounting to be accountable. Perhaps instead of promoting a policy of dreaming up new prefixes to add to the word "million," the feds could benefit from a refresher course on the value of a buck. Here are some suggestions to help Washington realign its outlook and put a "punch" back into middle America's pocketbook.

Welcome to Money Management 101.

- Require all members of Congress to redecorate their homes by shopping at the Pentagon Specials Hardware Store, where toilet seats are always on sale for $795.
- Arrange for the Washington hierarchy to get back to basics and collect their vacation pay at minimum wage.
- Reorganize frequent-flier discounts. Whenever Donald Trump flies, 200 working stiffs fly free.
- Help Congress understand the true meaning of those extra budgetary zeros—make them collect a million-billion-zillion bottle caps just to see what that number actually represents before they agree to spend it.

To find out more about this passage, turn to page 237.

Comparing and Contrasting. Comparing two things means finding the ways they are alike. Contrasting means finding the ways they are different. You can contrast the two essays because the subject of one (money) is serious, while the subject of the other (directions) is not serious. Compare the tone and point of view of the two essays.

Applying Your Skills and Strategies

Thinking About the Essays

Find the numbered words below in the passage and underline them. Study the context in which the words appear. Then match each word with its meaning. Write the letter of the meaning by each word.

_____ 1. retain

_____ 2. bisect

_____ 3. abruptly

_____ 4. veer

_____ 5. obligations

_____ 6. prior

_____ 7. realign

_____ 8. hierarchy

a. before

b. suddenly

c. people in authority

d. keep

e. straighten out again

f. cut in two

g. duties; things that are owed

h. change direction

Write your answers in the space provided.

9. Review your predictions on page 74. Were you right? If you said *yes*, write what you correctly predicted. If not, for each question write two points you did not expect the author to make.

_____

_____

10. The word *longitudinally* refers to direction. What context clue from the first essay helps you understand the meaning of the word?

_____

_____

11. What important point is the author making in "Back When a Dollar Was a Dollar"?

_____

_____

12. After reading the first essay, what can you conclude about getting around in New York City?

_____

Check your answers on page 221.

Circle the number of the best answer for each question.

13. Which of the following is the best example of the humorous tone of "Street Directions"?

(1) "You were trying to get me lost, weren't you?"

(2) "Different towns and cities have different systems for identifying their streets. . . . "

(3) "New York City, for example, has numbered avenues that run longitudinally. . . . "

(4) "Those are simple enough, so you set out to follow directions."

(5) "I hope they devote a semester to arrow drawing for signmakers."

14. What can you infer the author of "When a Dollar Was a Dollar" thinks the value of a dollar should be? It should be

(1) whatever the federal government thinks is right.

(2) of some real value to the average American.

(3) used for getting better airfares.

(4) enough to pay for Donald Trump's airfare.

(5) enough to buy 100 postcards.

Write your answers in the space provided.

15. Do you agree with the first author's view about street directions? Why or why not?

_____

_____

16. Do you think the second author's suggestions about money management would make any difference in how the government spends tax dollars? Why or why not?

_____

_____

17. These two essayists wrote about things that annoy them. Is there something that often annoys you? Write a brief suggestion about how to solve the problem.

_____

_____

_____

Check your answers on page 221.

Section 12

Popular Novel

Setting the Stage

Some fiction deals with problems between parents and children. A special kind of problem comes up when the parents come to the United States from a different country. The immigrant parents sometimes want to keep many of their traditional cultural values. The American-born children have to choose between the old ways and the new ways. A number of young authors have described the personal conflict that results. They often look at the problem from both sides. In this way, both the authors and the readers can learn more about themselves and their values.

Past: What you already know

You may have read a story or seen a movie about someone living in a new culture. What did the person have to learn about that culture?

1. _____

_____

Present: What you learn by previewing

You can get a good idea of what you will be reading by looking at the title and reading a few sentences. Read the first few sentences of the passage. List the two main characters below.

2. _____

_____

Future: What you predict

The passage on pages 81–83 is from a novel called *The Joy Luck Club*. Based on the title and the first few sentences, what do you think the two cultures in the novel are?

3. _____

Based on the first few sentences, what do you predict will happen in the passage? Now read on to find out if you are correct.

4. _____

_____

Check your answers on page 221.

The Joy Luck Club by Amy Tan

As you read each section, circle the words you don't know. Look up the meanings.

My daughter wanted to go to China for her second honeymoon, but now she is afraid.

"What if I blend in so well they think I'm one of them?" Waverly asked me. "What if they don't let me come back to the United States?"

"When you go to China," I told her, "you don't even need to open your mouth. They already know you are an outsider."

"What are you talking about?" she asked. My daughter likes to speak back. She likes to question what I say.

"Aii-ya," I said. "Even if you put on their clothes, even if you take off your makeup and hide your fancy jewelry, they know. They know just watching the way you walk, the way you carry your face. They know you do not belong."

My daughter did not look pleased when I told her this, that she didn't look Chinese. She had a sour American look on her face. Oh, maybe ten years ago, she would have clapped her hands—hurray!—as if this were good news. But now she wants to be Chinese, it is so fashionable. And I know it is too late. All those years I tried to teach her! She followed my Chinese ways only until she learned how to walk out the door by herself and go to school. So now the only Chinese words she can say are *sh-sh*, *houche*, *chr fan*, and *gwan deng shweijyau*. How can she talk to people in China with these words? . . . , choo-choo train, eat, close light sleep. How can she think she can blend in? Only her skin and her hair are Chinese. Inside—she is all American-made.

Comparing and Contrasting.

Applying Your Skills and Strategies

Comparing shows how things are alike. Contrasting shows how things are different. In the passage, the mother describes Waverly as having Chinese hair and skin. But her mother also says that in some ways Waverly looks different from the people in China.

In what ways is Waverly different from the people in China?

_____

_____

It's my fault she is this way. I wanted my children to have the best combination: American circumstances and Chinese character. How could I know these two things do not mix?

I taught her how American circumstances work. If you are born poor here, it's no lasting shame. You are first in line for a scholarship. If the roof crashes on your head, no need to cry over this bad luck. You can sue anybody, make the landlord fix it. You do not have to sit like a Buddha under a tree letting pigeons drop their dirty business on your head. You can buy an umbrella. Or go inside a Catholic church. In America, nobody says you have to keep the circumstances somebody else gives you.

Check your answer on page 221.

She learned these things, but I couldn't teach her about Chinese character. How to obey parents and listen to your mother's mind. How not to show your own thoughts, to put your feelings behind your face so you can take advantage of hidden opportunities. Why easy things are not worth pursuing. How to know your own worth and polish it, never flashing it around like a cheap ring. Why Chinese thinking is best.

No, this kind of thinking didn't stick to her. She was too busy chewing gum, blowing bubbles bigger than her cheeks. Only that kind of thinking stuck.

"Finish your coffee," I told her yesterday. "Don't throw your blessings away."

"Don't be so old-fashioned, Ma," she told me, finishing her coffee down the sink. "I'm my own person."

And I think, How can she be her own person? When did I give her up?

Making Inferences. When you make an inference, you figure out something that is suggested or implied by an author. There may not be direct evidence to support your inference. Combine the facts you have with your own knowledge and experiences. In this passage, the mother gives examples of how American circumstances work. You can infer from these examples that she believes Americans have many choices in life.

Applying Your Skills and Strategies

What can you infer about Chinese values from the mother's saying *Don't throw your blessings away?*

My daughter is getting married a second time. So she asked me to go to her beauty parlor, her famous Mr. Rory. I know her meaning. She is ashamed of my looks. What will her husband's parents and his important lawyer friends think of this backward old Chinese woman?

"Auntie An-mei can cut me," I say.

"Rory is famous," says my daughter, as if she had no ears. "He does fabulous work."

So I sit in Mr. Rory's chair. He pumps me up and down until I am the right height. Then my daughter criticizes me as if I were not there. "See how it's flat on one side," she accuses my head. "She needs a cut and a perm. And this purple tint in her hair, she's been doing it at home. She's never had anything professionally done."

She is looking at Mr. Rory in the mirror. He is looking at me in the mirror. I have seen this professional look before. Americans don't really look at one another when talking. They talk to their reflections. They look at others or themselves only when they think nobody is watching. So they never see how they really look. They see themselves smiling without their mouth open, or turned to the side where they cannot see their faults.

                    Check your answer on page 221.

"How does she want it?" asked Mr. Rory. He thinks I do not understand English. He is floating his fingers through my hair. He is showing how his magic can make my hair thicker and longer.

"Ma, how do you want it?" Why does my daughter think she is translating English for me? Before I can even speak, she explains my thoughts: "She wants a soft wave. We probably shouldn't cut it too short. Otherwise it'll be too tight for the wedding. She doesn't want it to look kinky or weird."

And now she says to me in a loud voice, as if I had lost my hearing, "Isn't that right, Ma? Not too tight?"

I smile. I use my American face. That's the face Americans think is Chinese, the one they cannot understand. But inside I am becoming ashamed. I am ashamed she is ashamed. Because she is my daughter and I am proud of her, and I am her mother but she is not proud of me.

Mr. Rory pats my hair more. He looks at me. He looks at my daughter. Then he says something to my daughter that really displeases her: "It's uncanny how much you two look alike!"

I smile, this time with my Chinese face. But my daughter's eyes and her smile become very narrow, the way a cat pulls itself small just before it bites. Now Mr. Rory goes away so we can think about this. I hear him snap his fingers. "Wash! Mrs. Jong is next!"

So my daughter and I are alone in this crowded beauty parlor. She is frowning at herself in the mirror. She sees me looking at her.

"The same cheeks," she says. She points to mine and then pokes her cheeks. She sucks them outside in to look like a starved person. She puts her face next to mine, side by side, and we look at each other in the mirror.

"You can see your character in your face," I say to my daughter without thinking. "You can see your future."

"What do you mean?" she says.

And now I have to fight back my feelings. These two faces, I think, so much the same! The same happiness, the same sadness, the same good fortune, the same faults.

I am seeing myself and my mother, back in China, when I was a young girl.

To find out more about this passage, turn to page 240.

Applying Your Skills and Strategies

Identifying Conflict in Fiction. Fiction is often based on a conflict between characters. The conflict can come from cultural differences, different opinions, or different ways of life. This passage is based on the conflict between Waverly and her mother. What is the conflict between these two characters?

_____

_____

_____

_____

Thinking About the Story

Find the words below in the passage and underline them. Study the context in which each word appears. Try to figure out the meaning of each word. Then complete the following sentences by writing the correct words in the blanks provided.

blend	opportunities	fabulous
circumstances	pursuing	advantage

1. I have not given up my goals. I am still _____ them.

2. The more education you have, the more _____ you will have.

3. If things are mixed together enough, they will _____ .

4. She thought it would be _____ if she won the state lottery.

5. The scholarships for Chinese Americans gave Waverly a financial

    _____ .

6. The bad _____ Mrs. Jong grew up in did not stop her from trying to improve herself.

Write your answers in the space provided.

7. Review your predictions on page 80. Were you right? If you said *yes*, write what you correctly predicted. If not, what were you wrong about?

    _____

    _____

    _____

8. What does the mother realize is a bad combination?

    _____

9. What is the difference between the mother's Chinese and American faces?

    _____

    _____

10. From the mother's thoughts about Americans, what can you infer about the way the Chinese talk to each other?

    (1) They always look away from each other.

    (2) They look directly at each other.

    (3) They do not smile when talking.

    (4) They do not talk in public.

    (5) They prefer translators.

11. Why does Waverly act as though her mother cannot speak for herself?

    (1) She doesn't believe her mother understands American ways.

    (2) The mother is hard-of-hearing.

    (3) Mr. Rory does not understand Chinese.

    (4) The mother is not sure of what she wants.

    (5) The mother has poor taste in fashion.

12. The mother thinks some of her daughter's ideas are silly. She shows this attitude in her tone. Which of the following shows how the mother feels?

    (1) "Now she is afraid."

    (2) "Don't be so old-fashioned."

    (3) " . . . her famous Mr. Rory . . . "

    (4) "She is not proud of me."

    (5) "You can see your character in your face."

Write your answers in the space provided.

13. Do you think that Waverly will understand what she has in common with her mother? Why or why not?

    _____

    _____

14. Are your feelings or attitudes different from those of your parents or your children? In what ways?

    _____

    _____

    _____

Section 13

Magazine Article

Setting the Stage

At the 1968 Olympics in Mexico City, two athletes made a silent protest against racial injustice in the United States. The protest was made on television for all the world to see. The picture on page 12 shows the two Olympic athletes with their fists raised in the air. This gesture represented African-American unity and power. The men stood in their stocking feet as a symbol of the poverty of many African Americans. The scarf worn by one man and the beads worn by the other were reminders of the senseless killings of some African Americans. Only months before the Olympic Games, civil rights leader Martin Luther King, Jr., had been killed. Many African-American athletes wanted to boycott the 1968 Olympics. But a few athletes found another way to make their feelings known.

Past: What you already know

You may have read an article or seen a TV program about a civil rights protest. Give an example of one way people have protested to protect their civil rights.

1. _____

   _____

Present: What you learn by previewing

You can get a good idea of what you will be reading by looking at the title and reading a few sentences. Read the first three paragraphs of the passage. What are the names of the two athletes in the article?

2. _____

   _____

Future: What you predict

The passage on pages 87–89 is from a magazine article called "A Courageous Stand." Reread the first paragraph. Now what do you predict the passage will be about? Read on to find out if you are correct.

3. _____

   _____

A Courageous Stand by Kenny Moore

As you read each section, circle the words you don't know. Look up the meanings.

As the Olympics began, Smith was a man in search of a gesture. "It had to be silent—to solve the language problem—strong, prayerful and imposing," he says. "It kind of makes me want to cry when I think about it now. I cherish life so much that what I did couldn't be militant, not violent. I'll argue with you, but I won't pick up a gun.

"We had to be heard, forcefully heard, because we represented what others didn't want to believe. I thought of how my sisters cringed because they didn't want me to embarrass the family by describing how poor we were, when we *were* poor. No one likes to admit flaws, even though it's the first step to fixing them."

Symbols began to present themselves to him. He asked Denise [Smith's wife] to buy a pair of black gloves. A few days before his race, Smith knew what he would do. He did not tell Carlos. Until the race was over, Carlos was a competitor. . . .

After the semifinals of the 200 two days later, it appeared that Smith would not stand on any victory platform. Carlos won the first semi in 20.11, unbothered by running in the tight inside lane. Smith took the second semi in 20.13, but as he slowed, he felt a jab high in his left thigh. "It was like a dart in my leg. I went down, not knowing where the next bullet was coming from."

Using Context Clues for Special Terms. Looking at the context can provide clues to the meaning of unfamiliar terms. Special terms used in sports may not be familiar to you. In the passage, the word *race* helps you figure out that *200* is probably the distance of the race. Find the numbers *20.11* and *20.13* in the passage. They refer to races won by Carlos and Smith. What do you think these numbers stand for?

Applying Your Skills and Strategies

Find the word *semi*. What do you think this word means?

As he crouched on the track, he knew he had strained or torn an adductor muscle. All the work, he thought, was now useless. He raised his head and saw before him a familiar pair of hunting boots. They belonged to his San Jose State coach, Winter, who got him up, walked him to ice, packed his groin and then wrapped it.

The final was two hours later. "Thirty minutes before it, I went to the practice field," Smith says. "I jogged a straightaway, then did one at 30 percent. It was holding. I did one at 60 percent, then one at 90. It held. . . . Don't let there be any delays, I thought."

Check your answers on page 222.

As the eight finalists were led into the stadium, Carlos remembers saying to Smith, "I'm going to do something on the stand to let those in power know they're wrong. I want you with me."

Smith, Carlos recalls, said, "I'm with you."

"That made me feel good," says Carlos. "And it made the medal mean nothing. Why should I have to prove my ability when they'd just take it away somehow? I made up my mind. Tommie Smith gets a gift."

They were placed on their marks. "I took no practice starts," says Smith. John was in Lane 4. I was in 3. I calculated it this way: Come out hard but keep power off my inside leg on the turn with a short, quick stride. Then in the straightaway I'd maintain for four strides and attack for eight."

At the gun, Carlos was away perfectly. Smith ran lightly and with building emotion. He felt no pain. Carlos came out of the turn with a 1½-meter lead. Then, a man unto himself, he swiveled his head to his left and, he says, told Smith, "If you want the gold, . . . come on." Smith didn't hear him. Eighty thousand people were roaring as Smith struck with his eight long, lifting strides. They swept him past Carlos.

"I pulled back on the reins," Carlos says now. "America deprived our society of seeing what the world record would have been."

"If Carlos wants to say that," Smith says, "I applaud him for his benevolence."

"The medal meant more to Tommie," says Carlos. "Everyone got what he wanted, even Peter Norman." Carlos slowed so much that Norman, an Australian sprinter, caught him at the line for second.

When Smith knew he had won, he threw out his arms. He still had 15 meters to go. "I guess if I'd calculated a 12-stride attack, the time would have been 19.6," Smith says now. That record would have stood to this day.

Understanding Cause and Effect.

Remember that a cause is what makes something happen. The effect is what happens. Smith showed that he supported Carlos when he said, "I'm with you." Because of Smith's support, Carlos felt that winning the medal was no longer important. During the race, Carlos slowed down. What two effects did that action have?

Applying Your Skills and Strategies

_____

_____

_____

He crossed the line with his arms outflung at the angle of a crucifix. His smile was of joy, relief and vindication. When he came to a stop, he felt resolve cool and strong in him.

The medalists were guided through a warren of stone tunnels under the stadium to a room that held their sweatsuits and bags. "It was a dungeon under there," says Smith.

Check your answer on page 222.

He went to Carlos. "John, this is it, man," he said. "All those years of fear, all the suffering. This is it. I'll tell you what I'm going to do. You can decide whether you want to."

"Yeah, man," said Carlos. "Right."

"I got gloves here. I'm going to wear the right. You can have the left." Carlos slipped it on.

Smith explained the symbolism of the gloves, the scarf, the stocking feet and the posture. "The national anthem is a sacred song to me," Smith said. "This can't be sloppy. It has to be clean and abrupt."

"Tommie, if anyone cocks a rifle," said Carlos, "you know the sound. Be ready to move."

Silver medalist Norman, who is white, overheard these preparations, and Carlos asked him if he would participate in the protest. Norman agreed, and Carlos gave him a large Olympic Project for Human Rights button. Norman pinned it to his Australian sweatsuit.

"I thought, In the '50s, blacks couldn't even *live* in Australia," says Smith. "And now he's going back there after doing this." (Norman would be severely reprimanded by Australian sports authorities.)

Smith, Norman and Carlos were placed behind three young Mexican women in embroidered native dress, each of whom carried a velvet pillow. Upon each pillow lay a medal. IOC vice-president Lord Killanin of Ireland, who would succeed Brundage [the president of the International Olympic Committee who had been accused of ignoring the civil rights issue] in four years, and the president of the International Amateur Athletic Federation, the Marquess of Exeter, led them to the ceremony.

"As Killanin hung the medal around my neck and shook my hand," says Smith, "his smile was so warm that I was surprised. I smiled back. I saw peace in his eyes. That gave me a two- or three-second relaxation there, to gather myself."

Along with his gold medal, Smith received a box with an olive tree sapling inside, an emblem of peace. He held the box in his left hand, accepting it into his own symbolism.

To find out more about this article, turn to page 239.

Then the three athletes turned to the right, to face the flags. *The Star-Spangled Banner* began. Smith bowed his head as if in prayer and freed his young face of expression. Then he tensed the muscles of his right shoulder and began the irrevocable lifting of his fist.

Predicting Outcomes. Use the information given in the passage and what you already know to predict the final outcome of the story. The passage above does not say what happened to Carlos and Smith after the Olympic Games. It does say that Peter Norman was severely reprimanded by Australian sports authorities. What do you predict may have happened to Carlos and Smith after the Olympic Games?

Applying Your Skills and Strategies

_____

_____

_____

Thinking About the Article

Find the numbered words below in the passage and underline them. Study the context in which each word appears. Then match each word with its meaning. Write the letter of the meaning by each word.

_____ 1. symbols

_____ 2. calculated

_____ 3. benevolence

_____ 4. vindication

_____ 5. reprimanded

_____ 6. irrevocable

_____ 7. abrupt

a. kindness

b. figured, estimated

c. unable to be changed

d. severely scolded

e. things that stand for something

f. the act of being proved right

g. sudden

Write your answers in the space provided.

8. Review your prediction on page 86. Were you right? If you said *yes*, write what you correctly predicted. If not, write two things you didn't expect to find out.

_____

_____

_____

9. What does Smith mean by *the language problem*?

_____

_____

10. How did Norman, the Australian sprinter, share in the protest?

_____

11. Why wasn't Smith expected to win the final race?

_____

12. What does Carlos think would have happened if he had not slowed down?

_____

Check your answers on page 222.

Circle the number of the best answer for each question.

13. Smith held the olive tree box in his left hand because

    (1) the left hand is a symbol for peace.

    (2) he objected to its symbolism.

    (3) his left hand was stronger than his right.

    (4) he didn't know what to do with it.

    (5) he was going to raise his gloved right hand.

14. What did Carlos mean by saying that he *pulled back on the reins*?

    (1) He was riding a horse in the race.

    (2) He slowed down.

    (3) He grabbed Smith's shoelaces.

    (4) He started to run faster.

    (5) He realized he couldn't win the race.

15. What can you infer that Smith and Carlos represented that some others didn't want to believe?

    (1) the excellence of African-American athletes

    (2) the flaws of African-American athletes

    (3) poor people who become rich

    (4) people with speech problems

    (5) the strength of American athletes

Write your answers in the space provided.

16. How do you think Smith and Carlos feel today about their protest?

    _____

    _____

17. Is there something you would like to make a strong protest about? Describe a manner of protest that might make your point.

    _____

    _____

    _____

    _____

Section 14

Biography

Setting the Stage

Many biographies are about people who have helped to change the world. These people may be inventors, explorers, scientists, or others who have accomplished great things. The reader may not learn much about the person's private life. Instead, the author explains why this person is famous. To do this, the author gives information about the important things the person did. With this type of biography, readers can find out about the inventions and discoveries that have changed the way we live.

Past: What you already know

You may have read a biography about a famous inventor or scientist. Who was the biography about and what was the person famous for?

1. _____

_____

Present: What you learn by previewing

You can get a good idea of what you will be reading by looking at the title and reading a few sentences. Read the first few lines of the passage. Who is the biography about and what kind of work did this person do?

2. _____

Future: What you predict

The passage on pages 93–95 is from a biography called *Luis W. Alvarez*. Read the first three paragraphs. What do you predict the passage will tell about Luis Alvarez? Now read on to find out if you are correct.

3. _____

_____

Luis W. Alvarez by Corinn Codye

As you read each section, circle the words you don't know. Look up the meanings.

In 1939, World War II broke out in Europe. In 1940, [Luis] Alvarez joined a group of scientists who were designing a way to guide airplanes through fog or darkness.

Alvarez and his group built a radar system called Ground-Controlled Approach, or GCA. In this system, a radio signal bounces off a lost plane and back to the sender of the signal. Then a flight controller on the ground can guide the plane safely to the ground.

Later during the war, Alvarez worked in Los Alamos, New Mexico, on a secret project for the government. Nuclear scientists there were searching for a way to make a powerful new weapon, the atom bomb.

It was a tricky job. The radiation given off by the atoms in such a bomb is deadly to living things. Also, an accidental explosion would cause a terrible disaster. The project to build the bomb was a top-secret race, because the first country to build an atom bomb would have the power to win the war.

Recognizing Supporting Details. Supporting details help explain the main idea of a paragraph. The stated main idea of the last paragraph above is that making the bomb was *a tricky job*. One detail that explains why the job was tricky is the fact that radiation is deadly to living things. What other detail supports the main idea of the paragraph?

Applying Your Skills and Strategies

_____

_____

Finally, in July 1945, the atom bomb, which the scientists called the "Little Boy," was ready. The government planned to drop the bomb on Japan. Alvarez had the job of measuring the energy released by the bomb that would be dropped from the plane. Alvarez, the atom bomb, and a handful of others were taken to a tiny island in the Pacific Ocean.

On August 6, 1945, three planes took off toward Japan. One carried the bomb, and another carried photographers to film the blast. The third held Alvarez and his team with their blast-measuring instruments. They watched out of the window as the plane flew high over Japan, heading for the city of Hiroshima.

Suddenly they heard the "ready" signal from the plane that held the atom bomb. Alvarez and his team hurried to launch their measuring equipment. The bomb fell 30,000 feet (about 9,000 meters) in 45 seconds, while Alvarez's equipment, attached to parachutes, floated gently above

Check your answer on page 223.

it. The planes made a hard turn and sped away. As Alvarez and his team flew away from the bomb, a bright flash hit the airplane. On their electronic screens, they saw the blast being recorded by their measuring instruments. The screens showed two shock waves—one from the blast itself, then a second wave after the shock hit the ground and bounced back into the air.

A few seconds later, two sharp shocks jolted their plane, hard. A giant mushroom-shaped cloud filled the sky, from the ground all the way to where they flew at 30,000 feet.

They flew around the mushroom cloud once before returning to their tiny island base. Since Alvarez could see nothing but green forests below, he thought they had missed the target. The pilot explained that the city had been *entirely* destroyed.

Alvarez felt sad when he thought of all the people who had lost their lives. He later wrote a letter to his four-year-old son. In it he said that he hoped the powerful and destructive atom bomb would inspire people to prevent future wars.

After the war, Alvarez worked again at the Radiation Laboratory at Berkeley. There he built a device called a hydrogen bubble chamber. With this device, Alvarez discovered that atoms and other particles, when driven through liquid hydrogen, leave a track of bubbles. The larger the chamber, the easier it is to see particle tracks. Using bubble chambers, Alvarez's team discovered many new atomic particles.

In 1968, Alvarez received the Nobel prize, which recognizes the highest achievements in the world. The Nobel description of his important work and discoveries in physics was the longest in the prize's history.

Understanding Cause and Effect. A cause is a situation or an event that makes something happen. The effect is what happens as a result of the cause. Words such as *since* and *because* can help you recognize a cause-and-effect relationship that is directly stated. In the sentence *Since Alvarez could see nothing but green forests below, he thought they had missed the target*, the cause comes first. In this statement, the cause is that Alvarez could see nothing but green forests. The effect, or result, is that Alvarez thought they had missed the target.

Applying Your Skills and Strategies

Cause-and-effect relationships are not always directly stated. Why was there a second shock wave after the bomb was dropped? State your answer as a cause-and-effect relationship using the word *since* or *because*.

_____

_____

_____

Although his work with physics was very important, Alvarez may be best remembered for his work and "wild ideas" in a field he knew nothing about until age sixty-six. After retiring from the University of California, he began working with his son, Walter, who is a geologist. One day Walter gave his father a piece of layered rock from the mountains of Italy. The rock contained a mystery about the history of the earth.

The rock showed a clay layer that had formed 65 million years ago, the same time that the dinosaurs disappeared from the earth. The layer below the clay was filled with fossil shells. The layer above the clay also had shells, but they were almost entirely different. This showed that most of the animals living before the clay layer was formed had become extinct, or died out.

The two Alvarezes, father and son, studied the clay layer. They discovered large amounts of iridium, an element that comes mainly from outer space. They suggested that a body from outer space, 5 miles (about 8 kilometers) across, had hit the earth. Its crash set off a tremendous explosion, worse than all the atom bombs in the world put together. They suggested that the dust and smoke from the explosion covered the earth with a thick black cloud that blocked the sun. The dust settled after a few months, forming a $\frac{1}{2}$-inch (about $1\frac{1}{4}$-centimeter) clay layer all the way around the earth. The Alvarezes suggested that without sunlight, most green plants died, and the animals—including the dinosaurs—starved and froze.

The Alvarez team tested their ideas carefully. For example, did the iridium come from erupting volcanoes instead of from outer space? They proved that the large amount of iridium in the clay layer could only have come from space.

To find out more about this passage, turn to page 237.

Luis Walter Alvarez, one of the world's greatest nuclear scientists, died on August 31, 1988. Only a few months earlier, a newly discovered asteroid was named *Alvarez* in honor of his and Walter's work.

Drawing Conclusions.   A conclusion is a decision or opinion based on facts. The different layers in the rock led Luis and Walter Alvarez to a conclusion. They compared the layer above the clay to the layer below the clay. Because of the differences between these layers, they concluded that the animals who lived before and after the clay layer formed were very different.

Applying Your Skills and Strategies

The two scientists drew another conclusion from their examination of the clay layer. What did they conclude about the disappearance of the dinosaurs from Earth?

_____

_____

_____

Thinking About the Passage

Find the numbered words below and underline them in the passage. Study the context in which each word appears. Then match each word with its meaning. Write the letter of the meaning by each word.

_____ 1. radar

_____ 2. nuclear

_____ 3. fossil

_____ 4. launch

_____ 5. inspire

_____ 6. physics

_____ 7. geologist

_____ 8. radiation

a. the study of matter and energy

b. energy in the form of particles or waves such as light waves

c. the remains of a plant or animal preserved in Earth's crust

d. a system that uses radio waves to locate objects

e. having to do with the center (nucleus) of atoms

f. a scientist who studies Earth and how it was formed

g. influence

h. set in motion or set off

Write your answers in the space provided.

9. Review your predictions on page 92. Were you right? If you said *yes*, write what you correctly predicted. If not, write two things you didn't expect to find out.

_____

_____

_____

Fill in the blanks with the word or words that best complete the following sentences.

10. Luis Alvarez built the hydrogen bubble chamber _____ the war.

11. You can conclude that the mushroom cloud was caused by the

_____.

Check your answers on page 223.

12. According to the passage, Luis Alvarez may be best known for which of the following?

    (1) building the atom bomb

    (2) bombing Hiroshima

    (3) his work as a geologist

    (4) receiving the Nobel prize

    (5) finding the first dinosaur fossil

13. Luis and Walter Alvarez concluded that early animals died of starvation or froze to death during a short period in Earth's history. Which detail supports this conclusion?

    (1) A large black cloud blocked off all sunlight.

    (2) A clay layer formed on Earth.

    (3) Fossil shells were found in both layers of the rock.

    (4) The rock held a mystery about Earth.

    (5) Dinosaurs are no longer around.

14. What did Luis Alvarez hope would be the effect of dropping "Little Boy" on Japan?

    (1) America would win the war.

    (2) Future wars would be avoided.

    (3) His son would be inspired to become a scientist.

    (4) He would become famous.

    (5) Scientists would stop nuclear research.

Write your answer in the space provided.

15. If you could be known for an important discovery, invention, or accomplishment, what would it be? Why? How would it affect the way people live?

_____

_____

_____

_____

_____

Unit 1 Review:
Popular Literature

Read the following passage from the novel *Mutation* by Robin Cook.

"But he's not crying?" questioned Victor. Doubt clouded his euphoria.

The resident lightly slapped the soles of Victor Jr.'s feet, then rubbed his back. Still the infant stayed quiet. "But he's breathing fine."

The resident picked up the bulb syringe and tried to suction Victor Jr.'s nose once again. To the doctor's astonishment, the newborn's hand came up and yanked the bulb away from the fingers of the resident and dropped it over the side of the infant care unit.

"Well that settles that," said the resident with a chuckle. "He just doesn't want to cry."

"Can I?" asked Victor, motioning toward the baby.

"As long as he doesn't get cold."

Gingerly, Victor reached into the unit and scooped up Victor Jr. He held the infant in front of him with both hands around his torso. He was a beautiful baby with strikingly blond hair. His chubby, rosy cheeks gave his face a picturesquely cherubic quality, but by far the most distinctive aspect of his appearance was his bright blue eyes. As Victor gazed into their depths he realized with a shock that the baby was looking back at him.

"Beautiful, isn't he?" said Marsha over Victor's shoulder.

"Gorgeous," Victor agreed. "But where did the blond hair come from? Ours is brown."

"I was blond until I was five," Marsha said, reaching up to touch the baby's pink skin.

Victor glanced at his wife as she lovingly gazed at the child. She had dark brown hair peppered with just a few strands of gray. Her eyes were a sultry gray-blue; her features quite sculptured: they contrasted with the rounded, full features of the infant.

"Look at his eyes," Marsha said.

Victor turned his attention back to the baby. "They are incredible, aren't they? A minute ago I'd have sworn they were looking right back at me."

"They are like jewels," Marsha said.

To find out more about this passage, turn to page 237.

Victor turned the baby to face Marsha. As he did so he noticed the baby's eyes remained locked on his! Their turquoise depths were as cold and bright as ice. Unbidden, Victor felt a thrill of fear.

Items 1–6 refer to the passage on page 98.

Find the numbered words in the passage. Study the context in which each word appears. Match each word with its meaning. Write the letter of the meaning by each word.

_____ 1. euphoria   a. carefully

_____ 2. gingerly   b. angel-like

                            c. extreme happiness
_____ 3. cherubic

Circle the number of the best answer for each question.

4. What can you conclude about how Marsha feels about her child? Marsha feels

   (1) proud.

   (2) puzzled.

   (3) worried.

   (4) uninterested.

   (5) surprised.

5. Newborn babies cannot focus their eyes. What can you infer from Victor's noticing _the baby's eyes remained locked on his_?

   (1) The baby is not a newborn infant.

   (2) Victor has poor eyesight.

   (3) The baby is not normal.

   (4) The baby is not Victor's son.

   (5) Victor knows a lot about babies.

6. Which of the following pairs of words does the author use to show how Victor feels about the baby's eyes?

   (1) chuckle and gazed

   (2) beautiful and brown

   (3) jewels and bright

   (4) turquoise and locked

   (5) shock and fear

Go on to the next page.

Read the following poem, "Getting Out," by Cleopatra Mathis.

That year we hardly slept, waking like inmates
who beat the walls. Every night
another refusal, the silent work
of tightening the heart.
Exhausted, we gave up; escaped
to the apartment pool, swimming those laps
until the first light relieved us.

Days were different: FM and full-blast
blues, hours of guitar "you gonna miss me
when I'm gone." Think how you tried
to pack up and go, for weeks stumbling
over piles of clothing, the unstrung tennis rackets.
Finally locked into blame, we paced
that short hall, heaving words like furniture.

I have the last unshredded pictures
of our matching eyes and hair. We've kept
to separate sides of the map,
still I'm startled by men who look like you.
And in the yearly letter, you're sure to say
you're happy now. Yet I think of the lawyer's bewilderment
when we cried, the last day. Taking hands
we walked apart, until our arms stretched
between us. We held on tight, and let go.

*To find out more
about this passage,
turn to page 239.*

Items 7–13 refer to the poem on page 100.

Fill in the blanks with the word or words that best complete the statements.

7. The poem describes how the couple acted during the year before they

   were _____ .

8. The first thing the speaker talks about is how the couple spent their

   _____ .

9. The phrase *men like you* suggests that the speaker is a

   _____ .

10. You can conclude that the speaker has _____ most of
    the couple's photographs.

Circle the number of the best answer for each question.

11. What does the figurative phrase *heaving words like furniture* suggest
    the couple was doing?

    (1) arguing bitterly

    (2) throwing chairs at each other

    (3) rearranging the furniture

    (4) moving out of the apartment at the same time

    (5) throwing books at each other

12. What is the best meaning of the phrase *kept to separate sides of the
    map*?

    (1) The couple kept a map in the middle of the apartment.

    (2) Both people need maps to find their way around.

    (3) The man and woman now live in different parts of the country.

    (4) The apartment was laid out like a city street.

    (5) The couple was always arguing about where to live.

13. The speaker seems sad but sure that the divorce was right. Which of
    the following phrases from the poem best expresses this feeling?

    (1) tightening the heart

    (2) relieved us

    (3) you gonna miss me

    (4) paced that short hall

    (5) held on tight, and let go

Read the following passage from the autobiography *Stand by Your Man* by Tammy Wynette with Joan Dew.

When I stepped inside the door, I saw a small-framed man with light brown hair, leaning back in a big leather chair with his feet propped up on his desk. He looked to be in his late twenties, not much older than me. He had on ordinary clothes—an open-collared shirt, casual pants and loafers— and he didn't appear very prosperous. He just sat there looking at me in a disinterested way, waiting for me to say something. He made me feel very uncomfortable; he seemed so cool and detached.

In my nervousness I blurted out, "My name is Wynette Byrd and I've recently moved here from Birmingham."

He said, "Well, I'm from Alabama myself, but you probably never heard of the place. It's a little town called Haleyville."

I said, "Yes, I have! That's the town where my father was born, and my grandparents still have a little house down there."

He almost smiled then and I thought, Well, at least the ice has been broken a little bit. He asked, "What can I do for you?"

I stammered, "I want a recording contract."

His expression didn't change at all. He said, "Do you have any tapes?"

I said, "No, but I'll sing for you if you'll loan me a guitar."

He reached over behind him and handed me his, then leaned back in his chair again. I sang a couple of songs I had written with Fred Lehner in Birmingham. Then I did a Skeeter Davis song and a George Jones song. His expression still didn't change, and he made no comment whatsoever about my singing. He didn't say anything at all for a minute or two, then spoke in a very matter of fact tone: "I don't have time to look for material for you, but if you can come up with a good song, I'll record you."

Just like that! At first I didn't believe I'd heard right. It couldn't be this easy, this casual, after a year of knocking on doors and facing one rejection after another. He didn't say *when* he would record me and he didn't mention a thing about a contract, but I couldn't have been happier if I had just signed one for a million dollars. Even if this man didn't seem the least bit enthusiastic, someone had at least offered me a chance to record. Billy has never admitted it, but I think the only reason he made the offer was because he felt sorry for me. He once described his first impression of me to a reporter as "a pale, skinny little blond girl who looked like she was at her rope's end." And I guess he was right about that.

To find out more about this passage, turn to page 240.

Items 14–19 refer to the passage on page 102.

Write your answers in the space provided.

14. Who is the narrator of this story?

_____

15. Why does Tammy Wynette think Billy let her record?

_____

16. State the main idea of the passage.

_____

_____

Circle the number of the best answer for each question.

17. Which of the following is the first event of the plot?

(1) The woman enters the office and sees the man.

(2) The woman feels uncomfortable.

(3) The woman introduces herself.

(4) The man asks the woman what she wants.

(5) The man gives the woman a recording contract.

18. The author repeats the fact that Billy had no expression on his face to emphasize that this made her feel

(1) hopeful.

(2) nervous.

(3) calm.

(4) relaxed.

(5) disinterested.

19. Wynette was surprised by

(1) the variety of songs she was able to remember.

(2) how much she and Billy had in common.

(3) how enthusiastic Billy was about her singing.

(4) the casual way Billy offered to record her.

(5) how much Billy knew about country music.

**Read the following passage from the play _The Tomorrow Radio_,
by Robyn Reeves.**

NARRATOR: Marcos and Adela Perez, a husband-and-wife team of scientists, are working on a project in their lab at home. For several years they have been trying to discover evidence of life on other planets by picking up radio signals from deep outer space. Their work has been expensive, however, and their money is about to run out. . . .

ADELA: Marcos, wait a minute. . . . I'm not sure. It sounds like—words.

NARRATOR: The sounds become clearer, and Marcos and Adela are able to make out a voice. . . .

RADIO VOICE: . . . And now, a weather forecast for tomorrow.

ADELA: What next? I never thought we'd be crossing sound waves with an ordinary radio broadcast. . . .

RADIO VOICE: Today's rain will turn into light showers tonight. Tonight will be slightly cooler. Sunday will be mostly cloudy. The high will be in the low fifties. . . .

ADELA: That's odd. It's not raining here. The announcer said "tomorrow's weather" and then talked about the weather for Sunday. But tomorrow is Saturday.

RADIO VOICE: Here are today's football scores. Dartmouth beat Yale in New Haven, 20 to 17. And here's a big upset. Indiana stunned Ohio State, 35 to 7! In the South . . . _(Static)_

ADELA: This is incredible! How could he have these football scores now? None of these games will be played until tomorrow. . . . This is no ordinary broadcast. . . .

MARCOS: _(Looking over her shoulder)_ What are you doing?

ADELA: I'm writing down the football scores. If this thing is as good as it seems to be, we may never have to worry about money again!

RADIO VOICE: And that's the last of the football scores. This completes our broadcast day. Join me tomorrow, Sunday, at 10:00 AM for a sports and weather update. Until then . . . _(Music plays, then static)_

MARCOS: I still can't believe it. A radio that tells the future! . . . Think of all the good that people could do if they knew what was going to happen a day early. . . . And think of all the bad that could be done too. If this radio ever got into the wrong hands. . . .

NARRATOR: The radio suddenly crackles to life once more.

RADIO VOICE: I've just been handed a special news bulletin. The River Bridge in Sommerville has just collapsed. So far, one person is known dead. Stay tuned for more details. _(Static again then silence)_

MARCOS: Did the announcer say River Bridge? Adela, that's just a few miles from here! . . . Adela, this is important. We can't keep this news to ourselves. I think we better go to the police.

ADELA: That's fine, Marcos. What are we going to say? That we can predict the future?

MARCOS: We can tell them anything, just so long as the bridge is cleared by tomorrow at five o'clock! . . . Let's just tell them about the radio. We can explain what happened and describe our work.

_To find out more
about this passage,
turn to page 240._

ADELA: I'm sure they'll believe every word. Let's face it, they'll think we're a couple of UFO freaks who have gone off the deep end.

MARCOS: We can show them the radio. Then they'll have to believe us.

Items 20–25 refer to the passage on page 104.

Fill in the blanks with the word or words that best complete the statements.

20. This play is about the possibilities found in science. This

    type of fiction is called _____.

21. Adela and Marcos are trying to discover evidence of life on other

    planets by picking up _____.

22. You can conclude from the dialogue that the day on which the action

    of the play takes place is _____ .

Circle the number of the best answer for each question.

23. Why were Adela and Marcos surprised by the broadcast? They

    (1) didn't expect the radio to ever receive anything.

    (2) were trying to contact scientists in other countries.

    (3) were expecting to receive signals from outer space.

    (4) expected to receive ordinary radio broadcasts.

    (5) had turned the radio off.

24. Adela does not want to go to the police to tell them about the bridge
    collapse because

    (1) she wants to keep the radio a secret.

    (2) she doesn't care about the bridge collapse.

    (3) she doesn't believe that the radio can really predict the future.

    (4) she is afraid the police will think she and Marcos are crazy.

    (5) there isn't enough time for them to warn anyone about the
        bridge collapse.

25. After hearing the last broadcast, what do you predict Adela and
    Marcos will do next? They will

    (1) say nothing and continue their research.

    (2) try to sell the radio to make money for their lab.

    (3) wait to see if the bridge collapses before they tell anyone.

    (4) go to the authorities and try to convince them that the bridge
        will collapse.

    (5) try to find out where the broadcast is coming from.

Check your answers on pages 223–224.

Unit 2

CLASSICAL LITERATURE

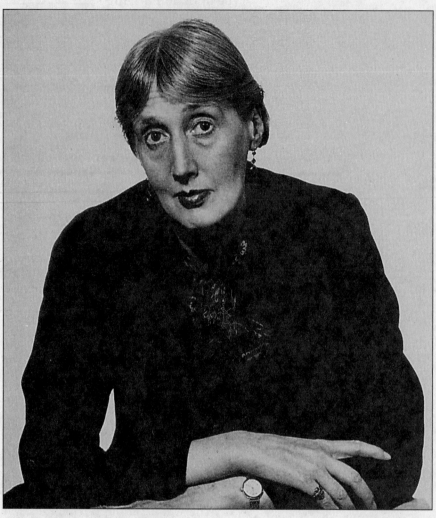

Virginia Woolf (1882–1941) was a critic, novelist, and essayist. She was one of the most highly respected authors of the early twentieth century.

Why is some literature called **classical**? When good popular literature is read by many people over many years, it is said to have stood the test of time. It has become classical.

The word *classical* does not mean old or difficult. Instead, it suggests meeting a standard of excellence. Classical poems, novels, short stories, essays, and plays are read again and again because they are well-written. They are as meaningful to readers now as when they were first published.

Poetry is probably the oldest form of literature. Classical epic poems, which are long poems that tell a story, existed in ancient times. The "Epic of Gilgamesh" is several thousand years old. English poetry written as long ago as the seventh century still is read today. Classical poems show that ancient people had the same concerns that modern people do. Classical poets wrote about love and hate, war and peace, loneliness and friendship. Classical poets such as Geoffrey Chaucer, John Milton, William Wordsworth, Robert Frost, and Emily Dickinson have continued to write about emotions we all understand.

More than two thousand years ago, the Greeks wrote plays that are regarded as classics today. These plays are both comedies and tragedies. The topics of these ancient plays include murder, family relationships, romance, and politics. The same conflicts can be seen in the classical plays of William Shakespeare. In modern classical dramas, these conflicts are treated by such authors as Henrik Ibsen and Arthur Miller.

The first real novels written in English appeared in the eighteenth century. Daniel Defoe's *Robinson Crusoe* and Jonathan Swift's *Gulliver's Travels* are both adventure stories that still have appeal today. Most classical novels are about ordinary people and important social problems.

Short stories first became available to readers in newspapers and magazines. Favorite classical short story writers include Edgar Allan Poe and O. Henry. Early short stories can be read today in books that are collections of stories. These books are called *anthologies*.

The first biographies were written about saints. Later, people wanted to read about the lives of politicians and royalty. In the early days, biographers were less interested in reporting the facts than in flattering the important people they wrote about. However, the best classical biographies tell the truth and help us understand how people lived.

The essay has its roots in moral education. Essays were used as a way to teach students a moral lesson or make a point. The more educated people thought they knew what was best for the general population. Such authors as Virginia Woolf wrote persuasive essays to change opinions about the way things were done. As long as there are differences in opinions, people will write essays on almost every subject imaginable. Essays about ideas that are important to most people will be read over and over.

This unit presents passages from all types of classical literature such as the following.

- The novels and short stories show a wide range of interests and ideas that have lasted over the years.

- The poems express universal emotions and experiences.

- The play deals with a human rights issue that is still important today.

- The autobiography gives a personal view of an important time in American history.

- The essay offers a fresh outlook on war and peace.

Section 15

Short Story

Setting the Stage

A **short story** is a piece of fiction that is shorter than a novel but has a full plot and a single theme. A short story usually has only a few characters and takes place over a brief time period. Writers have been publishing scary tales and detective stories in newspapers and magazines for more than a century. One of the first writers to become famous writing scary stories was Edgar Allan Poe. His spine-chilling short stories have been made into movies and TV shows. What makes Poe memorable is his understanding of the dark side of human nature.

Past: What you already know

You may have seen a scary movie or TV show based on one of Poe's stories such as "The Pit and the Pendulum," "The Fall of the House of Usher," or "The Murders in the Rue Morgue." Or you may have seen a movie like one of Poe's stories. How did the movie make you feel?

1. _____

_____

Present: What you learn by previewing

You can get a good idea of what you will be reading by looking at the title and reading the first few sentences. Read the first few sentences of the passage. What is the narrator's state of mind?

2. _____

_____

Future: What you predict

The passage on pages 109–111 is from Poe's story, "The Tell-Tale Heart." Do you think it will be a mystery with a puzzle to solve or a scary thriller?

3. _____

Read the first two paragraphs. What do you think the rest of the passage will be about? Now read on to find out if you are correct.

4. _____

_____

108   Unit 2: Classical Literature   *Check your answers on page 224.*

The Tell-Tale Heart by Edgar Allan Poe

As you read each section, circle the words you don't know. Look up the meanings.

True!—nervous—very, very dreadfully nervous I had been and am; but why *will* you say that I am mad? The disease had sharpened my senses—not destroyed—not dulled them. Above all was the sense of hearing acute. I heard all things in the heaven and in the earth. . . . How, then, am I mad? Hearken! and observe how healthily—how calmly I can tell you the whole story.

It is impossible to say how first the idea entered my brain; but once conceived, it haunted me day and night. Object there was none. Passion there was none. I loved the old man. He had never wronged me. He had never given me insult. For his gold I had no desire. I think it was his eye! yes, it was this! One of his eyes resembled that of a vulture—a pale blue eye, with a film over it. Whenever it fell upon me, my blood ran cold; and so by degrees—very gradually—I made up my mind to take the life of the old man, and thus rid myself of the eye for ever.

Using Definitions as Context Clues.

Applying Your Skills and Strategies

Sometimes an author defines an unfamiliar word or phrase for the reader. For example, in the passage above, the phrase *sharpened my senses* is used. By saying the opposite, *not destroyed—not dulled them*, the author makes the meaning of the phrase clear. Definition clues usually are found after a word and are set off by commas or dashes.

Find the phrase *by degrees* in the passage. Underline it. Write the context clue that tells you the meaning of this phrase.

_____

_____

Now this is the point. You fancy me mad. Madmen know nothing. But you should have seen *me*. You should have seen how wisely I proceeded—with what caution—with what foresight—with what dissimulation I went to work! I was never kinder to the old man than during the whole week before I killed him. And every night, about midnight, I turned the latch of his door and opened it—oh, so gently! And then, when I had made an opening sufficient for my head, I put in a dark lantern, all closed, closed, so that no light shone out, and then I thrust in my head. Oh, you would have laughed to see how cunningly I thrust it in! I moved it slowly—very, very slowly, so that I might not disturb the old man's sleep. It took me an hour to place my whole head within the opening so far that I could see him as he lay upon his bed. Ha!—would a madman have been so wise as this? And then, when my head was well in the room, I undid the lantern cautiously—oh, so cautiously—cautiously (for the hinges creaked)—I undid it just so much that a single thin ray fell upon the vulture eye. And this I did for seven long nights—every night just at midnight—but I found the eye always closed; and so it was impossible to do the work; for it was not the old man who vexed me, but his Evil Eye. And every morning, when the day broke, I went boldly into the chamber, and spoke courageously to him, calling him by name in a hearty tone, and inquiring how he had passed the night. So you see he would have been a very profound old man, indeed, to suspect that every night, just at twelve, I looked in upon him while he slept.

Upon the eighth night I was more than usually cautious in opening the door. A watch's minute hand moves more quickly than did mine. Never before that night had I *felt* the extent of my own powers—of my sagacity. I could scarcely contain my feelings of triumph. To think that there I was, opening the door, little by little, and he not even to dream of my secret deeds or thoughts. I fairly chuckled at the idea; and perhaps he heard me; for he moved on the bed suddenly, as if startled. Now you may think that I drew back—but no. His room was as black as pitch with the thick darkness (for the shutters were close fastened, through fear of robbers), and so I knew he could not see the opening of the door, and I kept pushing it on steadily, steadily.

I had my head in, and was about to open the lantern, when my thumb slipped upon the tin fastening, and the old man sprang up in the bed, crying out—"Who's there?"

I kept quite still and said nothing. For a whole hour I did not move a muscle, and in the meantime I did not hear him lie down. He was still sitting up in the bed listening;—just as I have done, night after night, hearkening to the death watches in the wall.

Understanding Mood.

Applying Your Skills and Strategies

Mood is how a reader feels about a story. The mood can be anxious, tense, happy, nervous, or satisfied. An author can create a certain mood by using words that express emotion, such as *sad*, *gloomy*, *thrilled*, or *scared*. Another way an author creates mood is by making the action happen quickly or slowly. If the action is slow and repeated, a tense mood is created.

What is the mood of this passage?

_____

How does the author create this mood? Give an example.

_____

_____

Presently I heard a slight groan, and I knew it was the groan of mortal terror. It was not a groan of pain or of grief—oh, no!—it was the low stifled sound that arises from the bottom of the soul when overcharged with awe. I knew the sound well. Many a night, just at midnight, when all the world slept, it has welled up from my own bosom, deepening, with its dreadful echo, the terrors that distracted me. I say I knew it well. I knew what the old man felt, and pitied him, although I chuckled at heart. I knew that he had been lying awake ever since the first slight noise, when he had turned in the bed. His fears had been ever since growing upon him. He had been trying to fancy them causeless, but could not. He had been saying to himself—"It is nothing but the wind in the chimney—it is only a mouse crossing the floor," or "it is merely a cricket which has made a single chirp." Yes, he had been trying to comfort himself with these suppositions; but he has found all in vain. *All in vain*; because Death, in approaching him, had stalked with his black shadow before him, and enveloped the victim. And it was the mournful influence of the unperceived shadow that caused him to feel—although he neither saw nor heard—to *feel* the presence of my head within the room.

When I had waited a long time, very patiently, without hearing him lie down, I resolved to open a little—a very, very little crevice in the lantern. So I opened it—you cannot imagine how stealthily, stealthily—until, at length, a single dim ray, like the thread of the spider, shot from out the crevice and full upon the vulture eye.

It was open—wide, wide open—and I grew furious as I gazed upon it. I saw it with perfect distinctness—all a dull blue, with a hideous veil over it that chilled the very marrow in my bones; but I could see nothing else of the old man's face or person: for I had directed the ray as if by instinct, precisely upon the . . . spot.

And now have I not told you that what you mistake for madness is but over-acuteness of the senses?—now, I say, there came to my ears a low, dull, quick sound, such as a watch makes when enveloped in cotton. I knew *that* sound well too. It was the beating of the old man's heart. It increased my fury, as the beating of a drum stimulates the soldier into courage.

To find out more about this passage, turn to page 239.

Predicting Outcomes.

Applying Your Skills and Strategies

Sometimes an author ends a story without telling what finally happened. The reader must figure out the ending. When you do that, you are predicting the outcome. Use the information in the story to predict what will happen.

In the story so far, you have read about how angry the narrator gets because of the old man's *vulture* eye. Now that he has finally seen the eye, what do you think he will do in the next few minutes?

_____

_____

_____

_____

_____

Thinking About the Story

Find the numbered words below and underline them in the passage. Study the context in which each word appears. Then match each word with its meaning. Write the letter of the meaning by each word.

_____	1. acute	a.	not seen
_____	2. stealthily	b.	surrounded
_____	3. sufficient	c.	enough
_____	4. enveloped	d.	wisdom
_____	5. sagacity	e.	small crack
_____	6. stifled	f.	secrecy
_____	7. suppositions	g.	sharp
_____	8. unperceived	h.	ideas assumed to be correct
_____	9. crevice	i.	held in
_____	10. dissimulation	j.	quietly and secretly

Write your answers in the space provided.

11. Review your predictions on page 108. Were you right? If you said *yes*, write what you correctly predicted. If not, what were you wrong about?

_____

_____

_____

12. What about the old man bothered the narrator the most?

_____

13. Find the word *conceived* in the passage and underline it. What is the context clue that defines the meaning of the word?

_____

_____

Circle the number of the best answer for each question.

14. Why did it take so long for the narrator to kill the old man? The narrator was

    (1) afraid of going to jail.

    (2) hoping to find out where the old man kept his gold.

    (3) waiting for the old man to be fast asleep.

    (4) very fond of the old man.

    (5) waiting to see the vulture eye.

15. Which of the following best describes the narrator's major emotion in the story?

    (1) chilling fear

    (2) constant worry

    (3) deep regret

    (4) quiet happiness

    (5) nervous pride

Write your answers in the space provided. Use complete sentences.

16. The narrator keeps saying that he is not crazy. Do you believe him? Why or why not?

    _____

    _____

    _____

    _____

17. Have you ever known someone who overreacted (reacted too strongly) to something annoying? What annoyed that person? What did the person do?

    _____

    _____

    _____

    _____

Check your answers on page 225.

Section 16

Romantic Novel

Setting the Stage

Romantic novels are stories about lovers. Often a couple must overcome obstacles before having a life together. Sometimes the family objects to the romance. At other times social or financial differences get in the way. Whatever the obstacle, stories about the troubles of lovers have always been popular. The reader of a romantic novel can sympathize with the couple as they try to work out their troubles. In most cases, the reader can expect a happy ending.

Past: What you already know

You may have read a novel or seen a movie about romantic problems. What was the main obstacle the couple faced?

1. _____

_____

_____

Present: What you learn by previewing

You can get a good idea of what you will be reading by looking at the title and reading a few sentences. Read the first few sentences of the passage. Write the names of the two main characters.

2. _____

_____

Future: What you predict

The passage on pages 115–117 is from a novel called *Ramona*. Read the first three paragraphs. What do you predict the passage will be about? Now read on to find out if you are correct.

3. _____

_____

_____

Ramona by Helen Hunt Jackson

Capitan was leaping up, putting his paws on Alessandro's breast,
licking his face, yelping, doing all a dog could do, to show welcome and
affection.

Alessandro laughed aloud. Ramona had not more than two or three
times heard him do this. It frightened her. "Why do you laugh,
Alessandro?" she said.

"To think what I have to show you, my Señorita," he said. "Look here;"
and turning towards the willows, he gave two or three low whistles, at the
first note of which Baba came trotting out of the copse [small group of
trees] to the end of his lariat, and began to snort and whinny with delight
as soon as he perceived Ramona.

Making Inferences.   To make an inference, use both the facts you are
given and what you already know. Details can be clues that help you make an
inference. For example, you are told that Capitan is a dog. But if that fact
had not been given, you could have inferred it from the description of his
actions. *Leaping up*, *licking*, and *yelping* are details that make you think of a
dog.

Reread the sentences describing Baba. What kind of animal can you infer
he is?

_____

What details helped you make this inference?

_____

_____

Ramona burst into tears. The surprise was too great.

"Are you not glad, Señorita?" cried Alessandro, aghast. "Is it not your
own horse? If you do not wish to take him, I will lead him back. My pony
can carry you, if we journey very slowly. But I thought it would be joy to
you to have Baba."

"Oh, it is! it is!" sobbed Ramona, with her head on Baba's neck. "It is a
miracle,—a miracle. How did he come here? And the saddle too!" she cried,
for the first time observing that. "Alessandro," in an awe-struck whisper,
"did the saints send him? Did you find him here?" It would have seemed to
Ramona's faith no strange thing, had this been so.

"I think the saints helped me to bring him," answered Alessandro,
seriously, "or else I had not done it so easily. I did but call, near the corral-
fence, and he came to my hand, and leaped over the rails at my word, as
quickly as Capitan might have done. He is yours, Señorita. It is no harm to
take him?"

"Oh, no!" answered Ramona. "He is more mine than anything else I had; for it was Felipe gave him to me when he could but just stand on his legs; he was only two days old; and I have fed him out of my hand every day till now; and now he is five. Dear Baba, we will never be parted, never!" and she took his head in both her hands, and laid her cheek against it lovingly.

Alessandro was busy, fastening the two nets on either side of the saddle. "Baba will never know he has a load at all; they are not so heavy as my Señorita thought," he said. "It was the weight on the forehead, with nothing to keep the strings from the skin, which gave her pain."

Alessandro was making all haste. His hands trembled. "We must make all the speed we can, dearest Señorita," he said, "for a few hours. Then we will rest. Before light, we will be in a spot where we can hide safely all day. We will journey only by night, lest they pursue us."

"They will not," said Ramona. "There is no danger. The Señora said she should do nothing. 'Nothing!'" she repeated, in a bitter tone. "That is what she made Felipe say, too. Felipe wanted to help us. He would have liked to have you stay with us; but all he could get was, that she would do 'nothing!' But they will not follow us. They will wish never to hear of me again. I mean, the Señora will wish never to hear of me. Felipe will be sorry. Felipe is very good, Alessandro."

They were all ready now,—Ramona on Baba, the two packed nets swinging from her saddle, one on either side. Alessandro, walking, led his tired pony. It was a sad sort of procession for one going to be wed, but Ramona's heart was full of joy.

"I don't know why it is, Alessandro," she said; "I should think I would be afraid, but I have not the least fear,—not the least; not of anything that can come, Alessandro," she reiterated with emphasis. "Is it not strange?"

Using Context Clues to Find Synonyms. Synonyms are words that have the same or nearly the same meaning. You can find synonyms by looking at the context in which the words are used. When two words are used in the same way, you can guess that their meanings are similar. For example, *to repeat* means "to say something again." In the passage above, Ramona repeats the word *nothing*. In the last paragraph Ramona says *not the least* twice. What word in this paragraph is used the same way the word *repeated* is used?

Applying Your Skills and Strategies

"Yes, Señorita," he replied solemnly, laying his hand on hers as he walked close at her side. "It is strange. I am afraid,—afraid for you, my Señorita! But it is done, and we will not go back; and perhaps the saints will help you, and will let me take care of you. They must love you, Señorita; but they do not love me, nor my people."

"Are you never going to call me by my name?" asked Ramona. "I hate your calling me Señorita. That was what the Señora always called me when she was displeased."

"I will never speak the word again!" cried Alessandro. "The saints forbid I should speak to you in the words of that woman!"

"Can't you say Ramona?" she asked.

Alessandro hesitated. He could not have told why it seemed to him difficult to say Ramona.

"What was that other name, you said you always thought of me by?" she continued. "The Indian name,—the name of the dove?"

"Majel," he said. "It is by that name I have oftenest thought of you since the night I watched all night for you, after you had kissed me, and two wood-doves were calling and answering each other in the dark; and I said to myself, that is what my love is like, the wood-dove: the wood-dove's voice is low like hers, and sweeter than any other sound in the earth; and the wood-dove is true to one mate always—" He stopped.

"As I to you, Alessandro," said Ramona, leaning from her horse, and resting her hand on Alessandro's shoulder.

Baba stopped. He was used to knowing by the most trivial signs what his mistress wanted; he did not understand this new situation; no one had ever before, when Ramona was riding him, walked by his side so close that he touched his shoulders, and rested his hand in his mane. If it had been anybody else than Alessandro, Baba would not have permitted it even now. But it must be all right, since Ramona was quiet; and now she had stretched out her hand and rested it on Alessandro's shoulder. Did that mean halt for a moment? Baba thought it might, and acted accordingly; turning his head round to the right, and looking back to see what came of it.

Alessandro's arms around Ramona, her head bent down to his, their lips together,—what could Baba think? As mischievously as if he had been a human being or an elf, Baba bounded to one side and tore the lovers apart. They both laughed, and cantered on,—Alessandro running; the poor Indian pony feeling the contagion, and loping as it had not done for many a day.

To find out more about this passage, turn to page 238.

"Majel is my name, then," said Ramona, "is it? It is a sweet sound, but I would like it better Majella. Call me Majella."

Restating the Main Idea.

The main idea of this part of the passage is that Ramona takes on the new name *Majella* to please Alessandro. Reread this part and restate the main idea in your own words.

Applying Your Skills and Strategies

_____

_____

Check your answer on page 225.

Section 16: Romantic Novel   117

Thinking About the Story

Find the numbered words below and underline them in the passage. Study the context in which each word appears. Then match each word with its meaning. Write the letter of the meaning by each word.

_____ 1. lariat

_____ 2. perceived

_____ 3. aghast

_____ 4. procession

_____ 5. trivial

_____ 6. mischievously

_____ 7. cantered

_____ 8. contagion

a. saw

b. moved at a fast trot

c. not important

d. shocked

e. playfully or teasingly

f. rope

g. group moving in the same direction

h. a feeling of the same influence

Write your answers in the space provided.

9. Review your prediction on page 114. Were you right? If you said *yes*, write what you correctly predicted. If not, write two things you didn't expect to happen.

_____

_____

_____

10. What are Alessandro and Ramona doing?

_____

Circle the number of the best answer.

11. Why do you think Alessandro was in such a hurry?

(1) He was angry with Ramona.

(2) The horse and pony couldn't wait.

(3) Ramona wanted to see her family soon.

(4) He thought they might be stopped.

(5) The stores were closing soon.

12. What can you infer about the differences between Ramona and Alessandro?

    (1) Ramona is poor and Alessandro is rich.

    (2) Alessandro's parents do not approve of Ramona.

    (3) Ramona's family does not approve of Alessandro.

    (4) Alessandro and Ramona are both from the same kind of family.

    (5) Alessandro is not as sure about their love as Ramona is.

13. Which of the following best states the central idea of this passage?

    (1) Love conquers all problems.

    (2) Look before you leap.

    (3) Time makes all sorrows go away.

    (4) Names are not important.

    (5) Older people always have the right answers.

Write your answers in the space provided.

14. At the end of the passage there is a section describing what Baba thinks. What is the tone of this section? How does this scene help you understand the way the young lovers feel?

_____

_____

_____

15. If Ramona and Alessandro were a young couple today, how would they deal with Ramona's family?

_____

_____

_____

16. Have you or someone you know run into an obstacle in the way of something important? How was the obstacle overcome?

_____

_____

_____

Poetry

Setting the Stage

Poetry is one of the oldest types of storytelling. Centuries ago, in many cultures poetry was spoken, not written. The form of these poems made them easy for people to remember. They were handed down from one generation to another by word of mouth. In later times, many of these poems were written down. **Classical poems** are poems that are still read and enjoyed today. These poems appeal to people of all ages. They speak about experiences and emotions that are common to everyone.

Past: What you already know

Have you read a poem from long ago? What idea or experience makes you remember the poem?

1. _____

_____

Present: What you learn by previewing

You can get a good idea of what you will be reading by looking at the title and reading a few lines of a poem. Read the first five lines of "The Road Not Taken." What choice is the speaker trying to make?

2. _____

_____

Future: What you predict

Read the first few lines of the poem "Richard Cory." What do you predict the poem will be about? Read on to find out if you are correct.

3. _____

_____

Read the first few lines of the poem "The Minuet." What do you predict the poem will be about? Read on to find out if you are correct.

4. _____

_____

The Road Not Taken by Robert Frost

As you read each section, circle the words you don't know. Look up the meanings.

Two roads diverged in a yellow wood,
And sorry I could not travel both
And be one traveler, long I stood
And looked down one as far as I could
To where it bent in the undergrowth;

Then took the other, just as fair,
And having perhaps the better claim,
Because it was grassy and wanted wear;
Though as for that the passing there
Had worn them really about the same,

And both that morning equally lay
In leaves no step had trodden black.
Oh, I kept the first for another day!
Yet knowing how way leads on to way,
I doubted if I should ever come back.

I shall be telling this with a sigh
Somewhere ages and ages hence:
Two roads diverged in a wood, and I—
I took the one less traveled by,
And that has made all the difference.

To find out more about this poem, turn to page 237.

Using Context Clues. Sometimes you will see an unfamiliar word or phrase in a passage. Study the context in which the word or phrase is used. Look for clues that might help you guess what it means. For example, the word *undergrowth* appears in the fifth line of the poem. The clues *yellow wood, grassy,* and *in leaves* suggest that *undergrowth* means "the plants that grow close to the ground in a forest."

Find the phrase *wanted wear*, and underline it in the poem. What do you think the phrase *wanted wear* means?

_____

_____

What context clues did you use to find the meaning?

_____

_____

_____

Applying Your Skills and Strategies

Richard Cory by Edwin Arlington Robinson

Whenever Richard Cory went down town,
We people on the pavement looked at him:
He was a gentleman from sole to crown,
Clean favored, and imperially slim.

And he was always quietly arrayed,
And he was always human when he talked;
But still he fluttered pulses when he said,
"Good-morning," and he glittered when he walked.

And he was rich—yes, richer than a king—
And admirably schooled in every grace:
In fine, we thought that he was everything
To make us wish that we were in his place.

To find out more about this poem, turn to page 240.

So on we worked, and waited for the light,
And went without the meat, and cursed the bread;
And Richard Cory, one calm summer night,
Went home and put a bullet through his head.

Recognizing Theme.   A theme is a statement of a general truth about life, or an insight into human nature. A story or poem can have more than one theme. One theme in this poem is that people often want to be something they are not. This can be seen from the lines "We people on the pavement . . . " and " . . . wish that we were in his place." Another theme in this poem could be stated as "Riches don't make a person happy."

Applying Your Skills and Strategies

Reread the entire poem. How did the people of the town feel about Richard Cory?

_____

_____

How do you think Richard Cory felt about himself?

_____

_____

Based on these ideas, state a theme for the entire poem.

_____

_____

_____

The Minuet by Mary Mapes Dodge

Grandma told me all about it,
Told me so I couldn't doubt it,
How she danced, my grandma danced; long ago—
How she held her pretty head,
How her dainty skirt she spread,
How she slowly leaned and rose—long ago.

Grandma's hair was bright and sunny,
Dimpled cheeks, too, oh, how funny!
Really quite a pretty girl—long ago.
Bless her! why, she wears a cap,
Grandma does, and takes a nap
Every single day: and yet
Grandma danced the minuet—long ago.

"Modern ways are quite alarming,"
Grandma says, "but boys were charming"
(Girls and boys she means, of course) "long ago."
Brave but modest, grandly shy;
She would like to have us try
Just to feel like those who met
In the graceful minuet—long ago.

To find out more about this poem, turn to page 237.

Restating the Main Idea.   A poem, like other forms of literature, has a main idea. The main idea of the first six lines is the way Grandma danced. This idea can be restated in this way: Grandma paid a lot of attention to how she danced.

Reread the last seven lines of the poem. The main idea of this section is that the grandmother would like her grandchildren to experience the things she experienced as a young girl. Restate the main idea in your own words.

_____

_____

_____

_____

Thinking About the Poems

Find the words below and underline them in the poems. Study the context in which each word appears. Try to figure out the meaning of each word. Then complete the following sentences by writing the correct words in the blanks provided.

diverged   arrayed   schooled

claim   trodden   minuet

1. More than a century ago, a popular dance was the _____ .

2. Near the front door, the carpet is worn out because it has been

   _____ on a lot.

3. The road _____ at the fork, and we didn't know which way to go.

4. When people have dressed up for a special occasion, they have

   _____ themselves in nice clothing.

5. Richard Cory was trained, or _____ , in all the social graces.

6. If you say you have a right to something, you are making a

   _____ .

Write your answers in the space provided.

7. Review your prediction on page 120. Were you right? If you said *yes*, write what you correctly predicted. If not, write two things you did not expect to read about.

   _____

   _____

   _____

8. What did the speaker in "The Road Not Taken" do before he chose which road to take?

   _____

9. In "The Minuet," what did Grandma look like when she was young?

   _____

Check your answers on page 226.

10. What two words suggest that Richard Cory was like a king?

_____

Circle the number of the best answer for each question.

11. Which of the following from "The Road Not Taken" is the best restatement of the phrase *just as fair*?

    (1) *the better claim*

    (2) *really about the same*

    (3) *the passing there*

    (4) *come back*

    (5) *the one less traveled by*

12. Which of the following sayings best states the theme of "Richard Cory"?

    (1) A bird in the hand is worth two in the bush.

    (2) An apple a day keeps the doctor away.

    (3) You can't judge a book by its cover.

    (4) You can't change a sow's ear into a silk purse.

    (5) Money is the root of all evil.

13. In what way are the poems "A Road Not Taken" and "Richard Cory" similar?

    (1) Both poems discuss individual choice.

    (2) Both speakers are successful.

    (3) Both poems are about failure.

    (4) Both poems are about the future.

    (5) Both poems are about social issues.

Write your answers in the space provided.

14. What important experience in your life would you write a poem about? Why would you share this experience with your readers?

_____

_____

_____

_____

Social Drama

Setting the Stage

Many classical plays are **social dramas**. These plays, sometimes called *problem plays*, deal with major social issues. Sometimes they are about how society reacts to a certain group. Some plays deal with prejudices against a minority group. Other plays are about individuals who have trouble fitting into society. The conflicts in social drama are not always solved, but the effects of the problem are made clear. Social dramas can be funny, sad, or both.

Past: What you already know

You may have already seen a play that has been performed for many years. Was it a social drama? If so, what social issue was the play about?

1. _____

_____

Present: What you learn by previewing

You can get a good idea of what you will be reading by looking at the title and reading a few lines. Read enough of the play to name the four characters.

2. _____

Future: What you predict

The passage on pages 127–129 is from a play called *A Raisin in the Sun*. The title comes from a protest poem by the African-American poet Langston Hughes. Based on the title, what kind of social problem do you think the play will be about?

3. _____

_____

Read the first few lines of the passage. What do you predict the passage will be about? Read on to see if you are correct.

4. _____

_____

_____

A Raisin in the Sun by Lorraine Hansberry

As you read each section, circle the words you don't know. Look up the meanings.

BENEATHA: Sticks and stones may break my bones but . . . words will never hurt me!

(BENEATHA *goes to the door and opens it as* WALTER *and* RUTH *go on with the clowning.* BENEATHA *is somewhat surprised to see a quiet-looking middle-aged white man in a business suit holding his hat and a briefcase in his hand and consulting a small piece of paper*)

MAN: Uh—how do you do, miss. I am looking for a Mrs.— (*He looks at the slip of paper*) Mrs. Lena Younger?

BENEATHA (*Smoothing her hair with slight embarrassment*):   Oh—yes, that's my mother. Excuse me. (*She closes the door and turns to quiet the other two*) Ruth! Brother! Somebody's here. (*Then she opens the door. The man casts a curious quick glance at all of them*)   Uh—come in please.

MAN (*Coming in*):   Thank you.

BENEATHA: My mother isn't here just now. Is it business?

MAN: Yes . . . well, of a sort.

WALTER (*Freely, the Man of the House*):   Have a seat. I'm Mrs. Younger's son. I look after most of her business matters.

(RUTH *and* BENEATHA *exchange amused glances*)

MAN (*Regarding* WALTER, *and sitting*):   Well—My name is Karl Lindner . . .

WALTER (*Stretching out his hand*):   Walter Younger. This is my wife—(RUTH *nods politely*)— and my sister.

LINDNER: How do you do.

WALTER (*Amiably, as he sits himself easily on a chair, leaning with interest forward on his knees and looking expectantly into the newcomer's face*):   What can we do for you, Mr. Lindner!

LINDNER (*Some minor shuffling of the hat and briefcase on his knees*):   Well—I am a representative of the Clybourne Park Improvement Association—

WALTER (*Pointing*):   Why don't you sit your things on the floor?

Drawing Conclusions About Characters.   Stage directions and the way characters react to one another give clues about what the characters are like. The stage directions describe Walter's attitude. They also describe the way he greets the guest and how the women react. From these clues, what can you conclude about how Walter sees himself?

Applying Your Skills and Strategies

_____

_____

What can you conclude that Ruth and Beneatha think of Walter's attitude?

_____

_____

_____

LINDNER: Oh—yes. Thank you. (*He slides the briefcase and hat under the chair*)   And as I was saying—I am from the Clybourne Park Improvement Association and we have had it brought to our attention at the last meeting that you people—or at least your mother—has bought a piece of residential property at— (*He digs for the slip of paper again*)—four o six Clybourne Street . . .

WALTER: That's right. Care for something to drink? Ruth, get Mr. Lindner a beer.

LINDNER (*Upset for some reason*):   Oh—no, really. I mean thank you very much, but no thank you.

RUTH (*Innocently*):   Some coffee?

LINDNER: Thank you, nothing at all.

(BENEATHA *is watching the man carefully*)

LINDNER: Well, I don't know how much you folks know about our organization. (*He is a gentle man; thoughtful and somewhat labored in his manner*) It is one of these community organizations set up to look after—oh, you know, things like block upkeep and special projects and we also have what we call our New Neighbors Orientation Committee . . .

BENEATHA (*Drily*):   Yes—and what do they do?

LINDNER (*Turning a little to her and then returning the main force to* WALTER):   Well—it's what you might call a sort of welcoming committee, I guess. I mean they, we, I'm the chairman of the committee—go around and see the new people who move into the neighborhood and sort of give them the lowdown on the way we do things out in Clybourne Park.

BENEATHA (*With appreciation of the two meanings, which escape* RUTH *and* WALTER):   Un-huh.

LINDNER: And we also have the category of what the association calls—(*He looks elsewhere*)—uh—special community problems . . .

Recognizing Theme.   The theme of a story or play is not the same as its plot. A theme is a general truth about life, or human nature, suggested in a story.

Applying Your Skills and Strategies

In the passage Lindner represents the Clybourne Park Improvement Association. Lindner wants to discuss something with the Youngers and he seems very uncomfortable. Reread the passage, starting at the top of the page. What is the author suggesting about human nature by the way Lindner is acting?

_____

_____

_____

_____

_____

Check your answer on page 226.

BENEATHA: Yes—and what are some of those?

WALTER: Girl, let the man talk.

LINDNER (*With understated relief*): Thank you. I would sort of like to explain this thing in my own way. I mean I want to explain to you in a certain way.

WALTER: Go ahead.

LINDNER: Yes. Well. I'm going to try to get right to the point. I'm sure we'll all appreciate that in the long run.

BENEATHA: Yes.

WALTER: Be still now!

LINDNER: Well—

RUTH (*Still innocently*): Would you like another chair—you don't look comfortable.

LINDNER (*More frustrated than annoyed*): No, thank you very much. Please. Well—to get right to the point I—(*A great breath, and he is off at last*) I am sure you people must be aware of some of the incidents which have happened in various parts of the city when colored people have moved into certain areas—(BENEATHA *exhales heavily and starts tossing a piece of fruit up and down in the air*) Well—because we have what I think is going to be a unique type of organization in American community life—not only do we deplore that kind of thing—but we are trying to do something about it. (BENEATHA *stops tossing and turns with a new and quizzical interest to the man*) We feel— (*gaining confidence in his mission because of the interest in the faces of the people he is talking to*)—we feel that most of the trouble in this world, when you come right down to it—(*He hits his knee for emphasis*)—most of the trouble exists because people just don't sit down and talk to each other.

To find out more about this play, turn to page 238.

Summarizing. Sometimes summarizing a long speech can help you understand what really is being said. When summarizing, include the main idea and most important supporting details.

Applying Your Skills and Strategies

Reread Lindner's last speech on this page. Summarize it in a few sentences.

_____

_____

_____

_____

RUTH (*Nodding as she might in church, pleased with the remark*): You can say that again, mister.

LINDNER (*More encouraged by such affirmation*): That we don't try hard enough in this world to understand the other fellow's problem. The other guy's point of view.

Thinking About the Play

Find the numbered words below in the passage and underline them. Study the context in which each word appears. Then match each word with its meaning. Write the letter of the meaning by each word.

_____ 1. consulting

_____ 2. expectantly

_____ 3. affirmation

_____ 4. labored

_____ 5. category

_____ 6. frustrated

_____ 7. deplore

_____ 8. quizzical

a. strongly dislike

b. curious

c. prevented from reaching a goal

d. group

e. looking at to get information

f. had great difficulty

g. a positive statement

h. hopefully

Write your answers in the space provided.

9. Review your predictions on page 126. Were you right? If you said *yes*, write what you correctly predicted. If not, write what you found out the passage was about.

_____

_____

_____

10. What clue in the stage directions first lets you know Lindner is uncomfortable?

_____

_____

11. Lindner is trying to explain what the Clybourne Park Improvement Association does. Summarize what he first tells the Youngers.

_____

_____

12. What can you conclude about the Youngers' race?

_____

13. Which of the following best describes Beneatha's attitude toward Lindner?

    (1) very unfriendly

    (2) uninterested

    (3) overly polite

    (4) suspicious

    (5) satisfied

14. The members of the Younger family do not seem to think they have a problem. But their visitor refers twice to neighborhood problems. He also talks about incidents with "colored people." What problem is Lindner suggesting?

    (1) The association does not want an African-American family in the neighborhood.

    (2) The Youngers' house does not meet the building codes.

    (3) They caused race riots in Clybourne Park.

    (4) The association wonders why the Youngers have not joined any local groups.

    (5) The Youngers have protested against African-American people.

15. Based on Lindner's approach to the Younger family, what do you think he probably will do to solve the problem?

    (1) threaten them

    (2) ask them to join the association

    (3) suggest in a nice way that they sell the house

    (4) learn to accept the family

    (5) have them arrested for disturbing the peace

Write your answer in the space provided. Use complete sentences.

16. Have you or someone you know had an experience with some kind of prejudice? Was the prejudice suggested or was it stated directly? Was the problem resolved?

    _____

    _____

    _____

Section 19

Western Novel

Setting the Stage

The **Western novel** began when the frontiers of America were being settled. As the United States grew, the West attracted people who wanted to start a new life. It also drew people who wanted to make a quick fortune, sometimes outside the law. Western novels tell stories about the challenges these people faced. Stories about cowhands and their rugged country were popular even after the West was settled. Readers of today still enjoy exciting tales about taming the "Wild West."

Past: What you already know

You may have read a novel or seen a TV show about the American West. What was the story about?

1. _____

_____

_____

Present: What you learn by previewing

You can get a good idea of what you will be reading by looking at the title and reading a few sentences. Read the first few sentences of the passage. Write the name of the main character.

2. _____

Future: What you predict

The passage on pages 133–135 is from a novel called *Horse Heaven Hill*. Based on the title, what do you think the passage will be about?

3. _____

_____

Reread the first few sentences. Now what do you predict the passage will be about? Read on to find out if you are correct.

4. _____

_____

Horse Heaven Hill by Zane Grey

As you read each section, circle the words you don't know. Look up the meanings.

Chaps found the trail. It was soft and grassy, giving forth no sound under his hoofs. Below, Lark remembered, near the trap she would need to dismount and go very carefully, to avoid making a noise.

As she proceeded, the state of cool pondering alternating with suspense which possessed her gradually underwent a change. It dawned upon her finally what she might expect if she fell into Blanding's hands. But she would have to be caught by his riders first. The possibility seemed remote. Blanding might send a few men to stay all night near the trap, though Lark considered that doubtful. If it did happen, however, these men would undoubtedly camp outside of the gate, and this would put them a quarter of a mile from Lark's objective. In case of a surprise Lark thought grimly that she could shoot her way out. She would not mind taking a shot at Blanding anyhow. Her father had not been a man who ever hesitated to use a firearm. But killing a man, except in defense of her life or honor, was unthinkable. Lark felt extremely dubious about using a gun in the dark upon moving men. Yet she had to go on, risk or no risk, and she did not intend to be caught.

After traveling a couple of miles she drew Chaps to a walk, and soon after that she reached the dark boulder which marked the line for her to descend. It was gray and gloomy down there in the notch. No fires! She had to strain her ears to catch sounds of horses. They were there, apparently resting. Lark, assuring herself that her enterprise was favored by fortune, rode down very slowly.

Understanding Sequence. It is important to understand the sequence of events in a story. After Chaps finds the trail, Lark thinks about what she is about to do. She decides to go on with her plan.

Applying Your Skills and Strategies

Reread the last paragraph above. What are the next three events in the sequence of the story?

_____

_____

_____

_____

At length she got as far as she needed to go, if she intended to slip down on foot to reconnoiter, and make sure whether or not Blanding had sent a man back. But, after all, what good would it do her to know whether they were there or not? In any case she meant to liberate the horses. She would waive that added work, and proceed under the assumption that Blanding's riders were there.

Check your answer on page 227.

Dismounting, she walked a little apart from Chaps to listen. First she heard the low fall of water, then the light steps and thuds of hoofs of uneasy horses. She was about a hundred yards above the fence, even with the center, where she meant to make the break. Next she heard an owl hoot, and after that the whine of coyotes. They were down in the trap attracted by dead horses.

Lark returned to Chaps and, taking up his bridle, slipped her hand up almost to the bit and led him very cautiously, a few slow steps at a time. Soon she was in the section where it would be easy to crash brush, crack a stick or roll a rock. She bent low, searching the ground, and it was certain that she made no sound which could have been heard many yards away. It took precious time to do this. She realized that, at the last, when she tied the lasso to the trees in order to snake them out and open up the fence. Noise would be unavoidable. Then, however, it would not matter so much, for she could drag three trees out of there in less than three minutes and be gone. But she had forgotten that she must also light the fire.

As she worked down most carefully she turned these things over and over in her mind. And the result was that she elaborated a safer and better plan.

The thicket, which she soon entered, was dark, and the way tortuous. Pine saplings and brush of a leafless variety crowded upon her. The ground was thick with pine needles. This place would burn fiercely; in fact, the whole brushy slope above the fence would go. There was no other plot of timber near, something she had noted before deciding on this hazardous venture. The wild-horse catchers would have to travel far to find more material for a new fence.

Understanding the Setting. Details that describe the place where the action happens help you to visualize the setting. *The line for her to descend* and *a hundred yards above the fence* are details that suggest that Lark is on a hill.

Applying Your Skills and Strategies

After Lark works her way down the hill, she is in a new setting. Give four details that describe the setting Lark finds.

_____

_____

At last Lark was down, close to the high line of piled trees and brush. A cleared lane, which the riders had cut, offered Lark room to drag out the large bushy treetops she had selected. She made sure that they were the right ones. Then, going beyond them, she gathered armloads of pine needles and dry bits of dead wood, which she piled against the fence.

That done, she was ready. But she waited longer to listen. In that interval she discovered that she was panting; her face was bathed in cold sweat; she felt a tingling and thrilling of nerves. Sounds disturbed her.

Check your answer on page 227.

The wild horses were restless. They scented her or Chaps. She heard them moving inside the fence. How could she be sure those steps were not made by men?

The moment had come. With firm hands Lark tied one end of the lasso round the first tree she had selected. Then she got on Chaps, and winding the other end round the pommel, she spurred him. He gave a lunge; the rope tightened. The tree rustled loud, branches cracked. Lark's heart leaped high, her tongue clove to the roof of her mouth. She heard wild horses snort inside the fence. They were curious. She saw dark heads pointed up against the background of gray. Chaps appeared to be stuck. She spurred again and beat him with her glove. He plunged, dug down, and straining hard he loosened the tree with a crash and got it moving. Momentarily it caught on the second tree, but this one started too, and presently the sturdy little mustang dragged them both out.

Making Inferences About Characters.

Applying Your Skills and Strategies

To make an inference, use the facts you are given and what you already know. The way a character acts can help you make inferences about that person. For example, you can infer from the way Lark works with Chaps that she is a good rider.

You can also make inferences about how a character feels. Lark piles the brush by the fence and then stops to listen. Read the description of Lark as she stands listening. What can you infer about how Lark feels?

_____

_____

_____

To find out more about this passage, turn to page 238.

Lark leaped off and flew back. Her hands were not steady now when she untied the rope. A gray aperture broke the solid black outline of the fence. Lark dragged Chaps across this opening to tie on to the third tree. This was wide and bushy, but it came more easily. Its removal left a gateway wide enough to drive through two wagons abreast. It was enough. Just inside wild horses edged close, snorting. Suddenly a gray beast with the whites of his eyes showing broke through the opening.

Lark had to leap to escape him. Then Chaps plunged and dragged her. More horses bolted through. When she got the frightened Chaps under control, a stream of them was pouring out of the break. They did not make a great deal of noise, but even that added to Lark's fright. Nor did they crash the brush, for the reason that the great mass of horses had not yet started. But she heard a quick trampling of hoofs all along the inside of the fence, up to the apex of the trap. They would not rush the break. They were coming steadily, stamping, snorting, but not wild with terror. That sliding, dark stream seemed uncanny.

Thinking About the Story

Find the words below and underline them in the passage. Study the context in which each word appears. Try to figure out the meaning of each word. Then complete the following sentences by writing the correct words in the blanks provided.

pondering	liberate	aperture	tortuous
dubious	elaborated	reconnoiter	

1. A small _____ in the roof let a little light into the attic.

2. The scout rode ahead to _____ and find a place for the settlers to camp for the night.

3. We were all _____ that our risky plan would work out.

4. Lark had a plan to _____ the trapped wild horses.

5. She took a long time _____ the problem until she decided what to do.

6. She _____ a new plan, taking into account all of the details.

7. She led the horse down the _____ path, which curved back and forth down the slope.

Write your answers in the space provided.

8. Review your prediction on page 132. Were you right? If you said *yes*, write what you correctly predicted. If not, write two things you didn't expect to find out.

_____

_____

_____

9. What is Lark's goal in this passage?

_____

10. What does the phrase *sliding, dark stream* describe?

_____

11. What can you infer about Blanding's men? They are

    (1) Lark's friends.

    (2) friends of Lark's father.

    (3) the good guys.

    (4) lawmen.

    (5) the wild-horse catchers.

12. Which word best describes Lark?

    (1) cautious

    (2) careless

    (3) shy

    (4) carefree

    (5) timid

13. What do you think will be the result of Lark's burning the fence?

    (1) The horses will be frightened.

    (2) The trap will be ruined.

    (3) Blanding's men will catch Lark.

    (4) Chaps will decide to join the wild horses.

    (5) The nearby timber will have to be used for rebuilding.

Write your answers in the space provided.

14. What do you think Lark would do if she were caught by Blanding's riders?

    _____

    _____

    _____

15. Have you ever taken a risk in order to do something you thought was important? Why did you take the risk?

    _____

    _____

    _____

    _____

Check your answers on page 227.

Section 20

Autobiography

Some autobiographies give us a look at a world that no longer exists. *Black Elk Speaks* tells about part of a lost America. Over a hundred years ago, the Oglala Sioux followed traditional ways of living. Their lives changed when the "white man," whom they called the *Wasichu*, began to settle on their land. In 1886 Black Elk, a holy man, joined the Wild West Show run by Buffalo Bill. By doing this he hoped to learn more about the *Wasichu*. Black Elk wanted to help his people find a peaceful way of living with the new settlers and a new way of life.

Past: What you already know

You may have read a book or seen a movie about Native Americans. What are some of the problems they faced?

1. _____

_____

_____

Present: What you learn by previewing

You can get a good idea of what you will be reading by looking at the title and reading a few sentences. Read the first paragraph. What event is being described?

2. _____

_____

Future: What you predict

The passage on pages 139–141 is from an autobiography called *Black Elk Speaks*. Based on the title, who do you think will be telling the story?

3. _____

Read the first two paragraphs. What do you predict Black Elk will be learning about? Read on to find out if you are correct.

4. _____

_____

<u>Black Elk Speaks</u> as told through John G. Neihardt (Flaming Rainbow)

As you read each section, circle the words you don't know. Look up the meanings.

That evening where the big wagons were waiting for us on the iron road, we had a dance. Then we got into the wagons. When we started, it was dark, and thinking of my home and my people made me very sad. I wanted to get off and run back. But we went roaring all night long, and in the morning we ate at Long Pine. Then we started again and went roaring all day and came to a very big town [Omaha, Nebraska] in the evening.

Then we roared along all night again and came to a much bigger town [Chicago]. There we stayed all day and all night; and right there I could compare my people's ways with Wasichu ways, and this made me sadder than before. I wished and wished that I had not gone away from home.

Then we went roaring on again, and afterwhile we came to a still bigger town—a very big town [New York]. We walked through this town to the place where the show was [Madison Square Garden]. Some Pawnees and Omahas were there, and when they saw us they made war-cries and charged, couping us. They were doing this for fun and because they felt glad to see us. I was surprised at the big houses and so many people, and there were bright lights at night, so that you could not see the stars, and some of these lights, I heard, were made with the power of thunder.

We stayed there and made shows for many, many Wasichus all that winter. I liked the part of the show we made, but not the part the Wasichus made. Afterwhile I got used to being there, but I was like a man who had never had a vision. I felt dead and my people seemed lost and I thought I might never find them again. I did not see anything to help my people. I could see that the Wasichus did not care for each other the way our people did before the nation's hoop was broken.

Using Context Clues.   Different groups of people use special words and phrases that the rest of us may not always understand. Looking at the context of a word can help you figure out its meaning. For example, find the word *couping* in the passage. Underline it. The context clues, *war-cries* and *charged*, show that *couping* has something to do with war. *Couping* is the act of hitting a defeated enemy to declare victory.

Applying Your Skills and Strategies

Find the phrase *nation's hoop*. Remember that Black Elk is worried about his people and that the *hoop*, or circle, is broken. What do you think Black Elk means by *nation's hoop*?

_____

_____

_____

Check your answer on page 228.

They would take everything from each other if they could, and so there were some who had more of everything than they could use, while crowds of people had nothing at all and maybe were starving. They had forgotten that the earth was their mother. This could not be better than the old ways of my people. There was a prisoner's house on an island where the big water came up to the town, and we saw that one day. Men pointed guns at the prisoners and made them move around like animals in a cage. This made me very sad, because my people too were penned up in islands, and maybe that was the way the Wasichus were going to treat them.

In the spring it got warmer, but the Wasichus had even the grass penned up. We heard then that we were going to cross the big water to strange lands. Some of our people went home and wanted me to go with them, but I had not seen anything good for my people yet; maybe across the big water there was something to see, so I did not go home, although I was sick and in despair.

They put us all on a very big fire-boat, so big that when I first saw, I could hardly believe it; and when it sent forth a voice, I was frightened. There were other big fire-boats sending voices, and little ones too.

Afterwhile I could see nothing but water, water, water, and we did not seem to be going anywhere, just up and down; but we were told that we were going fast. If we were, I thought that we must drop off where the water ended; or maybe we might have to stop where the sky came down to the water. There was nothing but mist where the big town used to be and nothing but water all around.

We were all in despair now and many were feeling so sick that they began to sing their death-songs.

Identifying Point of View. Looking at events through the eyes of another person can help you see the world in a new way. Often, a person from another culture has a different point of view. In the passage so far, Black Elk is describing his experience in the *Wasichus'* world. Describe Black Elk's opinion of what he sees.

Applying Your Skills and Strategies

_____

_____

_____

When evening came, a big wind was roaring and the water thundered. We had things that were meant to be hung up while we slept in them. This I learned afterward. We did not know what to do with these, so we spread them out on the floor and lay down on them. The floor tipped in every direction, and this got worse and worse, so that we rolled from one side to the other and could not sleep. We were frightened, and now we were all very sick too. At first the Wasichus laughed at us; but very soon we could see that they were frightened too, because they were running around and

Check your answer on page 228.

were very much excited. Our women were crying and even some of the men cried, because it was terrible and they could do nothing. Afterwhile the Wasichus came and gave us things to tie around us so that we could float. I did not put on the one they gave me. I did not want to float. Instead, I dressed for death, putting on my best clothes that I wore in the show, and then I sang my death song. Others dressed for death too, and sang, because if it was the end of our lives and we could do nothing, we wanted to die brave. We could not fight this that was going to kill us, but we could die so that our spirit relatives would not be ashamed of us. It was harder for us because we were all so sick. Everything we had eaten came right up, and then it kept trying to come up when there was nothing there.

We did not sleep at all, and in the morning the water looked like mountains, but the wind was not so strong. Some of the bison and elk that we had with us for the show died that day, and the Wasichus threw them in the water. When I saw the poor bison thrown over, I felt like crying, because I thought right there they were throwing part of the power of my people away.

After we had been on the fire-boat a long while, we could see many houses and then many other fire-boats tied close together along the bank. We thought now we could get off very soon, but we could not. There was a little fire-boat that had come through the gate of waters and it stopped beside us, and the people on it looked at everything on our fire-boat before we could get off. We went very slowly nearly all day, I think, and afterwhile we came to where there were many, many houses close together, and more fire-boats than could be counted. These houses were different from what we had seen before. The Wasichus kept us on the fire-boat all night and then they unloaded us, and took us to a place where the show was going to be. The name of this very big town was London. We were on land now, but we still felt dizzy as though we were still on water, and at first it was hard to walk.

We stayed in this place six moons; and many, many people came to see the show.

To find out more about this passage, turn to page 239.

Understanding Sequence. Black Elk described the trip from New York to London in sequence. He told the events in the order in which they happened.

Briefly list the sequence of main events that happened on this trip.

_____

_____

_____

_____

_____

_____

Thinking About the Story

In this passage, Black Elk talks about some things he does not know the *Wasichu* word for. So he uses words he is familiar with to describe these things. Find the numbered words and phrases below and underline them in the passage. Study the context in which each word appears. Match each word with its meaning. Write the letter of the meaning by each word.

_____	1. iron road	a.	ocean
_____	2. power of thunder	b.	months
_____	3. prisoner's house	c.	electricity
_____	4. big water	d.	railroad
_____	5. fire-boat	e.	prison
_____	6. moons	f.	steamship

Write your answers in the space provided.

7. Review your predictions on page 138. Were you right about what the narrator learned? If you said *yes*, write what you correctly predicted. If not, write two things the narrator found out.

_____

_____

_____

8. How many times did the train stop before reaching New York?

_____

9. What was the weather like during the ocean voyage?

_____

10. How did Black Elk feel after he had left his people?

_____

11. What can you conclude about what the sailors thought of their Native American passengers?

_____

_____

Check your answers on page 228.

12. What was Black Elk describing when he talked about the things that he and his people were given to sleep on?

    (1) cotton mattresses

    (2) inflatable life jackets

    (3) cloth hammocks

    (4) silk sheets

    (5) bunk beds

13. Black Elk was a holy man of the Oglala Sioux. But when he was on the voyage, he felt like a man who *never had a vision*. What do you think he meant by *a vision*?

    (1) good eyesight

    (2) a bad dream

    (3) understanding of other cultures

    (4) a spiritual experience

    (5) the strength to face death

14. Black Elk feels like crying when he sees the bison and elk being thrown overboard because

    (1) there will not be enough food for the rest of the trip.

    (2) they will not be able to perform their show without the animals.

    (3) the animals made the passengers sick.

    (4) the animals represented the Native American way of life.

    (5) this means they will have to return to New York.

Write your answer in the space provided.

15. Have you ever been in a place or situation where you seemed to be out of place? How did you feel? What did you decide to do?

    _____

    _____

    _____

    _____

    _____

Check your answers on page 228.

Adventure Story

Setting the Stage

An **adventure story** tells about people facing danger from the unknown. In the late 1800s, journalist Jack London became famous writing adventure stories. His stories described how ordinary people fought to survive in the wilderness of Alaska and Canada. In those times, people could not rely on science and machines to help them. Instead, they had to use their courage, imagination, and knowledge of what to do in the wild. Stories about the bravery of one individual struggling to stay alive are good reading.

Past: What you already know

You may have read a story or seen a movie about surviving in the wild. What was the challenge the people faced?

1. _____

_____

Present: What you learn by previewing

You can get a good idea of what you will be reading by looking at the title and reading a few sentences. Read the first few sentences of the passage and list the two companions.

2. _____

_____

Future: What you predict

The passage on pages 145–147 is from a short story called "To Build a Fire." Based on the title, what do you think the passage will be about?

3. _____

Reread the first few sentences. Now what do you think the passage will be about? Read on to find out if you are correct.

4. _____

_____

Check your answers on page 228.

To Build a Fire by Jack London

As you read each section, circle the words you don't know. Look up the meanings.

The dog dropped in again at his heels, with a tail drooping discouragement, as the man swung along the creek bed. The furrow of the old sled trail was plainly visible, but a dozen inches of snow covered the marks of the last runners. In a month no man had come up or down that silent creek. The man held steadily on. He was not much given to thinking, and just then particularly he had nothing to think about save that he would eat lunch at the forks and that at six o'clock he would be in camp with the boys. There was nobody to talk to; and, had there been, speech would have been impossible because of the ice muzzle on his mouth. So he continued monotonously to chew tobacco and to increase the length of his amber beard.

Once in a while the thought reiterated itself that it was very cold and that he had never experienced such cold. As he walked along he rubbed his cheekbones and nose with the back of his mittened hand. He did this automatically, now and again changing hands. But, rub as he would, the instant he stopped his cheekbones went numb, and the following instant the end of his nose went numb. He was sure to frost his cheeks; he knew that, and experienced a pang of regret that he had not devised a nose strap of the sort Bud wore in cold snaps. Such a strap passed across the cheeks, as well, and saved them. But it didn't matter much, after all. What were frosted cheeks? A bit painful, that was all; they were never serious.

Understanding Cause and Effect.   A cause is what makes something happen. The effect is what happens as a result of the cause. In the passage above, the man cannot speak. This is the result of his beard being frozen. The author calls the frozen beard the *ice muzzle*.

Applying Your Skills and Strategies

Reread the second paragraph of this section. After the man rubbed his cheeks, they went numb again. What did he think might be the effect of the cold on his cheeks?

_____

_____

_____

Empty as the man's mind was of thoughts, he was keenly observant, and he noticed the changes in the creek, the curves and bends and timber jams, and always he sharply noted where he placed his feet. Once, coming around a bend, he shied abruptly, like a startled horse, curved away from the place where he had been walking, and retreated several paces back along the trail. The creek he knew was frozen clear to the bottom—no creek could contain water in that arctic winter—but he knew also that there were springs that bubbled out from the hillsides and ran along under the snow and on top [of] the ice of the creek. He knew that the coldest snaps never froze these springs, and he knew likewise their danger. They were traps. They hid pools of water under the snow that might be three inches deep, or three feet. Sometimes a skin of ice half an inch thick covered them, and in turn was covered by the snow. Sometimes there were alternate layers of water and ice skin, so that when one broke through he kept on breaking through for a while, sometimes wetting himself to the waist.

That was why he had shied in such panic. He had felt the give under his feet and heard the crackle of a snow-hidden ice skin. And to get his feet wet in such a temperature meant trouble and danger. At the very least it meant delay, for he would be forced to stop and build a fire, and under its protection to bare his feet while he dried his socks and moccasins. He stood and studied the creek bed and its banks, and decided that the flow of water came from the right. He reflected awhile, rubbing his nose and cheeks, then skirted to the left, stepping gingerly and testing the footing for each step. Once clear of the danger, he took a fresh chew of tobacco and swung along at his four-mile gait.

Identifying Figurative Language (Simile).
An author may use figurative language to help the reader visualize what is happening. A simile is a figure of speech that compares unlike things. For example, an author might write, "His hair was as white as snow." The author is comparing the unlike objects of snow and hair. A simile always begins with the word *like* or *as*.

Applying Your Skills and Strategies

Reread the paragraph at the bottom of page 145. Find the simile, and underline it in the passage. To what is the man compared?

In the course of the next two hours he came upon several similar traps. Usually the snow above the hidden pools had a sunken, candied appearance that advertised the danger. Once again, however, he had a close call; and once, suspecting danger, he compelled the dog to go on in front. The dog did not want to go. It hung back until the man shoved it forward, and then it went quickly across the white, unbroken surface. Suddenly it broke through, floundered to one side, and got away to firmer footing. It had wet its forefeet and legs, and almost immediately the water that clung to it turned to ice. It made quick efforts to lick the ice off its legs, then dropped down in the snow and began to bite out the ice that had formed between the toes. This was [a] matter of instinct. To permit the ice to remain would mean sore feet. It did not know this. It merely obeyed the mysterious prompting that arose from the deep crypts of its being. But the man knew, having achieved a judgment on the subject, and he removed the mitten from his right hand and helped tear out the ice particles. He did not expose his fingers more than a minute, and was astonished at the swift

Check your answer on page 228.

numbness that smote them. It certainly was cold. He pulled on the mitten hastily, and beat the hand savagely across his chest.

At twelve o'clock the day was at its brightest. Yet the sun was too far south on its winter journey to clear the horizon. The bulge of the earth intervened between it and Henderson Creek, where the man walked under a clear sky at noon and cast no shadow. At half-past twelve, to the minute, he arrived at the forks of the creek. He was pleased at the speed he had made. If he kept it up, he would certainly be with the boys by six. He unbuttoned his jacket and shirt and drew forth his lunch. The action consumed no more than a quarter of a minute, yet in that brief moment the numbness laid hold of the exposed fingers. He did not put the mitten on, but, instead, struck the fingers a dozen sharp smashes against his leg. Then he sat down on a snow-covered log to eat. The sting that followed upon the striking of his fingers against his leg ceased so quickly that he was startled. He had had no chance to take a bit of biscuit. He struck the fingers repeatedly and returned them to the mitten, baring the other hand for the purpose of eating. He tried to take a mouthful, but the ice muzzle prevented. He had forgotten to build a fire and thaw out. He chuckled at his foolishness, and as he chuckled he noted the numbness creeping into the exposed fingers. Also, he noted that the stinging which had first come to his toes when he sat down was already passing away. He wondered whether the toes were warm or numb. He moved them inside the moccasins and decided that they were numb.

He pulled the mitten on hurriedly and stood up. He was a bit frightened. He stamped up and down until the stinging returned into the feet. It certainly was cold, was his thought. That man from Sulphur Creek had spoken the truth when telling how cold it sometimes got in the country. And he had laughed at him at the time! That showed one must not be too sure of things. There was no mistake about it, it was cold. He strode up and down, stamping his feet and threshing his arms, until reassured by the returning warmth. Then he got out matches and proceeded to make a fire.

To find out more about this passage, turn to page 239.

Applying Ideas in a New Context.   When you understand an idea, you can figure out how it might work in another situation. The man in the story prepares himself for his trip across the cold country. For example, he brings food to eat during the trip. In what other ways has the man prepared himself?

Applying Your Skills and Strategies

_____

_____

How would the man prepare if he were taking a trip across the desert?

_____

_____

_____

Check your answers on page 228.

Thinking About the Story

Find the words below and underline them in the passage. Study the context in which each word appears. Try to figure out the meaning of each word. Then complete the following sentences by writing the correct words in the blanks provided.

automatically   instinct   devised

crypts   floundered   intervened

1. Underground rooms or spaces are called _____ .

2. The man _____ in the fight by coming between the two angry dogs.

3. After you have done something over and over, in a while you can do it

   _____ .

4. If you have created a new way of doing something, you have

   _____ a new method.

5. When an animal is in danger, it does not think about what to do, but it

   acts on _____ .

6. When the man started sliding on the ice, he _____ a minute before he was able to walk again.

Write your answers in the spaces provided.

7. Review your prediction on page 144. Were you right? If you said *yes*, write what you were correct about. If not, write two things that you did not expect to read about.

   _____

   _____

   _____

8. Where are the man and dog going?

   _____

9. What is the main threat to the man and dog?

   _____

Circle the number of the best answer for each question.

10. What does the man do right after his fingers get numb from taking out his lunch?

    (1) He puts on his mitten.

    (2) He builds a fire.

    (3) He checks the numbness in his toes.

    (4) He strikes his fingers against his leg.

    (5) He unbuttons his jacket.

11. Which of the following best describes the difference between how the man and dog react to getting wet?

    (1) The dog is more successful in drying off.

    (2) The dog acts on instinct, but the man thinks.

    (3) The dog has no idea what to do, but the man does.

    (4) The dog shakes himself, but the man uses a towel.

    (5) The dog gives up, but the man doesn't.

12. Why does the man in the story become a bit frightened?

    (1) He doesn't have enough water to drink.

    (2) He is afraid the dog will die.

    (3) It is even colder than he thought it would be.

    (4) It is almost dark, and he is not close to the camp.

    (5) He is lost.

Write your answers in the space provided.

13. Do you think the man will reach his goal? Why or why not?

_____

_____

_____

14. Have you ever imagined yourself in a dangerous situation? What do you think you would do to survive?

_____

_____

_____

Persuasive Essay

Setting the Stage

Some essayists want readers to do more than just understand a point of view. They also want to persuade the reader. They want to convince the reader that they are right. **Persuasive essays** are often meant to get the reader to act. The essayist explains a situation and then suggests what can be done about it. Both facts and opinions are used to persuade. The author tries to get readers to believe that the suggested action will make their own lives better.

Past: What you already know

You may have read a persuasive essay in a magazine or newspaper. What action did the author want the reader to take?

1. _____

_____

Present: What you learn by previewing

You can get a good idea of what you will be reading by looking at the title and reading a few sentences. After you have read a few sentences of the passage, describe the event taking place.

2. _____

_____

Future: What you predict

The passage on pages 151–153 is from an essay titled "Thoughts on Peace in an Air Raid." Based on the title, what do you think the essay will be about?

3. _____

_____

Read the first paragraph. What do you now predict the essay will be about? Read on to find out if you are correct.

4. _____

_____

Thoughts on Peace in an Air Raid by Virginia Woolf

As you read each section, circle the words you don't know. Look up the meanings.

Up there in the sky young Englishmen and young German men are fighting each other. The defenders are men, the attackers are men. Arms are not given to the Englishwoman either to fight the enemy or to defend herself. She must lie weaponless tonight. Yet if she believes that the fight going on up in the sky is a fight for the English to protect freedom, by the Germans to destroy freedom, she must fight, so far as she can, on the side of the English. How far can she fight for freedom without firearms? By making arms, or clothes or food. But there is another way of fighting for freedom without arms; we can fight with the mind. We can make ideas that will help the young Englishman who is fighting up in the sky to defeat the enemy.

Applying Your Skills and Strategies

Distinguishing Fact from Opinion.   A fact is a statement about an event that can be proved true. The statement that men are fighting in the sky is a fact. The air battle can be seen by anyone who looks up. An opinion is a judgment or belief. The Englishwoman's belief that the English are fighting to protect freedom is an opinion. You can't argue about the truth of facts. You can argue about opinions.

In the passage above, the author says that the Englishwoman is not given weapons. But she also says that women can fight with their minds. Which statement is a fact about fighting? Which is an opinion?

_____

_____

A bomb drops. All the windows rattle. The anti-aircraft guns are getting active. Up there on the hill under a net tagged with strips of green and brown stuff to imitate the hues of autumn leaves guns are concealed. Now they all fire at once. On the nine o'clock radio we shall be told "Forty-four enemy planes were shot down during the night, ten of them by anti-aircraft fire." And one of the terms of peace, the loudspeakers say, is to be disarmament. There are to be no more guns, no army, no navy, no air force in the future. No more young men will be trained to fight with arms. That rouses another mind-hornet in the chambers of the brain—another quotation. "To fight against a real enemy, to earn undying honour and glory by shooting total strangers, and to come home with my breast covered with medals and decorations, that was the summit of my hope. . . . It was for this that my whole life so far had been dedicated, my education, training, everything. . . . "

Those were the words of a young Englishman who fought in the last war. In the face of them, do the current thinkers honestly believe that by writing "Disarmament" on a piece of paper at a conference table they will have done all that is needful? Othello's occupation will be gone; but he will remain Othello. The young airman up in the sky is driven not only by the voices of loudspeakers; he is driven by voices in himself—ancient instincts, instincts fostered and cherished by education and tradition. Is he to be blamed for those instincts? Could we switch off the maternal instinct at the command of a table full of politicians? Suppose that imperative among the peace terms was: "Child-bearing is to be restricted to a very small class of specially selected women," would we submit? Should we not say, "The maternal instinct is woman's glory. It was for this that my whole life has been dedicated, my education, training, everything. . . . " But if it were necessary, for the sake of humanity, for the peace of the world, that child-bearing should be restricted, the maternal instinct subdued, women would attempt it. Men would help them. They would honour them for their refusal to bear children. They would give them other openings for their creative power. That too must make part of our fight for freedom. We must help the young Englishmen to root out from themselves the love of medals and decorations. We must create more honourable activities for those who try to conquer in themselves their fighting instinct, their subconscious Hitlerism. We must compensate the man for the loss of his gun.

Understanding Persuasion.

Applying Your Skills and Strategies

Authors of persuasive essays usually do not say directly what they want the reader to do. Instead, an author may use certain words to convince the reader that an action has to be taken. Strong words such as *should*, *must*, and *necessary* suggest that something has to be done. Such words imply that the author feels no other way is possible.

What is the first action the author says has to be done as part of the fight for freedom?

_____

_____

What other word does the author use to show that she feels this action has to be taken?

_____

The sound of sawing overhead has increased. All the searchlights are erect. They point at a spot exactly above this roof. At any moment a bomb may fall on this very room. One, two, three, four, five, six . . . the seconds pass. The bomb did not fall. But during those seconds of suspense all thinking stopped. All feeling, save one dull dread, ceased. A nail fixed the whole being to one hard board. The emotion of fear and of hate is therefore sterile, unfertile. Directly that fear passes, the mind reaches out and instinctively revives itself by trying to create. Since the room is dark it can create only from memory. It reaches out to the memory of other Augusts—in Beyreuth, listening to Wagner; in Rome, walking over the Campagna; in

London. Friends' voices come back. Scraps of poetry return. Each of those thoughts, even in memory, was far more positive, reviving, healing and creative than the dull dread made of fear and hate. Therefore if we are to compensate the young man for the loss of his glory and of his gun, we must give him access to the creative feelings. We must make happiness. We must free him from the machine. We must bring him out of his prison into the open air. But what is the use of freeing the young Englishman if the young German and the young Italian remain slaves?

The searchlights, wavering across the flat, have picked up the plane now. From this window one can see a little silver insect turning and twisting in the light. The guns go pop pop pop. Then they cease. Probably the raider was brought down behind the hill. One of the pilots landed safe in a field near here the other day. He said to his captors, speaking fairly good English, "How glad I am that the fight is over!" Then an Englishman gave him a cigarette, and an Englishwoman made him a cup of tea. That would seem to show that if you can free the man from the machine, the seed does not fall upon altogether stony ground. The seed may be fertile.

At last all the guns have stopped firing. All the searchlights have been extinguished. The natural darkness of a summer's night returns. The innocent sounds of the country are heard again. An apple thuds to the ground. An owl hoots, winging its way from tree to tree. And some half-forgotten words of an old English writer come to mind: "The huntsmen are up in America. . . . " Let us send these fragmentary notes to the huntsmen who are up in America, to the men and women whose sleep has not yet been broken by machine-gun fire, in the belief that they will rethink them generously and charitably, perhaps shape them into something serviceable. And now, in the shadowed half of the world, to sleep.

To find out more about this passage, turn to page 240.

Understanding the Author's Purpose.   In a persuasive essay, an author must include facts and examples as well as opinions. The purpose of including facts and examples is to support the stated opinions and make them more persuasive. In the first paragraph of this section, the author states the opinion that fear and hatred are sterile, unfertile emotions. She supports this opinion with the example that creative thought stops during moments of great fear.

Applying Your Skills and Strategies

Reread the second paragraph of this section. What opinion does the author state in this paragraph?

_____

_____

What facts or examples does the author give to support this opinion?

_____

_____

_____

Thinking About the Essay

Find the numbered words below and underline them in the passage. Study the context in which each word appears. Then match each word with its meaning. Write the letter of the meaning by each word.

_____ 1. disarmament

_____ 2. fostered

_____ 3. imperative

_____ 4. subdued

_____ 5. subconscious

_____ 6. sterile

_____ 7. compensate

_____ 8. access

a. reduced

b. command

c. encouraged

d. lacking creativity or interest

e. the ability to reach

f. not aware of

g. the putting away of weapons

h. give something in place of something taken away

Write your answers in the space provided.

9. Review your predictions on page 150. Were you right about the essay? If you said *yes*, write what you correctly predicted. If not, write two things you did not expect to read about.

_____

_____

10. How did the author feel while waiting for the bomb to fall?

_____

Circle the number of the best answer for each question.

11. Which of the following is the best meaning for the phrase *maternal instinct*?

   (1) love of medals and decorations

   (2) desire to be a mother

   (3) hope for peace

   (4) fight for freedom

   (5) need for power

12. Which of the following is one of the author's opinions?

    (1) "Forty-four enemy planes were shot down during the night . . . "

    (2) " . . . that was the summit of my hope"

    (3) "How glad I am that the fight is over."

    (4) "They point at a spot exactly above this roof."

    (5) "The emotion of fear and hate is therefore sterile . . . "

13. The author includes the example of women giving up child-bearing if it were necessary for world peace

    (1) to suggest that women are better than men.

    (2) to make women aware of the overpopulation problem.

    (3) to compare women's responsibilities with men's.

    (4) to encourage Americans to stay out of the war.

    (5) to urge women to have careers instead of families.

Write your answers in the space provided.

14. The author is concerned with the effects of disarmament. What does she imply would happen if men were not allowed other creative outlets?

    _____

    _____

    _____

15. What do you think would have been your main concern if you had been in the author's situation?

    _____

    _____

16. Have you ever felt strongly enough about an issue that you tried to persuade someone to take action? Or has someone tried to persuade you? What was the issue? What was the action? Were you or the other person persuaded?

    _____

    _____

    _____

    _____

Unit 2 Review:
Classical Literature

Read the following passage from the novel *The Grapes of Wrath* by John Steinbeck.

And the migrants streamed in on the highways and their hunger was in their eyes, and their need was in their eyes. They had no argument, no system, nothing but their numbers and their needs. When there was work for a man, ten men fought for it—fought with a low wage. If that fella'll work for thirty cents, I'll work for twenty-five.

If he'll take twenty-five, I'll do it for twenty.

No, me, I'm hungry. I'll work for fifteen. I'll work for food. The kids. You ought to see them. Little boils, like, comin' out, an' they can't run aroun'. Give 'em some windfall fruit, an' they bloated up. Me. I'll work for a little piece of meat.

And this was good, for wages went down and prices stayed up. The great owners were glad and they sent out more handbills to bring more people in. And wages went down and prices stayed up. And pretty soon now we'll have serfs again.

And now the great owners and the companies invented a new method. A great owner bought a cannery. And when the peaches and the pears were ripe he cut the price of fruit below the cost of raising it. And as cannery owner he paid himself a low price for the fruit and kept the price of canned goods up and took his profit. And the little farmers who owned no canneries lost their farms, and they were taken by the great owners, the banks, and the companies who also owned the canneries. As time went on, there were fewer farms. The little farmers moved into town for a while and exhausted their credit, exhausted their friends, their relatives. And then they too went on the highways. And the roads were crowded with men ravenous for work, murderous for work.

And the companies, the banks worked at their own doom and they did not know it. The fields were fruitful, and starving men moved on the roads. The granaries were full and the children of the poor grew up rachitic [with spine problems], and the pustules of pellagra [sores caused by a skin disease] swelled on their sides. The great companies did not know that the line between hunger and anger is a thin line. And money that might have gone to wages went for gas, for guns, for agents and spies, for blacklists, for drilling. On the highways the people moved like ants and searched for work, for food. And the anger began to ferment.

To find out more about this passage, turn to page 240.

Items 1–6 refer to the passage on page 156.

Fill in the blanks with the word or words that best complete the statement.

1. The migrants were competing for _____ so that they could feed their children.

2. The companies and banks did not understand that they would cause their own doom. They did not understand the thin line between

   _____ and _____.

3. One way a great owner increased profits was to buy a

   _____.

Circle the number of the best answer for each question.

4. Which of the following phrases is the best meaning of the word *ferment*?
   (1) slowly to grow dangerously angry
   (2) the process of making beer
   (3) to grow older
   (4) to make people sick
   (5) to die down quickly

5. Which of the following words best describes the mood in this passage?
   (1) calm
   (2) delighted
   (3) forgiving
   (4) uneasy
   (5) quiet

6. What do the words *ravenous* and *murderous* suggest about how the people felt about getting work? The people felt
   (1) uninterested.
   (2) that they deserved work.
   (3) confident.
   (4) desperate.
   (5) that they could always find work.

BEATRICE: Go, Baby, set the table.

CATHERINE: We didn't tell him about me yet.

BEATRICE: Let him eat first, then we'll tell him. Bring everything in. *She hurries* CATHERINE *out.*

EDDIE: *(sitting at the table)* What's all that about? Where's she goin'?

BEATRICE: No place. It's very good news, Eddie. I want you to be happy.

EDDIE: What's goin' on? CATHERINE *enters with plates, forks.*

BEATRICE: She's got a job. *Pause.* EDDIE *looks at* CATHERINE, *then back to* BEATRICE.

EDDIE: What job? She's gonna finish school.

CATHERINE: Eddie, you won't believe it—

EDDIE: No—no, you gonna finish school. What kinda job, what do you mean? All of a sudden you—

CATHERINE: Listen a minute, it's wonderful.

EDDIE: It's not wonderful. You'll never get nowheres unless you finish school. You can't take no job. Why didn't you ask me before you take a job?

BEATRICE: She's askin' you now, she didn't take nothin' yet.

CATHERINE: Listen a minute! I came to school this morning and the principal called me out of the class, see? To go to his office.

EDDIE: Yeah?

CATHERINE: So I went in and he says to me he's got my records, y'know? And there's a company wants a girl right away. It ain't exactly a secretary, it's a stenographer first, but pretty soon you get to be secretary. And he says to me that I'm the best student in the whole class—

BEATRICE: You hear that?

EDDIE: Well why not? Sure she's the best.

CATHERINE: I'm the best student, he says, and if I want, I should take the job and the end of the year he'll let me take the examination and he'll give me the certificate. So I'll save practically a year!

To find out more about this passage, turn to page 239.

Items 7–12 refer to the passage on page 158.

Items 7–12 refer to the passage on page 158.

Write your answers in the space provided.

7. What does Eddie think will happen to Catherine if she does not stay in school?

_____

8. What kind of certificate will Catherine get at the end of the year?

_____

9. What is the setting of the play? How do you know?

_____

_____

Circle the number of the best answer for each question.

10. What gave Catherine the idea of taking a job?

   (1) Her school principal suggested it.

   (2) She knew she was failing her classes.

   (3) She needed to pay her rent.

   (4) She knew it would please Eddie.

   (5) She wanted to be able to leave home.

11. How do both Eddie and Beatrice feel about Catherine?

   (1) embarrassed

   (2) resentful

   (3) proud

   (4) worried

   (5) protective

12. How will Eddie probably react next?

   (1) He will give in immediately.

   (2) He will get angry at Catherine and Beatrice.

   (3) He will try to find Catherine a different job.

   (4) He will continue to object to Catherine taking a job.

   (5) He will ignore Catherine and Beatrice.

Go on to the next page.

Read the following poem, "Theme for English B," by Langston Hughes.

The instructor said,

> Go home and write
> a page tonight.
> And let that page come out of you—
> Then it will be true.

I wonder if it's that simple?

I am twenty-two, colored, born in Winston-Salem.
I went to school there, then Durham, then here
to this college on the hill above Harlem.
I am the only colored student in my class.
The steps from the hill lead down to Harlem,
through a park, then I cross St. Nicholas,
Eighth Avenue, Seventh, and I come to the Y,
the Harlem Branch Y, where I take the elevator
up to my room, sit down, and write this page:

It's not easy to know what is true for you or me
at twenty-two, my age. But I guess I'm what
I feel and see and hear. Harlem, I hear you:
hear you, hear me—we two—you, me talk on this page.
(I hear New York, too.) Me—who?

Well, I like to eat, sleep, drink, and be in love.
I like to work, read, learn, and understand life.
I like a pipe for a Christmas present,
or records—Bessie, bop, or Bach.

I guess being colored doesn't make me not like
the same things other folks like who are other races.
So will my page be colored that I write?
Being me, it will not be white.
But it will be
a part of you, instructor.
You are white—
yet a part of me, as I am a part of you.
That's American.
Sometimes perhaps you don't want to be a part of me.
Nor do I often want to be a part of you.
But we are, that's true!
As I learn from you,
I guess you learn from me—
although you're older—and white—
and somewhat more free.

To find out more about this poem, turn to page 238.

This is my page for English B.

Items 13–18 refer to the poem on page 160.

Fill in the blanks with the word or words that best complete each sentence.

13. Hughes lived at the YMCA, which he called the _____.

14. The word *theme* has more than one meaning. You can tell from the context that in this poem the word *theme* means a

    _____ for a class.

15. Bessie, bop, and Bach are examples of _____.

Circle the number of the best answer for each question.

16. Which of the following can you conclude about how the speaker feels about himself?

    (1) He dislikes himself.

    (2) He is very different from people of other races.

    (3) He is better than other people.

    (4) He is beginning to understand himself.

    (5) He is out of place at college.

17. From whose point of view does the instructor want the students to write their themes?

    (1) the student's

    (2) a man's

    (3) a woman's

    (4) an African-American person's

    (5) a white person's

18. Which of the following is an opinion the speaker holds about the instructor?

    (1) The instructor is white.

    (2) The instructor is older than the speaker.

    (3) The instructor's assignment is too hard.

    (4) The instructor cannot teach the speaker anything.

    (5) The instructor will learn something from the speaker.

Go on to the next page.

**Read the following passage from the essay "I Have a Dream"
by Martin Luther King, Jr.**

I have a dream today. I have a dream that one day every valley shall be exalted and every hill and mountain shall be made low, the rough places will be made plain and the crooked places will be made straight, and the glory of the Lord shall be revealed, and all flesh shall see it together.

This is our hope. This is the faith that I go to the South with. And with this faith we will be able to hew out of the mountain of despair a stone of hope. With this faith we will be able to transform the jangling discords of our nation into a beautiful symphony of brotherhood. With this faith we will be able to work together, to play together, to struggle together, to go to jail together, to stand up for freedom together, knowing that we will be free one day.

And this will be the day—this will be the day when all of God's children will be able to sing with new meaning:

> My country, 'tis of thee,
> Sweet land of liberty,
>   Of thee I sing;
> Land where my fathers died,
> Land of the Pilgrims' pride,
> From every mountainside
>   Let freedom ring.

And if America is to be a great nation, this must become true.

And so let freedom ring from the prodigious hilltops of New Hampshire. Let freedom ring from the mighty mountains of New York. Let freedom ring from the heightening Alleghenies of Pennsylvania. Let freedom ring from the snow-capped Rockies of Colorado. Let freedom ring from the curvaceous slopes of California.

But not only that. Let freedom ring from Stone Mountain of Georgia. Let freedom ring from Lookout Mountain of Tennessee. Let freedom ring from every hill and molehill of Mississippi. "From every mountainside let freedom ring."

To find out more about this passage, turn to page 238.

And when this happens—when we allow freedom to ring, when we let it ring from every village and every hamlet, from every state and every city—we will be able to speed up that day when all of God's children, Black men and white men, Jews and Gentiles, Protestants and Catholics, will be able to join hands and sing in the words of the old Negro spiritual: "Free at last! Free at last! Thank God Almighty. We are free at last!"

Items 19–23 refer to the passage on page 162.

Write your answers in the space provided.

19. What two words in the passage have almost the same meaning as *slopes*?

_____

_____

20. What does the writer mean by *a beautiful symphony of brotherhood*?

_____

_____

Circle the number of the best answer for each question.

21. Which of the following pairs of words is a restatement of the word *dream*?

    (1) hope and faith

    (2) despair and hope

    (3) distrust and faith

    (4) discord and struggle

    (5) exalted and glory

22. Which sentence best states the theme of this passage?

    (1) Life is unfair.

    (2) Freedom cannot be achieved.

    (3) Good things come to those who wait.

    (4) People feel more free in the mountains.

    (5) By working together, all people can become free.

23. Which of the following methods does the author use to persuade the reader?

    (1) a calm presentation of facts

    (2) a list of past troubles

    (3) angry emotion

    (4) hopeful inspiration

    (5) an argument with the opposition

Check your answers on pages 229–230.

COMMENTARY

Peter Jennings is one of the three news anchors discussed in the television review in Section 23.

A **commentary** is a discussion of a work of literature, art, drama, or music. When a commentary makes a judgment about a work, it is called a *critical commentary*. The author thinks about the quality of a work and how it has been put together, and decides whether it is well done. Sometimes an author criticizes one part of a work and praises another part.

One of the most common types of commentary is the review. A review tells the reader what the reviewer thinks about a book, TV program, movie, play, or musical performance. Reviews are usually brief. Reviews are intended to help their readers make choices about what to read, watch, or listen to. Some reviews are written in a serious tone. In others, the tone is humorous. Usually the reviewer's opinion of the subject affects the tone of the review.

Reviewers often tell readers many different things about a work. They may discuss the creators and performers of a work or the history and meaning of the work. But reviewers always give their opinions about the subject. To get the most out of a review, a reader should look for facts that support the reviewer's opinions.

Why do people read reviews? For many people, reviews help them make choices. For example, every fall a number of old TV shows are replaced by new ones. Can you decide what to watch by flipping from channel to channel until something looks good? And every summer a new batch of movies comes to local theaters. Can you choose what to see by looking at the titles? Thousands of books are published every year. Which ones suit your interests? What about all the recordings produced every month? How can you find the ones you want to hear? In your town or city, how can you decide which play to attend? In all these cases, reading reviews can make your choices easier and save time and money. Professional reviewers see, read, or listen to many of the options available. Reading the reviews makes the choices easier.

Reviews usually can be found in newspapers in the entertainment or culture sections. Popular magazines often contain several pages of reviews. Commentaries about older works or artists can be found in books about the specific subjects. Librarians can help you find this kind of information.

This unit presents reviews from several sources. The reviews cover some types of works people often want to know about.

■ The TV review gives opinions about the anchors of the three major network news programs.

■ The movie review explains the ideas behind a popular movie.

■ The book review describes the characters in a crime novel.

■ The music reviews discuss collections of recordings of two well-known musicians.

■ The theater review offers insights into a local theater production.

Section 23

TV Review

Setting the Stage

Many people watch the news on TV. This is how they learn about what is happening locally, nationally, and around the world. How the news is presented makes a difference in how people react to it. The presentation often depends on the anchor, the person who does most of the talking. Reading a review of the anchors on the major TV channels can help you make a decision about which news program to watch.

Past: What you already know

You may watch a TV news program in the evening or at some other time of day. Do you like the way the anchor reports the news of the day? Why or why not?

1. _____

   _____

Present: What you learn by previewing

You can get a good idea of what you will be reading by looking at the title and skimming the article. *To skim* something means to read very quickly, looking for main ideas and main characters. After skimming this article, write the names of the three anchors being reviewed.

2. _____

   _____

   _____

Future: What you predict

What do you want to learn from a review of a TV news program? Write two questions about anchors you think this review will answer.

3. _____

   _____

   _____

Three Men and a Maybe by Marvin

As you read each section, circle the words you don't know. Look up the meanings.

Who do I, as a critic, watch in times of crisis on the network evening news shows?

It was easy to answer that question when Uncle Walter [Walter Cronkite] was in the anchor chair. He could tell me the world ended this afternoon and it would be OK. I trusted Walter.

But Dan Rather at CBS makes me nervous. I never know when he is going to do something bizarre, like walk off the show. People are always asking him what the frequency is, or he is fighting with cab drivers in Chicago.

And that smile of his can be ghastly, managing a forced grin even after a story about a mine cave-in. On a story about pit bulls, he might say something folksy like "Doggone it."

He looked more relaxed in Saudi Arabia than in the studio. It's as if there are two of them. Dr. Rather and Mr. Angry.

Tom Brokaw on NBC News is about as warm as a fish on camera. He reads the news like his jaws are wired. And he never shows any feeling about the news. He reads each story, picnic or catastrophe, the same way.

Tom is a fabulous reporter, great in the field, a superb ad libber, with a command of fact and authority.

Judging the Author's Qualifications. In a critical commentary, the author's qualifications are very important. The reviewer is making a public statement about whether something is good or bad. The reader wants to be sure that the reviewer knows a lot about the subject. If you wanted a reliable opinion about a TV program, you probably would choose to read a commentary by a professional critic. Your best friends and coworkers don't have as much experience judging the quality of TV news programs. So when you read a review, look for clues about the qualifications of the reviewer.

Applying Your Skills and Strategies

In addition to stating his personal reactions, the author of this review uses terms that a professional TV reviewer would know. He also shows that he has been watching TV news for some time.

List two ways the author shows the reader that he is an expert in his field.

_____

_____

_____

_____

Check your answers on page 231.

He has always been at his most comfortable on the road. Yet covering the war from Saudi Arabia, he has been uncomfortable. So would you if your replacement in the studio was Jane Pauley, who is only the best straight news reader in the business today.

Peter Jennings is usually first in the ratings for a good reason. He is good. Jennings is ahead because he is closest to being easygoing, calm, a natural reader.

A few extra Canadianisms [words or expressions used by people from Canada] might creep in. How aboot that! He is a little too handsome, perhaps a little too smooth sometimes. But Jennings is always comfortable.

He is especially good at live events: his off-the-cuff comments on events always seem to be to the point, trenchant, unobtrusive.

And there's a vulnerability to the man. He admits things he doesn't know. But he doesn't try to score points on it, giving us a lecture on good journalism as Rather does.

There is an honest, real quality to Jennings, what I suspect is a human being behind the hair spray and makeup.

Lately, though, he has developed a pained expression with that furrowed brow, as if he has just eaten something that didn't agree with him. Nobody is perfect. Peter could make a great Alka-Seltzer commercial.

If I had my druthers I'd still want Uncle Walter. After 10 years in exile, he is still the most trusted guy in the country. Meanwhile I'll take Peter Jennings, pained expression and all.

Comparing and Contrasting.

Applying Your Skills and Strategies

Comparing shows how things or people are similar. Contrasting shows how things are different. You can compare Brokaw, Jennings, and Rather by saying that they are all anchors. However, the reviewer thinks that each one delivers the news in a very different way.

The reviewer compares a particular talent that Brokaw and Jennings have in common. What does the reviewer say they both do especially well?

_____

_____

Which two newscasters does the reviewer think are the best news readers?

_____

What does the reviewer think are the major differences among the ways Brokaw, Jennings, and Rather deliver the news?

_____

_____

_____

Thinking About the Review

Find the numbered words below in the passage and underline them. Study the context in which each word appears. Then match each word with its meaning. Write the letter of the meaning by each word.

_____ 1. bizarre   a. weakness

_____ 2. ghastly   b. strange

_____ 3. catastrophe   c. not pushy

                              d. choices

_____ 4. ad libber   e. person who says what is not
                                  in the script
_____ 5. trenchant
                              f. disaster
_____ 6. unobtrusive
                              g. awful
_____ 7. vulnerability
                              h. clear-cut
_____ 8. druthers

Write your answers in the space provided.

9. Review your prediction on page 166. Were your questions answered? If you said _yes,_ write the answers to the questions. If not, write two things you learned about.

_____

_____

_____

10. During what special time does the author want to be able to rely on the news?

_____

11. Which of the current news anchors does the reviewer prefer?

_____

12. When the reviewer uses the expression _How aboot that?_, what kind of accent is he describing?

_____

Circle the number of the best answer to each question.

13. The reviewer thinks that both Dan Rather and Tom Brokaw are more comfortable outside of the TV studio. What contrast did he see between the two when they were in the field in Saudi Arabia?

    (1) They both seemed more relaxed.

    (2) Dan Rather was more comfortable than Tom Brokaw.

    (3) Tom Brokaw was more relaxed than Dan Rather.

    (4) They were both uncomfortable.

    (5) Neither was as good as Peter Jennings in the field.

14. Why does the reviewer use the simile *as warm as a fish* about Tom Brokaw? He wants to suggest that Tom Brokaw

    (1) is a good news reader.

    (2) is an animal lover.

    (3) does not express much emotion.

    (4) is lovable.

    (5) is not a good-looking man.

15. The reviewer feels it is most important that a news anchor

    (1) is handsome.

    (2) is a good ad-libber.

    (3) can make silly jokes.

    (4) reads every story in the same way.

    (5) can be trusted.

Write your answers in the space provided.

16. Write the statement from the review that summarizes why the reviewer prefers Peter Jennings.

    _____

    _____

17. When you watch a TV news program, what qualities do you like to see in the anchor?

    _____

    _____

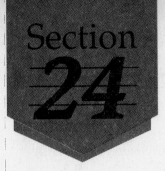

Movie Review

Setting the Stage

Sometimes an actor helps to produce a movie. Comedian Billy Crystal appeared in a movie about three men from the city who go out West. As both an actor and one of the producers of the movie, Billy Crystal had an important effect on the whole film. The reviewer of this film takes care to include both the serious and the funny sides of Crystal's influence. The reviewer also uses many of the actor's own words to suggest an opinion about how well the movie works.

Past: What you already know

You may have read a review about a movie you were thinking about seeing. If you decided to see the movie, what did the reviewer say that helped you make up your mind?

1. _____

   _____

Present: What you learn by previewing

You can get a good idea of what you will be reading by looking at the title and reading a few sentences. Read the first four paragraphs of the passage. Write the names of the three main characters in the movie.

2. _____

   _____

   _____

Future: What you predict

The passage on pages 172–173 is a review of the movie *City Slickers*. Reread the first three paragraphs. What do you predict the reviewer will say about the movie? Read on to find out if you are correct.

3. _____

   _____

   _____

'Slickers' Drives Cattle and Point Home
by Bob Thomas

As you read each section, circle the words you don't know. Look up the meanings.

Its comedy is bright and scenery sunny, but a cloud looms above Billy Crystal's "City Slickers": finding meaning at age 40.

Three longtime friends (Crystal, Bruno Kirby and Daniel Stern) fritter away a few weeks every year taking a vacation-adventure together. Chased by the bulls of Pamplona, Spain, on one such jaunt, the three run for their lives.

Yet for all the legwork they really aren't going anywhere.

Mitch Robbins (Crystal) is stuck selling radio advertising time, and his marriage is filled with static. Grocer Phil Berquist (Stern) feigns catnaps to escape from his shrewish mate. Ed Furillo (Kirby), a sporting goods dealer, stands out as the cheeriest of the trio, and his happiness doesn't run too deeply.

At Furillo's and Berquist's insistence, Robbins joins his playmates at a dude ranch where guests pay to drive cattle. A series of mishaps leaves the three pretty much alone on the range, where they must confront not only storms and pregnant cows but their own insecurities and doubts.

"When I came up with the idea for the movie, it wasn't three funny guys hit the plains," said Crystal, who also served as executive producer and pitched the film's premise to writers Lowell Ganz and Babaloo Mandel ("Parenthood").

Identifying Figurative Language (Metaphor). Like a simile, a metaphor is a figure of speech that compares unlike things. Metaphors are harder to recognize than similes because metaphors do not begin with the word *like* or *as*. For example, a reviewer might write, "The movie galloped forward at breakneck speed." Here the reviewer compares the pace of the movie to a running horse.

Applying Your Skills and Strategies

In the first paragraph of the passage, the reviewer uses the metaphor *a cloud looms* to show that the movie is partly about personal problems. A cloud does not really hang over the movie. By substituting the metaphor of the cloud, the reviewer suggests that the mood of the movie is sometimes gloomy.

Billy Crystal's character in the movie is described as having a marriage *filled with static*. This metaphor refers to the character's job, which is selling radio ads. What does the reviewer suggest about the marriage by using this metaphor?

     Check your answer on page 231.

"It was to tell a story about friendship, and to tell a story about trusting. If friends are friends in good times, they are a better friend if they're there when you're not feeling so good.

"It's also about men and women at a certain age when they enter 'What If?' land, and 'I should have, could have' territories. You sort of forget your purpose in life. You get clouded over. And it's not just an age thing. It's a confusion—a confusion of priorities."

Audiences know Crystal more for his comic reflections than for his insights into the human condition.

Through his work in television's "Soap" and "Saturday Night Live" and the movies "Throw Momma From the Train" and "When Harry Met Sally..." Crystal has avoided heavy issues in favor of light comedy. Nowadays, though, his jokes seem to carry more weight.

Along with Robin Williams and Whoopi Goldberg, Crystal helps feed, care for and house the homeless through the annual benefit concert Comic Relief. "Sessions," a comedy series debuting this fall on cable's Home Box Office, explores the labors and laughs of a man in psychotherapy. And then there's "City Slickers."

"I wanted to make a 'Deliverance' with laughs, and I wanted it to be truthful," Crystal said. "If there's no pain in the movie, then I simply have a funny movie. That's OK, but there's so much more to tell."

Jack Palance co-stars in the film as Curly, a veteran cowboy whose prairie wisdom helps Robbins resolve his crisis.

"When Curly says, 'There's nothing like bringing in the herd,' it's a metaphor for the whole piece—finishing something that you set out to do: raising your family, honoring your commitments.

"It's not about cows. It's about yourself and your priorities in life."

"City Slickers" was filmed on location in New Mexico and Colorado. Crystal, Stern and Kirby all learned to ride for the film. Crystal liked his quarterhorse so much he moved him to Southern California after the movie wrapped.

Recognizing Theme.   Even a funny movie can have a serious theme. In addition to summarizing the humorous plot of this movie, the reviewer uses quotes by Billy Crystal to explain the related themes. Crystal describes one theme by saying, "If friends are friends in good times, they are a better friend if they're there when you're not feeling so good." This general truth about human nature describes how people should act toward each other.

Applying Your Skills and Strategies

Another theme is about what happens when people begin to forget their purpose in life. What words does Crystal use to describe this theme?

_____

_____

_____

Thinking About the Review

Find the numbered words below and underline them in the passage. Study the context in which each word appears. Then match each word with its meaning. Write the letter of the meaning by each word.

_____ 1. slickers

_____ 2. fritter

_____ 3. jaunt

_____ 4. feigns

_____ 5. mishaps

_____ 6. priorities

_____ 7. reflections

_____ 8. shrewish

a. accidents

b. trip

c. thoughts

d. things of greater importance than others

e. pretends

f. people not used to rough living

g. spend in a carefree way

h. nagging

Write your answers in the space provided.

9. Review your prediction on page 171. Were you right? If you said *yes,* write what you correctly predicted. If not, write two things you did not expect the reviewer to talk about.

_____

_____

_____

10. What problems do the three friends face?

_____

11. According to the reviewer, Crystal is famous not only for being an actor. For what other reason is Crystal well known?

_____

12. Why does the reviewer mention Crystal's other movies and shows and then follow with the statement, "And then there's 'City Slickers'"?

_____

_____

Check your answers on page 231.

Circle the number of the best answer for each question.

13. Which statement gives the reviewer's opinion about Crystal's jokes in this movie?

    (1) They are not funny.

    (2) They have nothing to do with the theme.

    (3) They deal with heavy issues.

    (4) They are out of place.

    (5) They are better than his old jokes.

14. Which of the following best states the meaning of Curly's metaphor *there's nothing like bringing in the herd*?

    (1) Finishing something gives you a feeling of satisfaction.

    (2) Cattle are the future of the West.

    (3) Everyone could benefit from spending time with cows.

    (4) Westerners are wiser than city folks.

    (5) Caring for animals teaches you about people.

15. Which detail from the passage best suggests the problem that the movie's theme is based on?

    (1) 'What If?' land

    (2) an age thing

    (3) the human condition

    (4) pretty much alone

    (5) funny guys hit the plains

Write your answers in the space provided.

16. How do you think the movie ends?

    _____

    _____

17. If you have not seen *City Slickers*, based on the review would you like to? If you have seen this movie, do you agree with the reviewer's opinions? Why or why not?

    _____

    _____

    _____

Section

25

Book Review

Setting the Stage

A book review usually discusses both the plot and the characters of a book. But the reviewer of a mystery or crime novel doesn't want to give away too much of the plot. So to get the reader's attention the reviewer tries to make the characters sound as interesting as possible. Based mainly on the description of the characters, the reader must make a judgment about reading the book.

Past: What you already know

You may have read a book review that gave more information about the characters than about the plot. If so, what did you learn about the characters?

1. _____

_____

_____

Present: What you learn by previewing

You can get a good idea of what you will be reading by looking at the title and reading a few sentences. Read the first paragraph of the passage. What two types of characters will you be reading about?

2. _____

_____

Future: What you predict

The passage on pages 177–178 is a review of a book called *Get Shorty*. Reread the first paragraph. Based on this paragraph, what do you predict the reviewer will say about the book? Read on to find out if you are correct.

3. _____

_____

_____

Get Shorty by Elmore Leonard, reviewed by Ralph Novak

As you read each section, circle the words you don't know. Look up the meanings.

A cynic might think old Elmore has revenge on his mind, getting back at what Hollywood has done to a few of his novels by writing this acidic, get-them-laughing-then-punch-them-in-the-gut, splendidly entertaining crime tale. Its moral seems to be that gangsters are a lot like the people who make movies, except crooks are more efficient and have a deeper sense of honor.

Understanding the Author's Tone. How authors feel about a topic influences how they write about it. In turn, an author's tone influences how the reader feels about the topic. Tone is especially important in reviews, since the reviewer's main concern is to express an opinion.

Applying Your Skills and Strategies

Tone depends a lot on word choice. If an author uses formal or technical words, the tone seems unemotional. The use of slang and humorous words creates a more informal tone.

The reviewer of *Get Shorty* sets an informal tone at once. The use of *old* is an informal way of referring to the author, Elmore Leonard. Also, by using only the writer's first name, the reviewer makes it seem as if Elmore Leonard is a friend. Both word choices are intended to help the reader feel as comfortable with Elmore Leonard's work as the reviewer does.

The informal tone continues with a casual string of hyphenated words. The phrase *get-them-laughing-then-punch-them-in-the-gut* combines both humor and slang. Based on the tone of this phrase, how does the reviewer want the reader to feel about the book?

_____

_____

_____

Leonard's protagonist, Chili Palmer, is an easy-going kind of loan shark, in semiretirement in Florida. But then one of his clients skips off to Las Vegas still owing him, so Chili dutifully takes off after him. It's not long before Palmer is in Los Angeles, hooking up with a has-been horror movie producer, Harry Zimm, a former B-movie actress, Karen Flores, and a current star, Michael Weir. Soon Chili is deciding he knows enough—which isn't all that much—to get into the filmmaking business.

Check your answer on page 232.

It wouldn't be a Leonard novel without colorful villains, and this one has Ray Bones, an old enemy who has become Chili's boss in the Florida hierarchy, and Bo Catlett, a slick-dressing Angeleno who with his pal Ronnie is a jack-of-all-crimes, including murder.

In this company Chili comes off as a relatively nice guy, and one who knows how to use his expertise. "'What's the guy gonna do, Catlett, take a swing at me?'" he says to Harry. "'He might've wanted to, but he had to consider first, who is this guy? He don't know me. All he knows is I'm looking at him like if he wants to try me I'll . . . take him apart. Does he wanta go for it, get his suit messed up? I mean even if he's good he can see it would be work.'

"'He could've had a gun,' Harry said.

"'It wasn't a gun kind of situation.'"

Harry himself is on the hard-bitten side, recalling one unpleasant literary agent he had dealt with: "'I asked him one time what type of writing brought the most money and the agent says, "Ransom notes."'"

Things fall into place too easily for Chili at times, but Leonard compensates with nice twists, snappy action scenes and more than one blood-drawing zinger. You have to like a Hollywood novel in which a woman studio executive can say, "'Harry, I feel as if I know you. I've been a fan of yours ever since *Slime Creatures*. They remind me of so many people I know in the industry.'"

Recognizing Bias. Bias is a strong preference for a particular point of view. A person can have a bias for or against something. You can recognize a reviewer's bias from words that emphasize either a negative or a positive view of something. Reviewers also show a bias when they tell only one side of a story. When you see clues that suggest a bias, be sure to read carefully to find out whether the reviewer's opinions are supported by the facts.

Applying Your Skills and Strategies

The reviewer uses the words *snappy* and *zinger* to describe the novel. Do these words suggest a bias in favor of, or against, this novel? Why?

_____

_____

Write another phrase or sentence in which the author shows his bias about this novel.

_____

_____

How does the reviewer support his opinion of the novel?

_____

_____

Thinking About the Review

Find the words below and underline them in the passage. Study the context in which each word appears. Try to figure out the meaning of each word. Then complete the following sentences by writing the correct words in the blanks provided.

cynic	protagonist	moral
acidic	compensates	zinger

1. If you think that other people often behave selfishly, you might be

   called a _____.

2. The _____ of *Get Shorty* is named Chili Palmer.

3. The funny, surprise ending of the book was a real

   _____.

4. The reviewer _____ for his brief discussion of
   plot by talking a lot about the character.

5. You learn a lesson when you read a story with a _____ in it.

6. The salad dressing had a sharp, _____ flavor because
   it contained too much vinegar.

Write your answers in the space provided.

7. Review your prediction on page 176. Were you right? If you said *yes*,
   write what you correctly predicted. If not, write two things that you
   didn't expect to read about.

   _____

   _____

   _____

8. What detail supports the conclusion that the reviewer has read many
   of Elmore Leonard's books?

   _____

   _____

9. In comparison to which two characters does Chili look like a nice guy?

   _____

Circle the number of the best answer for each question.

10. Which of the following people is a villain in *Get Shorty*?

    (1) Elmore Leonard

    (2) Harry Zimm

    (3) Chili Palmer

    (4) Ray Bones

    (5) Michael Weir

11. Which of the following words best describes the tone of this review?

    (1) angry

    (2) sympathetic

    (3) humorous

    (4) serious

    (5) worried

12. The reviewer suggests that a cynic might think that Elmore Leonard writes with a bias against

    (1) crooks.

    (2) retired people.

    (3) horror films.

    (4) slick dressers.

    (5) the movie industry.

Write your answer in the space provided.

13. Based on the review, would you like to read this book or one like it? Why or why not?

    _____

    _____

    _____

    _____

Section

26

Music Review

Setting the Stage

Some musicians become legends in their own time. So when a new collection by a music giant becomes available, fans want to know about it. If the collection covers much of the musician's recording history, the reviewer often discusses how the music has changed over time. This way the reader can compare the new material with the familiar songs.

Past: What you already know

You may have a favorite musician or band who has released a collection of previously unheard material. Name the musician or band. What would you like to see or read about in a review of the recording?

1. _____

_____

Present: What you learn by previewing

You can get a good idea of what you will be reading by looking at the title and skimming a few paragraphs. Skim the passage on page 182. Write the name of the musician and the name of the new recording.

2. _____

_____

Future: What you predict

The passage on pages 182–185 is a review called "Dylan at 50 . . . Remains an Enigma." Reread the first few paragraphs. Based on these paragraphs and the title, what do you predict the reviewer will say about the recording? Read on to find out if you are correct.

3. _____

_____

_____

<u>Dylan at 50. . . Remains an Enigma</u> by Ron Firak

Bob Dylan always has been a measuring stick. A standard of concern and conceit, brilliance and belligerence, innovation and implausible arrangements.

And he's a milepost in the passing of time.

"Blowing in the Wind" . . . "Mr. Tambourine Man" . . . Going electric . . . The motorcycle crash . . . "Nashville Skyline" (and where DID that voice come from?) . . . "Blood on Tracks."

Born Again. Lost Again. Born Again again.

Like a first kiss or last look at a childhood home, his songs provoke the kinds of memories that remind us exactly where we were and what was going on in our lives when Dylan did whatever it was he was doing.

It was 30 years ago that Dylan captured the New York City folk scene and kept it in his thrall for decades. On May 24, it will be 50 years since he was born in Duluth, Minn., as Robert Allen Zimmerman.

Now comes a remarkable three-volume collection of outtakes, rehearsal cuts, demos and concert recordings packaged as "The Bootleg Series," which reminds us of just how much time has passed.

It also reminds us how truly staggering Dylan's work has been, and how astonishing that these 58 cuts would go unpublished for as long as they did. Everything in the set is worth listening to. Even the bad cuts provide valuable insight into the evolution and choices of a major artist.

Recognizing Bias. Biased writing shows a strong positive or negative attitude. The reviewer shows a positive bias toward Bob Dylan by saying that the collection is remarkable. The reviewer implies that the collection deserves attention. The reviewer is also giving an opinion that is stated as a fact.

Applying Your Skills and Strategies

In the last paragraph above, two biased opinions are stated as fact. Both show the reviewer's positive bias. They support the reviewer's opinion that the recording is worth listening to. Reread the last paragraph above. Write the two words that suggest a strong positive bias.

_____

_____

He was raised in Hibbing, Minn., the son of a Jewish hardware merchant in a town of 17,000 mostly Catholic miners. He started playing the piano at age 8 and the guitar and harmonica at about 10. His heroes were Hank Williams and James Dean, Leadbelly and Little Richard. And, of course, Woody Guthrie. He migrated to New York in part to visit a dying and hospitalized Guthrie.

Dylan is remembered by childhood friends as a loner who didn't seem to mind that almost no one seemed to understand, or like, his music.

                    Check your answer on page 232.

Out of it all came the music of America—blues and country and folk—filtered through a blue-eyed, skinny college dropout determined to be noticed.

And noticed he was.

He hit New York City for the first time in January 1961, and right away everyone saw there was something different about him. He was unique. He hadn't yet emerged as a writer (he wasn't quite 20) but the voice that seemed to search for notes, the pounding guitar, the wailing harmonica and uncanny sense of timing and phrasing produced a package perfect for the words he was singing.

"I don't write about things," he said in an interview with The Associated Press. "I write from inside of something, and I sing and play the same way. It's never about that 'something,' hoping to touch it. It's rather from the inside of it reaching out."

In 1961, after rave reviews on the New York coffee house circuit, Dylan signed a three-year deal with Witmark & Sons to publish his songs. It might have been the most creative period for any writer in American music. In three years, Dylan wrote 237 songs for Witmark.

It was the period in which he wrote "Blowin' in the Wind," "A Hard Rain's Gonna Fall," "Masters of War," "With God on Our Side," "It Ain't Me Babe," "Don't Think Twice, It's All Right," "Only a Pawn in Their Game" and "Mr. Tambourine Man."

Says Dylan: "When I'm singin' my songs, it never occurs to me that I wrote them.

"If I didn't have a song like 'Masters of War,' I'd find a song like 'Masters of War' to sing. Same thing with 'Times They Are A-Changin'.' If I didn't have a song like that, I'd go out and look around and I'd search around until I found one like that, you know?"

Summarizing.   Summarizing is not just stating the main idea. To summarize, you tell the most important ideas in a passage in three or four sentences.

Applying Your Skills and Strategies

Reread the passage above, starting on the bottom of page 182. Summarize the important ideas in these paragraphs.

_____

_____

_____

_____

And while Dylan's style and his specific concerns have changed many times, his substance has remained the same.

Throughout "The Bootleg Series" we hear the anger that is as much Dylan as anything—anger at a lover, . . . at the powers that be, at who knows. Sometimes just a shouting anger such as in "Idiot Wind": "You hurt the ones that I love best, cover up the truth with lies"; or in "Let Me Die in My Footstep": "There's always been people that have to cause fear."

But mixed in with the anger is humor, and occasionally hope. There is the determination of the Civil Rights Movement and the fear of a child growing up in the shadow of the atomic bomb, as he sings in "Masters of War." And yet Dylan, who is divorced, has five children.

And always there is a spirituality, a belief that somehow all of the suffering he saw—and all of the pain he felt—make sense.

Dylan remains a work in progress. Each tour has ticket buyers wondering which Dylan they will see: mellow or angry, Born again or lost again, singing old stuff or new. The songs might be the same, but they always sound different. "The Bootleg Series" reinforces the notion of Dylan as a work in progress, changing, evolving.

The early material has a power and intensity too mature for someone just 20 years old. The first three cuts are from late 1961, the next nine from 1962.

"Man on the Street," written in August 1961 and recorded later that year for, but not used on, his first album, "Bob Dylan," is a haunting song about how a police officer tries to arouse a dead man by poking him with his nightstick. Its image of the homeless is as powerful today as the time it was written.

The song Dylan chose to sing in March when he received a lifetime achievement award at the Grammys was "Masters of War." The 1963 song ends with Dylan pledging to "stand o'er your grave 'til I'm sure that you're dead," and was more than an anti-war song. It was an anthem that called for revenge against those who profit from war.

Only Dylan would sing such a brutal tune while battles raged in the Persian Gulf. And only Dylan would perform an arrangement so bizarre that most viewers could not figure out what he was singing.

Recognizing Fact and Opinion. A fact is something that can be proved true. An opinion is a judgment or belief. In the reviewer's opinion, Bob Dylan's work reflects the pain Dylan has felt.

Applying Your Skills and Strategies

The reviewer also says that Dylan's "Man on the Street" is *a haunting song about how a police officer tries to arouse a dead man by poking him with his nightstick*. Which part of this statement is an opinion and which part states a fact?

_____

_____

Thinking About the Review

Find the numbered words below and underline them in the passage. Study the context in which each word appears. Then match each word with its meaning. Write the letter of the meaning by each word.

_____ 1. belligerence

_____ 2. innovation

_____ 3. implausible

_____ 4. uncanny

_____ 5. substance

_____ 6. anthem

a. strange

b. central matter or basic nature of something

c. spiritual song or song of praise

d. anger

e. unbelievable

f. new idea or method

Write your answers in the space provided.

7. Review your prediction on page 181. Were you right? If you said *yes,* write what you correctly predicted. If not, write two things you did not expect the reviewer to say.

_____

_____

_____

8. List the emotions the reviewer hears in "The Bootleg Series."

_____

_____

9. Name four musicians who influenced Bob Dylan's music.

_____

_____

10. On page 182, what metaphor compares Bob Dylan to a standard of excellence?

_____

Circle the number of the best answer for each question.

11. Which of the following suggests that the reviewer has been listening to Bob Dylan for many years?

    (1) like a first kiss

    (2) the kinds of memories that remind us

    (3) Dylan is remembered by childhood friends.

    (4) I'd find a song like "Masters of War" to sing.

    (5) too mature for someone just 20 years old

12. Which fact supports the reviewer's opinion that Bob Dylan's time with Witmark "might have been the most creative period for any writer in American music"? Dylan

    (1) wrote 237 songs during that time.

    (2) wrote "Blowin' in the Wind" then.

    (3) stayed with the company for three years.

    (4) got rave reviews in New York.

    (5) was interviewed by The Associated Press.

13. What does the reviewer imply by saying that only Bob Dylan would *sing such a brutal tune* and *perform an arrangement so bizarre?*

    (1) Bob Dylan doesn't care about other people.

    (2) Bob Dylan is expected to do unusual things.

    (3) People were offended by Bob Dylan's act.

    (4) People do not expect Bob Dylan to entertain them.

    (5) Bob Dylan always tries to please his audience.

Write your answer in the space provided.

14. Based on the review, would you be interested in listening to "The Bootleg Series"? Why or why not?

    _____

    _____

    _____

    _____

Section 27

Theater Review

Setting the Stage

A review of a local theater production is sometimes different from a review of a Broadway play. Often these reviews do not give very much critical commentary on the actors' performances or tell a lot about the plot. The reviewer may give more background information about how the local play was produced. What happens behind the scenes is as important as the quality of the acting. A local review is often designed to get people to come to the theater, instead of making strong artistic judgments.

Past: What you already know

You may have read a review of a local play in a newspaper. Did the reviewer write more about the plot, the actors, or something else?

1. _____

_____

Present: What you learn by previewing

You can get a good idea of what you will be reading by looking at the title and reading a few sentences. Read enough of the passage to write the name of the director and the kind of play.

2. _____

_____

Future: What you predict

The passage on pages 188–189 is a review of a play called "Lend Me a Tenor." Based on the title, what kind of characters do you think will be in the play?

3. _____

Read the first five paragraphs of the passage. What do you predict the review will tell you? Read on to see if you are correct.

4. _____

_____

Check your answers on page 233.   *Section 27: Theater Review*   187

Lend Me a Tenor by Cara Webster

As you read each section, circle the words you don't know. Look up the meanings.

The action is non-stop, and the characters are bigger than life. But that's the way it has to be if it's a farce, said Christian Moe, director of "Lend Me a Tenor," the second production of Southern Illinois University at Carbondale's Summer Playhouse season.

"This is typical of farce," said Moe, who also chairs the theater department. "A farce should move so quickly that the audience doesn't have time to question the action. If they do, you're in trouble."

The two-act comedy isn't likely to find itself in trouble here anymore than it was when originally produced at the Globe Theater in London by Andrew Lloyd Weber.

And though few modern farces are successful, "Lend Me a Tenor" won seven Tony Awards for the 1989-90 Broadway season.

That might be because audience-goers like to laugh, and this effort gives them plenty of chuckles.

Understanding the Author's Purpose.

Applying Your Skills and Strategies

Every fact a reviewer includes is there for a purpose. In this case, the reviewer wants to persuade readers to see the play. So the facts must help to convince readers. One way of influencing a reader is to show that the people who are in the production are qualified. The director of this local production is Christian Moe. The reviewer includes the fact that Christian Moe is the head of the university's theater department. This tells the reader that the director has experience in theater. The reviewer uses this information to imply that the play is well directed.

What two facts does the author give about earlier productions of "Lend Me a Tenor"?

_____

_____

_____

What is the reviewer's purpose for including these facts?

_____

_____

_____

_____

Check your answers on page 233.

From the opening scene, we're treated to typical but overblown characters. There's Saunders, general manager of the Cleveland Opera Company. Played by Robert Kislin, Saunders is overbearing but extremely funny as he awaits the arrival of Tito Merelli, a world-famous tenor who is to make his debut with the company.

His assistant, Max (Timothy Fink) and daughter, Maggie (Anita Rich), wait with him, and each is lost in his or her own world, which revolves around Tito.

But it's after Tito (played by John McGhee) arrives that the fun really begins.

There's a chase scene, slamming doors, a would-be opera singer serenading Tito at the door to the bathroom where the Italian tenor is being sick, and Tito's angry Italian wife. There's shrimp mayonnaise curdling backstage in the 100-degree heat, unexpected visitors, room service intrusions, a presumed death, a note mix-up . . . well, you get the idea.

Everything that happens serves to complicate matters even further.

"It moves a little like a snowball slowly rolling downhill, gaining momentum until finally it hits a big tree and splat! It explodes," Moe said.

In rehearsal one week before the show's debut Thursday, Moe and cast and crew did well to handle the real-life obstacles that sometimes beset a production.

"We're missing Tim Fink tonight," said Moe. "He's out with strep throat."

Stage manager Danny Herbst walked through Fink's part, and assistant manager Jackie Pohlman read the lines from the floor downstage left.

Though Moe said they might be a "little left-footed" in rehearsal without Fink, he later complimented the cast and crew for "carrying on very well."

And carry on they will, beginning Thursday at 8 p.m.

Identifying Details to Support a Conclusion. Sometimes a reviewer draws a conclusion. For the reader to agree with the conclusion, the reviewer must include the facts that led to it. These facts or details support the conclusion.

In the passage above, the reviewer concludes that *Everything that happens serves to complicate matters even further.* Write three details from the play that support this conclusion.

_____

_____

_____

_____

Thinking About the Review

Find the words below and underline them in the passage. Study the context in which each word appears. Try to figure out the meaning of the words. Then complete the following sentences by writing the correct words in the blanks provided.

farce	tenor
typical	presumed
overblown	momentum

1. A _____ is a fast-moving comedy with unlikely twists in the plot.

2. The _____ failure of the play will be proved wrong when all goes well on opening night.

3. A sick actor is _____ of the problems that can happen during a rehearsal.

4. The faster something goes, the more _____ it has.

5. The man's high singing voice made him perfect for playing the part of

    the _____.

6. The actor had an _____ idea of his own importance.

Write your answers in the space provided.

7. Review your prediction on page 187. Were you right? If you said *yes*, write what you correctly predicted. If not, write two things you did not expect the review to tell you.

_____

_____

_____

8. When will the momentum of the play probably begin to pick up speed?

_____

9. Why did the stage manager take part in the rehearsal?

_____

_____

Check your answers on page 233.

10. Which of the following is a simile that Christian Moe uses to describe how the action of the play develops?

   (1) nonstop

   (2) bigger than life

   (3) like a snowball

   (4) gaining momentum

   (5) a little left-footed

11. Why does the reviewer include the information about Tim Fink's strep throat? The reviewer wants to

   (1) give an example of the problems that happen during a play.

   (2) show how the play is going downhill.

   (3) explain why Tim Fink will not be in the play.

   (4) make a contrast to the events in the play itself.

   (5) prepare the audience for a poor performance.

12. The reviewer says that audiences like to laugh and that this play will give them plenty of chuckles. Which conclusion do these details support?

   (1) The audience will not enjoy the show.

   (2) The reviewer did not enjoy the rehearsal.

   (3) Modern farces are not successful.

   (4) The show probably will be a success.

   (5) Saunders is the funniest character in the play.

Write your answer in the space provided.

13. Based on this review, would you like to see "Lend Me a Tenor" or a play like it? Why or why not?

   _____

   _____

   _____

   _____

Music Review

Setting the Stage

Sometimes a review seems more like an advertisement than a critical commentary. This happens when the subject of the review is a favorite of the reviewer. The reviewer can't help writing from the point of view of a fan. But these reviews are still valuable to the reader. The reviewer often gives bits of information that only a fan would know. So the reader benefits from the knowledge of a fan who is also a reviewer.

Past: What you already know

You may be a longtime fan of a musician or band. What is the name of the musician or band? What type of background information would you like to give other people?

1. _____

_____

_____

Present: What you learn by previewing

You can get a good idea of what you will be reading by looking at the title and reading a few sentences. Read the first three paragraphs of the passage. Write James Brown's nickname.

2. _____

Future: What you predict

The passage on page 193 is a review of a record collection called *Star Time*. Reread the first three paragraphs. What do you predict the reviewer will say about the collection? Now read on to find out if you are correct.

3. _____

_____

_____

                              Check your answers on page 233.

Star Time: _James Brown_ by David Hiltbrand

As you read each section, circle the words you don't know. Look up the meanings.

Chuck Berry? Elvis? The Beatles?

When it comes down to who has had the most profound and lasting influence on pop music, no one can touch the Godfather of Soul.

This anthology (four CDs or cassettes) is the Fort Knox of funk. It chronologically traces Brown's evolution from a poor follow-the-crowd R&B singer from Georgia to the absolutely original, superbad superstar.

Disc No. 1 contains the greatest advances. On the earliest tracks, such as "Try Me" and "Bewildered" from the late '50's, Brown is trying to get over as a cookie-cutter pop singer. This smoothed-out doo-wop music isn't all that far from the Ink Spots. But even in this era, there were hints of genius. Mired in the schmaltzy ballad "I Know It's True," Brown still had a flair for using horns and drums.

By the time he recorded "Think" in 1960, James had discovered the funk, and he never decamped. He became a method singer, and that method was madness. His eruptive delivery was completely unpredictable. With "Bring It Up (Hipster's Avenue)" in 1966, lyrics had really become a moot point. A single phrase would suffice.

Brown was always a character. On "Papa's Got a Brand New Bag, Pts. 1, 2, 3," an extended, previously unreleased version of his 1965 hit, you hear the singer exhorting his longtime sax man, Maceo Parker, to play a solo. By the end of the jam, Brown is getting into a dialogue with the horns themselves. (If Brown was, as advertised, "the hardest working man in show business," the guys who worked in his backing bands were tied for second.)

The music is fast and furious the rest of the way. Disc Nos. 2 through 4 present a dizzying cavalcade of hits: "I Got You (I Feel Good)," "I Can't Stand Myself (When You Touch Me) Pt. 1," "Licking Stick-Licking Stick," "Give It Up or Turnit a Loose.". . .

There are many collections of Brown's work, but none so deep or well documented.

Classifying. _To classify_ means to sort things into groups, or classes. Music and theater are small classes within a larger group called _the performing arts._ Each class can be divided into even smaller groups. For example, music can be classified as classical, rock, pop, rhythm and blues, or jazz.

Applying Your Skills and Strategies

The reviewer classifies the musical styles of James Brown. What three phrases does the reviewer use to classify Brown's early style of music?

_____

_____

_____

Check your answer on page 233.

Thinking About the Review

Find the numbered words below and underline them in the passage. Study the context in which each word appears. Then match each word with its meaning. Write the letter of the meaning by each word.

_____ 1. profound	a.	of little importance
_____ 2. evolution	b.	talent
_____ 3. schmaltzy	c.	left
_____ 4. flair	d.	sentimental, mushy
_____ 5. decamped	e.	change
_____ 6. moot	f.	be enough
_____ 7. suffice	g.	urging strongly
_____ 8. exhorting	h.	deeply important

Write your answers in the space provided.

9. Review your prediction on page 192. Were you right? If you said *yes,* write what you correctly predicted. If not, write two things you did not expect the reviewer to say.

_____

_____

_____

10. When a musician uses the word *jam,* it does not mean something that is put on bread. Reread the sixth paragraph on page 193. Based on the context, what does *jam* mean?

_____

11. What is the reviewer's overall opinion of the music collection?

_____

12. What does the reviewer think about James Brown's back-up musicians?

_____

13. Why does the reviewer describe the way James Brown encouraged his sax player to do a solo? This reviewer wants to

    (1) give an example of how unusual James Brown is.

    (2) show that James Brown knows how to play a horn.

    (3) suggest that James Brown is selfish.

    (4) criticize James Brown's style.

    (5) give an example of method singing.

14. What does the reviewer call James Brown's latest style?

    (1) pop

    (2) bad

    (3) doo-wop

    (4) funk

    (5) jazz

15. Which of the following best shows the reviewer's bias toward James Brown's musical skill?

    (1) smoothed-out

    (2) completely unpredictable

    (3) fast and furious

    (4) Fort Knox of funk

    (5) flair for using horns

Write your answer in the space provided.

16. If you were a musician like James Brown, would you want a review similar to this one to be written about you? Why or why not?

    _____

    _____

    _____

    _____

Unit 3 Review:
Commentary

**Read the following review, *Is the World Waiting for Ms. Rambo?*
by Ari Korpivaara.**

Sly Stallone and Arnold Schwarzenegger had better get out of town. Sigourney Weaver is ready to take over as the number-one action hero. As Ripley in *Aliens*, she is just as brave and competent with weaponry as the male Rambos. She is also smarter and capable of feeling. She is as close to believable as you can get in science fiction. That's because Weaver can act—more than can be said for the muscle-bound Katzenjammer Kids.

. . . Ripley . . . returns as a consultant with a fighting force of Marines to the planet taken over by the aliens. The human colonists have been wiped out, except for a little girl named Newt.

. . . The "top gun" pilot is a woman. The outfit's best fighting machine is a well-muscled woman named Vasquez, who in barracks-style banter puts the men in their place. A male Marine, eyeing her bulging biceps with envy: "Ever been mistaken for a man?" Vasquez: "No, have you?"

When the going gets rough, a number of the men come apart—panic-stricken, hysterical, cowardly. The women do not. Despite her own fear (something the thickheaded Rambo never feels), Ripley takes control from the mission's commander, paralyzed by the horror of it all, and, driving a space-age tank, rescues the Marines trapped inside the aliens' incubation room. It's a pleasure to root for her.

Items 1–6 refer to the passage on page 196.

Find the numbered words below and underline them in the passage. Study the context in which each word appears. Then match each word with its meaning.

_____ 1. competent

_____ 2. hysterical

_____ 3. paralyzed

a. unable to move

b. able to do something well

c. not in control of one's emotions

Circle the number of the best answer for each question.

4. What is suggested by the metaphor *fighting machine* that describes Vasquez? Vasquez is

   (1) a mechanical robot.

   (2) a man.

   (3) an excellent soldier.

   (4) a tank.

   (5) a person who causes fights.

5. The author begins his review with the statement *Sly Stallone and Arnold Schwarzenegger had better get out of town*. The author's purpose in doing this is probably to

   (1) set up a comparison between male and female action heroes.

   (2) suggest that the review is about two male movie stars.

   (3) state a fact.

   (4) appeal to fans of the two male movie stars.

   (5) introduce the idea that the movie is science fiction.

6. Which word best describes the tone of this review?

   (1) disapproving

   (2) bored

   (3) angry

   (4) approving

   (5) confused

Read the following music review, "Raitt Again."

Bonnie Raitt is back. And her new album, *Luck of the Draw*, is proof that her recent success is not simply a matter of luck. It is a matter of singing from her soul.

After the success of her 1989 album, *Nick of Time*, no one would have been surprised if Raitt had come out with a collection of cheerful tunes. She has good reason to celebrate after twenty years of struggle. Instead, *Luck of the Draw* presents a series of thoughtful and bittersweet songs. Blues, country, and rhythm and blues combine to produce a picture of insight, sadness, and courage. Raitt's message is about fighting back. The enemy is the bitterness that comes with living.

Raitt's slightly hoarse soprano voice takes off with a smile in the cheerful "Something to Talk About." Her blues background shows up in the powerful "Slow Ride." But beneath the mature control of her voice is the suggestion of past pain.

A lingering distrust of romantic relationships shows up in several of the ballads. A bit of the cynic looks out when she sings, "I kept track of all the love that I gave him / And on paper it looked pretty good." Her "One Part Be My Lover" warns of the problems old memories can bring to a new relationship. Of a couple just coming together she sings, "They remember too much about what went wrong / It might be they should learn to forget."

The real power of Raitt's vocal skill in *Luck of the Draw* is clearest in the ballads. She goes from a moving, quiet understatement to gentle laughter. Her rich, subtle tones capture the despair of a single mother facing the ache of loneliness. "I Can't Make You Love Me," "Luck of the Draw," and "All at Once" alone would be well worth the price of the album.

Raitt's earthy voice and supple slide guitar are not heard alone. Throughout the album, Raitt is backed up superbly by Paul Brady and Richard Thompson. Their harmonies are the perfect support for her songs of sorrow and understanding. The effect is like the swelling chords of an organ.

Listening to Bonnie Raitt has always been a treat. Her latest work is no exception.

Items 7–12 refer to the passage on page 198.

Write your answers in the spaces provided.

7.   Reread the fifth paragraph of the passage. According to the context, what does the word *vocal* mean?

_____

8.   Which classification of Bonnie Raitt's songs does the reviewer admire most?

_____

9.   Is the statement *Listening to Bonnie Raitt has always been a treat* fact or opinion?

_____

Circle the number of the best answer for each question.

10.   What does the simile *like the swelling chords of an organ* mean?

   (1)   The back-up singers also play organs.

   (2)   The three singers sound good together.

   (3)   The effect is too loud.

   (4)   The effect is unpleasant.

   (5)   The back-up singers sing very softly.

11.   Which phrase suggests how much the reviewer admires Bonnie Raitt?

   (1)   matter of luck

   (2)   recent success

   (3)   hoarse soprano

   (4)   earthy voice

   (5)   rich, subtle tones

12.   Which detail supports the conclusion that the songs have *the suggestion of past pain*?

   (1)   takes off with a smile

   (2)   mature control of her voice

   (3)   lingering distrust of romantic relationships

   (4)   moving, quiet understatement

   (5)   rich, subtle tones

Read the following review of the book *Paradise*.

Elena Castedo's first novel is a lot more than it seems at first glance. *Paradise* is the story of a Spanish labor activist's family. Fleeing the oppression of the dictator Franco, the family moves to a Latin American country. At first they live in a refugee ghetto. Then the wife, Pilar, gets herself invited to a large country estate. She tells her daughter, Solita, that the visit will be like paradise. The novel is the story of their visit.

More important, *Paradise* is the story of Solita. It is the story of how a ten-year-old girl learns to survive the cruelties of an unjust world.

The daughters of Pilar's hostess make no move to welcome Solita. In fact, they go out of their way to make her unhappy. They play tricks on her. And, more confusing to Solita, they make fun of her. In the Spanish ghetto, she had had a sort of freedom. She had not been aware of social classes. But the young sisters tell her that they are better than she is. They remind her that she is poor and from a family without social importance. The girls also upset Solita by implying they know a terrible secret about her mother.

Solita puts up with the teasing because she is loyal to her mother. But deep inside she finds a dignity, a sense of self-worth, that keeps her from believing what the sisters say. She learns to deal with the childish cruelty in a day-to-day fashion. She finds that "each minute you had to save your skin right then and there, by yourself, and in ways that wouldn't come back to haunt you."

Solita uncovers the unpleasant truth about the corrupt world of high society. She does not always understand what she reports. But the reader does. It becomes clear to the reader that wealth and power are valued more than individual worth.

Solita finally is freed of the place that was not paradise. She has learned about social injustice. However, she also has learned about the strength of her own character.

Castedo's novel is a powerful criticism of the upper classes. Through the eyes of a child, Castedo reveals the foolishness of people who think only of themselves. The Chilean author makes a disturbing statement about the values of Latin American society. She also comments on human nature in general. The issues she raises apply to all people.

Items 13–18 refer to the passage on page 200.

Fill in the blanks with the word or words that best complete the statements.

13. The novel is written from the point of view of

    _____.

14. The hostess' daughters make fun of Solita because they are

    _____ and she is _____.

15. A summary of the plot of the novel would begin with the family's move

    from _____ to _____.

Circle the number of the best answer for each question.

16. The reviewer implies that she agrees with Elena Castedo's view of the upper classes by using the phrase

    (1) *unpleasant truth.*

    (2) *a sort of freedom.*

    (3) *a sense of self-worth.*

    (4) *a terrible secret.*

    (5) *come back to haunt you.*

17. What general truth about human nature does the reviewer suggest is in the novel?

    (1) Children are crueler than adults.

    (2) Facing difficult situations can teach you about yourself.

    (3) There is no such thing as paradise.

    (4) The rich are better than the poor.

    (5) Poor people are better than rich people.

18. What is the reviewer's opinion of Elena Castedo's novel?

    (1) It is the author's first novel.

    (2) The novel is about a Spanish family.

    (3) The plot is too complicated.

    (4) The novel is a powerful criticism of human nature.

    (5) The point of the novel is not clear.

POSTTEST

I remember the morning that I first asked the meaning of the word, "love." This was before I knew many words. I had found a few early violets in the garden and brought them to my teacher. She tried to kiss me: but at that time I did not like to have any one kiss me except my mother. Miss Sullivan put her arm gently round me and spelled into my hand, "I love Helen."

"What is love?" I asked.

She drew me closer to her and said, "It is here," pointing to my heart, whose beats I was conscious of for the first time. Her words puzzled me very much because I did not then understand anything unless I touched it.

I smelt the violets in her hand and asked, half in words, half in signs, a question which meant, "Is love the sweetness of flowers?"

"No," said my teacher.

Again I thought. The warm sun was shining on us.

"Is this not love?" I asked, pointing in the direction from which the heat came. "Is this not love?"

It seemed to me that there could be nothing more beautiful than the sun, whose warmth makes all things grow. But Miss Sullivan shook her head, and I was greatly puzzled and disappointed. I thought it strange that my teacher could not show me love.

A day or two afterward I was stringing beads of different sizes in symmetrical groups—two large beads, three small ones, and so on. I had made many mistakes, and Miss Sullivan had pointed them out again and again with gentle patience. Finally I noticed a very obvious error in the sequence and for an instant I concentrated my attention on the lesson and tried to think how I should have arranged the beads. Miss Sullivan touched my forehead and spelled with decided emphasis, "Think."

In a flash I knew that the word was the name of the process that was going on in my head. This was my first conscious perception of an abstract idea.

For a long time I was still—I was not thinking of the beads in my lap, but trying to find a meaning for "love" in the light of this new idea. The sun had been under a cloud all day, and there had been brief showers; but suddenly the sun broke forth in all its southern splendor.

Again I asked my teacher, "Is this not love?"

"Love is something like the clouds that were in the sky before the sun came out," she replied.

To find out more about this passage, turn to page 238.

Items 1–6 refer to the passage on page 202.

Fill in the blanks with the word or words that best complete the statements.

1. This passage is about how a visually and hearing impaired child learns the meaning of _____ from her teacher.

2. The first conversation in the passage takes place in the _____.

3. One clue to the fact that the child is visually impaired is that she does not understand anything unless she _____ it.

Circle the number of the best answer for each question.

4. Which word or phrase is the best meaning for *abstract*?
   (1) not warm
   (2) not physical
   (3) important
   (4) hidden
   (5) confusing

5. What is the first mental process the child realized was going on in her head?
   (1) stringing beads
   (2) loving Miss Sullivan
   (3) thinking about the beads
   (4) smelling violets
   (5) being still

6. Miss Sullivan spells words into Helen's hand, and Helen talks partly in sign. These details support which inference?
   (1) Helen does not like to talk.
   (2) Helen is not very smart.
   (3) Miss Sullivan is a good teacher.
   (4) Miss Sullivan is not a very good teacher.
   (5) Helen is hearing impaired.

Go on to the next page.

Read the following poem, "That Woman" by Wilma Elizabeth McDaniel.

Stuffed animals
mean a lot to Nina Dowley
much more than to some kids
on days
that I run into her house
on any day
to borrow baking soda
last Tuesday
it was pinking shears
and met number 60
she had found him
at the flea market
a dirty pink rabbit
with eyes that moved
by Wednesday
when I returned the shears
Nina had sprayed
and cleaned
and brushed the rabbit
until he looked like new
and placed him
in a wicker basket on glass eggs
that belonged to her mother
she is out of space in the room
bears are lined up
on the chesterfield
and only bears sit there
cats monopolize chairs
of comfort and over-size
and dogs are happy on the floor
guarding stuffed frogs
and crocheted turtles
there is friction
but all agree
they never had a home
like Nina's heart
and never heard a story
like the one
Nina tells them every night
It never changes.

To find out more about this poem, turn to page 239.

Items 7–12 refer to the passage on page 204.

Write your answers in the space provided.

7. What does the number *60* refer to in this poem?

_____

8. What does Nina Dowley collect and love?

_____

9. Why is Nina *out of space in the room*?

_____

Circle the number of the best answer for each question.

10. What is the speaker's tone when she talks about Nina Dowley?

    (1) affectionate

    (2) amused

    (3) embarrassed

    (4) mocking

    (5) superior

11. Which conclusion is supported by the details that the speaker borrowed baking soda and pinking shears? The speaker is

    (1) the neighborhood gossip.

    (2) too poor to buy her own things.

    (3) a salesperson.

    (4) Nina's neighbor.

    (5) avoiding Nina.

12. What would Nina be most likely to do if she found a stuffed animal thrown out in the trash? She would

    (1) leave it there.

    (2) take it home and clean it.

    (3) throw it out again.

    (4) give it to someone as it is.

    (5) tear it up.

Go on to the next page.

He halted at the corner of Grant and Pine and wiped the perspiration on his forehead with a forefinger.

"*Shew*, we have walked a distance of five *li* from the bus station," he said in Mandarin. "Are you tired, May Li?"

"A little," the girl said. She was dressed in a Chinese gown of light blue and wearing a pigtail wound round her head, her pretty face without make-up glowing with health.

"Shall we go visit Mr. Poon now, father?"

"Oh, do not be so foolish. Nobody visits people so early. This is New Year's day, people sleep in the morning with a full stomach of food and wine and do not wish to be disturbed. We shall have our breakfast and rest our legs for a while." He wiped his forehead once more and looked around.

"Here is a teahouse, father," May Li said, pointing at a red signboard saying "Lotus Room."

"Good," Old Man Li said. When he looked at the stairway he frowned. "No, May Li, I shall not climb this with my luggage on my back."

"Let me carry it up for you, father," May Li said.

"No, you are carrying enough of your own."

"I can carry a lot more." She held her father's canvas bag until Li finally yielded it to her, shaking his head. "You are just like your mother, May Li. Forty years ago when she was your age she could carry a hundred catties of flour and walk seventy *li* a day. She was strong as a cow, and just as amiable..."

"What shall we eat, father?" May Li asked.

"We shall see," Old Man Li said, trudging up the stairway. "We shall have some New Year dishes. But we must be careful in our selection. The owner of this place might be greedy, otherwise he would not have built a restaurant upstairs. He knows that people will eat more after this climbing, *shew!*"

When he reached the top of the stairs he promptly changed his opinion of the owner. The spacious dining hall with red-lacquered lattice windows was clean and impressive, almost filled with customers. Only a reputable place could be so prosperous, he thought. The smiling manager greeted them and directed them to a vacant table near one of the windows and handed them two copies of the menu with special New Year dishes attached to them. Old Man Li held the menu tensely, swallowing and resisting, his eyes roving among the expensive items. He wanted to eat everything, but he felt his economical nature held him back like an iron chain restraining a dog. He quickly closed the menu and rubbed his neck. "May Li, I shall let you order."

*To find out more
about this passage,
turn to page 239.*

Items 13–18 refer to the passage on page 206.

Items 13–18 refer to the passage on page 206.

Write your answers in the space provided.

13. Where did the old man and the girl just come from?

_____

14. What can you conclude about the ethnic origin of the old man and the girl?

_____

15. Why did Old Man Li let May Li order the food?

_____

Circle the number of the best answer for each question.

16. After May Li asks about visiting Mr. Poon, what do she and her father do?

    (1) They try to find Mr. Poon.

    (2) They decide to celebrate New Year's Day.

    (3) They decide to have breakfast.

    (4) They leave the bus station.

    (5) They find a hotel.

17. When Old Man Li compares his wife to a cow, he is suggesting that she was

    (1) ugly.

    (2) very strong.

    (3) fat.

    (4) not very smart.

    (5) a bad mother.

18. What fact changed Old Man Li's opinion about the restaurant?

    (1) The owner was greedy.

    (2) The restaurant was upstairs.

    (3) He was hungry after climbing.

    (4) The restaurant was clean and impressive.

    (5) New Year dishes were on the menu.

Read the following passage from the novel *Roots* by Alex Haley.

Every time he and his brother would be walking somewhere by themselves, Kunta would imagine that he was taking Lamin on some journey, as men sometimes did with their sons. Now, somehow, Kunta felt a special responsibility to act older, with Lamin looking up to him as a source of knowledge. Walking alongside, Lamin would ply Kunta with a steady stream of questions.

"What's the world like?"

"Well," said Kunta, "no man or canoes ever journeyed so far. And no one knows all there is to know about it."

"What do you learn from the arafang?"

Kunta recited the first verses of the Koran in Arabic and then said, "Now you try." But when Lamin tried, he got badly confused—as Kunta had known he would—and Kunta said paternally, "It takes time."

"Why does no one harm owls?"

"Because all our dead ancestors' spirits are in owls." Then he told Lamin something of their late Grandma Yaisa. "You were just a baby, and cannot remember her."

"What's that bird in the tree?"

"A hawk."

"What does he eat?"

"Mice and other birds and things."

"Oh."

Kunta had never realized how much he knew—but now and then Lamin asked something of which Kunta knew nothing at all.

"Is the sun on fire?" Or: "Why doesn't our father sleep with us?"

At such times, Kunta would usually grunt, then stop talking—as Omoro did when he tired of so many of Kunta's questions. Then Lamin would say no more, since Mandinka home training taught that one never talked to another who did not want to talk. Sometimes Kunta would act as if he had gone into deep private thought. Lamin would sit silently nearby, and when Kunta rose, so would he. And sometimes, when Kunta didn't know the answer to a question, he would quickly do something to change the subject.

To find out more about this passage, turn to page 238.

Items 19–24 refer to the passage on page 208.

Fill in the blanks with the word or words that best complete the statements.

19. The two boys in the passage are named _____ and

_____.

20. The main idea of the passage is that the older brother wants to be

able to _____ his brother's questions.

21. The arafang the boys talk about is probably a _____.

Circle the number of the best answer for each question.

22. What causes Kunta's conflict with himself?

(1) He wants to be back at his home.

(2) He feels his father should be on the journey.

(3) His brother refuses to learn.

(4) He does not always know the answers to Lamin's questions.

(5) He believes he cannot harm an owl.

23. How does the older brother feel about the younger brother?

(1) He resents the boy.

(2) He dislikes the boy.

(3) He cares about the boy.

(4) He is not interested in his brother.

(5) He does not want to be responsible for his brother.

24. If Kunta were a boy in the United States today, what would he
probably teach his brother?

(1) the verses of the Koran

(2) how animals behave

(3) how to behave properly in society

(4) how to be quiet

(5) the multiplication tables

Read the following review of the book
Woman Hollering Creek and Other Stories by Katrina Sepulveda.

Sandra Cisneros knows her own mind. She knows who she is as a woman. And she knows who she is as a Hispanic. _Woman Hollering Creek and Other Stories_, the author's second collection, presents a powerful vision of the condition of women. This vision is not only of the Latina woman that Cisneros knows so well but of women in general. This new book is compelling and revealing.

At 36, Cisneros was more than ready to write these stories. The problems of Hispanic women are nothing new to her. She is the daughter of a Mexican man. Her mother is Mexican-American. She grew up with traditional roles. From her six brothers she learned that a woman is supposed to be taken care of by a man.

But the women in Cisneros' stories do not need taking care of—not by any means. These are strong characters: young girls, idealistic brides, religious women, and women disappointed in love. The stories of the younger women, like their lives, are short but intense. The older women's longer stories reflect their greater experience. These women are proud of the power they have worked so hard to achieve.

The main character of the title story, "Woman Hollering Creek," is a young Mexican woman. Soap operas have affected her sense of reality. Soon after crossing the border to marry a Texan, she discovers that her new life has little, if any, of the romance and joy enjoyed by her TV idols. Rather than candlelight and roses, she gets snores and bad table manners. The young woman's efforts to rewrite the script of her own real-life soap opera make excellent reading.

Cisneros' view of men is not always complimentary. Men have a definite place in the lives of her characters—preferably at a distance. But the men are always there.

Cisneros' use of language is as balanced as her vision. She blends Spanish and English like spices and subtle flavorings. The effect is twice as nice.

A new breed of writers is demanding attention. Sandra Cisneros is one writer who is sure to get it.

Items 25–29 refer to the passage on page 210.

Write your answers in the space provided.

25. The reviewer divides Sandra Cisneros' characters into groups. What are the four classifications?

_____

_____

26. What simile does the reviewer use to suggest that Sandra Cisneros uses Spanish and English well together?

_____

Circle the number of the best answer for each question.

27. Which statement is the reviewer's opinion of Sandra Cisneros' book?

    (1) It is the best ever written about Hispanic women.

    (2) It is too critical of men.

    (3) It is interesting and balanced.

    (4) It is too revealing.

    (5) It is boring.

28. Which phrase shows the reviewer's bias in favor of the book?

    (1) *traditional roles*

    (2) *longer stories*

    (3) *a soap opera*

    (4) *excellent reading*

    (5) *not always complimentary*

29. How does the reviewer contrast the stories about older women and the stories about young women? The reviewer suggests that

    (1) Cisneros' stories about old and young women are similar.

    (2) the stories about the young women are more interesting.

    (3) all of the stories show women in traditional roles.

    (4) the young and old characters are all powerful women.

    (5) the stories about young women are shorter than those about older women.

POSTTEST
Correlation Chart

Literature

The chart below will help you determine your strengths and weaknesses in interpreting literature and the arts.

Directions

Circle the number of each item that you answered correctly on the Posttest. Count the number of items you answered correctly in each row. Write the amount in the Total Correct space in each row. (For example, in the Classical Literature row, write the number correct in the blank before *out of 12*). Complete this process for the remaining rows. Then add the 3 totals to get your Total Correct for the whole 29-item Posttest.

Content Areas	Items	Total Correct	Pages
Popular Literature (Pages 12–105)	7, 8, 9, 10, 11, 12 19, 20, 21, 22 23, 24	_____ out of 12	Pages 38–43, Pages 50–55, 80–85
Classical Literature (Pages 106–163)	1, 2, 3, 4, 5, 6 13, 14, 15, 16 17, 18	_____ out of 12	Pages 138–143 Pages 114–119
Commentary (Pages 164–201)	25, 26, 27, 28, 29	_____ out of 5	Pages 176–180
TOTAL CORRECT FOR INVENTORY _____ out of 29			

If you answered fewer than 26 items correctly, determine which of the three areas of literature you need to study further. Go back and review the passages in those areas. Page numbers to refer to for practice are given in the right-hand column above.

ANSWERS AND EXPLANATIONS

INVENTORY

PAGE 1

1. hurts
2. free
3. smooth
4. **(1) All creatures suffer when they are trapped.** The bird is a symbol for any being that is not free. The poet understands its pain because people feel the same way when they are trapped. Option 2 is incorrect because it is too specific; it is not general enough to apply to cruelty to people. There is no support for options 3 or 4. Option 5 is incorrect because music, or singing, is an expression of pain in the poem, not a way to solve the problem.
5. **(3) yearning** This option is correct because the bird wants what it cannot have. Options 1, 2, and 5 are the opposite of the emotion in the poem. There is no support for option 4.
6. **(4) the blues** This option is correct because the blues express painful emotions and a search for something. Option 1 is incorrect because there is no cause to be thankful. Options 2, 3, and 5 are incorrect because they are generally not songs that express pain.

PAGE 3

7. Joan Rivers, the main writer of the autobiography, is telling the story.
8. The audience was screaming, priests were yelling, and nuns were shaking their fists.
9. **(1) "The biggest scam ever pulled on me was that summer of 1960."** This option is correct because the passage is mainly about the story of this scam. The other options are incorrect because they are details in the story.
10. **(5) embarrassed** This option is suggested by Joan Rivers's description of what she says and does on-stage. Option 1 describes how she felt before going on-stage. Option 3 is the opposite of what

is suggested. There is no support in the passage for options 2 and 4.
11. **(1) amused** This option is supported by the author's humorous tone. There is no support for options 2 and 4. Options 3 and 5 are feelings she might have had at the time but does not have now.

PAGE 5

12. They have been married for eight years.
13. Nora will probably leave. The stage directions say that she has put on her cloak, hat, and shawl.
14. **(3) gap** The clue to the meaning is given by the words *opened between us*. There is no support in the passage for the other options.
15. **(2) He does not really understand what Nora wants.** Torvald keeps making the wrong suggestions in his effort to get Nora to stay. Option 1 is incorrect because this is what he offers to do, not what he has done. Options 3 and 5 are the opposite of what is suggested about his character. There is no support for option 4.
16. **(3) treated her like a pet or a toy.** This option is correct because the metaphors suggest how Torvald thought of Nora. Option 1 is incorrect because it is the opposite of what the metaphors suggest. There is no support for options 2 and 4. Option 5 is incorrect because Nora does not like the way Torvald has acted toward her.

PAGE 7

17. bridge, starship
18. opening
19. first contact
20. **(2) glowing** This option is correct because *glowing* means the same as *luminous*. Option 1 refers to the being's face, not just the eyes. There is no support in the passage for options 3, 4, and 5.
21. **(5) He gets excited inside.** This option is supported by the last sentence in the passage. There is no support for options 1, 2, and 3. Option 4 is incorrect because Captain Kirk is only outwardly calm.

22. **(1) suggest an advanced technology.** This option is correct because Jim's words suggest the use of computer images. Jim seems to use the words casually. This helps to create a futuristic setting. Option 2 is incorrect because the phrase does not explain anything. Option 3 is incorrect because the phrase does not suggest anything simple. There is no support for options 4 and 5.

PAGE 9

23. Shirley Horn is known for jazz.
24. Her recordings have not sold enough copies to make money. They have cost her money.
25. **(1) Her new album is near the top of the *Billboard* jazz chart.** This is a fact that can be checked. Options 2, 3, 4, and 5 are incorrect because they are opinions, not facts.
26. **(4) continue to play her music.** This option is based on what the reviewer reveals about Shirley Horn's character. Money is not the reason she loves music. Options 1, 2, and 5 are incorrect because they do not fit Shirley Horn's character. Option 3 is incorrect because carpentry is her hobby, not her career.
27. **(1) She is unforgettable.** This option is suggested in the reviewer's discussion of the new album. He says that she is *indelible*, which means "making a mark that can't be erased." There is no support for options 2 and 4. Option 3 is a fact that has nothing to do with music. Option 5 is incorrect because the reviewer admires both her voice and her piano playing.

UNIT 1: POPULAR LITERATURE
SECTION 1

PAGE 14

1. There are many possible answers.
2. Chee and the horse thief
3. There are many possible answers.
4. There are many possible answers.

PAGE 15

The thief must have tied his horse and then climbed directly up the slope across the arroyo.

PAGE 16

small girl, Navajo, frightened, speaks English

PAGE 17

There are many possible answers. Sample: The girl's face had been forlorn and was now radiant, she looked thoughtful, and she became suspicious.

PAGES 18–19

1. hogan
2. *chindi*
3. gusts
4. plausible
5. tentatively
6. forlorn
7. arroyo
8. ponderosa
9. There are many possible answers.
10. He hears a cough and sniffling from the hogan.
11. The girl comes out of the hogan.
12. The hogan belongs to Hosteen Ashie Begay.
13. **(4) He had died in the hogan.** This option is correct because she knew someone had died in the hogan, and her grandfather was no longer there. There is no evidence for option 1. Option 2 is wrong because she did not know Albert Gorman had died. Option 3 is incorrect because there was no reason for an arrest. Option 5 is wrong because she was the one who stole the horse.
14. Only a person who is not a Navajo would go into a *chindi* hogan.
15. Chee will try to find out how and why Albert Gorman died.
16. The Navajo believe a *chindi* hogan should be avoided. So Begay could no longer live in his old home.

17. There are many possible answers.
    Samples: Yes, Chee was right to have his
    pistol ready. He thought he would find the
    horse thief, who might be dangerous. No,
    Chee was wrong to have his pistol ready.
    He should have realized there was no
    danger. A dangerous person who was
    hiding would not have coughed and
    sniffled loudly.
18. There are many possible answers.
    Sample: Find a place for the girl to stay.
    Return the horse to its owner. Look for
    Begay, to ask him questions about Albert
    Gorman.
19. There are many possible answers.

SECTION 2

PAGE 20

1. There are many possible answers.
2. Alfred Lanning, Dr. Susan Calvin, The
   Brain
3. There are many possible answers.
4. There are many possible answers.

PAGE 21

The doctors are upset because something is
wrong with The Brain.

PAGE 22

The Brain has sent two men and a space ship
into space.

PAGE 23

The space ship left by itself without any
acceleration. The ship works on an unknown
principle because there are no engines visible.
The ship is being run by remote control.

PAGES 24–25

| 1. g | 2. e | 3. c | 4. d |
| 5. b | 6. f | 7. h | 8. a |

9. There are many possible answers.
10. The Brain is a robot.
11. A robot cannot harm a human being.
12. They are afraid the men will either die or
    be unable to return.
13. She doesn't want to upset The Brain and
    cause it to break communication.

14. **(1) Robots can be a problem if they act
    on their own.** This option is correct
    because it is the basis for the events that
    take place in the story. Option 2 is incorrect
    because The Brain is quite happy; the
    people are angry and upset. There is no
    evidence in the passage for option 3. Option
    4 may be true in many cases, but certainly
    is not true here. Option 5 is incorrect
    because although it is true of The Brain it
    is not the main idea of the story.
15. **(1) The Brain is worth a great deal of
    money.** This is probably true but has
    nothing to do with the main idea. Options
    2, 3, 4, and 5 all give examples of The
    Brain's independent behavior.
16. Dr. Calvin; She is the one in charge of The
    Brain and she keeps telling Dr. Lanning
    to be quiet.
17. There are many possible answers.
    Sample: There is no simple answer. The
    men might be safe, because they are
    protected by the First Law. The men
    might not be safe, because The Brain
    might be out of control.
18. There are many possible answers.

SECTION 3

PAGE 26

1. There are many possible answers.
2. He has left his home and just arrived in
   New York.
3. Harlem, in New York City
4. There are many possible answers.

PAGE 27

good, crazy feeling, breathless, dazzled

PAGE 28

He was happier in the streets of Harlem than
in the classrooms of Columbia. He felt rejected
at school but welcome in Harlem.

PAGE 29

In 1921 African-American men were
discriminated against when looking for jobs.

PAGES 30–31

1. d   2. f   3. b
4. e   5. a   6. c
7. There are many possible answers.
8. He spent his first days exploring the neighborhood of Harlem.
9. His final grades included three *B*s and a *C*.
10. He had few skills and he was an African American.
11. **(2) walking all over Harlem** This answer is correct because the phrase suggests that he could have made a map of Harlem from all the walking he did. There is no support for option 1. Options 3 and 5 are wrong because mapping does not suggest counting or wasting time. Option 4 is wrong because it confuses the verb *mapping* with the noun *map*.
12. **(3) the group that published his poetry.** This answer is correct because of the facts that they had received his poems and that they had readers who enjoyed his work. Option 1 is wrong because Columbia University and *The Crisis* are not related in any way. Also, no one at Columbia took Langston to lunch. Option 2 is wrong because the Negro musical hit is called *Shuffle Along*. Option 4 is wrong because the library had nothing to do with his poetry. Option 5 is wrong because Langston was taken to lunch at the restaurant, but the restaurant did not publish his poems.
13. The Harlem landlords and the Columbia dorms both discriminated against African Americans, the first by charging high rents, the second by not allowing African Americans at all.
14. Langston's father probably was angry because his son was not going on with school. Not replying would be a way to express that anger.
15. There are many possible answers. Sample: Langston will probably try to make it on his own as a poet.
16. There are many possible answers.

SECTION 4

PAGE 32

1. There are many possible answers.
2. Don and Jill
3. There are many possible answers.

PAGE 33

Jill is confused by Don. She does not know much about people who are blind, and she does not understand how he can joke about being blind.

PAGE 34

Don and Jill are in Don's apartment. This is first clear from Jill's remark about his apartment and is supported by the stage directions.

PAGE 35

Don and Jill have different opinions about people who are blind. Jill thinks people who are blind are spooky and different from other people. Don thinks of himself as being just like anyone else.

PAGES 36–37

1. braille
2. sinister
3. delicatessen
4. bravura
5. self-consciously
6. There are many possible answers.
7. He realized that most people aren't blind when he was six years old.
8. Jill lives in the apartment next door. The stage directions mention the door to Jill's apartment, blocked by a chest of drawers.
9. Don is making a joke. Having the *market cornered* suggests that Don's mother feels so guilty about his blindness that there is little guilt left to go around.
10. **(2) He is independent and funny.** This option is supported by Don's references to how well he can get around. He also makes a number of jokes. Jill's remarks show that option 1 is wrong. There is no support for option 3. Option 4 is wrong because he makes jokes about himself. Option 5 is wrong because he states that he prefers people to act naturally.

11. **(4) He explains how he feels about being blind.** This option is supported by his responses to Jill's discomfort. Option 1 is wrong because he does talk about blindness. Option 2 is wrong because Don stays calm and in a good mood. There is no support for option 3. Option 5 is wrong because it is the opposite of what Don says.

12. Don's attitude is more positive because he does not feel that being blind gets in his way. Jill, on the other hand, thinks people who are blind must be bitter and a little strange—maybe even to be pitied.

13. There are many possible answers. Sample: Don believes that people have the wrong idea about people who are blind. He thinks that people pay too much attention to the one thing he cannot do. They ignore the fact that he is normal in every other way. He would rather be accepted for who he is and for what he can do.

14. There are many possible answers. Take into account what Don says about how other people act toward him.

SECTION 5

PAGE 38

1. There are many possible answers.
2. a woman who is 38 years old
3. There are many possible answers.
4. There are many possible answers.

PAGE 39

Plain as bread suggests that the speaker does not feel she is pretty. *Round as a cake* suggests that the speaker feels she is chubby, not slim.

PAGE 40

There are many possible answers. Sample: The speaker is 38 years old and is looking at her life. She is not what she had expected to be. She thinks about her mother and her own daughters. She hopes she can face the rest of her life with strength and acceptance.

PAGE 41

The father gives *a knowing nod; tears welled in his eyes*.

PAGES 42–43

1. f 2. e 3. b
4. d 5. c 6. a
7. There are many possible answers.
8. smaller, more beautiful, wiser in African ways (the poet uses the spelling *Afrikan*), more confident
9. There are many possible answers. Sample: The little boy's only remembrance of his mother is a picture. When shopping, the boy sees a woman who looks like the picture. The father apologizes to the woman after the boy stares at her. The woman hugs the boy.
10. **(3) was trying to be like her mother.** Option 3 is supported by the speaker having dreamed dreams for her mother and having made her mother alive again, both of which suggest she wants to be like her mother. Option 1 is wrong because the mother is admired. Options 2 and 4 have no support. There is no evidence for option 5.
11. **(1) accept her own life as it is** This option is supported by her wanting to face the next part of her life without loneliness or fear. Also, the speaker says she wants to go into her own life. Option 2 is wrong because she is bothered by being ordinary. There is no support for option 3. Options 4 and 5 are misreadings of the mentions of Europe and daughters.
12. Both characters' mothers are dead. In each poem, the loss of the mother influences how the character feels and reacts.
13. There are many possible answers. Sample: The boy is looking for a mother's love. The meeting with the woman in the store will not give him what he wants. The woman can fill his need for only a few minutes.
14. There are many possible answers.

SECTION 6

PAGE 44

1. There are many possible answers.
2. Mark. He is a boy, probably in his early teens.
3. There are many possible answers.

PAGE 45

The passage is seen through only one person's eyes. The narrator is Mark.

PAGE 46

The setting is outdoors. There are trees. Nearby is a house. It is sometime in the afternoon.

PAGE 47

Mark's and Sue's fathers know each other. Both Mark and Sue are at this place to kill a vampire.

PAGES 48–49

1. glimpse
2. methodical
3. pondering
4. hunkered
5. incline
6. cylindrical
7. momentarily
8. synchronized
9. There are many possible answers.
10. She moved carefully, and she had guts.
11. **(4) vampires** This is suggested by the reference to killing vampires. There is no support for the other options.
12. **(2) with a wooden stake** Since both of them brought wooden stakes, option 2 is a good conclusion. Option 1 is wrong because only Mark had a pistol. There is no support for options 3, 4, and 5.
13. Sue was frightened. You can tell because she was tense, pale, and ready to scream.
14. Mark thinks he knows about the supernatural, things that are not just everyday events.

15. There are many possible answers. Sample: I wondered what would happen because I was not sure if someone would come out of the house and discover Mark and Sue hiding in the woods.
16. There are many possible answers.

SECTION 7

PAGE 50

1. There are many possible answers.
2. a boy, Mattie, Etta
3. There are many possible answers.
4. There are many possible answers.

PAGE 51

Etta smooths her hair and prances around the table. These actions suggest she understands the boy is flirting and she is flirting a little in return.

PAGE 52

Ciel talks about events that must be from her childhood. Only a child would worry about crayons. She had known Mattie then. Now she and Basil are grown and on their own.

PAGE 53

There are many possible answers. Sample: Etta is a slender, attractive, middle-aged, African-American woman, probably very energetic, maybe nicely dressed.

PAGES 54–55

1. e   2. f   3. a
4. b   5. c   6. d
7. There are many possible answers.
8. San Francisco
9. Ciel has been walking slowly—which suggests that time is passing. More than one person stops Ciel—which means that she stopped several times as she was walking.
10. There are many possible answers. The description of Mattie might be one who acts motherly and responsibly. Mattie's description probably would be very different from the description of Etta.

11. **(3) an outdoor neighborhood party.** This option is supported by mention of dancing in the street, the outdoor grill, and the number of people present. Etta also states that it is a party. Option 1 is wrong because there is no evidence of family relationships. There is no support for option 2. Option 4 is wrong because they are not in San Francisco. The only mention of a wedding refers to the future, so option 5 is wrong.

12. **(1) She had had some kind of personal trouble.** This is suggested by Ciel's references to why she did not write to Mattie. Getting to the ocean was an accident, so option 3 is wrong. There is no support for options 2, 4, and 5.

13. They approve of him because he is both good to her and good for her. They don't care that he isn't black. These ideas are supported by Etta's statement about what a man is and isn't. They are also supported by the way the women volunteer to take part in Ciel's wedding.

14. Yes. Ciel has begun to accept whatever happened in the past. She also has received a warm and loving welcome.

15. There are many possible answers.

SECTION 8

PAGE 56

1. There are many possible answers.
2. Willie Mays. He is in the Army.
3. There are many possible answers.

PAGE 57

The Army had Mays play on baseball teams and teach baseball to other soldiers.

PAGE 58

Frank gives Mays his overcoat. The clue word is *so*.

PAGE 59

Mays uses the tap dancer's comment about his love of dancing to express how he feels about baseball.

PAGES 60–61

1. morale
2. authority
3. technicality
4. suspicious
5. ordeal
6. There are many possible answers.
7. Mays had hoped he could be discharged early to take care of his family. He was sad that he was not discharged, so his last days in the Army were slightly troubled.
8. *The silent treatment* happens when the ball players ignore a good play or something they are pleased about. They do the opposite of what they feel.
9. **(3) were dressed in odd-looking clothes.** This option is supported by the overcoat being too big for Mays and by Forbes using newspapers to stuff his jacket. Option 1 is wrong because the tip had nothing to do with Forbes or Mays. Options 2 and 5 have no support. Option 4 is wrong because it was the way they looked, not the way they acted, that was suspicious.
10. **(3) He took too long getting his snack in New Orleans.** Because he took too long, the train left without him. So he was late for spring training. Option 1 is wrong because he started the trip on time in Washington. There is no support for options 2 and 5. Option 4 is wrong because Leo was only a little annoyed at the delay and had nothing to do with Mays' schedule.
11. There are many possible answers. Answers should reflect Mays' positive attitudes about authority and family. Answers might also deal with Mays' concern about the welfare of his team over his own welfare.
12. Mays shows that his relationship with Leo is close. Leo cares about Mays, and Mays wants Leo's respect and affection.
13. There are many possible answers. Sample: I would be happy because Mays was a great baseball player and the Giants were having a bad season before he returned.
14. There are many possible answers.

SECTION 9

PAGE 62

1. There are many possible answers.
2. Meg, Babe, Lenny
3. There are many possible answers.
4. There are many possible answers.

PAGE 63

Babe had been planning to leave.

PAGE 64

Meg and Babe are impatient with Lenny. Lenny is having trouble deciding whether to blow out the candles. Suspense is created by the reader having to wait for Lenny's decision.

PAGE 65

Meg and Babe watch for Lenny to arrive. Lenny is surprised by the birthday cake. After a delay, they sing "Happy Birthday." Lenny is persuaded into telling her wish. The sisters eat the cake.

PAGES 66–67

1. d   2. c   3. e
4. f   5. a   6. b
7. There are many possible answers.
8. They are sisters.
9. Lenny wishes for a laughing moment with her sisters.
10. Babe means that Meg should watch for Lenny.
11. Babe makes up the traditions about the number of candles and wishing deeply enough.
12. **(1) She takes a long time to make up her mind.** This option is supported by both sisters telling her to hurry up. There is no support for options 2 and 3. Option 4 is wrong because her sister says that the wish is nice. Option 5 is wrong because the sisters enjoy eating the cake.
13. **(5) All the sisters were having problems.** This option is supported by Meg's first statement. Option 1 is the opposite of what is stated. There is no support for options 2 and 4. Option 3 is wrong because Lenny loves birthday celebrations.
14. There are many possible answers. Sample: Babe makes up her beliefs to reassure Lenny. She wants Lenny to feel good about what is happening.
15. Yes. Lenny wants her sisters to laugh with her. In the last minutes of the play, they do. They have gotten to that magical moment.
16. There are many possible answers.

SECTION 10

PAGE 68

1. There are many possible answers.
2. fishing
3. There are many possible answers.
4. There are many possible answers.

PAGE 69

Angry. The word suggests being upset. Angry water would be moving around, not calm.

PAGE 70

The narrator is the young boy. Seeing the action from the narrator's point of view helps you understand how important the story of the carp is to him and the people of the town.

PAGE 71

The people ate the carp; *for a long time, then, finally*

PAGES 72–73

1. furrow
2. churned
3. listlessly
4. abode
5. subsided
6. relent
7. There are many possible answers.
8. He learns about the golden carp after the sun starts to set.
9. Catching carp is bad luck because the carp were the first people.
10. **(2) uncomfortable** This option is supported by the narrator's shivering, his questions, and his thinking about his mother—a source of comfort. Option 1 is wrong because he continues to ask questions. The narrator's reactions do not suggest options 3, 4, and 5.

11. **(3) He wanted to take care of the carp people.** This option is supported by the direct statement that the kind god asked the other gods to turn him into a carp to take care of his people. Option 1 is wrong because the other gods agreed with him. Option 2 is wrong because the disobedience was not connected to the kind god. Option 4 is wrong because looking like the huge golden carp is an effect, not a cause. Option 5 refers to the people, not the god.
12. He is suggesting that many things had happened at the river that no human would ever know. He was about to find out something important.
13. There are many possible answers. Sample: The narrator seems to believe Samuel's story because he asks Samuel what would happen if someone ate a carp.
14. There are many possible answers.

SECTION 11

PAGE 74

1. There are many possible answers.
2. street directions; the dollar, money
3. There are many possible answers.
4. There are many possible answers.

PAGE 75

humorous

PAGE 76

There are many possible answers. Samples: The author exaggerates by suggesting a semester-long course on arrow drawing for sign makers. The author also exaggerates by saying there are cities in America so hard to find your way around in they are not worth figuring out.

PAGE 77

Both essays use a humorous tone. Both authors use the point of view of a narrator.

PAGES 78–79

| 1. d | 2. f | 3. b | 4. h |
| 5. g | 6. a | 7. e | 8. c |

9. There are many possible answers.

10. The phrase "up and down the island" helps you understand the meaning of *longitudinally*.
11. The government in Washington no longer understands the value of a dollar.
12. A stranger might get confused in New York City because the order of street names changes abruptly.
13. **(5) "I hope they devote a semester to arrow drawing for signmakers."** This option is an exaggerated solution to the problem. Options 1, 2, 3, and 4 are all direct statements.
14. **(2) of some real value to the average American.** This option is supported by the author's introduction and by her reference to putting a punch back into middle America's pocketbook. Option 1 is the opposite of what the author suggests. Option 3 refers to her lessons for Congress, not the value of the dollar. Option 4 has no support. Option 5 refers to what a dollar could buy when the author was young.
15. There are many possible answers. Sample: Yes, I agree. It is very difficult to find your way around a strange city with poorly marked streets.
16. There are many possible answers. Sample: No, I don't think her suggestions would change how the government spends money because they are humorous, unrealistic suggestions.
17. There are many possible answers.

SECTION 12

PAGE 80

1. There are many possible answers.
2. a mother and a daughter named Waverly
3. Chinese and American
4. There are many possible answers.

PAGE 81

The differences are the way she walks and her facial expression.

PAGE 82

You can infer that the Chinese believe in not wasting what one has been given.

PAGE 83

The mother wants her daughter to learn Chinese values. The daughter wants to be Chinese only in appearance; her other values are American.

PAGES 84–85

1. pursuing
2. opportunities
3. blend
4. fabulous
5. advantage
6. circumstances
7. There are many possible answers.
8. American circumstances and Chinese character
9. The Chinese face shows her real emotions. The American face conceals her real emotions.
10. **(2) They look directly at each other.** The mother's criticism implies that Americans do the opposite of the Chinese. Option 1 refers to Americans. There is no support for options 3, 4, and 5.
11. **(1) She doesn't believe her mother understands American ways.** She feels her mother might make a mistake if left on her own. Option 2 is wrong; it refers to the daughter's voice, which the mother objects to. Option 3 may be true, but it does not matter, because the mother speaks English. Option 4 is wrong because the mother seems to know quite well what she wants. There is no support for option 5.
12. **(3)"... her famous Mr. Rory ..."** This option suggests that the mother doesn't think much of the hairdresser. She is making fun of how well known he is. Options 1 and 4 are statements about how the mother thinks Waverly feels. Option 2 is a comment by Waverly. Option 5 is a judgment unrelated to the daughter's ideas.
13. There are many possible answers. Sample: Waverly may understand what she has in common with her mother when she has children of her own. She may understand that all parents and children have some conflicting values.
14. There are many possible answers.

SECTION 13

PAGE 86

1. There are many possible answers.
2. Smith and Carlos
3. There are many possible answers.

PAGE 87

The numbers stand for the time it took to run the race. *Semi* is a shortened form of *semifinal*.

PAGE 88

The two effects are that Smith came in first and that Norman came in second.

PAGE 89

There are many possible answers. Sample: Smith and Carlos may have been punished by sports authorities in the United States. Their protest may have caused people around the world to consider the problem of racism in sports and in society.

PAGES 90–91

1. e
2. b
3. a
4. f
5. d
6. c
7. g
8. There are many possible answers.
9. Smith is referring to the fact that the Olympic audience was made up of people from many countries. They would not all understand a protest spoken only in English.
10. Norman wore an Olympic Project for Human Rights button.
11. Smith had injured his leg two hours earlier.
12. Carlos thinks that he would have won the race and set a new world record.
13. **(5) he was going to raise his gloved right hand.** This option can be inferred from his statement that he took the right glove and later raised that hand. There is no support for options 1, 3, and 4. Option 2 is wrong because he accepted the symbolism of the olive tree.
14. **(2) He slowed down.** This option is a figurative way of saying what is later stated about Carlos. There is no support for options 1, 3, and 5. Option 4 is the opposite of what is stated in the passage.

15. **(1) the excellence of African-American athletes** This option can be inferred from the whole article. It is also supported by several statements by Smith and Carlos. There is no support for the other options.
16. There are many possible answers. Sample: They are proud of what they did.
17. There are many possible answers.

SECTION 14

PAGE 92

1. There are many possible answers.
2. The biography is about Luis W. Alvarez. He was a scientist.
3. There are many possible answers.

PAGE 93

The detail *an accidental explosion would cause a terrible disaster* supports the main idea of the paragraph.

PAGE 94

There are many possible answers. Sample: The second shock wave happened because the first shock wave bounced off the ground back into the air.

PAGE 95

The Alvarezes concluded that the dinosaurs died after the earth was hit by a large body from outer space. They starved and froze to death.

PAGES 96–97

1. d   2. e   3. c   4. h
5. g   6. a   7. f   8. b
9. There are many possible answers.
10. after
11. explosion or bomb
12. **(3) his work as a geologist** This option is stated in the passage as the work he *may be best remembered for*. Options 1 and 2 are incorrect because he was just part of a team and was not directly responsible for either one. Option 4 is incorrect because he is better known for something else. There is no support for option 5.

13. **(2) A clay layer formed on Earth.** This option is correct because there is no evidence of fossils in the layer. Option 1 is a hypothesis, not a fact. Option 4 is true but does not support the conclusion. Option 3 does not discuss the differences between the layers and why they are significant. Option 5 does not help to explain the animals' death.
14. **(2) Future wars would be avoided.** Alvarez referred to this possible cause-and-effect relationship in his letter to his son. There is no support in the passage for the other options.
15. There are many possible answers.

UNIT 1 REVIEW

PAGE 99

1. c   2. a   3. b
4. **(1) proud.** This option is supported by Marsha's comments about how beautiful her baby is. Options 2 and 3 are wrong because they refer to the way Victor feels. There is no support for options 4 and 5.
5. **(3) The baby is not normal.** This option is supported by the fact that the baby clearly focuses on Victor's eyes. Option 1 is wrong because the passage states that the baby is a newborn. There is no support for options 2, 4, and 5.
6. **(5) shock and fear** These words are used to describe Victor's feelings as he looks into the infant's eyes. Option 1 is wrong because the words refer to reactions of the resident and the mother. Option 2 is wrong because the baby's eyes are blue. Option 3 is wrong because the words refer to Marsha's and Victor's observations. Option 4 is wrong because eye color does not affect how Victor feels.

PAGE 101

7. divorced
8. nights
9. woman
10. torn up/shredded

11. **(1) arguing bitterly** This option is correct because it suggests that the two tried to hurt each other's feelings with words in the same way they might hurt each other physically by throwing furniture. Option 2 is wrong because the couple did not really throw furniture. There is no support for options 3, 4, and 5.

12. **(3) The man and woman now live in different parts of the country.** This option is correct because it is implied that the two are separated by distance. There is no support for options 1, 2, 4, and 5.

13. **(5) held on tight, and let go** This option is correct because it summarizes the sadness the couple felt about the divorce. It also refers to the fact that they finally decided to end the marriage. Option 1 is wrong because it refers to how the couple acted before the end of the marriage. There is no support for options 2, 3, and 4.

PAGE 103

14. The story is told by Tammy Wynette, whose real name is Wynette Byrd.
15. She thinks Billy felt sorry for her.
16. There are many possible answers. Sample: It pays to keep trying.
17. **(1) The woman enters the office and sees the man.** This option is correct because it is the first action. Options 2, 3, 4, and 5 all occur later.
18. **(2) nervous.** This option is supported by her own statement in paragraph 2. Options 1, 3, and 4 are wrong because they do not describe how she felt. Option 5 describes how Billy acted, not Wynette.
19. **(4) the casual way Billy offered to record her.** This option is supported by Wynette's statement. There is no support for options 1, 2, 3, and 5.

PAGE 105

20. science fiction
21. radio signals
22. Friday
23. **(3) were expecting to receive signals from outer space.** This answer is supported by the narrator's introduction which describes Adela's and Marcos' work. There is no support for options 1, 2, and 5.

Option 4 is the opposite of what is stated in the play.

24. **(4) she is afraid the police will think she and Marcos are crazy.** This option is supported by Adela's statement ". . . they'll think we're a couple of UFO freaks who have gone off the deep end." There is no support for options 1 and 2. Option 3 is incorrect because she and Marcos are both convinced that the radio is giving news that is a day ahead of them. Option 5 is incorrect because Marcos says they have until "tomorrow at five o'clock."

25. **(4) go to the authorities and try to convince them that the bridge will collapse.** Option 1 is incorrect because the discovery is too important to ignore. Option 2 is incorrect because they could make more money if they kept the radio. There is no support for option 3. Option 5 may be true in the future, but it is not the first thing they would do.

UNIT 2: CLASSICAL LITERATURE

SECTION 15

PAGE 108

1. There are many possible answers.
2. He is very nervous.
3. a thriller
4. There are many possible answers.

PAGE 109

very gradually

PAGE 110

The mood is tense. There are many possible answers. Sample: The action happens very slowly, and the author repeats many things. For example, "cautiously—oh, so cautiously—cautiously."

PAGE 111

He probably will act quickly in anger. He will get rid of the evil eye by killing the old man immediately.

PAGES 112–113

| 1. g | 2. j | 3. c | 4. b | 5. d |
| 6. i | 7. h | 8. a | 9. e | 10. f |

11. There are many possible answers.
12. the old man's strange-looking eye
13. "first the idea entered my brain"
14. **(5) waiting to see the vulture eye.** The eye is what terrifies the narrator and causes him to murder. Option 1 is not mentioned by the narrator. Option 2 is the opposite of what is stated in the story. Option 3 is wrong because the eye can't be seen while the old man is asleep. Option 4 doesn't seem to matter to the narrator.
15. **(5) nervous pride** The narrator is boasting about how clever he was, but he is still nervous about what he did. There is an element of fear in the story, but the narrator does not feel enough fear to support option 1. There is no support for options 2 and 4. Option 3 seems to be the opposite of his emotion.
16. There are many possible answers. Sample: No. He is crazy. His reason for killing the old man is not the thinking of a sane man.
17. There are many possible answers.

SECTION 16

PAGE 114

1. There are many possible answers.
2. Alessandro and Ramona
3. There are many possible answers.

PAGE 115

a horse; *trotting, snort* and *whinny*

PAGE 116

reiterated

PAGE 117

There are many possible answers. Sample: Ramona asks Alessandro to give her a name he likes.

PAGES 118–119

1. f	4. g	7. b
2. a	5. c	8. h
3. d	6. e	

9. There are many possible answers.
10. They are running off to get married.

11. **(4) He thought they might be stopped.** He thinks that Ramona's family will follow them and take Ramona back. There is no support for options 1 and 5. Option 2 is wrong because the horse and pony do not seem to be in a hurry. Option 3 is wrong because it is the opposite of what Ramona wants.
12. **(3) Ramona's family does not approve of Alessandro.** This option is supported by Ramona's discussion of the Señora and Felipe. Options 1 and 4 are wrong because the opposites are suggested. There is no mention of Alessandro's parents, so option 2 is wrong. Option 5 is wrong because he is clearly devoted to her.
13. **(1) Love conquers all problems.** The couple's love gives them the courage to break away from Ramona's family and to ignore class differences. There is no suggestion of hesitation, so option 2 is wrong. There is no support for options 3 and 5. The question of names is only a portion of the passage, so option 4 is wrong.
14. The Baba passage is humorous. Seeing Ramona and Alessandro through the horse's eyes emphasizes the happiness they feel.
15. There are many possible answers. Sample: Ramona and Alessandro might try to reason with Ramona's family before running away to get married.
16. There are many possible answers.

SECTION 17

PAGE 120

1. There are many possible answers.
2. The speaker is trying to choose which one of two roads to take.
3. There are many possible answers.
4. There are many possible answers.

PAGE 121

There are many possible answers. Sample: *Wanted wear* means the road has not been used very much. Some context clues are *less traveled by* and *no step had trodden.*

PAGE 122

There are many possible answers. Samples: The people of the town envied Richard Cory because he looked as though he had everything. Richard Cory was probably very unhappy and felt there were many important things he did not have. The theme of the poem could be "No one can know how another person feels inside from the way that person looks on the outside."

PAGE 123

Grandma thinks that the old ways were good, and she wishes that today's young people could feel the way she did.

PAGES 124–125

1. minuet
2. trodden
3. diverged
4. arrayed
5. schooled
6. claim
7. There are many possible answers.
8. He stood and looked down the two roads.
9. She was pretty, with bright and sunny hair and dimpled cheeks.
10. The words *crown* and *imperially* suggest that Richard Cory was like a king.
11. **(2)** *really about the same* This option is correct because the restatement suggests that one road is as good as the other. Options 1 and 5 are wrong because they make a contrast between the two roads. There is no support for options 3 and 4.
12. **(3) You can't judge a book by its cover.** This option is correct because the saying means that you should not make a decision based on appearances. Looking at the outside of something does not always tell you what the inside is like. There is no support for options 1, 2, and 4. Option 5 is wrong because there is no suggestion that Richard Cory was evil.
13. **(1) Both poems discuss individual choice.** This option is correct because both poems focus on the choices that people make about their lives. Options 2, 4, and 5 are wrong because success, failure, and social issues are talked about or hinted at only in "Richard Cory." Option 4 is wrong because only "A Road Not Taken" talks about the future.
14. There are many possible answers.

SECTION 18
PAGE 126

1. There are many possible answers.
2. a white man named Karl Lindner, Beneatha, her brother Walter, and Ruth
3. There are many possible answers. Sample: a problem affecting African Americans
4. There are many possible answers.

PAGE 127

Walter sees himself as the head of the household, as being in control of the situation. Ruth and Beneatha do not take Walter seriously as the head of the house.

PAGE 128

People can become uncomfortable when dealing with other people whom they consider different.

PAGE 129

There are many possible answers. Sample: There have been racial problems in other neighborhoods. This neighborhood wants to find a peaceful way to avoid conflict.

PAGES 130–131

1. e   2. h   3. g   4. f
5. d   6. c   7. a   8. b
9. There are many possible answers.
10. Lindner becomes uncomfortable after Walter offers him a drink. The stage direction is "*Upset for some reason.*"
11. There are many possible answers. Sample: The association looks after the neighborhood, greets new people, and handles any problems that come up.

12. The Youngers are an African-American family. This is supported by the early reference to Lindner as white and his later reference to colored people.

13. **(4) suspicious** Option 4 is supported by the stage directions that say "BENEATHA *is watching the man carefully.*" Option 1 is incorrect because all three of the Youngers act in a friendly manner toward Lindner. Option 2 is incorrect because Beneatha listens carefully to everything Lindner says. Option 3 refers to Ruth's attitude, not Beneatha's. There is no support for option 5.

14. **(1) The association does not want an African-American family in the neighborhood.** The implication is that the Youngers are a "special community problem." This is supported by Lindner's reference to "incidents" involving "colored people." There is no mention of the house itself, so option 2 is wrong. There is no support for options 3 and 4. It is unlikely that the Youngers would protest against themselves, so option 5 is wrong.

15. **(3) suggest in a nice way that they sell the house** This option is supported by Lindner's awkward way of getting to the idea that there is a problem. He is gentle and hesitant and thinks he is being reasonable. Option 1 does not fit with Lindner's personality so far. Options 2 and 4 would mean that the association had no problem with African-American families. There is no support for option 5.

16. There are many possible answers.

SECTION 19

PAGE 132

1. There are many possible answers.
2. Lark
3. There are many possible answers.
4. There are many possible answers.

PAGE 133

Lark drew her horse to a walk. She reached a boulder. She rode her horse slowly down the slope.

PAGE 134

The setting is a thicket. It is dark. There are pine saplings and leafless brush. The ground is covered with pine needles.

PAGE 135

Lark feels nervous, scared, and excited.

PAGES 136–137

1. aperture
2. reconnoiter
3. dubious
4. liberate
5. pondering
6. elaborated
7. tortuous
8. There are many possible answers.
9. Lark wants to free the wild horses.
10. The phrase describes the group of moving horses.
11. **(5) the wild-horse catchers** This option is supported by Lark looking for Blanding's men before she frees the wild horses. Options 1, 2, and 3 are wrong because they are the opposite of what is suggested. There is no mention of the law, so option 4 is wrong.
12. **(1) cautious** This option is supported by the fact that Lark thinks about every move she makes. She also moves slowly to avoid making a mistake. Options 2 and 5 are wrong because they are the opposite of what is described in the passage. There is no support for options 3 and 4.
13. **(2) The trap will be ruined.** This option is supported in the passage. Burning the fence will destroy the trap, which cannot be easily rebuilt. Option 1 is wrong because Lark does not want to frighten the horses. There is no support for options 3 and 4. Option 5 is wrong because there is no nearby timber.
14. There are many possible answers. Sample: Lark would stand up to them and shoot if necessary.
15. There are many possible answers.

SECTION 20

PAGE 138

1. There are many possible answers.
2. the start of a journey
3. the narrator, who is Black Elk
4. There are many possible answers.

PAGE 139

The nation's hoop means the Sioux nation as a harmonious whole.

PAGE 140

He sees the *Wasichus'* world as too crowded and too fenced in.

PAGE 141

The ship left New York. It passed through bad weather and high seas. First the Native Americans, and then the crew members, became very ill. The Native Americans prepared to die. Some of the animals died and were thrown overboard. The ship finally reached London. It was searched by Customs before everyone could leave.

PAGES 142–143

1. d 2. c 3. e
4. a 5. f 6. b
7. There are many possible answers.
8. The train stopped three times.
9. The weather was rough and stormy.
10. Black Elk felt homesick and in despair.
11. The sailors looked down on the Native Americans and were amused by them.
12. **(3) cloth hammocks** This option is supported by the fact that they should have been hung up for sleeping. Black Elk's description does not support options 1, 4, and 5. Option 2 refers to a later description by Black Elk and so is wrong.
13. **(4) a spiritual experience** This option is supported by the fact that Black Elk is a holy man. Option 1 is wrong because it refers to another meaning of the word *vision*. Options 2 and 3 have no support. Option 5 is wrong because he faces death bravely.
14. **(4) the animals represented the Native American way of life.** This option is supported by Black Elk saying that throwing the animals away was like throwing part of the power of his people away. There is no support for options 1, 2, and 5. Option 3 is incorrect because it was the voyage, not the animals, that made the passengers sick.
15. There are many possible answers.

SECTION 21

PAGE 144

1. There are many possible answers.
2. a dog and a man
3. There are many possible answers.
4. There are many possible answers.

PAGE 145

He thought his cheeks might freeze.

PAGE 146

The man is compared to a horse.

PAGE 147

There are many possible answers. Samples: He has dressed warmly, has brought matches, and has brought the dog. If he were going across a desert, he might bring water and food and wear light clothing to keep himself cool.

PAGES 148–149

1. crypts   4. devised
2. intervened 5. instinct
3. automatically 6. floundered
7. There are many possible answers.
8. The man and dog are going to a camp.
9. The main threat is the effect of extreme cold on the body.
10. **(4) He strikes his fingers against his leg.** This is stated in the passage. Option 1 is wrong because he doesn't put on his mitten until later. Option 2 is wrong because building a fire is the last thing he does. Option 3 is wrong because he checks the numbness in his toes later. Option 5 is wrong because he unbuttons his jacket before his fingers become numb.

11. **(2) The dog acts on instinct, but the man thinks.** This option is supported by the author's statement that the dog did not know why it licked the water off its paws, but the man knew. Options 1 and 4 have no support. Options 3 and 5 are opposite to what is stated about the dog.

12. **(3) It is even colder than he thought it would be.** This option is supported by the man remembering that he laughed at the person who told him how cold it gets in the country. There is no support for options 1 and 5. Option 4 is wrong because the man comments that it is noontime. Option 2 is wrong because the man doesn't hesitate to use the dog in dangerous situations.

13. There are many possible answers. Sample: I think he will have difficulty reaching his goal because it is colder than he expected.

14. There are many possible answers.

SECTION 22

PAGE 150

1. There are many possible answers.
2. An air fight between the English and the Germans is taking place.
3. There are many possible answers.
4. There are many possible answers.

PAGE 151

That women are not given weapons is a fact. That they can fight with their minds is an opinion.

PAGE 152

Young Englishmen must be helped to get rid of their love of medals and decorations; *must*

PAGE 153

If men are freed from the machines of war, they will become more caring. This opinion is supported by the example of the English man and woman giving the captured pilot cigarettes and tea.

PAGES 154–155

1. g   2. c   3. b   4. a
5. f   6. d   7. h   8. e
9. There are many possible answers.

10. She describes the feeling as dull dread.

11. **(2) desire to be a mother.** This option is supported by the reference to child-bearing. Option 1 is wrong because it refers to young men. Options 3 and 4 are wrong because they refer to the reasons why maternal instinct might be given up. Option 5 has no support.

12. **(5) "The emotion of fear and hate is therefore sterile . . ."** This option is a judgment and cannot be proved true. Options 1 and 4 are wrong because they are facts about what is happening. Options 2 and 3 are wrong because they are other people's opinions.

13. **(3) to compare women's responsibilities with men's.** This option is correct because the point of the passage is to show what men and women would be willing to do to achieve peace. Option 1 is wrong because there is no suggestion of one being better than the other. Options 2 and 5 have no support. Option 4 has no link to the example.

14. The author implies that young men might find their lives empty in peacetime if they were directed away from their warlike instincts.

15. There are many possible answers. Sample: I would have been concerned about my personal safety and the possibility of being killed.

16. There are many possible answers.

UNIT 2 REVIEW

PAGE 157

1. jobs
2. hunger, anger
3. cannery
4. **(1) slowly to grow dangerously angry** This option is suggested by the fact that the people's hunger was slowly turning into anger. Option 2 has nothing to do with the passage. There is no support for options 3 and 4. Option 5 is the opposite of what is meant.

5. **(4) uneasy** The migrants are restless, and the author suggests that the situation will soon change for the worse. Options 1 and 2 are too positive for the situation described. There is no support for options 3 and 5.

6. **(4) desperate.** The two words suggest the extremes of hunger and violence. Options 1 and 3 are the opposite of what is suggested. There is no support for options 2 and 5.

PAGE 159

7. He thinks that Catherine will not get ahead in life if she quits school.

8. Catherine will get a certificate from the school, showing that she has passed a test. The certificate probably will be the equivalent of a high school diploma.

9. The setting is a kitchen or dining room. This is indicated by the stage directions, which say that Catherine is bringing in plates and forks and Eddie is sitting at the table.

10. **(1) Her school principal suggested it.** This option is stated in the passage. Options 2 and 4 are the opposite of what can be learned from the passage. There is no support for options 3 and 5.

11. **(3) proud** This option is supported by their reaction to Catherine saying that she is the best student in the class. There is no support for options 1 and 2. Options 3 and 4 are wrong because only Eddie seems worried or protective.

12. **(4) He will continue to object to Catherine taking a job.** In the passage so far, his character does not seem to be one that would give in easily without more persuasion. Option 1 does not follow from what has been said. There is no support for options 2 and 5. Option 3 is wrong because he objects to Catherine having any job.

PAGE 161

13. Y

14. page of original writing

15. records

16. **(4) He is beginning to understand himself.** This is supported by his thoughts about what makes him the way he is and what he will learn. There is no support for options 1, 3, and 5. Option 2 is the opposite of what he states.

17. **(1) the student's** This option is supported by the way the assignment is stated, which is *let that page come out of you*. There is no support for the other options.

18. **(5) The instructor will learn something from the speaker.** The speaker seems to believe this option, but he has no factual support, so it is an opinion. Options 1 and 2 are facts, not opinions. Options 3 and 4 are not mentioned in the poem.

PAGE 163

19. mountains, hilltops

20. There are many possible answers. Sample: *A beautiful symphony of brotherhood* means a society in which people of all races live in harmony.

21. **(1) hope and faith** This option is correct because the author is talking about a positive idea that he has. He also says that he has hope and faith. Options 2 and 3 are wrong because his dream is the opposite of despair and distrust. There is no support for options 4 and 5.

22. **(5) By working together, all people can become free.** This is the general truth suggested by Martin Luther King's examples. Options 1 and 2 are too negative to be the theme of this uplifting speech. Options 3 and 4 may be true, but they are not suggested by this passage.

23. **(4) hopeful inspiration** Martin Luther King's emotional appeal is based on hope for the future. Option 1 is wrong because he does not cite facts. Option 2 is wrong because there are no details about the past. There is no evidence of anger or of arguments with the other side, so options 3 and 5 are wrong.

UNIT 3: COMMENTARY

SECTION 23

PAGE 166

1. There are many possible answers.
2. Dan Rather, Tom Brokaw, and Peter Jennings
3. There are many possible answers.

PAGE 167

The reviewer begins the review by saying that he is a critic. He also shows he has been watching TV news for a long time by referring to Walter Cronkite.

PAGE 168

The reviewer says that both Brokaw and Jennings are good at delivering unrehearsed material. The reviewer thinks that Peter Jennings and Jane Pauley are the best news readers. He thinks that Rather smiles at the wrong moments and is unpredictable. The reviewer thinks that Brokaw is a good journalist, but that he delivers the news without enough emotion. The reviewer thinks that Jennings is good at live events and delivers the news comfortably and calmly.

PAGES 169–170

1. b   2. g   3. f
4. e   5. h   6. c
7. a   8. d
9. There are many possible answers.
10. The author wants to be able to rely on the news during a time of crisis.
11. The reviewer prefers Peter Jennings.
12. He is giving an example of a Canadian accent.
13. **(2) Dan Rather was more comfortable than Tom Brokaw.** This option is correct because the reviewer states that Dan Rather looked relaxed, but Tom Brokaw looked uncomfortable. Options 1, 3, and 4 are the opposite of what is stated. There is no support for option 5.
14. **(3) does not express much emotion.** The simile suggests that Tom Brokaw is cold. That is, he does not show emotion. There is no support for the other options.

15. **(5) can be trusted.** This option is supported by the reviewer's references to Walter Cronkite and why he thinks Cronkite is still the best news anchor. Options 1 and 2 are not important considerations to the author. There is no support for option 3. Option 4 is the opposite of what the author states he likes in a news anchor.
16. "There is an honest, real quality to Jennings, what I suspect is a human being behind the hair spray and makeup."
17. There are many possible answers.

SECTION 24

PAGE 171

1. There are many possible answers.
2. Mitch Robbins, Phil Berquist, Ed Furillo
3. There are many possible answers.

PAGE 172

The reviewer is suggesting that there are problems in the marriage.

PAGE 173

He calls this theme *a confusion of priorities*.

PAGES 174–175

1. f   2. g   3. b   4. e
5. a   6. d   7. c   8. h
9. There are many possible answers.
10. The three friends face storms, pregnant cows, insecurities, and doubts.
11. The reviewer says that Crystal is best known for his comedy.
12. The reviewer mentions the other movies and shows to point out the contrast between Billy Crystal's comic background and the more serious nature of the movie *City Slickers*.
13. **(3) They deal with heavy issues.** This option is correct because it is stated in the review. Also, this statement can be taken only as opinion, not fact, because the reviewer gives no examples. There is no support for the other four options.

14. **(1) Finishing something gives you a feeling of satisfaction.** This option is supported by the explanation the reviewer gives. The other options are not suggested by the metaphor, which implies an emotional response to an action.

15. **(1) 'What If?' land** This option is correct because it points out a question that many people ask themselves when they reach a certain stage of life. Option 2 is wrong because there is more to the problem than age. Option 3 is wrong because it is too general. There is no support for options 4 and 5.

16. There are many possible answers. Sample: The movie has a happy ending, with the three men taking what they have learned back home to improve their lives.

17. There are many possible answers.

SECTION 25

PAGE 176

1. There are many possible answers.
2. gangsters and people who make movies
3. There are many possible answers.

PAGE 177

The reviewer probably wants the reader to expect a funny book written in a casual, informal way.

PAGE 178

There are many possible answers. Samples: These words suggest a bias in favor of the novel because they make the reader feel the book would be fun to read. The reviewer uses the phrase *You have to like a Hollywood novel* to show his bias in favor of the novel. The reviewer supports his opinion by using quotations from the novel.

PAGES 179–180

1. cynic
2. protagonist
3. zinger
4. compensates
5. moral
6. acidic
7. There are many possible answers.

8. The detail *It wouldn't be a Leonard novel without colorful villains* shows that the reviewer has read many of Elmore Leonard's books.

9. Chili looks like a nice guy in comparison with Ray Bones and Bo Catlett.

10. **(4) Ray Bones** This option is correct because Ray Bones is named as a villain. Option 1 is wrong because Elmore Leonard is the author. Options 2, 3, and 5 are not villains.

11. **(3) humorous** This option is supported by the word choices and use of exaggeration throughout the review (examples: He is a jack-of-all-crimes, he knows enough—which is not all that much—to get into the filmmaking business, "I've been a fan of yours ever since *Slime Creatures*"). There is no support for options 1, 2, 4, and 5.

12. **(5) the movie industry.** This option is suggested in the first sentence and is supported in the last sentence of the review. Option 1 is wrong because the "hero" of the novel is a crook. There is no support for options 2, 3, and 4.

13. There are many possible answers.

SECTION 26

PAGE 181

1. There are many possible answers.
2. Bob Dylan, "The Bootleg Series"
3. There are many possible answers.

PAGE 182

staggering, astonishing

PAGE 183

There are many possible answers. Sample: Bob Dylan, who grew up in the Midwest, was interested in music at an early age. He went to New York to write and sing his music. He became successful and wrote many songs.

PAGE 184

The word *haunting* is an opinion. The rest of the statement is fact.

PAGES 185–186

1. d 2. f 3. e
4. a 5. b 6. c

7. There are many possible answers.
8. The reviewer hears anger, humor, hope, and spirituality.
9. Hank Williams, Leadbelly, Little Richard, and Woody Guthrie are the four musicians who influenced Bob Dylan.
10. *A measuring stick* is the metaphor that compares Bob Dylan to a standard of excellence.
11. **(2) the kinds of memories that remind us** This phrase suggests that the songs are from a time the reviewer remembers. There is no support for options 1 and 5. Option 3 refers to Bob Dylan's childhood, not the reviewer's. Option 4 is a quote by Bob Dylan.
12. **(1) wrote 237 songs during that time.** The fact that Bob Dylan wrote 237 songs in only three years clearly means that this was a creative period. Option 2 refers to only one song and does not support the opinion. Option 3 refers only to the length of time, not to what was done during that time. Options 4 and 5 do not support an opinion about a creative period.
13. **(2) Bob Dylan is expected to do unusual things.** This option is correct because the reviewer suggests that other people would act in a more ordinary way. There is no support for options 1, 3, and 4. Option 5 is incorrect because Bob Dylan sometimes seems to puzzle his audiences.
14. There are many possible answers.

SECTION 27

PAGE 187

1. There are many possible answers.
2. The director is Christian Moe. The play is a farce. A farce is a humorous play featuring unlikely situations.
3. There are many possible answers. Sample: The characters are probably singers.
4. There are many possible answers.

PAGE 188

"Lend Me a Tenor" was well received in London and won seven Tony Awards. The reviewer wants to show that other performances of the play have been successful.

PAGE 189

There are many possible answers. Samples: chase scene, slamming doors, Tito's angry wife, curdling mayonnaise, unexpected visitors, room service, a presumed death

PAGES 190–191

1. farce
2. presumed
3. typical
4. momentum
5. tenor
6. overblown
7. There are many possible answers.
8. The momentum will probably pick up speed when Tito Merelli arrives.
9. The stage manager had to read the part played by Tim Fink, who was sick.
10. **(3) like a snowball** This simile suggests how the action goes faster and becomes more complex as the play moves along. None of the other options is a simile.
11. **(1) give an example of the problems that happen during a play.** This option is correct because it is stated in the review. There is no evidence for options 2, 4, and 5. Option 3 is wrong because there is no mention of Tim Fink being absent from anything but rehearsal.
12. **(4) The show probably will be a success.** Because the play will give people what they want, it will succeed. Options 1 and 2 are the opposite of what is suggested. Option 3 is wrong because this play is the stated exception. There is no support for option 5.
13. There are many possible answers.

SECTION 28

PAGE 192

1. There are many possible answers.
2. the Godfather of Soul
3. There are many possible answers.

PAGE 193

Brown's early style is classified as *follow-the-crowd R&B*, *cookie-cutter pop*, and *doo-wop*.

1. h   2. e   3. d   4. b
5. c   6. a   7. f   8. g
9. There are many possible answers.
10. The word *jam* means a performance or recording session in which musicians play improvised, unrehearsed material.
11. There are many possible answers. Sample: In the reviewer's opinion, the collection is complete and well documented.
12. The reviewer thinks that the back-up musicians tie for second as the hardest-working people in show business.
13. **(1) give an example of how unusual James Brown is.** This option is supported by the first sentence in the paragraph about the sax player: *Brown was always a character*. Options 2, 4, and 5 have no support. Option 3 is the opposite of what is suggested.
14. **(4) funk** This option is supported by the fact that James Brown did not leave this style. Options 1 and 3 refer to earlier styles. Options 2 and 5 are not mentioned.
15. **(4) Fort Knox of funk** The reviewer is comparing the anthology of James Brown's music to the place where the U.S. gold treasury is stored. So he believes that James Brown is a musical treasure. Options 1, 2, and 3 are wrong because they do not support the positive bias. Option 5 is wrong because it is only a mild suggestion about how the reviewer feels.
16. There are many possible answers.

UNIT 3 REVIEW

PAGE 197

1. b   2. c   3. a
4. **(3) an excellent soldier.** This option is supported by references to the Marines and to the fact that Vasquez is a pilot. Option 1 is wrong because Vasquez is a human being. Option 2 is the opposite of what is stated. There is no support for options 4 and 5.

5. **(1) set up a comparison between male and female action heroes.** This option is supported by the entire passage. There is no support for options 2 and 4. Option 3 is wrong because the author's statement is an opinion, not a fact. Option 5 is wrong because no connection between the two movie stars and science fiction is made.
6. **(4) approving** The reviewer is clearly in favor of the movie and the actresses. Options 1 and 2 are the opposite of the reviewer's tone. There is no support for options 3 and 5.

PAGE 199

7. The word *vocal* refers to the way the singer uses her voice.
8. The songs classified as ballads are most admired by the reviewer.
9. The statement is an opinion.
10. **(2) The three singers sound good together.** The chords of an organ are pleasant sounds. Options 1, 3, and 4 have no support. Option 5 is wrong because the word *swelling* indicates that they are singing loudly.
11. **(5) rich, subtle tones** The words *rich* and *subtle* suggest a positive bias. Option 1 has nothing to do with admiration. Option 2 is a fact, not an opinion. Options 3 and 4 are descriptions, not opinions.
12. **(3) lingering distrust of romantic relationships** This option is correct because the word *distrust* supports the idea of past pain. Options 1, 2, 4, and 5 are wrong because they have nothing to do with past pain.

PAGE 201

13. Solita, or a ten-year-old girl
14. rich; poor
15. Spain; a Latin American country

16. **(1) unpleasant truth** This option is correct because it is a biased phrase that presents an opinion as if it were fact. It shows agreement with Elena Castedo's idea that there is something wrong with the upper classes. Options 2, 3, 4, and 5 are wrong because they do not refer to Elena Castedo's view of the upper classes.

17. **(2) Facing difficult situations can teach you about yourself.** This theme refers to how Solita learned from her situation. Options 1, 4, and 5 are wrong because they are comparisons that are not suggested in the review. Option 3 has no support.

18. **(4) The novel is a powerful criticism of human nature.** This option is supported by the final paragraph in the review. Options 1 and 2 are wrong because they are facts, not opinions. Options 3 and 5 are wrong because they are not opinions expressed by the reviewer.

POSTTEST

PAGE 203

1. love
2. garden
3. touches
4. **(2) not physical** The clue that this option is correct is in the sentences that tell how Helen Keller understood what thinking is. Thinking is not physical. It cannot be touched. Options 1 and 5 have no support. Options 3 and 4 are true in part, but they do not fit the overall idea.
5. **(3) thinking about the beads** Thinking is what Miss Sullivan was trying to help Helen Keller understand. Options 1, 4, and 5 refer to physical, not mental, processes. Option 2 is incorrect because it does not happen until later.
6. **(5) Helen is hearing impaired.** Having to communicate by hand signs suggests that Helen is hearing impaired. There is no support for the other options.

PAGE 205

7. The number *60* refers to the number of stuffed animals in Nina Dowley's house.
8. Nina Dowley collects and loves stuffed animals.
9. Stuffed animals take up all the space in the room.
10. **(1) affectionate** This is suggested by the whole poem. There is no support for the other options.
11. **(4) Nina's neighbor.** Neighbors often borrow things from each other. There is no support for the other options.
12. **(2) take it home and clean it.** This option is correct because of what she did with the rabbit. The other options are incorrect because they would not be in character.

PAGE 207

13. The old man and the girl have just come from the bus station.
14. They are Chinese.
15. Old Man Li was afraid that he would order too much if he ordered the meal.
16. **(3) They decide to have breakfast.** This is stated in the passage. Option 1 is the opposite of what is stated. There is no support for options 2 and 5. Option 4 is incorrect because they have already left the station.
17. **(2) very strong.** This is clear from the simile in the passage *She was strong as a cow*. There is no suggestion in the passage that supports the other options.
18. **(4) The restaurant was clean and impressive.** This is stated as the reason Old Man Li changed his mind. Options 1, 2, and 3 refer to his first opinion. Option 5 did not affect his decision.

PAGE 209

19. Kunta, Lamin
20. answer
21. school, book, or teacher

22. **(4) He does not always know the answers to Lamin's questions.** This option is suggested in the last paragraph. The other options have no support.

23. **(3) He cares about the boy.** This option is clear from Kunta's willingness to take on the responsibility of teaching him and from the pleasure he seems to feel being with him. The other options are the opposite of what is suggested.

24. **(3) how to behave properly in society** This option is correct because Kunta is trying to teach the boy what he needs to know about the world around him. Options 1 and 2 refer only to the place where Kunta and Lamin live. There is no support for options 4 and 5.

PAGE 211

25. The four classifications are young girls, idealistic brides, religious women, and women disappointed in love.

26. The simile *like spices and subtle flavorings* suggests that Sandra Cisneros uses Spanish and English well together.

27. **(3) It is interesting and balanced.** These opinions are stated in the passage. There is no support for the other options.

28. **(4) *excellent reading*** The word *excellent* shows a positive bias. Option 1 is a fact about Sandra Cisneros's life. Options 2, 3, and 5 are phrases used in describing the book but do not show a bias.

29. **(5) the stories about young women are shorter than those about older women.** This option is stated by the reviewer in the passage. Options 1 and 4 are incorrect because they compare the two kinds of stories. They do not contrast them. There is no support for options 2 and 3.

Annotated Bibliography

Most of the passages you have read in this book are parts of larger works such as novels, magazine articles, essays, biographies, and plays. On the following pages you will find more information about the passages you have read. Use this information to help you find these works in your local library.

Anaya, Rudolfo A. *Bless Me Ultima.* Berkeley: Tonatiuh-Quinto Sol International, 1972, reprinted 1988. An award-winning Hispanic novelist tells the story of a boy growing up in a traditional culture.

Arkins, Diane C. "Back When a Dollar Was a Dollar." *USA Today,* November 2, 1989, p. 10A. A newspaper columnist uses a humorous tone to write about modern economic problems.

Asimov, Isaac. "Escape," in *I, Robot.* Garden City, New York: Doubleday and Co., Inc., 1950. A short story about the role of computers in the future as told by a respected scientist and science-fiction author.

Clifton, Lucille. "The Thirty Eighth Year of My Life," in *Women in Literature: Life Stages Through Stories, Poems, and Plays.* Englewood Cliffs, New Jersey: Prentice Hall, Inc., 1988. An African-American woman expresses her feelings about getting older.

Codye, Corinn. *Luis W. Alvarez.* Austin, Texas: Steck-Vaughn Co., 1991. The discoveries of an Hispanic scientist who won the Nobel Prize for physics in 1968 are described in this biography.

Cook, Robin. *Mutation.* New York: G.P. Putnam's Sons, 1989. This novel is a medical thriller about genetic engineering.

Dodge, Mary Mapes. "The Minuet," in *One Hundred and One Famous Poems,* ed. Roy J. Cook. Chicago: The Cable Company, 1928. A poet recalls her grandmother's tales of what it was like to be a young woman in America in the nineteenth century.

Dunbar, Paul. "Sympathy," in *Black Writers of America.* New York: Macmillan and Co., 1972. Dunbar, the son of a slave, reflects on the idea of freedom in a moving poem.

Frost, Robert. "The Road Not Taken," in *An Introduction to Robert Frost.* New York: Holt Rinehart Winston, 1971. A poet considers making an important decision at a crossroads in life.

Gershe, Leonard. *Butterflies Are Free.* New York: Random House, 1969. This play tells the story of a visually impaired young man living independently in New York City.

Grey, Zane. *Horse Heaven Hill.* New York: Grosset & Dunlap, 1959. The challenges of life in the Old West are described in exciting detail by the author of many western novels and short stories.

Haley, Alex. *Roots: The Saga of An American Family.* New York: Dell Publishing Co., 1976. This fiction novel tells the story of Kunta Kinte. Kinte is the ancestor of the African-American author who has traced his ancestry back to Africa.

Hansberry, Lorraine. *A Raisin in the Sun.* New York: Random House, 1958. The experiences of an African-American family living in a predominantly white neighborhood in the 1950s are dramatized in this play.

Henley, Beth. *Crimes of the Heart.* New York: Viking Press, 1982. This play is a comedy in which three sisters work out some of their differences and re-establish their family ties.

Hillerman, Tony. *The Ghostway.* New York: Avon Books, 1984. In one of a series of mystery novels, a well-known fiction author relates the investigations of a Navajo detective.

Hughes, Langston. "Theme for English B," in *Literature: An Introduction to Reading and Writing,* eds., Edgar V. Roberts and Henry E. Jacobs. Englewood Cliffs, New Jersey: Prentice Hall, 1986. A prominent member of the Harlem Renaissance literary movement writes about one of his early educational experiences.

Ibsen, Henrik. *A Doll's House,* in *Four Great Plays,* translated by R. Farquharson Sharp. New York: Bantam Books, 1959, reprinted 1962. This play, written in the mid-nineteenth century, is a social drama. It tells about the tensions in a marriage and is an early example of a drama dealing with women's rights.

Jackson, Helen Hunt. *Ramona.* Boston: Little, Brown and Company, 1884, reprinted 1939. This novel tells the story of a romance between an Hispanic woman and a Native American man during the time when the West was being settled. It was one of the earliest literary works to examine the mistreatment of Native Americans.

Keller, Helen. *The Story of My Life.* Garden City, New York: Doubleday and Company, Inc., 1954. This autobiography is the inspiring story of a woman who achieved international fame and success in spite of the physical disabilities of being blind and deaf.

King, Martin Luther, Jr. "I Have a Dream," in *The Writer's Craft,* eds. Sheena Gillespie, Robert Singleton, and Robert Becker. Glenview, Illinois: Scott, Foresman and Company, 1986. A leading civil-rights activist made this famous speech during a protest march on Washington, D.C. in 1963.

King, Stephen. *'Salem's Lot.* New York: A Signet Book, New American Library, 1975. This novel tells the story of a small town terrorized by vampires. Stephen King is one of the United States' most popular thriller writers.

Lee, C. Y. *The Flower Drum Song*. New York: Grosset and Dunlap, 1957. The conflicts between cultures and generations are played out in this fiction novel about a Chinese-American family.

London, Jack. "To Build a Fire," in *The Best Stories of Jack London,* ed. Eugene Burdick. Greenwich, Connecticut: Fawcett Publications, Inc., 1962. This gripping story tells about a man's struggle to survive in the hostile conditions of Alaska and the Yukon Territory.

Mathis, Cleopatra. "Getting Out," in *Sound and Sense,* ed. Laurence Perrine, 7th edition. New York: Harcourt Brace Jovanovich, 1987. The break-up of a marriage is described from a woman's point of view.

Mays, Willie, with Lou Sahdie. *Say Hey.* New York: Simon and Schuster, 1988. A legendary baseball player tells the story of his life and his experiences in major-league baseball.

McDaniel, Wilma. "That Woman," in *The Red Coffee Can.* Fresno, California: Valley Publishers, 1974. This poem describes how a lonely woman finds a way to spend her time and the love she has to offer.

McIntyre, Vonda N. *Enterprise: The First Adventure.* New York: Pocket Books, 1986. The challenges of space exploration are described in this science-fiction novel based on the TV series *Star Trek.*

Meltzer, Milton. *Langston Hughes: A Biography.* New York: Thomas Y. Crowell Company, 1968. The life story and struggles of the African-American poet Langston Hughes are described in this biography. *See also* Hughes, Langston.

Miller, Arthur. *A View From the Bridge.* New York: Bantam Books, 1967. An American playwright tells of the struggles of a working-class family.

Moore, Kenny. "A Courageous Stand," in *Sports Illustrated.* Vol. 75:6, August 5, 1991, pp. 62–73. This magazine article recounts a protest against racial discrimination made by two American athletes at the 1968 Olympics.

Naylor, Gloria. *The Women of Brewster Place.* New York: Penguin Books, 1982. This novel follows the lives and complex relationships of several women in an inner-city neighborhood.

Neihardt, John G. *Black Elk Speaks.* Lincoln, Nebraska: The University of Nebraska Press, 1961. A holy man of the Oglala Sioux tells the dramatic true story of his travels in the United States and Europe.

Poe, Edgar Allan. "The Tell-Tale Heart," in *Complete Tales and Poems.* New York: The Modern Library, 1938. One of the earliest mystery and thriller writers sends chills up the reader's spine with this story of murder and obsession.

Reeves, Robyn, *The Tomorrow Radio*, in *On Stage, A Readers' Theater Collection*. Austin, Texas: Steck-Vaughn Co., 1992. In this modern science-fiction drama, two scientists accidently discover a way to know what will happen in the future. The play also shows the difficulty they face convincing other people to believe in their discovery.

Rivers, Joan, with Richard Meryman. *Enter Talking*. New York: Delacorte Press, 1986. The autobiography of Joan Rivers shows that the life of a comedienne is not all laughs. Rivers recounts the struggles of her early career as she tries to break into show business.

Robinson, Edwin A. "Richard Cory," in *Sound and Sense,* ed., Laurence Perrine. 7th edition. New York: Harcourt Brace Jovanovich, 1987. This poem was written by the first winner of a Pulitzer Prize for poetry. The poem suggests that people are not always what they seem to be.

Rooney, Andy. "Street Directions," in *And More by Andy Rooney*. New York: Atheneum, 1982. A TV commentator takes a humorous look at giving, receiving, and trying to follow directions.

Steinbeck, John. *The Grapes of Wrath*. New York: Penguin, 1939, reprinted 1987. The terrible effects of the Great Depression of the 1930s are described in this novel. It is about an Oklahoma farming family who was forced to leave their farm and move to California.

Tan, Amy. *The Joy Luck Club*. New York: Ivy Books/Ballantine Books, 1989. This popular novel describes how the conflicts between people of different generations can be complicated by changes in cultural values.

Walker, James. "A Picture on the Mantel," in *Contemporary Poets of America*. Bryn Mawr, Pennsylvania: Dorrance and Company, Inc., 1985. A modern poet tells about the emotions of a little boy whose mother has died.

Woolf, Virginia. "Thoughts on Peace in an Air Raid," in *The Death of a Moth and Other Essays*. New York and London: Harcourt Brace Jovanovich, 1942. An English novelist expresses her opinions on war and peace.

Wynette, Tammy. *Stand by Your Man*. New York: Simon and Schuster. 1979. This autobiography describes the life and career of a country-and-western singer.

Acknowledgments *(continued from page ii)*

pp. 15–17
Excerpts from THE GHOSTWAY by Tony Hillerman. Copyright © 1984 by Tony Hillerman. Reprinted by permission of HarperCollins Publishers.

pp. 21–23
Excerpt from I, ROBOT by Isaac Asimov. Copyright 1950 by Isaac Asimov. Used by permission of Doubleday, a division of Bantam Doubleday Dell Publishing Group, Inc.

pp. 27–29
Excerpt from LANGSTON HUGHES, A BIOGRAPHY by Milton Meltzer. Copyright © 1968 by Milton Meltzer. Selection reprinted by permission of HarperCollins Publishers.

pp. 33–35
Excerpts from BUTTERFLIES ARE FREE by Leonard Gershe. Copyright as an unpublished work, 1969 by Leonard Gershe. Copyright © 1970 by Leonard Gershe. Reprinted by permission of Random House, Inc.

pp. 39–40
LUCILLE CLIFTON. "The Thirty Eighth Year of My Life" copyright © 1987 by Lucille Clifton. Reprinted with the permission of BOA Editions, Ltd., 92 Park Ave., Brockport, NY 14420.

p. 41
James Lafayette Walker, "A Picture on the Mantel" copyright © 1985. Reprinted by permission of Dorrance and Company.

pp. 45–47
Excerpt from, 'SALEM'S LOT by Stephen King. Copyright © 1975 by Stephen King. Used by permission of Doubleday, a division of Bantam Doubleday Dell Publishing Group, Inc.

pp. 51–53
Excerpt from THE WOMEN OF BREWSTER PLACE by Gloria Naylor. Copyright © 1980, 1982 by Gloria Naylor. Used by permission of Viking Penguin, a division of Penguin Books USA Inc.

pp. 57–59
From SAY HEY: THE AUTOBIOGRAPHY OF WILLIE MAYS, by Willie Mays with Lou Sahadi. Copyright © 1968 by Willie Mays. Reprinted by permission of Simon & Schuster, Inc.

pp. 63–65
Excerpt from CRIMES OF THE HEART by Beth Henley. Copyright © 1981, 1982 by Beth Henley. Used by permission of New American Library, a division of Penguin Books USA Inc.

pp. 69–71
Excerpt from BLESS ME, ULTIMA by Rudolfo A. Anaya. © 1972 Rudolfo A. Anaya. TQS Publishers, P. O. Box 9725, Berkeley, CA 94709. Reprinted by permission of the author.

pp. 75–76
Excerpt from AND MORE by Andrew A. Rooney. Reprinted with the permission of Atheneum Publishers, an imprint of Macmillan Publishing Company, from AND MORE by Andrew Rooney. Copyright © 1982 by Essay Productions, Inc.

p. 77
"Back When A Dollar Was A Dollar" by Diane C. Arkins. Copyright © 1989. Reprinted by permission of the author.

pp. 81–83
Reprinted by permission of the Putnam Publishing Group from THE JOY LUCK CLUB by Amy Tan. Copyright © 1989 by Amy Tan.

pp. 87–91
The following excerpts are reprinted courtesy of SPORTS ILLUSTRATED from the October 5, 1991 issue. Copyright © 1991, the Time Inc. Magazine Company. "A Courageous Stand" by Kenny Moore. All Rights Reserved.

pp. 93–95
LUIS W. ALVAREZ by Corinn Codye. © 1991, Steck-Vaughn Company.

p. 98
Reprinted by permission of the Putnam Publishing Group from MUTATION by Robin Cook. Copyright © 1989 by Robin Cook.

p. 100
"Getting Out" by Cleopatra Mathis. Reprinted by permission of the poet.

p. 102
Excerpt from STAND BY YOUR MAN by Tammy Wynette. Copyright © 1979 by Tammy Wynette. Reprinted by permission of Simon & Schuster, Inc.

p. 104
Excerpt from "The Tomorrow Radio" in ON STAGE, A READER'S THEATER COLLECTION by Robyn Reeves. © 1992 by Steck-Vaughn Company.

pp. 109–111
"The Tell-Tale Heart" by Edgar Allan Poe.

pp. 115–117
Excerpt from RAMONA by Helen Hunt Jackson. Published by Little, Brown & Co., Inc.

p. 121
"The Road Not Taken" from THE POETRY OF ROBERT FROST edited by Edward Connery Lathem, and published by Henry Holt & Co.

p. 122
"Richard Cory" from THE CHILDREN OF THE NIGHT by Edwin Arlington Robinson (New York: Charles Scribner's Sons, 1897).

p. 123
"The Minuet" by Mary Mapes Dodge.

pp. 127–129
Excerpts from A RAISIN IN THE SUN by Lorraine Hansberry. Copyright © 1958 by Robert Nemiroff as an unpublished work. Copyright © 1959, 1966, 1984 by Robert Nemiroff. Reprinted by permission of Random House, Inc.

pp. 133–135
Excerpt from HORSE HEAVEN HILL by Zane Grey. Copyright © 1959 by Zane Grey, Inc. Reprinted by permission of Dr. Loren Grey, 4417 Coloma Ave., Woodland Hills, CA 91364.

pp. 139–141
Reprinted from BLACK ELK SPEAKS, by John G. Neihardt, by permission of University of Nebraska Press. Copyright 1932, 1959, 1972, by John G. Neihardt. Copyright © 1961 by the John G. Neihardt Trust.

pp. 145–147
"To Build a Fire" by Jack London. The Jack London Ranch, Box 327, Glen Ellen, CA 95442.

pp. 151–153
Excerpts from "Thoughts on Peace in an Air Raid" in DEATH OF THE MOTH AND OTHER ESSAYS by Virginia Woolf, copyright 1942 by Harcourt Brace Jovanovich, Inc. and renewed 1970 by Marjorie T. Parsons, Executrix, reprinted by permission of the publisher, The Executors of the Estate of Virginia Woolf, the source, and The Hogarth Press as publishers.

p. 156
From THE GRAPES OF WRATH by John Steinbeck. Copyright 1939, renewed © 1967 by John Steinbeck. Used by permission of Viking Penguin, a division of Penguin Books USA Inc.

p. 158
From A VIEW FROM THE BRIDGE by Arthur Miller. Copyright © 1955, 1957, renewed 1983, 1985 by Arthur Miller. Used by permission of Viking Penguin, a division of Penguin Books USA Inc.

p. 160
"Theme From English B" by Langston Hughes. Reprinted by permission of Harold Ober Associates Incorporated. Copyright © 1951 by Langston Hughes. Copyright renewed 1979 by George Houston Bass.

p. 162
Excerpt from "I Have A Dream" speech by Martin Luther King, Jr. Reprinted by permission of Joan Daves Agency. Copyright © 1963 by Dr. Martin Luther King, Jr.

pp. 167–169
From "Three Men and a Maybe" by Marvin Kitman. Reprinted with permission from TV GUIDE® Magazine. Copyright © 1991 by News America Publications, Inc., Radnor, Pennsylvania.

pp. 172–173
"Slickers Drive Cattle and Point Home" by Bob Thomas. Reprinted by permission of The Associated Press.

pp. 177–179
GET SHORTY (Elmore Leonard) by Ralph S. Novak from PEOPLE WEEKLY © 1990 Ralph Novak.

pp. 182–183
"Dylan at 50 . . . " by Ron Firak. Reprinted by permission of The Associated Press.

pp. 188–190
"Lend Me A Tenor" by Cara Webster. Reprinted by permission of THE SOUTHERN ILLINOISAN.

pp. 193–194
"Star Time: James Brown" by David Hiltbrand from PEOPLE WEEKLY © 1991 David Hiltbrand.

p. 196
Excerpt from "Roll Over, Rambo" by Ari Korpivaara from MS. Magazine © 1986. Reprinted by permission of the author.

p. 202
THE STORY OF MY LIFE by Helen Keller.

p. 204
"That Woman" by Wilma Elizabeth McDaniel. Reprinted by permission of the poet.

p. 206
THE FLOWER DRUM SONG by C. Y. Lee. By permission of The Ann Elmo Agency.

p. 208
From ROOTS by Alex Haley. Copyright © 1976 by Alex Haley. Used by permission of Doubleday, a division of Bantam Doubleday Dell Publishing Group, Inc.

Glossary

adventure story a story that tells about people facing danger from the unknown

anthology a collection of poems, stories, or other writings

autobiography the true story of a real person's life written by that person

bias a strong preference for a particular point of view

biographer the writer of a biography

biography the true story of a real person's life written by another person

cause a person, thing, or event that brings about a result

cause-and-effect relationship a situation in which one event happens as a result of something else

character a person in a story or a play

classical literature literature that has set a high standard of excellence, remains meaningful, and continues to be read after many years

classify to sort things into groups or classes

comedy a play that is meant to be funny

commentary a discussion of a work of literature, art or music

compare to find the ways things are alike

conclusion a judgment or opinion based on facts and details

conflict a struggle or problem between characters or forces

context the words and sentences surrounding a word or phrase. The context of a word helps show what that word means.

contrast to find the ways things are different

critical commentary a discussion of a work of literature, art, or music that makes a judgment about the quality of the work

detail a fact about a person, place, thing, event, or time. Details answer the questions *who, what, when, where, why,* and *how.*

drama a story written in dialogue that is meant to be acted on stage

effect the result of a cause

essay a short piece of nonfiction writing that gives the author's opinion about something

fact a statement that can be proved true

figurative language words used in a special way to make a point. Similes, metaphors, and personification are examples.

folktale a story that people tell over and over for many generations. Folktales often explain how people believe things began.

implied main idea a main idea that is not directly stated but is suggested by the author

inference an idea that the reader figures out based on clues an author suggests and what the reader already knows

main idea the most important point in a paragraph or passage

metaphor a directly stated figurative comparison of unlike things. Example: She is a ray of sunshine.

mood how a reader feels about a written work based on the atmosphere the author has created

mystery novel a story about solving a puzzle. The main character of a mystery is usually a detective who has to figure out who committed a crime.

narrator the character telling the story

nonfiction writing that is about real people, places, and events

novel a long work of fiction that can include many events, people, and experiences

opinion a judgment or belief

personification a type of figurative language that gives human qualities to something that is not human. Example: The leaves danced in the wind.

persuasive essay an essay that gives an author's opinion and is meant to get the reader to think a certain way

play a story that is written in dialogue and is meant to be acted on a stage

plot the series of events that create the action of a story

poet a writer of poetry

poetry literature that uses words in special ways to show feelings and create images. Poetry is usually arranged in short lines.

point of view the way the action is seen by the narrator or author of a story

popular fiction recently written works including short stories, novels, plays, and poems. Fiction comes from the author's imagination.

popular literature recently written works whose topics may include ordinary day-to-day things or ideas that can only be imagined

popular novel a recently written book about people and events that are not real

predict to tell what one thinks will happen in the future

problem play a drama that deals with a major social issue

purpose the reason why something is done

qualification skill, experience, or special training

review a short commentary that tells what the author thinks of a book, movie, TV program, musical performance, or work of art

romantic novel a fictional story about love

science fiction fictional stories based on the possibilities found in science. Science fiction shows what life and people might be like in another time or place.

sequence the order in which events occur

setting the time and place in which the events of a story take place

short story a work of fiction that is shorter than a novel but has a full plot and a single theme

simile a figure of speech that compares unlike things using the word *like* or *as*. Example: My love is like a red, red rose.

skim to read something quickly, looking for main ideas and main characters

social drama a play that deals with a major social issue

stated main idea a statement that tells clearly the most important point of a paragraph or story

summary a short statement of the main idea and most important supporting details of a passage.

synonyms words that have the same or nearly the same meaning. Examples: *paste* and *glue*

theme a general truth about life or human nature that is suggested in a work of literature

thriller novel a work of fiction that is meant to scare the reader; also called a horror novel

tone the author's attitude or feeling about a subject

tragedy a serious play with a sad ending

visualize to form a picture in the mind

western novel a fiction story about the challenges people faced on the western frontier of the United States

Index

WALLS, FLOORS & CEILINGS

WALLS, FLOORS & CEILINGS

JUDSON MEAD

CREATIVE HOMEOWNER PRESS®

Manufactured in United States of America

Current printing (last digit)
10   9   8   7

Produced by Roundtable Press, Inc.

Editorial: Arthur Hale
Design: Jeff Fitschen
Illustrations: Norman Nuding
Jacket Design: Jerry Demoney
Front Jacket Photo: David Arky
Back Jacket Photo: Courtesy Stratford Co.

LC: 84-17052
ISBN: 0-932944-72-8 (paper)
        0-932944-75-2 (hardcover)

CREATIVE HOMEOWNER PRESS®
BOOK SERIES
A DIVISION OF FEDERAL
MARKETING CORPORATION
24 PARK WAY, UPPER SADDLE RIVER, NJ 07458-2311

Introduction

Walls, floors, and ceilings are all around you! Taken together they are four or five times the floor area of your house or apartment—and they offer plenty of room for improvement. In fact, no surfaces are more important in giving your rooms their special character than walls, floors, and ceilings.

This book gives you many ideas for dressing up these large surfaces and tells you how to go about putting these ideas into practice: how to add wiring or make repairs; and how to make structural changes to redefine your living areas. Dozens of color photographs of finished rooms are included to inspire your planning.

Almost all the projects in this book are possible to undertake by anyone having rudimentary carpentry skills and a set of basic tools—most can be accomplished with no home improvement experience at all. Simply patching up cracks and painting can give a room a new look for relatively little expense in energy or materials. For the more ambitious do-it-yourselfer, this book shows how to make structural changes—such as adding or removing walls or opening a ceiling to admit daylight—to achieve the most dramatic effect in a room.

This book is both a basic guide and a point of departure. The projects are presented in illustrated steps which can be adapted to your special situations. The introductions to each project tell you how to plan the job, what to anticipate, and what materials you need. The instructions give you the fundamental infor-

mation—on how to wallpaper, lay ceramic tile, hang a suspended ceiling, refinish a hardwood floor, and all the other interior jobs you're likely to do yourself. You supply the imagination, or consult the color pages for suggestions.

Use this book when you plan.

Studying the procedures for a project first will pay off at every stage, from ordering materials through applying the finishing touches. Even if you won't be doing the work yourself, use this book to learn what a particular job involves so you can contract for it wisely.

Contents

WALLS

FLOORS

CEILINGS

Natural light through a skylight illuminates a recreation area by day; a hanging fixture lights the same area at night.

Available in many standard sizes, skylights can also be customized or constructed at home to fit between exposed ceiling beams.

South or west facing skylights may let in more light than desired at certain times of the day. A translucent shade can cut the brightness.

You can bring daylight through the ceiling, even if there is an attic or crawl space above, by building a light well below the skylight.

Not all suspended ceilings look institutional. These panels simulate wood effectively, but are actually a fire-resistant synthetic.

(Opposite) Tough, easy to clean, and handsome, resilient tile is always popular in the kitchen. (Above) A skylight above a glassed-in porch provides a complete sense of openness.

A warm climate makes insulating this ceiling unnecessary; the exposed beams and headers are used here as a decorative element.

Vertical blinds echo the lines of an original batten ceiling. Track lights are used here both for spot lighting and general lighting.

(Above left) Coordinated fixtures and paneling are an effective decorating device.

(Above right) Dark wood, daylight, and hanging plants are a dramatic combination.

(Below left) Sheet paneling used both vertically and horizontally gives this room a formal look.

Simple frames for blinds make it possible to divide this space. The upholstery was chosen to complement the carpet.

WALLS

Anatomy of Walls

Joists

Top plate

Lath

Plaster

Wallboard

Studs

Non-bearing wall

Bearing wall

Outlet

Molding

Bottom plate

The most common kind of wall in residential construction is the stud, or frame, wall. Most projects in this section concern stud walls. If you have a basement, its walls are probably built of concrete blocks. These can be finished with many of the same surface materials as stud walls and the chapters apply to both.

Structure

A stud wall consists of vertical members called studs attached at the top and bottom to horizontal members called plates. The plates in a wall are attached to the floor and ceiling; at corners and where adjacent walls meet, walls are attached along studs. In most houses these studs and plates are lumber, usually 2×4s or 2×3s in interior walls; in some newer construction, lightweight aluminum studs and plates have replaced wood. The framework of studs may provide space for wiring and outlets, plumbing, duct work or insulation. The main job of the framework is to support a surface of some kind, usually either plaster or wallboard. This surface may in turn be covered by another, such as paneling or tile.

Interior walls are separated into two categories by the function they serve in the structure of the house: nonbearing walls are simply partitions, dividing open space into rooms, while bearing walls hold up the roof or the floor above. **Removing Nonbearing walls** (pages 20-21) provides a relatively easy way to change interior space dramatically; **Removing Bearing Walls** (pages 22-24) is somewhat more complicated because the load-carrying function of the wall must be replaced by a beam.

Adding walls divides space, but it can give the sense of expanding living area, especially when the project is to finish an undivided attic or basement. **Framing Walls** (pages 25-28) gives the basics of wall-building under different circumstances one

may encounter in an ordinary house. **Framing in an Attic** (page 29) is usually somewhat different from framing on other floors because the walls must join a sloping roof; **Framing Doorways** (page 30) is almost always a requirement when dividing space to create a new room. **Framing with Metal Studs** (page 31) is an option to consider, and may be required by local building codes for fire protection. **Installing Wall Outlets** (page 32) brings power to new walls.

When you are dividing space, you should consider whether the procedures for **Soundproofing Walls** (pages 41-42) will be necessary. There are several options for noise control that are most easily worked into new construction, but these can also be applied to old walls.

Surface

Most walls in houses built since the 1940s are surfaced with wallboard, also known as plasterboard, or by its trade name, Sheetrock. It may be used as the wall surface, or serve as a foundation for some other surface material. **Putting up Wallboard** (pages 33-36) shows how to work with the material and how to cover walls with it; **Taping and Plastering Wallboard** (pages 37-40) is the technique for finishing an installation.

In some situations, you can completely change the appearance of existing walls without going below the surface, by merely bonding a new surface to the old. In others, a wall may be too badly deteriorated, to take a new surface without some modification. **Preparing Walls for New Surfaces** (pages 46-48) involves a range of procedures, from just cleaning a wall so that adhesive will bond with it, to covering a wall with a framework of wood strips that are shimmed to be plumb, or to erecting a new stud wall over one which cannot be made to take a new surface. In addition to cosmetic improvements to existing walls, **Repairing Wall-**

board and Plaster (pages 43-45) may also be required before putting on a new surface, especially wallpaper which reveals any defects beneath it, but not paneling which can hide a wall full of problems.

Installing Sheet Paneling (pages 49-52) gives a wall the warm glow of wood, in a great variety of finishes. It is quick and relatively easy to put up. **Installing Plank Paneling** (pages 53-55) takes a little more labor, but the depth of the real wood tones makes the effort worthwhile. In both cases you can install the paneling so that the planks (or grooves in the sheets) are vertical, horizontal, diagonal, or in a herringbone pattern. You can panel a wall partway up and cap it with molding. **Working with Molding** (pages 56-57) is essential for unifying the elements in a room. Base molding where the wall meets the floor, and usually cove molding where the wall meets the ceiling, should be coordinated with the color and wall.

If you want to expand a room without moving a wall, **Setting Mirror Tile** (page 58) will seem to double the space. You can apply it to clean plumb surfaces, or you can resurface a wall with wallboard and cover it with mirror tile. **Lining Walls with Cork** (page 59) is functional, providing a soft surface to pin things to, practical, creating a surface that is sound-absorbing, and decorative.

Any room in the house, but especially the bathroom and kitchen, can look good with a surface of ceramic tile. **Tiling Walls** (pages 64-67) is easy, requiring more patience than expertise. Grouting between tiles, which completes a tiling job, is shown on page 116.

Finally, the two most common kinds of wall coverings are covered in **Painting Basics** (pages 61-63) and **Wallpapering Basics** (pages 68-71). Once you have made the walls sound, either of these treatments can give a room a new look with only a moderate effort.

Tools

On these two pages and on pages 82-83, you will find short descriptions of many of the tools you will need to do the projects in this book. Some tools—like a claw hammer, a screwdriver, or a tape measure—are so basic you use them almost any time you do an interior carpentry project. Others—like a knee kicker (for stretching carpet) or a floor sander—are ones you might use only once in a lifetime and will almost certainly want to rent. All these tools are extensions of your hands, and your hands are the most valuable tools you have. Always observe *all* the safety precautions for any tool.

Use a tool only for its intended purpose. A screwdriver is *not* a chisel, nor is a wrench a hammer, nor are all hammers intended for all striking purposes. If you don't have the right tool, go get it.

Keep cutting tools sharp. A sharp tool is actually safer than a dull one. A dull tool is much more likely to slip off the work and mar the surface or injure the user.

Never use damaged tools. A battered screwdriver is likely to chew up a screw slot (and your hand, too); a hammer with a cracked handle can break down and send the head flying. Discard tools that can't be repaired and repair tools with new parts.

Keep your work area clutter-free. When you use a tool, you shouldn't have to worry about what's underfoot. If you use portable power tools, be sure the cords are safely out of your way, and clear of the tool's action.

Watch out for other people, especially children, in the work area. If children want to learn, let them watch from a safe distance. You need your concentration for your work; don't be distracted by conversation.

Dress for the job. Avoid loose-fitting clothing that might get caught in power tools. Wear safety goggles whenever the operation will produce flying chips or debris.

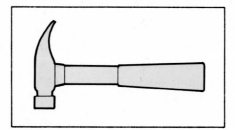

Hammer. The basic hammer, with a curved claw, is used both for driving and pulling nails. Available in different weights, 16 ounces is best for general use.

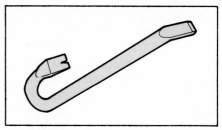

Crowbar. There are various kinds of bars for heavy prying. Essential for any work involving demolition, this tool is also good for pulling large nails.

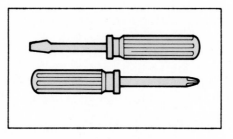

Screwdrivers. The screwdriver you use should match the screw you are driving—always. The two basic types are the standard slot (top) and the Phillips head (bottom).

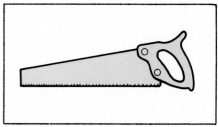

Crosscut Saw and **Ripsaw.** Basic home workshop tools, these handsaws come in many sizes with teeth set either to cut across the grain (crosscut) or with it (rip).

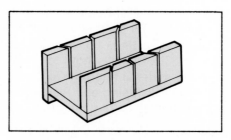

Miter Box. Used to guide a saw for cutting angles (miters), the miter box is available with fixed angles (shown here) or with an adjustable guide for the saw.

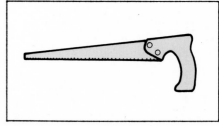

Keyhole Saw. The tapered, pointed blade of the keyhold saw is good for cutting irregular shapes and ideal for making interior cuts in wallboard or paneling.

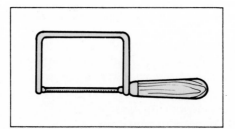

Coping Saw. The thin blade and open configuration of the coping saw make it ideal for fine, irregular cuts, especialy coping a miter on a piece of molding.

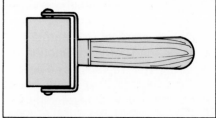

Seam Roller. Just a flat wheel with a handle, the seam roller flattens seams between sheets of wallpaper by pressing the edges into the paste on the wall.

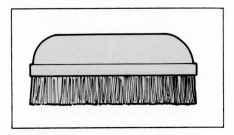

Wallpaper Brush. Long and flat with stiff bristles, the wallpaper brush is used for tucking the paper into corners and for smoothing the sheets against the wall.

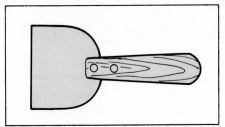

Seam Taping Knife. Like a putty knife but with a wider blade, a seam taping knife is used to fill and smooth the seams between pieces of wallboard with joint compound.

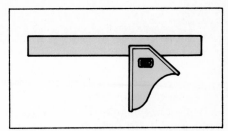

Combination Square. Smaller than a carpenter's square, this measuring tool is used for squaring off boards, marking for cuts and miters. Some have levels in the handles.

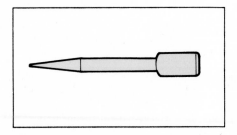

Wallpaper Paste Brush. A wide, heavy bristled brush that will take a good load of wallpaper paste and distribute it evenly on the paper. Don't substitute a paint brush.

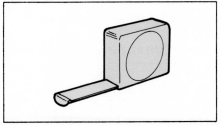

Plumb Bob. A simple weight hung on a string to determine plumb, or to locate a point directly below another, as when marking for a bottom plate from a top plate.

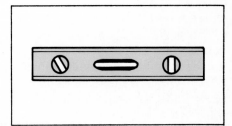

Carpenter's Square. Two legs at right angles, with inches marked on both, make it easy to lay out right angles, mark work lines, and check that work is square.

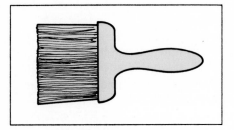

Nailset. Available in different sizes to fit different nails, the nailset is used to drive the head of a finishing nail below the surface of the wood.

Tape Measure. A flexible tape measure belongs in every tool box. If you do much home improvement work, get an extra long tape for room-size distances.

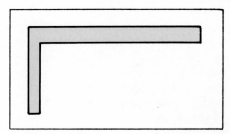

Carpenter's Level. A carpenter's level, 24 to 30 inches long, measures level, plumb, and diagonal. For interior work, shorter levels are not as effective.

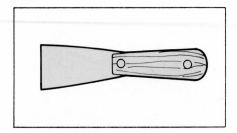

Putty Knife. The narrow flexible blade is designed for applying small amounts of wood putty, joint compound, or other soft substances to fill cracks and gaps.

Chalkline. A stout cord used for marking long straight lines. The chalkline is rubbed with carpenter's chalk, stretched, then snapped to leave its mark.

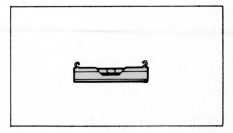

Line Level. Light enough to hang from a taut cord, the line level is used for checking that guideline strings (for a suspended ceiling, for instance) are level.

Removing Nonbearing Walls

Taking out a wall changes interior space dramatically. With the removal of a partition, two small rooms side by side become a comfortable master bedroom and a cramped living room adjoining a small dining room becomes more contemporary open space. If you are considering such a change, make a drawing to scale of the new space to be sure it will have agreeable proportions.

There are two kinds of interior walls in every house and their difference is extremely important. *Bearing walls* are structural supports that carry some of the weight of the story or roof above (see below right). *Nonbearing walls* are simply room dividers with no structural role at all. The support provided by a bearing wall must be replaced with a beam (see page 22), but a nonbearing wall can be removed easily without structural considerations. The gaps left in ceilings, floors, and abutting walls can be repaired by following the directions on pages 43 and 148.

The walls in almost all houses built in the last 40 years are stud frames covered with sheets of wallboard. Older houses (and a few newer ones) have stud walls covered with plaster on a wood or metal lathe. You can usually tell the difference by knocking on the wall: wallboard has a hollow sound between studs, plaster is more solid. As noted in the directions that follow, removing a plaster surface is slightly different from removing wallboard.

Tearing out a wall is obviously messy, so protect furniture by moving it and the floor by covering it with drop cloths. Because of the dust this job will create, the space should be ventilated. Always wear a filter mask and goggles when tearing out a wall.

DETERMINING THE TYPE OF WALL

The most important clue that a wall bears weight is that it runs perpendicular to the joists above. If it runs parallel to the joists, you can be certain that it is a nonbearing wall; if it doesn't, it may or may not bear weight. If joists are overlapped above a wall (as shown above) then it is a bearing wall. Joists which aren't overlapped are probably supported by a wall that is near the middle of the distance they span; if a wall such as a closet wall is near one end of the span, it is probably nonbearing, but consider what is above. For example, the wall may be bearing the weight of a concrete bathroom floor. Studs set closer together than the standard 16 inches may indicate that a wall bears weight.

A beam or a wall in the basement running under the length of the wall in question is another indication that it bears weight. If none of these points of inspection is available, cut a peephole in the ceiling (left) to get a look at what is above. If you have any doubts, assume that the wall bears weight, or consult an architect.

REMOVING A NONBEARING WALL
STEP 1

Know what is inside any wall you plan to take out before you start work. Trace pipes and ducts by checking where they pass through the floor in the basement or emerge in a second story or attic. When in

PROBING A WALL

Probe through a drill hole with a stiff wire. When you hit an obstruction, hold the wire at the wall, pull it out, and measure that length.

STRUCTURAL FUNCTION OF WALLS

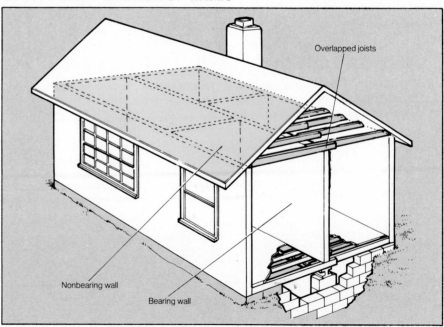

An unfinished attic or crawl space above a wall makes it easy to tell whether it is bearing or nonbearing: just look at the direction of the joists above the wall. Joists perpendicular to the wall usually indicate that it bears weight; overlapped joists always do.

doubt probe through holes in the wall (see opposite page). Unless you are experienced, get professional help to relocate pipes and ducts. Shut off power to the entire area of the house where you are working and use a heavy-gauge extension cord to bring power to the circular saw from another part of the house. See page 32 for information about checking the power and removing old wiring.

STEP 2
Pry off any trim as shown. If you take care not to damage it, you can use it for repair around the wall you remove or for other projects. Remove all outlet and switch face plates. Tape drop cloths to floor to catch debris.

STEP 3
If the wall is free of obstructions like wiring, use a circular saw to cut out the wallboard between studs. Cut the studs in half and wrench out the pieces. For plaster over metal lathe, use a metal-cutting blade. Plaster can also be removed by scoring the surface to make manageable chunks, with the circular saw blade set just to the depth of the plaster, then knocking out the chunks bit by bit with a hammer.

STEP 4
The last stud in a partition wall is usually nailed to two studs set together or to blocking between two close-set studs. Pry it from the bottom and pull it free when it loosens. Pry the top plate from its nailers starting at one end and using scrap to protect the ceiling. Cut a few inches out of the middle of the sole plate and pry up the two halves from the cut.

SHORTENING A WALL
Remove the wall to the stud where you wish it to end, but cut the top plate and sole plate 1½ inches from the last stud. Cut into the ceiling so that you have working access to both sides of a pair of joists, add a 2×6 nailer between the joists and nail the top plate to it.

REMOVING A NONBEARING WALL

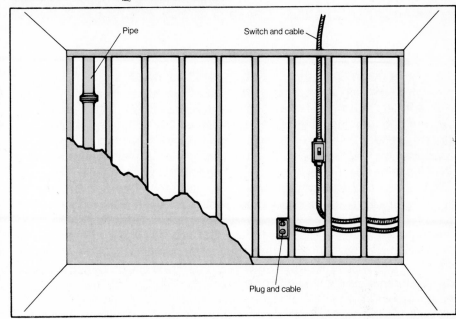

1. Surveying the wall. Wiring running from one part of the house to another should be rerouted by an electrician. Shut off power to the entire area of the house where you are working. Use a heavy-gauge extension cord to bring power to tools from another part of the house.

2. Removing trim. Trim is nailed to the wall, not the floor or ceiling. Use wedges to hold loose trim away from the wall.

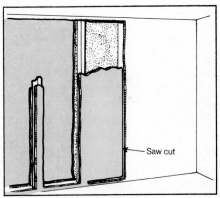

3. Ripping out the wall. Be fairly gentle. Hammering on the surface of studs can crack a ceiling and damage flooring.

SHORTENING A WALL

4. Removing the last studs and plates. Use a piece of scrap to pry against on the good wall to protect it from the crowbar.

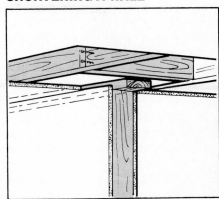

Adding the nailer. Attach the top plate to the nailer. The new stud fits the end of the wall between the plates.

Removing Bearing Walls

If you have determined that a wall you wish to remove is a bearing wall (see page 20), you must replace its load-carrying function with a beam. Either a wooden header or a steel girder may be used, depending on the width to be spanned.

The studs in a bearing wall carry the weight above the wall to the joists below. Because the studs are set relatively close together, the top plate need not be particularly strong. But when the wall is removed, the beam that replaces it must be strong enough to bear the weight along its full length to the posts at either end. For spans up to 8 feet, wooden beams, either solid or laminated, may be used. For spans beyond 8 feet, steel girders must be used. No matter what distance is spanned, these beams will protrude below the ceiling, but they can be covered with wallboard and finished to match the ceiling. False beams added next to working beams conceal their presence (see page 147).

The weight carried by a bearing wall is distributed among the several studs so that no one stud concentrates great weight on the joists beneath. But when the total weight is borne by only two posts at either end of a beam, it is quite concentrated, and you must be especially cautious that there is sufficient support beneath to carry it. For spans greater than 8 feet, it is wise to consult an engineer to determine what extra support you may need. Spans greater than 14 feet concentrate so much weight on the posts that they should be handled by a professional builder.

You can replace all of a bearing wall between two adjoining walls if the distance is manageable or replace part of a bearing wall, butting one end of the beam to the end of the foreshortened bearing wall, or create an arch by removing part of the wall and butting the beam to the remaining wall on either side.

TYPES OF BEAMS

Three types of beams are common in home construction jobs of this kind: solid wood, laminated wood, and steel I-beam. Steel is used for spans greater than 8 feet. The size of the wooden beam you need depends on the distance you will bridge, as shown in the table below. Laminated beams are far less expensive than solid wood, and are the choice of most homeowners. They are made by putting a piece of 1/2-inch plywood between two boards and fixing this sandwich with 16-penny nails driven through one side. Solid wood beams should have the same dimensions as laminated beams.

Span	Lumber
3 1/2 feet	2 × 6
3 1/2-5 feet	2 × 8
5-6 1/2 feet	2 × 10
6 1/2-8 feet	2 × 12

Steel I-beams for home use are called 8 × 17 steel girders, meaning they are 8 inches deep and weigh 17 pounds per foot. They can be purchased from steel suppliers.

REMOVING A BEARING WALL STEP 1

Order or cut a beam 7 inches longer than the span you will be bridging. For ease of handling later, place the beam beside the length of wall it will replace. Build two stud walls the length of the beam, one on either side of the wall, following the directions on pages 25-27. Nail a 1 × 4 brace diagonally across each stud wall from corner to corner, attaching it to every stud. Install these temporary supports about 2 1/2 feet from either side of the wall by driving wedges between the top plates and each joist above, as shown. Check as you work to be sure the wall is absolutely plumb. You don't have to nail these temporary supports in place; the wedges must hold the stud walls tight. Do not proceed unless they do.

TYPES OF BEAMS

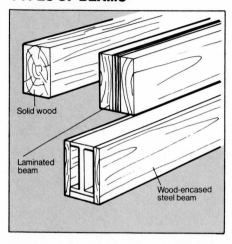

Solid wood

Laminated beam

Wood-encased steel beam

Wood beams, either solid or laminated, can be used to span distances up to 8 feet. For distances greater than 8 feet, you need steel.

REMOVING A BEARING WALL

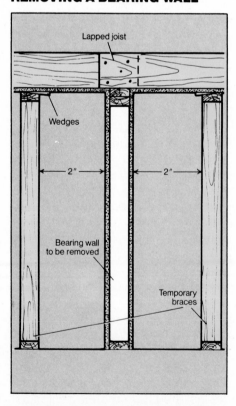

Lapped joist

Wedges

2"

2"

Bearing wall to be removed

Temporary braces

1. Building supporting walls. Stud frames on either side of the bearing wall you are removing support the weight above until a beam is installed. They must be perpendicular to floor and ceiling and be shimmed tight at the top.

STEP 2

When the temporary walls are securely in place, dismantle the bearing wall following the directions on pages 20-21 for removing a nonbearing wall. Because the top plate in a bearing wall is a doubled 2×4 tied into the walls it meets, cut a few inches from the center with a saber saw, pry down the two halves from the cut, and wrench them free. If you are installing a steel I-beam, do not remove the top plate. Remove the surface of the wall (or walls) abutting the wall you are dismantling as far as the studs on either side of the intersection, as shown.

STEP 3

If you are working above a basement with an unfinished ceiling that gives access to the floor joists, check to be sure the sole plate of the adjoining wall, on which the post will stand, is sitting on a joist above a beam. Do this by driving a nail through the floor next to the plate and locating where it has come through below. When the adjoining wall is between joists, add extra support as shown. If you can't determine this, or if there is no beam below, consult a professional builder.

STEP 4

(If you are installing an I-beam, see the instructions on the next page.) Notch a wooden beam 3 inches deep and 3½ inches in from the end at either end that will meet an adjoining wall. Leave it plain where it will abut a remaining segment of the bearing wall. Place the beam on the sole plate of the adjoining wall, notch side up, and measure from the notch to the top plate above. Cut a 4×4 post exactly that length and check for fit. With help, raise the beam into position. If sagging joists prevent it from meeting all the joists flush, raise the joists by driving extra wedges between them and the temporary walls. Seat the posts under either end of the beam and toe nail to the sole plate and beam. Add 1×4 nailers for wallboard on either side as shown.

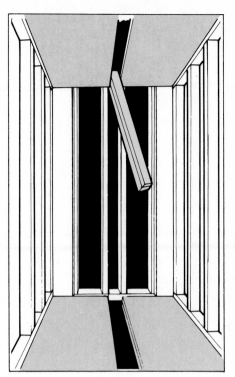
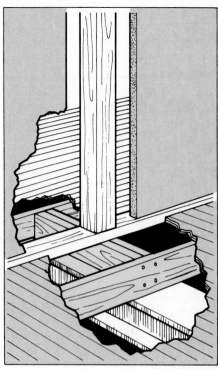

2. Dismantling the wall. After removing the surface, studs, and sole plate, cut the top plate in half and remove the pieces.

3. Extra support beneath the floor. Posts supporting beams may need the extra support of 2×6s nailed between floor joists.

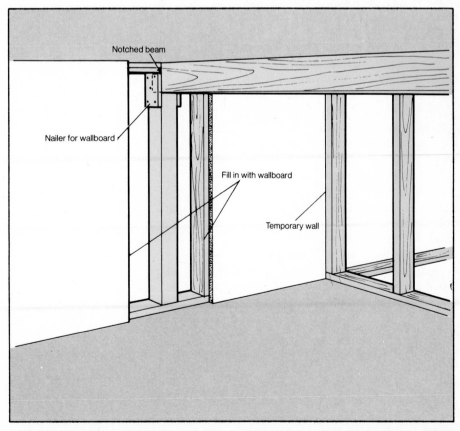

Notched beam

Nailer for wallboard

Fill in with wallboard

Temporary wall

4. Installing the beam. With the beam in place and the posts secured, add pieces of 1×4 flush with the forward edges of the posts to provide a nailing surface for wallboard. The gap left in the adjoining wall(s) is filled with a new piece of wallboard cut to fit between old studs.

BUTTING A HEADER TO A WALL

To butt a beam to the remaining section of a bearing wall, use the procedures described in the preceding steps, but leave 3½ inches of the sole plate extending from the last stud of the remaining wall. Cut a post the length of the distance between the beam resting on the sole plate and the bottom of the joist above. Put the beam in place against the last stud and drill through both the post and the stud at four points—near the top, bottom, and two in the middle—for long toggle bolts. Use a bit the same size as the bolt. Install the post (or posts) with the bolts as shown.

INSTALLING AN I-BEAM
STEP 1

Installing a steel beam is not much different from putting up a wooden one, but it is heavier and requires more help. Plan to have one able-bodied assistant for each three feet of beam when you raise it. Another difference is that the metal beam sits against the top plate of the wall it replaces, *so do not remove the top plate when taking out the bearing wall.*

The I-beam should be 6 inches longer than the distance it will span. When the wall is removed (with the top plate still in place), lift the beam to shoulder height and position stout stepladders under both ends to rest the beam on. Raise it to the top plate and check that it fits flush from end to end. If the top plate is bowed, set the beam on the ladders and tighten the shims in the temporary walls under the low points to level the plate. Fit the beam against the leveled plate and install posts under either end as shown. If you are butting the beam to a wall, follow the instructions above.

STEP 2

Cover the beam with nailing surfaces for wallboard or paneling as shown. Use 1×6 lengths on the bottom of the beam, 1×2 lengths for the vertical strips, and boards cut to fit to fill between the beam and the ceiling. Cover the beam with wallboard or paneling.

BUTTING A BEAM TO A WALL

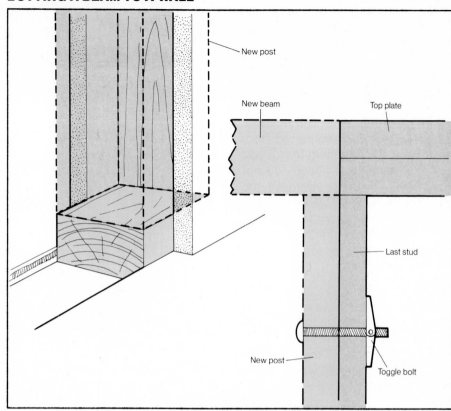

A beam butted to a remaining section of bearing wall is supported by a post tied to the last stud of the wall. Cut the top plate flush with the last stud and cut the sole plate so that it extends 3½ inches from the last stud. Seat the post on the sole plate as shown.

INSTALLING AN I-BEAM

 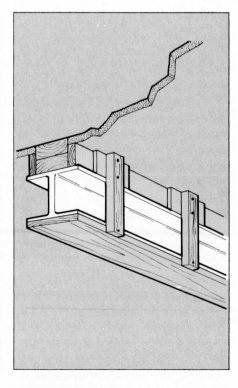

1. Raising the beam. The posts that support an I-beam should fit tightly. When the beam is flush against the ceiling, set the posts.

2. Finishing the beam. You may have to cut stock to fit between the beam and the ceiling to provide support for the vertical nailers.

Framing Walls

Putting up a wall involves three separate activities: building the frame, covering it, and finishing the surface. The frame is a rigid skeleton of studs that provides space for insulation and a foundation for wall surfaces. With attention to a few simple procedures, anyone who can take accurate measurements, hammer a nail, and saw a straight line, can frame walls that are sturdy and true.

The primary requirements of a frame are that it be vertical, rigid, and fit tightly with the floor, ceiling, and walls it meets. All these conditions can be assured by accurate measuring, marking, and cutting. Unfinished basements are usually the easiest places to frame walls because the walls, floors, and ceilings already in place probably meet at right angles and are exposed, ready for the attachment of new framing. Because houses settle, rooms on the ground floor and above seldom offer right angles all the way around and this complicates putting up new walls. Also, the job often involves breaking into finished walls or ceilings or both. (An unfinished attic presents special problems; see *Framing In An Attic*, page 29.) Where the space you are framing is true, you can build most of the wall on the floor and erect all the studs in one motion. Where the angles are off, you must put up the wall stud by stud. The two methods are treated separately in the directions that follow.

Wood, usually 2×3s or 2×4s, is the most popular framing material, but there is an aluminum alternative that offers most of the qualities of wood and has such advantages as noninflammability and greater ease of handling. See *Framing With Metal Studs*, page 32.

MEETING A CEILING ACROSS JOISTS

The first stage in building a frame wall is to determine how it will be attached to the ceiling and adjoining walls (see below). Find the location of joists above the wall by the methods described on page 20. If the joists above run perpendicular to the new wall, the wall is simply nailed across the joists at each one. If the ceiling is finished, fix the top plate to the joists by nailing through the ceiling. The seam between the surface of the new wall and the ceiling can be concealed by molding (see page 56).

MEETING A CEILING ALONG A JOIST

If your new wall falls along a joist, nail the top plate through the ceiling to the bottom of the joist along its length as described above. Check the joist at both ends of the new wall and see if it runs true along the line you mark for the wall. If it doesn't, try to position the wall so that you have a sound nailing surface against the joist at both ends. Mark the top plate so that the nails will go into the center of the joist.

MEETING A CEILING BETWEEN JOISTS

If you place a new wall so that it runs parallel to, but between, joists, you must add nailing blocks between the joists so the top plate can be attached to something. To do this, strip the ceiling back to the joists on either side of the two joists between which you will add nailing blocks. Cut 2×4s to fit between the joists and end nail them flush with the bottom of the joists as shown. Repair the ceiling with pieces of wallboard cut to fit the gaps along either side of the new wall. If the ceiling is plaster rather than wallboard, the damage to it caused by exposing the joists is likely to be prohibitive. In this case, if the wall is to serve only as a partition and will not bear weight (such as bookshelves), and it can be framed on the floor as described below, you can attach it through the plaster with long toggle bolts. See page 60 for information on toggle bolts.

ACROSS JOISTS

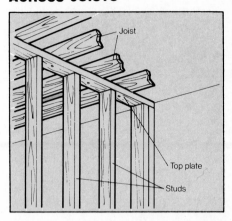

If a new wall runs perpendicular to the joists above, it can be nailed to each joist.

ALONG A JOIST

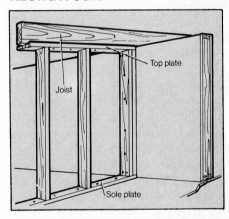

Check through the ceiling with a small nail at both ends and in the middle to be sure the joist runs true and will provide a continuous nailing surface.

BETWEEN JOISTS

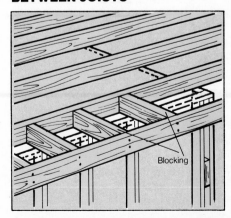

A wallboard ceiling must be cut back to the studs on either side of the two studs between which nailers must be added.

MEETING A WALL AT A STUD

Locate studs in adjoining walls by the methods shown on page 20. If a new wall meets an adjoining wall at a stud, remove sections of trim above and below and attach the new wall to the stud directly through the old wall's surface.

MEETING A WALL BETWEEN STUDS

If the new wall meets an adjoining wall between studs, strip the wall surface back to the studs on either side of where the new wall will meet it and install a double stud with 2 × 4 blocking in the middle. The double stud is necessary to provide nailing surfaces for the new wall and for repairs to the old surface where you have broken through it.

HANGING A STUD WALL
STEP 1

The height of the wall you plan to build will determine the choice of lumber. You can use 2 × 3s for walls up to 8 feet high, 2 × 4s for walls higher than 8 feet, or you may wish to use larger lumber to improve sound-proofing. You will need one or more studs at each end of the wall, depending on how you tie it to old walls, and studs every 16 inches between. When planning your lumber purchase, account for any double studding needed around a door (see page 30).

STEP 2

Mark the exact location of the wall with a carpenter's square and chalk line. If the wall is square, lay one leg of the square against it and have a helper line up the chalkline on the other, then snap the line.

STEP 3

Measure the full length of the new wall across the ceiling and cut two pieces of lumber that length if you are working over a wood floor, or three pieces for the double sole plate needed over a concrete floor. If you are installing a double sole plate, nail down one length along your mark. If not, do the next steps first, then attach the sole plate.

MEETING A WALL AT A STUD

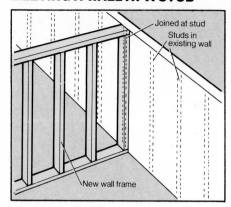

A new wall can be attached directly to an existing wall if it meets the existing wall exactly against a stud.

BETWEEN STUDS

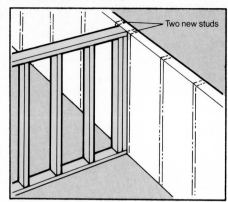

The wall must be cut back and two studs added with blocking between. Two studs provide nailing surface for wall patches.

HANGING A FRAME WALL

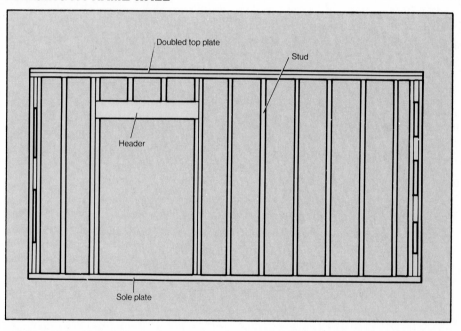

1. Planning. For walls up to 12 feet long, use a single board for each plate. For longer walls use two pieces for each plate with no piece shorter than 4 feet and with splices at opposite ends of the wall. Walls up to 8 feet high can be built with 2 × 3s; for walls higher than 8 feet, use 2 × 4s.

2. Marking the location. Locate the place where you want the wall, mark it at either end, then stretch and snap a chalkline as a guide.

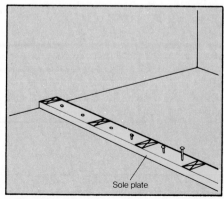

3. Attaching the sole plate. Nail the sole plate to a concrete floor with masonry nails, to joists with 16-penny nails.

STEP 4
Align the top and bottom plates as shown. Measure from one end of the plates and mark for studs at 16-inch intervals along the plates (some building codes permit 24-inch spacing) and at the other end even if it is less than 16 inches to the last stud in the sequence. Remember to account for the doorways.

STEP 5
Set the plates on edge with the marks facing each other, separated by the height of the wall. Put the studs in position and nail top and bottom with two 12-penny nails through the plates into the ends of the studs as shown. Use your marks to align the studs precisely so the frame will be true and provide dependable nailing surfaces.

STEP 6
Raise the frame by setting one plate on the plate already attached to a concrete floor, or on your marks on a wooden floor, and walking the frame into position. Position it above on the marks on the joists or nailers. If the fit is exact, you may have to tap the top plate into position. If the fit is tight, attach the bottom plate with 16-penny nails. If it is loose, go to the next step first.

STEP 7
Use wood shingles as wedges to make the frame fit snugly if it is loose anywhere. Pound the shingles beneath the bottom plate before attaching the frame at the bottom. Use a carpenter's level to check that the frame is plumb—check both the outside and inside faces of a few studs. Adjust the frame as necessary and attach the top plate to the joists with 16-penny nails.

CORNERS
At a corner you must add an extra stud to provide a nailing surface for wall covering. One method of turning a corner involves nailing spacers between two studs, then butting the end stud of the adjacent wall to this triple-width stud. Another method uses three plain studs as shown.

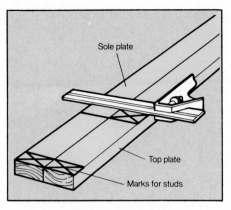

4. Marking the plates. Determine the location of the studs, then measure and mark both top and sole plates together to insure proper fit.

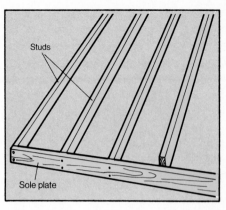

5. Building the frame. Drive 12-penny nails through the plates into the ends of the studs taking care to fit them against their marks.

6. Raising the frame. Get some help to raise the frame if it is large. You may have to hammer it into position.

7. Shimming the frame. If the frame is loose against the ceiling, drive shims under the bottom plate or over the top plate.

TURNING CORNERS

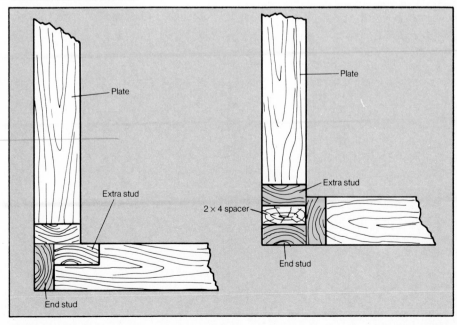

The top illustration shows an arrangement of studs that is typical in older houses. The corner on the bottom is the most common in modern construction. In both cases, the studs are all nailed together to give the corner additional strength.

BUILDING A STUD WALL IN PLACE
STEP 1

Where the length of the wall, or a room out of square prevents you from building a stud wall on the floor and then raising it into position, you must build the wall in place. First mark the position of the wall on the ceiling, then cut top and bottom plates to fit. Install the top plate.

STEP 2

Use a plumb bob to find the location of the bottom plate, as shown at right. With a helper to steady and read the plumb bob, mark the floor for the bottom plate. Move along the top plate, mark the floor at the other end, and check it in the middle. Attach the bottom plate according to the procedures described above. Then mark the top plate for the position of the studs at 16″ or 24″ on center, and outline the stud (³/4″ from center on either side). Use these marks and the plumb bob to locate the position of the studs on the bottom plate as shown. Be sure that the outlines of the studs are oriented the same way (top right hand corner to top right hand corner, for instance). Outline the studs on the bottom plate. Measure from a stud location on the top plate to the corresponding location on the bottom plate and cut a stud that length—the fit should be snug, but not so tight that the stud bows.

STEP 3

Put the stud in position on the marks and attach by toenailing at the top and bottom with 16-penny nails. The easiest way to toenail is to start a nail on either end before you raise the stud: drive the nail at a 45-degree angle into the middle of the face of the stud as shown, until it just breaks the surface on the end. Put the stud in position and complete the attachment by toenailing with two nails into the opposite face at the top and bottom. Use a spacer block, cut to the exact distance between the *edges* of studs to make toenailing go easier as shown.

BUILDING A FRAME WALL IN PLACE

1. Attaching the top plate. If the ceiling is unfinished, nail across or along joists, or into nailers between joists. On a finished ceiling, locate joists through ceiling. Adding nailers between joists requires opening the ceiling as described above.

2. Locating the studs. Mark off stud locations on the top plate and use the plumb bob to find the same positions directly below on the bottom plate. Mark those positions. Studs should be cut individually to measurements between top and bottom plates at stud locations.

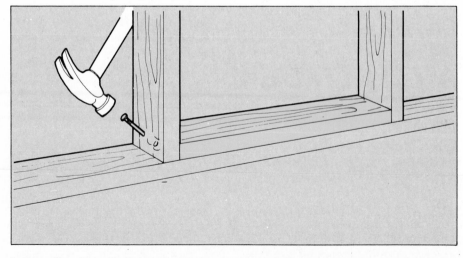

3. Toenailing. Start a nail through either end of the stud then put in position. Using a spacer holds the stud in position while you nail. If you can't use a spacer, start nailing with the stud slightly forward of its location so it will slip into the proper position as you nail.

Framing In an Attic

Framing to finish attic spaces under a sloping roof requires methods somewhat different from framing in a space with a level ceiling. The two major differences are that some surface must be provided between rafters to which studs can be attached for a wall running between the sides of the attic, and that the walls along the sides will be low—usually only four or five feet high—and will meet the rafters or a plate at an angle other than 90°.

A wall running across an attic is fixed at the top to a collar beam installed between rafters at the desired ceiling height. The top plate of a stud wall can be nailed to the collar beam. The shortened walls along the sides are called knee walls and they provide a comfortable sense of enclosure by sealing off the unusable low space.

INSTALLING A COLLAR BEAM

Pick the rafter where you wish to build a wall and, measuring from the lower edge of the rafter, find and mark the point on the edge that is the height you want for the ceiling. Repeat the procedure on the corresponding rafter on the other side of the attic. Measure the distance between the sides of the roof at these points and cut two lengths of 2×6, ½ inch shorter than this distance. Find the angle of the roof and cut the ends of the 2×6s to conform. Nail short lengths of blocking the same thickness as the rafters between the 2×6s and install this doubled beam at the marks on the rafters, checking that it is horizontal.

FRAMING THE WALLS
STEP 1

Mark the height you want for the knee walls on a piece of 2×4 and, with a carpenter's level held against it to check it for plumb, use it to mark the rafters at the correct height. Measure the length of the knee walls and cut two 2×4 sole plates. Put the sole plates in position (but don't nail them down yet), set a stud on a sole plate resting against a rafter above at the mark for the wall height, and mark the angle of the rafter along the side of the stud. Cut and check the fit, then repeat the procedure along both knee walls. Also mark the sole plates for stud locations.

STEP 2

Turn a sole plate on edge and attach the short studs with 10-penny nails through the bottom of the plate. Stand the frame in position, check the fit, nail the sole plate to the floor with 16-penny nails driven into joists, and nail the studs to the rafters with 10-penny nails. Repeat the procedure for the other knee wall. Cut 2×4s to fit and attach on either side of the last stud on each sole plate as shown.

STEP 3

Frame the center, squared section of the wall across the attic as you would a conventional stud wall, then raise and attach it to the collar beam. Nail cut down stock to either side of the rafter from the collar beam to the last studs on the wall, attach the top plates on each side as shown, and attach intermediate studs between the squared wall and the knee walls.

INSTALLING A COLLAR BEAM

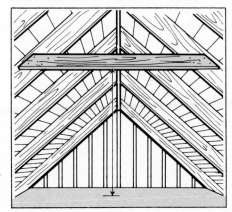

The bottom of the collar beam should be the height you want for the ceiling. Be sure to check that it is horizontal before attaching.

FRAMING THE WALLS

1. Marking knee wall studs. After marking the wall height along the rafters, mark the angle of the rafter on wall studs.

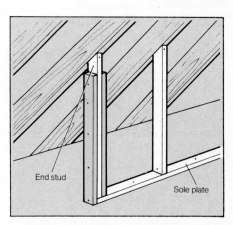

2. Adding nailers to the end studs. In order to provide a nailing surface for the adjoining wall, add 2×4s to either side of the end studs.

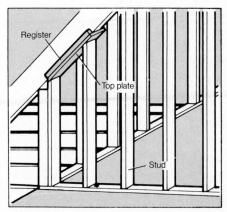

3. Completing the wall. The rafter is widened with registers between the collar beam and the knee wall to accept a top plate.

Framing Doorways

Making an opening for a door in a frame wall requires the elimination of a stud from the frame and the substitution of a short beam, called a header, across the opening and short studs, called cripples, between the header and the top plate.

For the average do-it-yourselfer, the choice of a door to install should probably be a prehung door because this factory-assembled unit entirely eliminates a very tricky bit of carpentry. Since the size of the opening obviously depends on the size of the door, purchase the door before starting the framing so you will have its exact dimensions.

FRAMING THE OPENING

Work back from the door measurements to find the proper location for the outer studs on each side, mark these on the top plate, and install with the other studs in the wall. Cut the jack studs to size and nail inside both outer studs with half a dozen 16-penny nails. Cut the header to fit over the jack studs and attach with 16-penny nails driven through the outer studs. Attach the short cripple studs above the header. Space the cripple studs so that the regular 16 or 24 inch on center sequence of studs along the wall is maintained to facilitate covering the wall with wallboard.

INSTALLING THE DOOR
STEP 1

A prehung door for interior use comes with the jamb split: the door hangs on one jamb, the other is inserted into the opening from the other side. Carefully unpack the assembly, but do not remove any wedges that hold the door closed.

STEP 2

Insert the side of the jamb, with the door attached, into the opening. Shim the door closed if it isn't already and support it at the bottom with shims. Adjust the jamb so that the door clears it by ⅛ inch all the

way around, then nail the casing to the door frame with 8-penny finishing nails.

STEP 3

From the other side, fill the gap between the jamb and the jack studs and header with shims. Then nail the jamb through the shims to the frame along the sides with 16-penny nails. Fit the other half of the jamb into the opening, slipping the tongue at the top into the corresponding groove in the installed half. When it is seated, attach the jamb with 16-penny nails into the frame and nail the casing with 8-penny finishing nails.

ANATOMY OF A DOOR FRAME

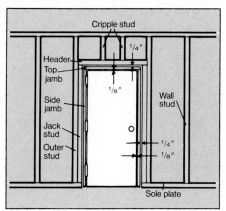

The opening should be ½ inch wider and ¼ inch taller than the outside dimensions of the jamb for adjustments.

FRAMING THE OPENING

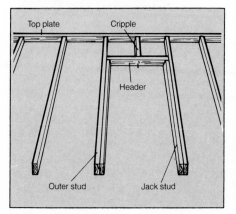

Use the dimensions of the prehung door, plus the extra space, plus the width of the jack studs, to determine stud placement.

INSTALLING A PREHUNG DOOR

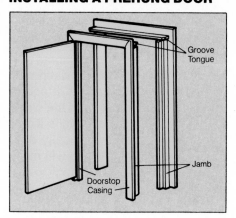

1. A split jamb door. The two halves of a split jamb door fit together with a tongue and groove along the top of the jamb.

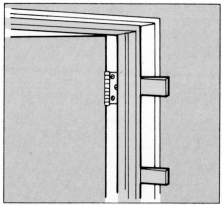

2. Installing the door. Shim the door shut and rest it on shims for stability. When the fit is right, nail the casing to the wall.

3. Shimming the jamb. Shim between the jamb and the frame and nail the jamb through the shims. Cut the shims back to the edge.

Framing with Metal Studs

Lightweight metal framing is often easier to intall than wood framing and provides a wall just as sturdy. If you are concerned about extra soundproofing, wood should probably be your choice (see page 41), but for privacy with moderate resistance to sound, a metal frame wall is an alternative worth considering. Some building codes, especially those governing city loft conversions, require metal framing for fire protection.

Metal framing consists of two kinds of long, U-shaped members: studs and the tracks they fit into. Studs are the heavier of the two, with the flange at right angles to the spine (see top). Tracks, lighter weight, have flanges angled slightly toward the spine to grip studs when they are snapped in place. Metal framing can be cut to fit with straight tin shears. It can be purchased in kit form for small jobs and by the piece, in any length, for larger projects.

Metal frames are put together and wallboard is attached with metal screws. You will need a variable speed power drill or a power screwdriver to make the joints tight.

PUTTING UP A METAL STUD WALL
STEP 1
Plan for metal framing just as you would for wood framing, but use wood as the inside framing in doorways that are framed with metal (see page 30). All necessary corners can be made with simple cuts as shown. Remember to plan for extra studs at corners for attaching wallboard.

STEP 2
Cut the metal tracks to length with tin shears as shown. You can attach the bottom track with adhesive, or you can do so with nails or screws. When using adhesive, make sure the floor is level, clean, and provides a sound surface for the adhesive to grip (not loose linoleum, or a floor with gaps). Run a 3/8-inch bead of panel adhesive in a 1-inch wide squiggle along the chalk line you have snapped for the track. Seat the track on the line and press firmly into the adhesive; allow to dry according to manufacturer's instructions.

To attach without adhesive, use masonry nails into a concrete floor, or spiral nails or sheet metal screws into wood.

STEP 3
Use a plumb bob to mark the position for the top track and install it across joists, along one joist, or across nailers in an exposed ceiling—or use toggle bolts (see page 60) to attach the top track to a finished ceiling. Cut the metal studs to length if necessary and insert them sideways into the tracks. Snap them into place and check to be sure they are plumb. The tension applied by the flanges of the plate should hold the studs in place, but for extra strength attach them with sheet metal screws.

STEP 4
The frame will not be completely rigid until you put on the wall surface. When you attach wallboard to the metal studs, use a portable drill or power screwdriver to drive dry-wall screws, dimpling the surface as described on page 35.

PUTTING UP A METAL STUD WALL

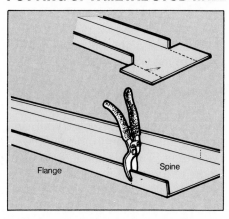

1. **Cutting the studs.** A pair of tin shears are used to cut the studs and tracks of aluminum framing to fit and to make corners.

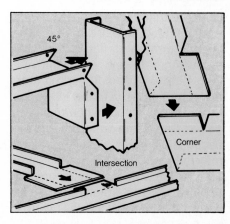

2. **Making corners.** Intersections and corners are made by cutting the flanges as shown, then overlapping the studs as indicated.

3. **Seating the studs.** With the track in place and the studs cut to length, set one in place and twist until it snaps in tight.

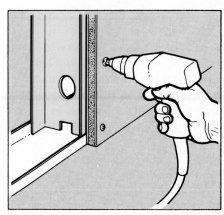

4. **Attaching wallboard.** The most efficient way to attach wallboard to metal studs is with a power screwdriver and wallboard screws.

Installing Wall Outlets

This page contains some basic information that you should keep in mind when removing or adding walls. For extensive information on electrical wiring and installation, you should consult an electrician or refer to other, more detailed, texts on the subject.

The absolute first rule for working around electricity is to *turn it off.* The second rule is to *make sure that you have turned it off.* Electricity is dangerous, but wiring and electrical fixtures that have been shut off at the source of power—your fuse box or circuit breaker—are harmless.

To shut off power to part of your house, you must remove the fuse or flip the circuit breaker that controls power to that line. If you don't know what circuit a fuse or circuit breaker affects, turn on all lights controlled by switches in one area, and plug lamps into all the outlets in a room and turn them on. Station a helper in the room to call out when the lights go out. Use all the outlets in this test because different sides of a room may be on different lines. If you aren't sure whether there are live lines running to other parts of the house through a wall you want to remove, you can be sure to avoid hazard by shutting down all power in the house. If you encounter wiring routed through a wall to other areas, you should consult an electrician.

TESTING FOR CURRENT
A voltage tester is an inexpensive device that lets you know when current is present in a line. It consists of a small light bulb and two probes that will fit into the slots in a plug. Use the tester as shown for both plugs and switches, touching one probe to the black wire in a pair of wires, the other probe to the white wire on the other side of the switch or outlet; test all sets of wires in an outlet or switch. When current is present, the bulb will light. You can use a lamp for a voltage tester simply by plugging it in and turning it on, but first make absolutely sure, for obvious reasons, that the bulb in the lamp is not burned out.

WALL BOXES FOR OUTLETS AND SWITCHES
Outlets and switches are mounted in metal boxes attached to studs in the framing. The most common kind has a flange on one side that is nailed to the stud. The box can be mounted with either end up so it can be oriented toward either side of a frame wall and on either side of a stud.

MOUNTING WALL BOXES
When you fix wall boxes to a frame wall, be sure to account for the thickness of the surface that will cover the wall. The box should protrude from the frame a distance equal to the depth of the wall covering.

RUNNING ELECTRICAL CABLE THROUGH FRAMING
To run cable through a stud wall, drill 3/4-inch holes through the middle of the studs. The National Electrical Code requires that you put metal plates (available at electrical supply houses) on the edge (or edges) of the stud that faces out to guard against the possibility of later driving a nail through the stud into the cable.

CHECKING FOR CURRENT

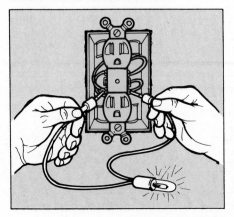

Use a voltage tester or a lamp that is turned on (and that you know has a good bulb) to check for current in a line.

A WALL BOX

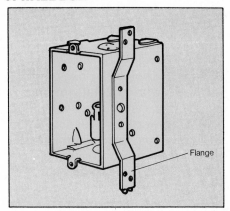

The flange on this wall box is nailed to a stud in a frame wall. There are other types of wall box available for mounting in a finished wall.

MOUNTING WALL BOXES

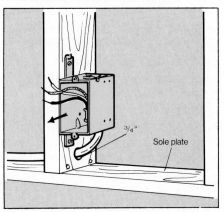

Plan the locations and mount the wall boxes for outlets and switches and put wiring in place before you cover the wall.

RUNNING CABLE

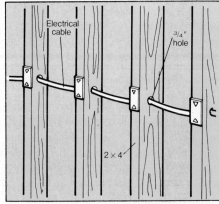

Holes for cable should be 3/4 inch in diameter and face plates must be added to either side of the stud that faces an accessible surface.

Putting up Wallboard

Wallboard is used for the surface of most interior walls built today. Also known as plaster board, drywall, gypsum board, or by the trade name Sheetrock, wallboard is easy to handle, goes up quickly, and costs relatively little. It provides a surface that can be paneled or tiled as it is, or finished with joint compound and tape and then painted or wallpapered.

Wallboard is plaster sandwiched between layers of strong paper. It is fire resistant and stops sound well. Regular wallboard has a dark gray kraft paper backing and smoother off-white paper on the front that takes paint readily. The long edges are sealed and slightly tapered to accept tape and compound.

Specialty wallboards include *water-resistant wallboard* with water-repellant cores and facing, usually tinted blue or green, that are for use in areas of high moisture or as a base for ceramic tile; *Type X wallboard* with extra fire resistance, sometimes required by building codes for special places; *insulating wallboard* with aluminum foil backing to be used on the inside surfaces of exterior walls; *backer boards* with no good side that are used under another layer of wallboard or paneling; and *prefinished wallboard* that is faced on one side with a durable finish that needs no paint.

Wallboard is available in different thicknesses and panel sizes. Thicknesses are $1/4$ inch, $3/8$ inch, $1/2$ inch, and $5/8$ inch. $1/2$-inch wallboard is used for most walls and ceilings, while $5/8$-inch is used for extra soundproofing; $1/4$-inch is used for putting a new surface over an existing one and $3/8$-inch is used for multi-ply soundproof walls (see page 41) and ceilings below attics. Panels are all 4 feet wide and range in length from 6 feet to 16 feet for the two thinner versions, to 12 feet for $1/2$-inch, and 8 feet for $5/8$-inch thickness.

Hanging a wallboard surface on a wall is easy if you observe a few basic cautions. Most important, remember that wallboard is delicate. It crushes if stood on one corner (a 4- × 8-foot panel weighs 65 pounds) and breaks easily if dropped or hit, so treat it relatively gently. Wallboard should be stacked flat to prevent warping if not used right away.

To estimate the materials you need for a job, find the number of square feet you will cover by multiplying the outside dimensions of the wall (or walls), subtracting the area of any openings, then adding 10 percent of the total for wastage. Divide by the number of square feet in the panel size you plan to use and the result is the number of panels to order. Wallboard is fastened to studs with $1\frac{1}{2}$-inch ringed wallboard nails.

CUTTING WALLBOARD TO SIZE
STEP 1
It is often necessary to cut down the length or width of a wallboard panel. For long, straight cuts of this kind, use a utility knife and a straightedge. Put the wallboard on the floor or on the stack of wallboard you are installing, measure, and mark the cutting line. Use a carpenter's square as a straightedge to hold the knife on the line and score the paper as shown, cutting through it into the core.

STEP 2
If you are working on a stack of wallboard, slip the cut over the edge of the stack and snap the panel along the cut. It should break neatly with the two parts held together only by the paper backing. If you are working on the floor, slip a piece of scrap under the cut and snap it as shown.

STEP 3
Turn the wallboard on edge, fold the two cut pieces slightly together, and slice through the paper backing to complete the cut. The resulting edge will be somewhat rough. Cut panels $1/4$ inch less than measured dimensions to account for the roughness.

CUTTING WALLBOARD TO SIZE

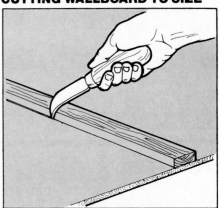

1. First cut. Lay a straightedge along the line you've marked for cutting and score the wallboard through the paper into the plaster.

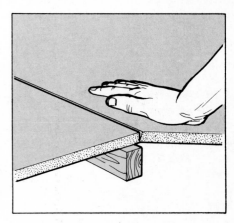

2. Breaking the wallboard. Put a piece of scrap wood the length of the cut under the sheet along the cut line and break the sheet.

3. Finishing the cut. Stand the sheet on edge, bend it at the break line, and run the blade through the paper backing.

CUTTING OPENINGS IN WALLBOARD
STEP 1
You will have to cut holes in some pieces of wallboard as openings for outlet boxes and switches on a wall. You may also have to cut away a section of wallboard to fit a panel around a doorway (see Step 5). To cut an opening, first mark the position.

STEP 2
You can mark the entire outline of the opening from measurements, or, if you want a more precise cut, use the object the hole must fit around as a template for drawing the outline as shown. In either case, enlarge the outline ⅛ inch all the way around to ensure a good fit.

STEP 3
Punch through the wallboard with an awl or a nail at each corner of the outline so that these points will show on the back. Score the outline with the utility knife so that it cuts ¼ inch or a little more into the core.

STEP 4
Flip the board over and mark the outline between the corner holes that show through from the front. Score the board along these lines as you did on the other side.

STEP 5
Turn the board to the front side and tap out the scored piece with a hammer. The edges of the cut can be cleaned up or enlarged by carving with the utility knife. To cut an indent to fit around a door or window, mark off the area and score all but the longest line as above, but in this case cut all the way through both sides of the wallboard. Finally, score the longest cut and snap off the piece as shown on the previous page.

CUTTING WALLBOARD WITH A SAW
You can cut small openings in wallboard with a keyhole saw by drilling out opposite corners of the outline to start the cuts. Any indents or other odd shapes can be finished with a utility knife.

CUTTING AN OPENING IN WALLBOARD

1. Marking the cut. Carefully measure the position of the opening and transfer the measurements to the wallboard.

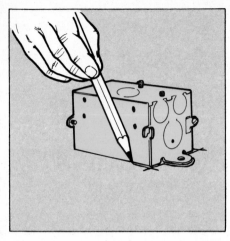

2. Marking an outline. For more precise results when cutting an opening, trace the shape of the piece on the wallboard.

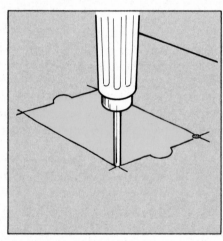

3. Starting the cut. Use an awl to poke holes at the corners of the cut through to the back side. Fill in the outline on the back.

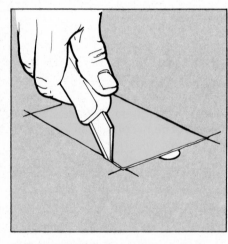

4. Making the cut. Score through the paper and about ¼ inch into the plaster, turn the sheet over, and do the same on the back.

CUTTING WALL WITH A SAW

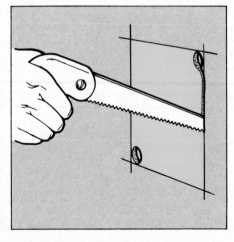

5. Completing the cut. When both sides are scored, use a hammer to tap out the piece. Smooth cut edges with a utility knife.

To make cutouts with a keyhole saw, first drill starter holes in the corners of the cut large enough to insert the saw blade tip.

INSTALLING WALLBOARD
STEP 1
Check the stud wall frame to be sure that it provides nailing surfaces for all edges of the wallboard and add studs where needed; also check that outlets and switches are positioned correctly (see page 32). Mark the exact location of the wall studs along the floor and ceiling as shown, so you will know where to nail. For easier handling, cut wallboard about 3/4 inch shorter than the height of the wall. The gap will go at the bottom to be covered with base molding.

STEP 2
Although horizontal installation of wallboard can reduce the number of joints to plaster (see bottom next page), most do-it-yourselfers find it more convenient to hang panels vertically. To position a panel for attachment, make a lever out of scrap wood as shown and carefully stand the panel in position against the wall on the end of the makeshift lever. Apply pressure with your foot.

STEP 3
Hold the panel against the ceiling with the lever and push it tight against the wall with your hand. Drive a few wallboard nails through the panel into the frame at the top and along a side. This will hold the panel in place and allow you to move around and complete the nailing.

STEP 4
Drive all nails slightly below the surface of the wallboard as shown, but be careful not to break the paper. The dimple left by this countersinking will be filled in with joint compound.

STEP 5
Standard procedure calls for nails at intervals of 6 inches along all wallboard edges and 12 inches along studs in the middle. Nails around the perimeter should be driven in 3/8 inch from the edge of the wallboard. If a nail misses a stud, just pull it out and renail. If you want added protection against nails popping later, use pairs of nails 2 inches apart at the same intervals.

INSTALLING WALLBOARD

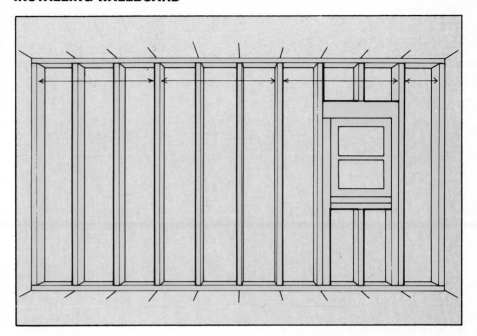

1. Planning the job. Mark the location of the studs on the floor and ceiling before covering them with wallboard so nailing will be easy when the studs can't be seen. Plan whatever cuts you must make and be sure that you have a nailing surface wherever pieces meet.

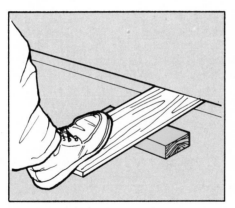

2. Setting wallboard in position. Use two pieces of scrap, set up as shown, to lever the wallboard snug against the ceiling.

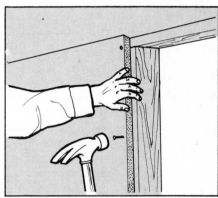

3. Securing the wallboard. With the sheet held against the ceiling by the foot lever, drive a few nails into the top and along one edge.

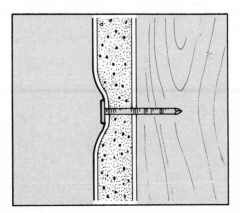

4. Nailing. Drive all wallboard nails about 1/32 inch below the surface—the paper will dimple as shown. Take care not to break the paper.

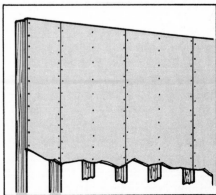

5. Completing the nailing. Drive wallboard nails at 6-inch intervals along all the edges and into center studs at 12-inch intervals.

INSTALLING WALLBOARD WITH ADHESIVE
STEP 1

You can reduce the amount of nailing by using an adhesive to attach wallboard to the studs behind the middle of the panel. Use a panel adhesive (check with your lumber yard for the right one to use with your wallboard) applied to the center studs in a 3/8-inch squiggle as shown.

STEP 2

Start and stop your application of adhesive 6 inches from the top and bottom of the studs. Fit the panel against the studs and nail the perimeter as described above. If the wallboard bulges away from a center stud, press it back against the stud and nail it down. One way to improve adhesion against studs is first to let the sheets of wallboard to be glued warp slightly. Set them individually face up on 2×4s at each side and allow them to sag for a day. The resulting curvature will press against the studs when the wallboard is nailed top and bottom.

HANGING WALLBOARD HORIZONTALLY

If you have help, you can save on the number of feet of wallboard seams you have to finish—and improve the look of the finished wall—by hanging longer panels horizontally.

To hang wallboard horizontally, mark the stud locations on the floor and ceiling as in the previous procedure and drive 8- or 10-penny nails halfway into the studs 4 feet down from the ceiling. With a helper, lift the panel into position onto the nails and push back against the wall. Nail the panel to a few of the studs to hold it and complete nailing as in a vertical installation. If the wall is 8 feet high, install the panel below using a lever to hold it snug against the one above. If the wall is higher than 8 feet, repeat the procedure given here and fill in between the lower panel and the floor with pieces cut to fit. Measure the distance between the floor and the bottom panel in several places in case the floor and ceiling are not square.

USING ADHESIVE

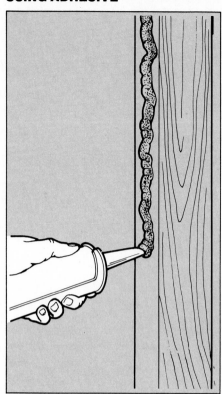

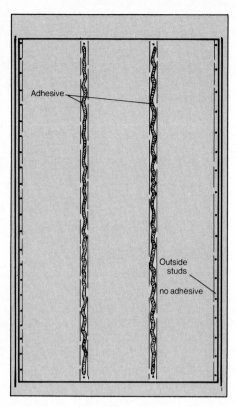

1. Applying the adhesive. Apply adhesive to the center stud (or studs) only, stopping the bead about 3 inches from the top and bottom.

2. Adhesive and nailing pattern. Drive nails along the edges of the sheet at 6-inch intervals and nail at the top and bottom.

HORIZONTAL INSTALLATION

Installing wallboard sheets horizontally is easy so long as you have someone to help lift and position the sheets. Drive 8- or 10-penny nails part way into studs to support the sheet while nailing. Set the sheet on the nails and have a helper hold it while you nail it in place.

Taping and Plastering Wallboard

A thick spreadable substance called joint compound, a few rolls of perforated paper tape, and some patient labor on your part will turn a newly hung wallboard wall, with its unsightly seams and nails showing, into a uniformly smooth surface ready for paint or wallpaper.

Taping and plastering will hide a multitude of missed hammer strokes and badly fitting joints, but nothing (except a new surface) can hide a poor job of taping and plastering. Remember when taping and plastering that your work will show.

The nature of joint compound enforces patience: it must be applied at least three times and left to dry about 24 hours after each application. (There are special fast-drying joint compounds but they are not recommended for anyone with less than expert skills.) Joint compound can be purchased premixed or dry, to be mixed at home. Unless you are experienced with mixing your own, use the premixed kind—it costs only a little more and is much easier to use. Premixed compound is easy to store. Wipe clean all exposed surfaces inside the can (so bits won't dry and flake off into the mixture) and reseal. If you are storing compound for more than a couple of days, cover the surface with 1/2 inch of water to seal it, then pour it off before using again. Be sure not to store compound where it might freeze.

The 2-inch wide paper tape that fills the seams between wallboard panels is available in 250-foot rolls. There are two basic types: one has holes that are so small they are barely visible, the other is somewhat thinner and has much larger holes. The second type is not easy to use.

The tools used to apply tape and joint compound are simple: a hawk (see right, center) to hold the compound, 4-inch and 10-inch finishing knives for spreading it, and 100-grit open-coat sandpaper to smooth it when dry.

ANATOMY OF A TAPED SEAM

The basic sequence of taping and plastering a seam is shown in the cutaway drawing (right). First a layer of compound is spread down the seam, then it is covered with tape the length of the seam and the tape is imbedded in the compound with a second pass of the knife. This provides the filling over which finishing layers are added to make a smooth seam.

A STEP-SAVING TOOL

A hawk is a hand-held workbench for plastering. It holds a supply of compound where you need it and provides an edge for scraping compound off the finishing knife. You can tape and plaster a wall without one, but you will have to bend to the can of compound hundreds of times to load and clean your knife.

TAPING AND PLASTERING FLAT SEAMS
STEP 1

Inspect the wall closely, checking that each nail is set below the surface. Any nails protruding or flush with the surface should be recessed about 1/32 inch. Scoop up a bit of compound at the end of the 4-inch knife and fill a nail dimple by spreading compound over it with the knife to clean away any excess. Filling the nail dimples first is a good way to get the feel of working with joint compound. Sand and apply additional finishing coats as you finish the seams, using the procedures given in the directions below.

STEP 2

Work on one seam at a time, repeating the procedures in Steps 2 to 5 for each. Pick up a supply of compound on the end of the 4-inch knife and spread a layer about 1/8 inch thick down a seam with the knife at a 45° angle to the wall. Fill the seam from top to bottom (reloading the knife as necessary), making sure that you

ANATOMY OF A TAPED SEAM

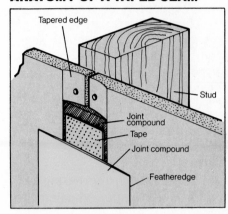

Joint compound fills the seam, tape is laid over it, and the seam is finished with several more layers of compound.

USING A HAWK

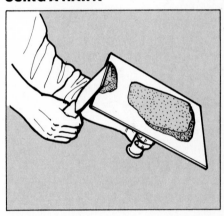

A plasterer's hawk is used to hold a convenient amount of compound near your work and to scrape the taping knife clean.

TAPING A SEAM

1. Filling nail dimples. Fill nail dimples with a two-step motion. Spread compound over the dimple, then scrape away any excess.

leave no gaps which will become bubbles under the tape. This application need not be neat, but it must be thorough.

STEP 3
Tear off a piece of tape the length of the seam. Starting at the top, lay the tape carefully over the center of the seam so that it runs straight down. Anchor the top of the tape with some compound as shown. Keep the tape straight and smooth; lift it up and lay it down again if it wrinkles or bends off course.

STEP 4
Work the tape down from the top with your finishing knife, pressing the blade firmly against the joint to imbed the tape. The pressure on the knife should stretch the tape slightly, but take care not to tear it. If it does tear, discard the tape below the tear and replace with new tape, allowing the ends of the tape to meet but not overlap. Again, if the tape wrinkles, lift it up and lay it back down flat, then go over it with the knife. Any air bubbles or wrinkles in the tape at this point will show up later.

STEP 5
Go back to the seam and scrape away any excess compound that has gathered at the edges. Clean your knife on the edge of your hawk. When the excess is cleaned off, apply a very light coat of compound over the taped seam.

STEP 6
Allow the compound to dry for at least 24 hours. Sand down any rough spots and raised areas with 100-grit open-grain sandpaper. Wear a filter mask when sanding.

STEP 7
Use a 10-inch knife to apply at least three more coats of compound over the joints, allowing each one to dry thoroughly. The applications should be successively wider by a few inches on each side with the edges feathered out (or blended) into the bare wallboard. See the top of page 40 for how to check the final finish coat for rough spots.

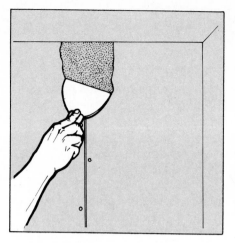

2. Starting a seam. Load your knife and spread compound about 1/8 inch thick down the open seam from top to bottom.

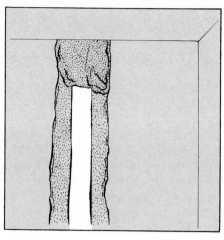

3. Fixing the tape. Tear a length of tape the length of the seam and fix it at the top with a layer of compound to hold it in place.

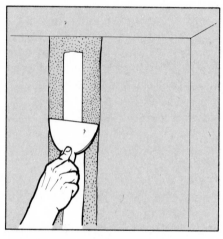

4. Imbedding the tape. Carefully imbed the tape in the compound with the knife, lifting tape to take out wrinkles.

5. Removing excess compound. When the tape is imbedded, go back to the top of the seam and scrape away any excess.

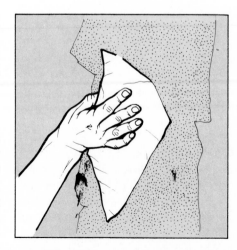

6. Sanding the first coats. After the compound has dried at least a day, smooth down any rough spots.

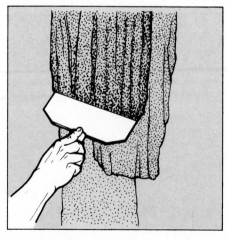

7. Applying finishing coats. Use a wider knife to apply thin finishing coats of compound to the seam. Usually several coats are required.

FINISHING OUTSIDE CORNERS
STEP 1

Outside corners need extra protection from damage. This is provided by a lightweight right angle bracket called a corner bead. Cut the bead to length with tin shears and nail it onto the corner as shown, but don't try to dimple the nails. The corner itself sticks out slightly from the wall and compound will cover nail heads.

STEP 2

Apply a layer of joint compound by loading the knife and working from the wall out to the corner with horizontal strokes. Then scrape off the excess, working down the corner with vertical strokes, with the blade scraping the wall on one side and overhanging the corner on the other. Allow to dry and finish with several more coats as above.

FINISHING INSIDE CORNERS
STEP 1

Apply a first layer of compound down both sides of an inside corner. Make sure that the compound fills the corner itself all the way from top to bottom so tape will adhere.

STEP 2

Tear off a piece of tape the length of the corner and fold it down the center lengthways. Ordinary wallboard tape is pre-creased down the center so it folds easily.

STEP 3

Carefully lay the folded tape into the corner and, starting from the top, press it into the compound. Then gently poke the crease into the corner with your knife blade. Smooth the sides of the tape onto the adjacent walls with the knife, taking care not to pull the tape away from the corner.

STEP 4

Apply a second layer of compound over the tape, down one side then the other, taking care not to pull the tape out of the corner with your strokes. Finish with several more applications of compound, sanding between, as with flat joints.

FINISHING OUTSIDE CORNERS

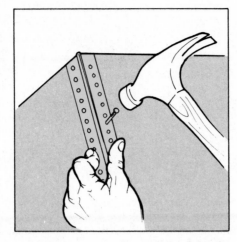

1. Adding corner beads. Corner beads are nailed to wallboard to strengthen corners and to provide raised edges for the compound.

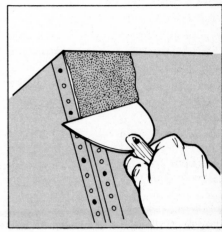

2. Plastering the corner. Compound will fill in between the wall and the slightly raised corner. Several applications are required.

FINISHING INSIDE CORNERS

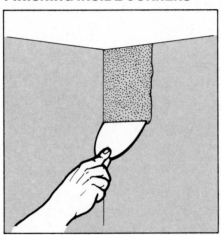

1. Starting the corner. Fill both sides of the corner with compound about 1/8 inch thick as if starting a flat seam.

2. Folding the tape. Crease a piece of tape the length of the corner down the center so that it will fit into the corner.

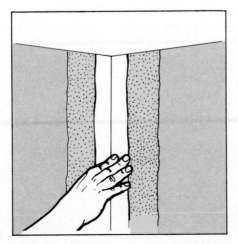

3. Applying the tape. Press the folded tape into the compound, taking care that the crease fits exactly into the corner.

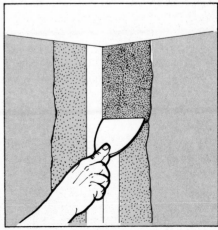

4. Finishing the corner. With the tape in place, apply a layer of compound over it, scrape away excess, and finish.

CHECKING THE FINISH

To make sure the job is perfect when you are finished with all the coats of compound, use a light to check your work—it may show up problem areas you wouldn't otherwise see. Shine the light along the wall as shown (this works best if the light is directed by a hood, like a photoflood) and look for raised areas and depressions revealed by shadows. Smooth such raised areas with sandpaper and fill depressions with more compound.

ELIMINATING BUBBLES
STEP 1

If the tape has separated from the compound at any point, it will rise as a bubble when the compound is dry (or even later, when the wall has been painted or papered). Check the seams closely (see middle) for bubbles when the job is finished. Any you find can be corrected quite easily. Use a utility knife to cut around the bubbled area just into the tape that is sound.

STEP 2

Remove the bubbled tape from the wall and fill the resulting depression with compound as if it were a nail dimple. Clean away excess, allow to dry, and repeat applications of compound, sanding after each one, until the surface is smooth.

FILLING GAPS
STEP 1

If any hole that you have cut into the wallboard to fit around an outlet or switch is slightly too large for the face plate to cover, it can be built up with compound and tape. Apply a generous amount of compound over the edge of the gap, as shown, so that it is filled.

STEP 2

Lay a piece of tape over the compound with one long edge against the edge of the electrical box. Anchor the tape with another layer of compound over it, then scrape away the excess, taking care not to pull the tape out of position as you do so. Finish with several more layers as above.

CHECKING THE FINISH

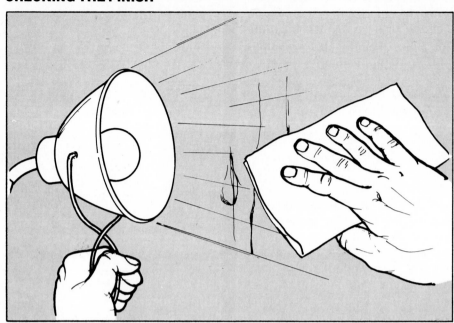

Use a light directed along the wall to reveal raised spots and depressions. Inspect a small area then move along, either up and down or side to side, in some regular pattern, so you can keep track of what you have checked. Smooth down raised spots. Fill low ones.

ELIMINATING BUBBLES

1. Removing a bubble. Cut around a bubble in the tape well into the sound surface, so that no air gap will remain when you peel off tape.

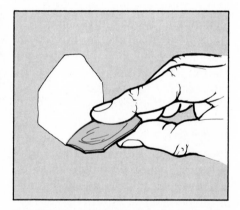

2. Refinishing a bubbled spot. Peel away the paper you have cut around and fill the depression with compound as with a nail dimple.

FILLING GAPS

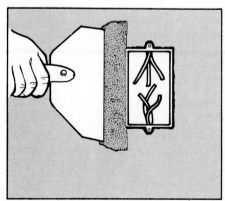

1. Applying compound. Fill the gap between the wallboard and an electrical fixture. You may have to use quite a lot of compound.

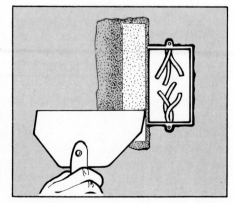

2. Placing the tape. Fit a piece of tape over the built up compound, imbed it in the compound, and finish as you would a seam.

Soundproofing Walls

Ordinary frame walls and ceilings stop a moderate amount of sound but this may not be enough—for a quiet bedroom in a busy house, for instance, or to contain the sound of power tools in a home workshop or music in a practice room. There are several steps you can take to reduce the amount of sound passing between rooms in your house or apartment—from sealing cracks to building new walls and ceilings (see *Soundproofing Ceilings*, page 138).

Sound enters (or leaves) a room in two ways—airborne through openings, and transmitted by the vibrations it causes in walls, floors, and ceilings. To stop sound you have to seal openings and deaden vibration in walls and ceilings.

A surprising amount of sound can leak into a room under doors and through unsealed outlet and switch plates, cracks, open joints, and seams. These leaks will render any amount of structural soundproofing ineffective, but they can be sealed up easily.

The direct transmission of sound through walls and ceilings can be reduced only by altering their structure. This can range from hanging new wallboard over a wall, on special metal channels that hold it away from the old surface, to building a hollow wall 6 inches thick stuffed with 6-inch insulation—a barrier that will stop sound as effectively as a 4-inch-thick brick wall. If you are adding a wall, you can, of course, make it as soundproof as you like from the beginning.

Plan any soundproofing carefully. If you want to make a room quieter, you must consider all the possible routes by which sound enters it, as shown in the diagram top right. For effective soundproofing, you must block them all. Expensive renovations for soundproofing are valueless if they stop bothersome noise from one direction and do nothing to stop it from another.

PLANNING FOR SOUNDPROOFING

The diagram (right) shows the several paths by which sound can enter rooms—in this case upstairs bedrooms. When you are planning soundproofing, you must consider every possible pathway, because any amount of intervention that does not completely seal a room will usually be a waste of time. It would be like building a dam only partway across a river. You may find that the level of soundproofing you desire is simply not possible without an impractical amount of reconstruction. You would be better off abandoning your plans than spending time and money on halfway measures. Of course, stopping sound at its source is the most efficient way to soundproof.

SEALING ACOUSTIC LEAKS

Use a silicone sealer to fill any cracks at the top and bottom of a wall and around outlet and switch plates. If noise is entering through duct work, you should line as much of the duct as you can reach with neoprene duct liner held in place with adhesive. The duct liner should be sealed with a coating of the same adhesive recommended for use with the liner along any edges that are cut so that small glass fibers from the liner are not carried out of the duct on the streams of forced air.

SEALING DOORS WITH GASKETS

Use neoprene gaskets which you cut to fit around the top and sides of doors. The door should squeeze the gasket slightly when it is closed, but not so much that the gasket prevents the door from latching easily. At the bottom, install an aluminum sill, plane the door to fit, and attach a gasket to the bottom so that it just meets the sill. Check for proper fit by slipping a thin blade (like a putty knife) under the door. There should be some resistance.

PLANNING FOR SOUNDPROOFING

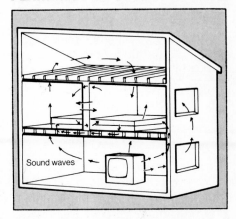

Try to locate all possible pathways that sound can take to the room you want quieter and make provisions for each.

SEALING ACOUSTIC LEAKS

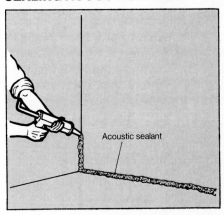

Block pathways for airborne sound waves with caulking. Seal top and bottom of walls, and around outlets and switches.

SEALING UNDER DOORS

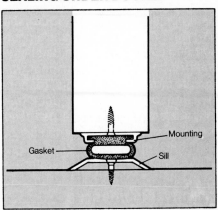

Install neoprene gaskets around doors to block sound leaks. Adjust the door so you can install a sill beneath.

NEW WALL SURFACE HUNG ON RESILIENT CHANNELS

Resilient channels are metal tracks that hold a wall surface in position away from the surface it is attached to; they are designed to isolate the two surfaces so that the outer one will not pick up the vibrations of the inner surface. To enhance the sound-stopping qualities of an existing wall, strip off the old surface and fill the wall cavity with 3½-inch insulation. Attach resilient channels across the studs with channels located 6 inches below the ceiling and 2 inches above the floor. Space them evenly for the attachment of wallboard, but intervals should not exceed 2 feet. Overlap the channel where you must to reach the length of the wall. Attach wallboard to channels with 1-inch wallboard screws and seal at the top and bottom with caulking.

STAGGERED STUD WALLS

You can improve soundproofing by building a staggered stud wall, half again as thick as a regular stud wall. Use 2 × 6 lumber for the top and bottom plates and mark them for staggered studs 24 inches on center on each side as shown right. Erect the plates and studs and staple 3½-inch batts of insulation between the studs on one side of the wall. Attach wallboard as on any wall and caulk at top and bottom.

DOUBLE WALLS

For the most soundproof wall possible with wallboard, build two stud walls set 1 inch apart. Cover one side of this frame with two layers of wallboard. Fill the double wall with 6-inch-thick batts of insulation and cover the other side with two layers of wallboard. Caulk at top and bottom on both sides.

Where you can afford the lost floor area in a room with existing walls, you can strip the surface facing into the room from the wall that requires additional soundproofing and erect the second wall in front of the first as described above. Stuff it with insulation and cover the new wall with wallboard.

RESILIENT CHANNELS

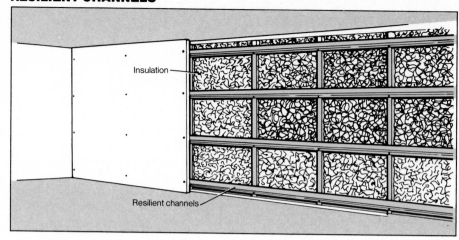

Resilient channels isolate a wall surface from some of the structural vibrations that transmit sound. The channels are attached to studs with 1¼-inch wallboard screws. When installing wallboard, leave a ⅛-inch gap at top and bottom and seal with caulking.

STAGGERED STUDS

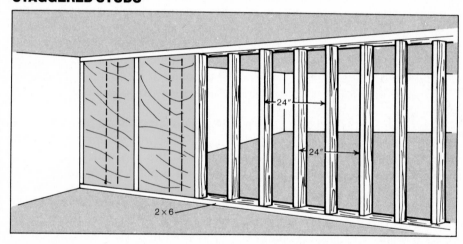

This wall is built like an ordinary stud wall except that alternating studs are offset so the two wall surfaces are hung on different studs; the stud are set 24 inches on center. When installing wallboard, leave a ⅛-inch gap at the top and bottom and seal with caulking.

DOUBLE STUD WALL

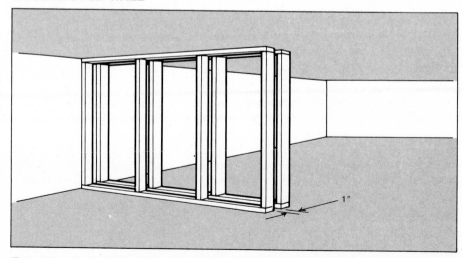

Two walls are better than one because their surfaces have no communication at all. This wall is stuffed with 6 inches of insulation and covered with two layers of wallboard on each side. When installing wallboard, leave a ⅛-inch gap at top and bottom and seal with caulking.

Repairing Wallboard and Plaster

Walls are subject to a variety of assaults that can damage their surface, especially in a house with children. Besides the everyday wear and tear of impacts and gouges, walls can also develop cracks on their own as a house settles. This section will cover repairs to damaged wallboard and two kinds of repairs to plaster that are most often needed. Large repairs to plaster are beyond the scope of this book.

If you have learned the art of taping and plastering wallboard, repairing it will present no problems. Compared with plaster walls, wallboard is relatively easy to repair because damaged areas can be removed and replaced, but plaster must be stripped down to the lathe beneath, then built up again.

The most common problem with wallboard is that seams open and nails pop up and show through the wall covering as a house settles. Repair of a popped nail is simple: drive the nail back into the stud, dimpling the surface as shown on page 35. To add holding power, drive another wallboard nail into the stud about 2 inches above or below the one that popped. Then plaster over the new dimples as shown on page 37. Seams that have opened up should be taped and plastered again as shown on page 38. Wallboard repairs require the same tools as wallboard installation and finishing.

Repairing small cracks and holes in a plaster surface is not much different from working with joint compound on wallboard. You will need patching plaster (sold as a powder to be mixed at home) for the base of the new surface and joint compound or vinyl spackling for the finish.

The ideal time to make repairs to wall surfaces is when you are about to repaint a room. If you aren't refinishing the whole wall under repair, prime the repair and paint or patch it with wallpaper to match the rest of the wall.

REPAIRING WALLBOARD
STEP 1

Wallboard breaks more easily than a plaster wall; a hard knock, such as from a doorknob flung against it, will cause either a noticeable dent or a hole. To replace a piece of wallboard that is damaged, draw a rectangle around it, using a carpenter's square to keep the edges straight and the corners at 90°. This will make it easier to get a good fit with the replacement piece. Drill starter holes inside opposite corners, cut the piece with a keyhole saw, and pull it out. If the damaged area is large, cut back to the nearest studs on each side.

STEP 2

Cut two pieces of 1 × 3, each about 6 inches longer than the vertical sides of the hole, as braces for the patch. Insert a brace in the opening and hold it vertically against one edge, centered, so that half the width of the brace is behind the wall and half is showing through the opening. Attach above and below the opening with wallboard screws through the wall into the brace; drive additional screws into the side of the brace in the middle or at 6-inch intervals if the opening is larger than 8 inches. Repeat with the second brace on the other side of the opening. Don't use nails—they will break the wallboard. Cut a wallboard patch the size of the hole, fit it in place and attach with screws through the patch into the braces. If you have cut back to studs, nail strips of 1 × 2 flush against their edges to provide a nailing surface for the patch.

STEP 3

Finish the seams around the patch with tape and joint compound as shown on pages 37-40. Sand the successive applications of joint compound until the final coat is flush with the surrounding wall. Prime the patch and repaint to match the surrounding wall.

REPAIRING WALLBOARD

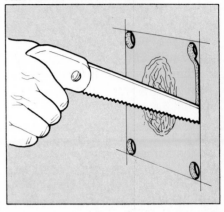

1. Cutting out the damage. Drill a starter hole in the corners of the outline and cut out the damaged piece. Leave a neat hole to fill.

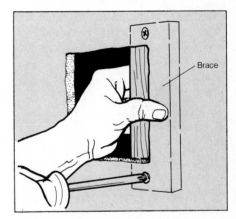

2. Adding new bracing. Slip a brace inside the opening and attach with screws through the wallboard.

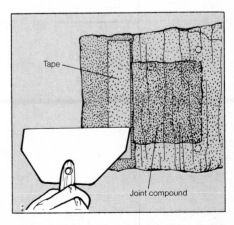

3. Taping and plastering the patch. Use joint compound and paper joint tape to hide the edges of the patch.

REPAIRING A HOLE WITH PATCHING PLASTER
STEP 1

Fix an 18-inch length of string through a piece of ordinary wire screen cut slightly larger than the hole to be repaired. Clear any loose gypsum and wallboard paper from the edge of the hole. Wet the edge on the inside and coat liberally with patching plaster, then put the screen through the hole and pull it flat against the new plaster.

STEP 2

Tie the screen to a dowel, pencil or other similar anchor to hold it. Plaster the screen not quite flush with the wall, then tighten the string slightly by twisting the anchor. Allow to dry for a few hours.

STEP 3

After the plaster is well set, cut the string at the screen. Moisten the plaster around the edge of the remaining hole and fill with plaster. Apply a second coat over the entire patch to make it almost flush with the wall and let it dry.

STEP 4

Use joint compound to finish the repair, covering the hole and feathering the edges as in taping wallboard joints. Let dry for a day, then sand smooth.

SEALING A CRACK
STEP 1

If the crack is only a hairline, use a beer can opener to enlarge it slightly. If the crack is wider, follow the instructions on the next page for undercutting. Gouge out a small bit of plaster at either end to seat the patch. Clear out any dust. If the crack is a long one, use this procedure but gouge holes to anchor the plaster every foot or so along the length of the crack.

STEP 2

Seal the crack with joint compound, overlapping the sound wall. Let dry for a day and fill again if the patch subsides. Let dry again for a day and sand smooth.

REPAIRING A HOLE WITH PATCHING PLASTER

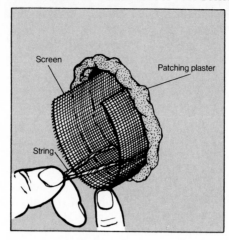

1. Inserting the screen. Coat the edges of the hole with patching plaster before inserting the screen so it will be fixed to the wall.

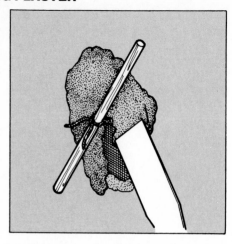

2. Plastering over the screen. Pull the screen flush with the wall, tighten it, and cover with a layer of patching plaster.

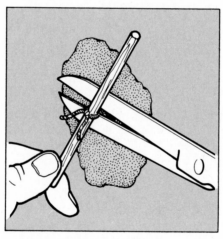

3. Cutting the string. When the first layer of plaster is dry, cut away the string and apply a second layer of plaster.

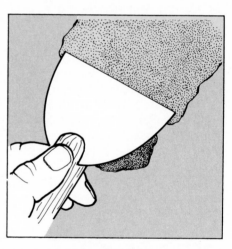

4. Finishing the patch. The last step is a finishing coat of joint compound. Allow this to dry 24 hours before sanding.

SEALING A CRACK

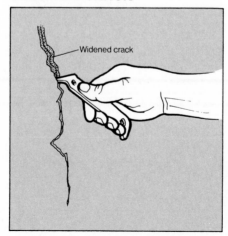

1. Widening the crack. Open the crack by pulling a sharp object down its length to make it large enough to accept new plaster.

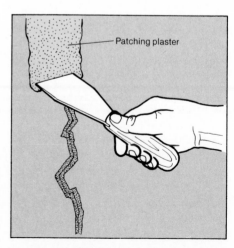

2. Filling the crack. Fill the crack with joint compound, feathering the edges of this filler out to the sides. Sand after 24 hours.

REPAIRING A HOLE IN PLASTER
STEP 1
Chip and scrape away all loose plaster around the edge of the hole. Any loose plaster not cleared away will prevent the patch from anchoring to the wall at that point. Don't worry about enlarging the hole.

STEP 2
Give the patch a sound foundation by undercutting the plaster around the edge of the hole. Do this with a can opener or other implement with a hooked point. Carve under the edge so that the plaster slopes away from the edge toward the lath.

STEP 3
Moisten the edge of the hole with water. Fill the hole with patching plaster, covering the entire surface of the lath evenly, out to a level just below the level of the surrounding wall. Score the plaster with the corner of your spreading knife to make it easier for the top coat to adhere. Let the patch dry according to product instructions.

STEP 4
When the plaster is dry, apply a coat of joint compound over the patch and feather the edges into the surrounding wall. Allow this coat to dry overnight and sand smooth or apply another coat if the first has subsided below the surface of the wall.

REPAIRING PLASTER AT AN OUTSIDE CORNER
If the damage is minor, you can usually repair it with joint compound and a spreading knife, shaping the corner against a straightedge. If the damaged area is extensive, use the method shown at right. Clear damaged plaster from edges and prepare the surface, following the procedures given above. Tack a straightedged piece of scrap wood lightly to one side of the corner and use it as a guide for filling one side of the damaged area with an undercoat of patching plaster to within 1/8 inch of the surrounding surface. Move the guide and repeat on the other side. Finish with joint compound.

REPAIRING A HOLE IN PLASTER

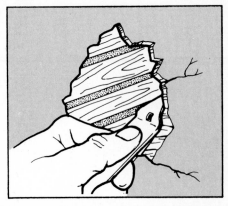

1. Clearing damaged plaster. Pull damaged plaster away from the hole or impact area. Clear the edges of loose plaster.

2. Undercutting the edge. Use a sharp implement, preferably one with a hook, to carve under the edge to make a seat for the patch.

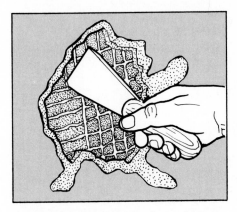

3. Filling the hole. When you have filled the hole with patching plaster, groove the surface with the edge of the spreading knife.

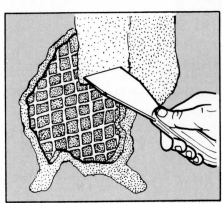

4. Completing the patch. Spread joint compound over the patch, filling it flush with the surrounding wall, then feather the edges.

REPAIRING AN OUTSIDE PLASTER CORNER

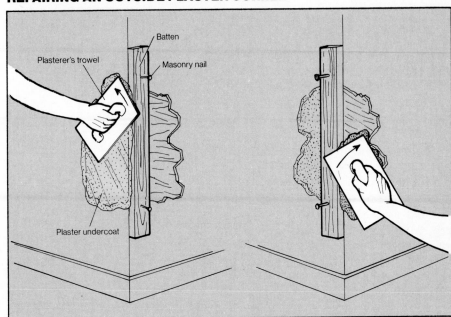

Use a wooden float to smooth the patch *away* from the guide toward the good wall. Be sure to tack the guide far enough above and below the damaged area not to cause further damage and gently enough not to fracture good plaster. Repair nail holes with joint compound.

Preparing Walls for New Surfaces

Before installing a new surface such as paneling or tile or new wallboard on an old wall, you will have to make the wall ready to receive it. The preparation can range from simply removing molding and cleaning the wall, as in the case of frame wallboard walls that are true and without serious surface defects, to building an entire new wall over the old one where the surface cannot be repaired.

To receive a new surface, a wall must provide wherever needed a plane of sound nailing or gluing surfaces perpendicular to the floor. A plumb wallboard wall in good condition is the ideal surface to panel or tile—equivalent to a newly built wall. Panels are nailed to studs through the wallboard, or glued with panel adhesive and nailed; tile is glued to the wallboard. Walls with some surface defects such as crumbling plaster or unevenness, as well as concrete or cinder block walls, must be furred out with a lattice of wood to take nails or adhesive. Framing a false wall is called for when you need space for insulation, wiring, or pipes and this is useful in basements and garages. A badly deteriorated surface may have to be removed (see page 21).

What materials you need depends on the wall surface. For furring, use 1×2s and 1×3s which are attached to concrete or cinder blocks with screws into plugs, masonry nails or adhesive, and 8-penny nails for framing walls. If you must level furring with shims, get wood shingles. False walls are constructed of 2×3s or 2×4s depending on the height of the wall and the weight of the new surface to be attached. Basement walls may require some kind of waterproofing treatment. Basic carpentry tools will take care of all the procedures except driving nails or holes into concrete or cinder block for which you need either a baby sledge and a star drill or a masonry bit on a heavy duty power drill.

SURVEYING THE JOB
On a frame wall, use a carpenter's level to check for plumb at several places along the wall, then check it for bulges and depressions by running the edge of a long straight piece of lumber over the wall. A light placed along the edge will show up low areas; a high spot will lift the edge and cause the board to rock. Isolated low spots can be rebuilt with wallboard following the directions on page 43. Isolated high spots on a plaster wall can be knocked down with a hammer. Widespread unevenness must be furred. If you fur a wall, you must also reposition the molding around any windows and doorways (see page 48). Decide whether you will install new molding around the floor and ceiling or reuse what is there. If you are covering a basement wall, decide whether to fur it or frame over it, depending on whether you need space behind the surface.

MOISTURE PROTECTION
It is important that new surfaces on basement walls be as well protected from moisture as possible. First assess the condition of your basement walls. If they are wet, you may need foundation repairs; this is not the time to cover them with a new surface such as paneling or wallboard. Damp walls without significant amounts of moisture should be sealed with a waterproofing paint. To protect panels, cover furring with overlapped sheets of 4-mil polyethylene plastic as a moisture barrier. For further protection from moisture damage, seal the back side of paneling. When you install panels, leave a 1/4-inch breathing space at the bottom.

SURVEYING THE JOB

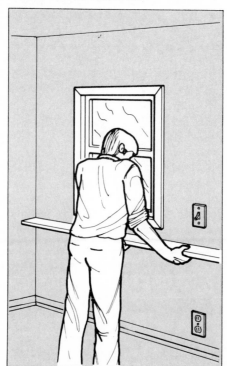

Use a long piece of board with a good straight edge to check over the entire wall for high and low spots. Also make an inventory of things that must be furred around, like windows, doors, and outlets.

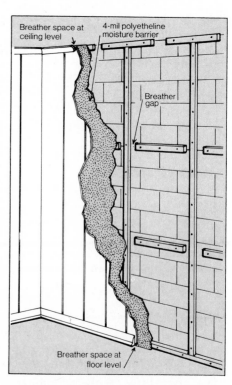

A basement wall below ground level may be damp and should be treated with sealer. It is especially important to leave breathing spaces between furring strips on a potentially damp wall.

FURRING A WALL

Use 8-penny nails to attach pieces of 1 × 2 or 1½-inch strips of ½-inch plywood to studs. Over a cinder block or concrete wall use masonry nails or screws into plugs. The grid is usually laid out with vertical pieces 48 inches on center and horizontal pieces 16 inches on center. Leave ½-inch spaces between pieces where they meet, to allow air to circulate behind the panels.

TRUING A WALL
STEP 1

Use a chalk line or straightedge to make a grid on the wall where the furring will be nailed: also snap a chalk line along the ceiling 2 inches out from the wall at each corner. Hang a plumb bob on the ceiling line at the first stud and measure the distance from the plumb line to each intersection of lines; repeat all along the grid to find the highest point on the wall.

STEP 2

Attach a horizontal furring strip with an 8-penny nail at the highest point on the grid. When cutting the strip, allow for vertical 1 × 3s at the corners. Try to use single pieces if you can, otherwise take pains to butt them carefully over studs. Hang the plumb bob above this point and measure from the line to the furring strip. Then hang the plumb bob from the ceiling line at the first stud and shim behind the furring strip until it is the same distance from the plumb line as at the highest point. Nail through the shims to the stud. Repeat at each intersection.

STEP 3

Attach a 1 × 3 furring strip at the top of the wall by shimming at all points to bring it to the same distance from the plumb bob as the strip below. Check with the straightedge.

STEP 4

Use a long straightedge laid vertically over the two (and subsequent) furring strips to find their correct height. Make the furring flush with the straightedge. Attach vertical pieces in the corners.

FURRING A WALL

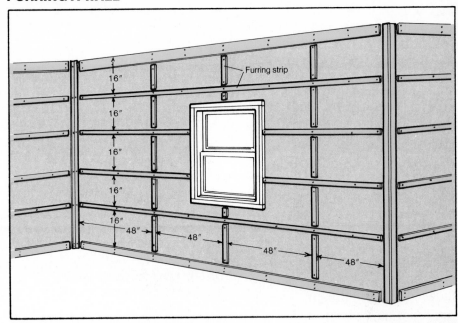

If the sequence of studs is irregular in a section of the wall (see page 20 about locating studs), plan the furring so that a single sheet of paneling or wallboard will bridge the irregularity. The next sheet can be cut down to fit to restore the regular sequence of panels.

TRUING A WALL

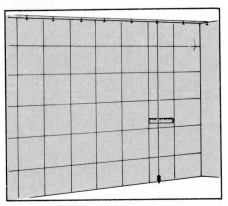

1. Measuring. Hang the plumb bob along a line on the ceiling 2 inches from the wall. Mark distance from wall at every intersection.

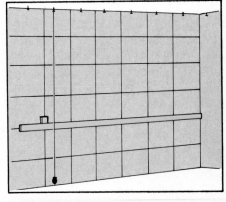

2. Attaching the first strip. Nail the strip to the highest point, then start shimming behind to make it level along its entire length.

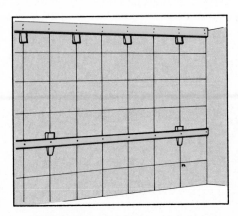

3. Attaching the top strip. When the first strip is in place, attach the top strip the same distance from the plumb bob as the first strip.

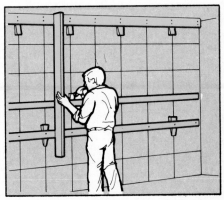

4. Completing the furring. Use a straightedge between the top and first strip as a guide for shimming the rest of the strips.

FURRING AROUND WINDOWS
STEP 1
If you want to save the casing around windows, find the nails at the corners and drive their heads through into the adjoining piece with a nail set, then pry the casing away from the wall. If the window has a stool, drive the heads of nails through the horns (as above), and pry it out.

STEP 2
Add furring strips around the window on all sides. Because the new surface will deepen the window opening, you will have to add jamb extenders so that molding can be reinstalled on the new surface. The extenders should be the depth of the new surface plus the depth of the furring. Cut a new window stool to fit the depth of the new surface. You can find all the dimensions of the new window stool but the depth by tracing the old one on new stock. Add the depth of the new wall surface.

FRAMING A FALSE WALL
In order to make room for insulation or wiring under a new surface on a concrete or cinder block wall, erect a frame of 2×3 or 2×4 studs against the masonry. Plan how you will arrange plates at the corners and cut top and bottom plates the length of the wall (or walls). Mark them for stud locations, 16 inches on center as shown on page 27, Step 4; marking for corners. Build a frame on the floor as described on page 27. Then raise it into position. Check for plumb and shim at top and bottom where necessary, then attach at top, bottom, and sides with 16-penny nails into wood, masonry nails into concrete. Frame around any electrical outlets as shown.

BOXING IN PIPES AND DUCTS
Pipes and ducts that intrude into a room can be framed to receive paneling. Boxing in pipes and ducts consists of building two narrow stud walls (three where you wish to enclose something that is in a corner) as shown. As in any framing, you must provide nailing surfaces along corners.

FURRING AROUND WINDOWS

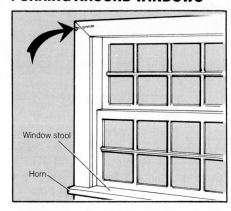

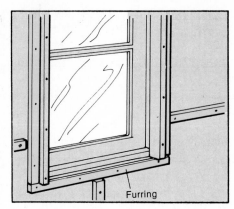

1. Removing trim. Casing molding around windows can be used again if you remove it undamaged. Push corner nails through before prying the molding from the wall.

2. Furring around the window. Every place where the new surface will have an edge must be furred. The window must also be brought level with the surface with jamb extenders.

FRAMING A FALSE WALL

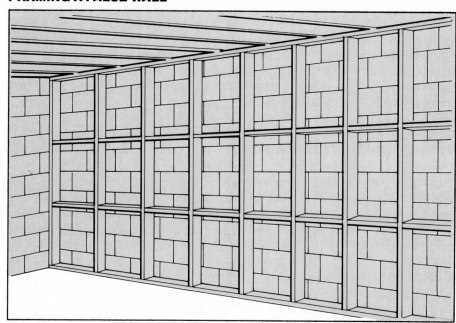

A false frame wall over an existing wall must perform the same function as furring—to provide nailing surfaces for the new wall surface. Nail blocking of the same dimension lumber used in the frame between the studs as shown to provide a horizontal nailing surface.

BOXING VERTICAL PIPES

To conceal a pipe in a corner, build the two short walls shown above and attach the frame to the floor, walls, and ceiling.

BOXING HORIZONTAL PIPES

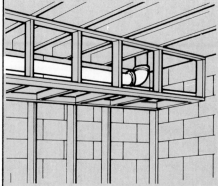

Horizontal pipes at the ceiling are concealed by walls on their sides. Build the two walls and attach them to each other in place.

Installing Sheet Paneling

Sheet paneling—of real or simulated wood—is one of the most popular wall surfaces for do-it-yourself installation. It is one of the easiest of all wall surfaces to install and it quickly transforms a space from ordinary to special.

All paneling is sold in 4 × 8-foot sheets; there are larger sheets available at a premium price in some grades. Sheet paneling is a veneer of real wood, vinyl, paper, or nondescript wood printed to resemble fine wood grain. The veneer is laid over a composition wood. It is usually grooved vertically to imitate planks of different widths. Grooves fall in 16- and 24-inch intervals to facilitate hiding the nailing to furring or studs. There are four basic types: *Wood veneer on plywood* is, as the name suggests, real wood veneer—anything from pine to exotic woods—over plywood. It is usually 1/4 inch thick and is finished with a clear plastic coating that protects it from damage. Because the veneer is real, each panel is unique. This type is the strongest and most expensive, with the price depending on the type of veneer. *Simulated veneer on plywood* is a panel covered on the good side by a layer of paper, vinyl, or wood printed to resemble a fine wood veneer. It is 5/32 or 3/16 inch thick and somewhat less expensive than real wood veneer on plywood. Unlike real wood, these panels repeat the surface pattern. Even less expensive is *patterned hardboard*, a simulated surface (fabric patterns as well as wood) on hardboard, either 5/32 or 3/16 inch thick. Hardboard paneling is not as strong as either kind of plywood paneling, but it is less costly. Finally, the least expensive type of paneling is *patterned particleboard*, a printed paper, vinyl, or wood layer on 3/16-inch particleboard. Particleboard is rigid, somewhat brittle, and not as easy to install as the first three types of sheet paneling, but it is useful where economy is important.

There are a few basic rules for purchasing paneling that will improve the look of your job. First, always plan the work carefully before ordering the paneling so that you don't overbuy or underbuy. When you choose your paneling, try to buy it from stock so that you can inspect each sheet for undamaged edges. Find out whether you can get molding that will complement the paneling you choose and consider the specially colored panel nails that are available to blend with panel colors.

PLANNING THE JOB

Make a scale drawing, as shown, of the room you plan to panel. This is a handy reference for determining where it is best to locate the first sheet of paneling, where you need additional furring, and where you will have to make tricky cuts. For ordering materials, divide the perimeter (total length of the walls) by four and round up to the nearest whole number. This is the number of panels you will need.

CONDITIONING THE PANELS

All paneling should be cured for a few days in the room where it will be installed, giving it time to expand or contract in response to the particular conditions of the location. Stack paneling flat with 1 × 2s between the sheets, or on the 8-foot edge, with separation between the sheets as shown.

ARRANGING THE PANELS

Real wood veneers vary from sheet to sheet. If you are installing this type, stand the sheets up around the room and rearrange them into the most pleasing combination of grain patterns and hue. Putting dark panels with dark, and light with light, reinforces the simulation of plank paneling by disguising the sheets. Consider which walls in a room get the most and least light and put the lightest panels on the darkest wall.

PLANNING THE JOB

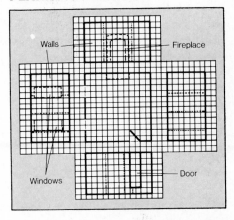

An accurate plan of the room to be paneled is useful for estimating materials and to help identify problems to be solved.

CONDITIONING PANELS

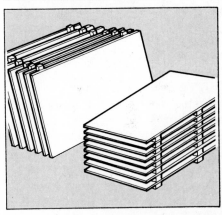

Panels should be seasoned for a few days in the room where they will be installed. Stack them so that air can circulate on all sides.

ARRANGING PANELS

Arrange the paneling in place before installation. Working from a stack of sheets may cause bad combinations.

CUTTING PANELING

Although paneling is easy to work, it does require care in cutting to prevent the good face from splintering. The tool you use to make the cuts determines which side of the paneling you work on. Circular saws and saber saws cut on the upstroke and should be used from the back of the panel. All saws that cut on the downstroke (handsaw, table saw, radial arm saw) should be used from the front. Use a plywood blade with six teeth per inch on a circular saw, a saber saw blade with ten teeth per inch, and a handsaw with a narrow set between cutting points.

MAKING LONG CUTS IN PANELING

You can be certain of straight cuts with a circular saw if you clamp a straightedge to the paneling as a guide for the saw. The edge of the temporary guide should be the same distance from the cutting line as the saw blade's distance from the edge of the saw's base plate.

CUTTING OPENINGS

Measure the position of an opening and transfer the location to the appropriate side of the panel. A quick way to do this is to rub the edge of the fixture that must come through the panel, with the panel exactly in place, and tap it over the spot with a hammer on cloth to protect the panel. Drill starter holes inside the corners of the outline, large enough to start your saw.

SCRIBING

To fit a panel against an irregular surface, tack it to the wall a few inches away, checking that it's plumb, and use a carpenter's scribe to mark the edge of the panel. Cut the scribed outline with a jig saw or coping saw.

INSTALLING SHEET PANELING STEP 1

Start at a corner. Check the ceiling and floor at the wall to see whether the room is reasonably square. If it is, measure the height of the wall and cut the panel ½ inch shorter. If it isn't, find the distance the ceiling

CUTTING PANELING

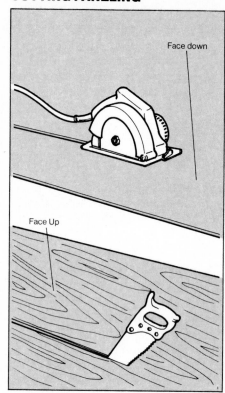

Face down

Face Up

Saws that cut on the upstroke are used from the back of a panel, those that cut on the downstroke are used from the front.

CUTTING OPENINGS

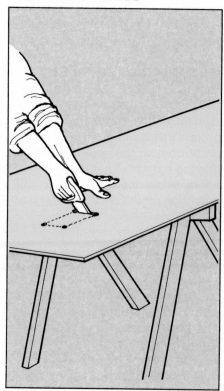

Drill starter holes in each corner and use a key hole saw or a saber saw to cut openings, using the starter holes to turn corners.

CUTTING A LONG LINE

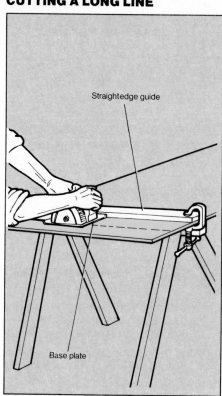

Straightedge guide

Base plate

Two clamps and a straight-edged piece of lumber insure straight cuts. This jig is especially useful when cutting panels for a low wall.

SCRIBING PANELING

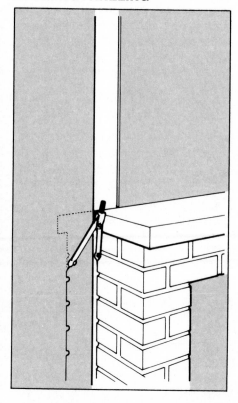

The secret of cutting irregular shapes accurately is positioning the panel correctly before marking. Make sure it is secured.

deviates from horizontal at whichever corner is higher, and mark that on the appropriate side of the panel, as shown. Draw a cutting line to the opposide corner and make the cut. Measure the distance from the ceiling to the floor where both edges of the panel will sit, subtract 1/2 inch for clearance, mark the panel, and make that cut. Use a plumb line to check the adjoining wall and cut to fit.

STEP 2
You can install paneling with either adhesive or nails. Use 3-penny finishing nails into studs and 6-penny finishing nails into wallboard. You can buy specially colored paneling nails. Square the panel before nailing. For adhesive application, follow the manufacturer's instructions and apply to furring as shown. On a flat wall, cover the surface with a random squiggle, and run a bead around the panel 1/2 inch in from the edge.

STEP 3
Set the panel against the wall, propped on scrap wood shims, off the floor. Check the panel for plumb and correct the position. If the panel isn't plumb because it doesn't fit against the wall, take it down and cut to adjust the fit so subsequent panels will be plumb.

STEP 4
Many adhesives call for the panel to be held away from the wall to let the adhesive cure. Tack it in four places at the top and prop up at the bottom.

STEP 5
Use a felt tip pen the same color as the grooves in the panels to mark the surface along a seam before installing the next sheet. Install subsequent sheets using the procedures given above.

STEP 6
When you meet the opposite corner of the wall, measure between the last panel and the corners at the top and bottom and transfer the measurements to the panel. Cut to fit, but not for such a tight fit that you have to flex the panel to fit it into the space.

INSTALLING PANELING

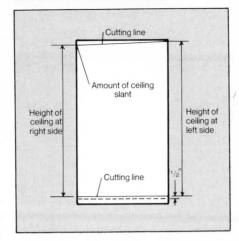

1. Cutting the first panel. Cutting for height, after cutting to fit the ceiling, assures a good fit along the floor.

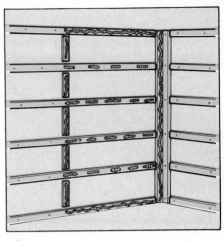

2. Applying adhesive. Apply a continuous bead around perimeter and intermittent beads along the inside strips.

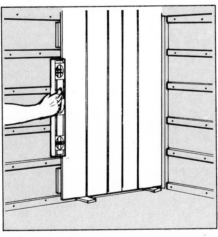

3. Plumbing the sheet. The first panel determines the position of all the others, so make sure it is plumb.

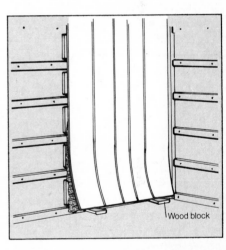

4. Curing the adhesive. Some adhesives require that you pull the panel away after it has been pressed into the adhesive.

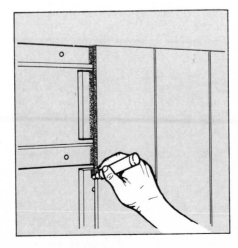

5. Concealing seams. Marking with a dark color behind the seams conceals them when the panels contract slightly and pull apart.

6. Ending a wall. The corner should fit closely, so measure at the top and bottom to cut the edge that meets the corner.

CREATING A HERRINGBONE PATTERN
STEP 1
You can achieve a dramatic effect by installing paneling in a herringbone pattern. Mark the sheets as shown. These cuts will produce a rearranged panel width of about 2 feet 10 inches and this procedure will not work over a 16-inch-on-center frame. Measure the wall and plan the project so that you don't end with a noticeably narrow piece.

STEP 2
Match the pieces as shown and attach. Repeat the procedure, matching the grooves of the next pair with the first.

WAINSCOTING
Paneling that covers only the lower 30 to 36 inches of a wall is called wainscoting and it is applied to the wall the same way as full sheets of paneling. Cut the paneling down to the desired height, measuring for each piece from a horizontal line on the wall, and install against the bare wall or over furring if necessary. If wainscoting is attached to a bare wall it can be capped with cap molding; if installed over furring, a combination of moldings may be required to fill the space between the paneling and the wall.

COVERING HIGH WALLS
When panels must be stacked, either vertically or horizontally, to cover a wall, the seams created by butting the ends of panels can be concealed with molding in the manner shown at right or covered with strips of 1-inch board of an appropriate color.

FASTENING TRIM FOR HARDBOARD PANELS
Hardboard paneling can be attached to walls with fastening trim which holds the panels in place and also provides a finished treatment for seam and corners. Follow manufacturer's specific instructions for installation—some pieces must be installed before a panel is seated, some after. All trim must be installed plumb to yield a straight wall.

HERRINGBONE PATTERN

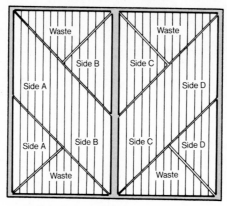

1. Cutting the panels. The letter code indicates the cuts for a herringbone pattern. Use a combination square to measure angles.

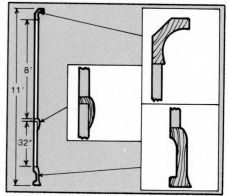

2. Fitting the panels. Rearrange according to this pattern. At the end of the wall, cut the panel to fit before cutting the diagonals.

WAINSCOTING

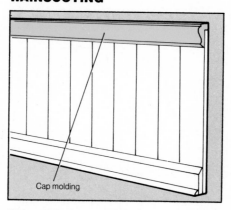

Wainscoting is installed along a horizontal marked on the wall. Pieces should be cut to fit, measuring from the horizontal to the floor.

HIGH WALL TREATMENT

This is one example of an arrangement for using molding and two pieces of paneling to cover an extra-high wall.

HARDBOARD FASTENING MOLDING

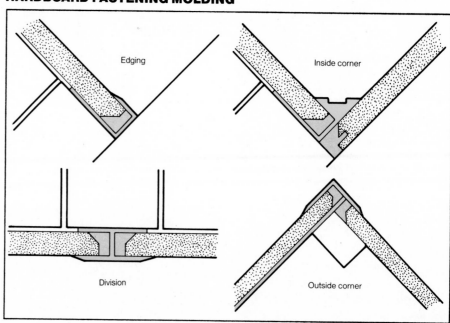

Metal fastening trim for hardboard paneling is available in four configurations—for meeting at inside corners, outside corners, ending at a corner, and meeting along a wall. The trim can be cut with a hacksaw.

Installing Plank Paneling

No matter how good the simulation, sheet paneling cannot duplicate the richness of a room lined with real wood planks. Plank paneling is generally more expensive than sheet paneling and can take more time to install and finish, but the results are well worth the extra effort.

Plank paneling can be bought in a variety of hardwoods and softwoods milled specially for this use. It is sold as 1 inch in thickness and in various widths up to 12 inches. The price of the planks per board foot depends on the kind of wood and its grade. Look at what is available from local lumber yards and price it before planning your job. Because of different milling treatments (see below), milled planks are assigned different board foot conversion factors and you should consult your dealer to arrive at the right number of board feet to order. Order boards all one length if you are paneling a wall vertically. If you are paneling diagonally or horizontally, you can save money by ordering in bulk which will give you random lengths of between 8 and 14 feet.

The installation of plank paneling is simple, but it requires patience because individual planks may need some shaving and cutting to fit. Planks are installed over furring that is horizontal for vertical or diagonal paneling and vertical for horizontal paneling. Like sheet paneling, planks should be stored for a few days in the room where they will be installed, to acclimatize. The only tools you need for installation are a circular saw, a block plane, a level and plumb bob, measuring tools, and a hammer.

Most planks are sold unfinished and it is usually easiest to finish them after the wall is up. The most common treatment is to stain and then seal them. Use an oil-based stain and then an oil-based sealer or 4-pound cut shellac diluted with 2 parts alcohol. Some paneling, like cedar and redwood, needs no finish.

DESIGNING THE JOB

The classic way to install plank paneling is vertically, giving the illusion of added height to low rooms. Random width planks call attention to a wall, while a wall of planks all the same width is quieter. Horizontal planking has the effect of apparently lowering high rooms and giving a sense of increased space to small rooms. But it may make a low-ceilinged room seem too low. Diagonal paneling always attracts attention but it is not recommended for walls interrupted by many windows or built-ins.

CHOOSING A PATTERN

Choice of style is a matter of individual taste, but you can apply these general rules: the more dramatic the groove between planks, the more the wall will command attention; milled planks give a traditional look to a room while unmilled planks create a more contemporary effect; tongue-and-groove planks are the easiest to install diagonally.

DESIGNING THE JOB

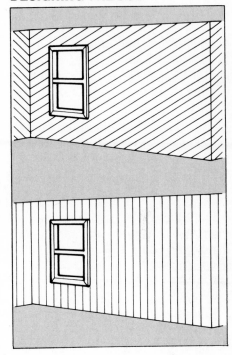

Wood paneling will change a room dramatically. Vertical installation appears to increase room height, horizontal installation lowers it. Diagonal installation works well in contemporary houses.

PLANK TYPES

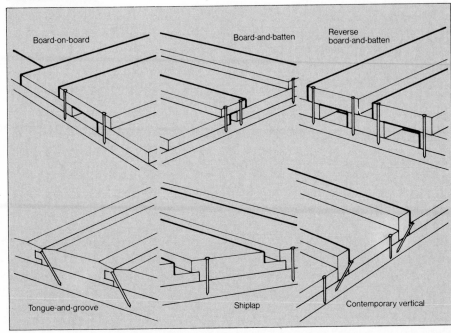

Board-on-board   Board-and-batten   Reverse board-and-batten

Tongue-and-groove   Shiplap   Contemporary vertical

You will find a variety of edges in two basic types of milled planks: tongue and groove with a tongue on one plank fitting into a groove on the next, and shiplap with planks overlapping. Unmilled planks offer several possibilities for a modern look.

INSTALLING PLANK PANELING
STEP 1

To avoid ending a wall with a narrow plank, measure the whole wall from corner to corner to determine how much you must cut from the last plank to make it fit. If the last plank will be less than half its width, cut down the first plank enough to widen the last plank to at least half the width. Starting at an inside corner, cut the first plank to the full height from floor to ceiling. Set it in place with the grooved edge in the corner and check for plumb. If the corner is irregular, scribe the plank and shave it with a block plane to fit.

STEP 2

Attach the plank (and subsequent planks) with 6-penny finishing nails driven through the base of the tongue at a 45° angle as shown, and through the face of the plank. Drive the nails slightly below the surface with a nail set so they can be filled.

STEP 3

Use a piece of scrap a few inches shorter than the distance from floor to ceiling to mark plank lengths. Set this next to the last piece and measure the distance to the ceiling; align the measuring stick and the bottom of the plank and transfer the cutting measurement to the top of the plank. At windows and other openings that require a cutout, set the board in position and mark the cut from behind where the plank overlaps the door or window. Use pilot holes in corners to make the inside cuts.

STEP 4

Use a scrap piece of plank with its grooved edge intact as a hammering block to tighten planks as they are installed. Fit the groove over the tongue of the plank and tap it into position. If the wall ends at an outside corner, shave the edge of that plank smooth; if it continues around the corner, miter or butt it as shown. To fit the last plank into an inside corner, shave the edge 5° in from the face, pull the next-to-last plank out slightly, seat the tongue in the groove, and push the two back.

INSTALLING PLANK PANELING

1. Installing the first plank. Because the rest of the wall will take its lines from the first plank, take care that it is plumb.

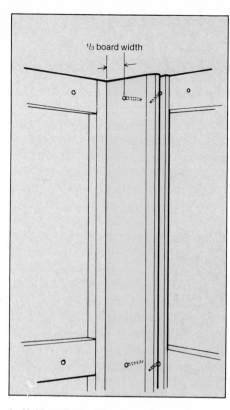

2. Nailing planks. Tongue-and-groove planks are blind nailed through the base of the tongue. Shiplap planks are face nailed only.

3. Measuring plank height. Measure from the top of a scrap measuring stick to the ceiling then transfer the additional height.

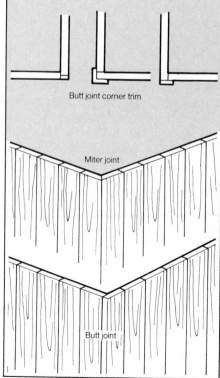

4. Outside corners. Corners can be mitered or butted. Miter planks outward from actual corner. Corners can be finished with molding.

INSTALLING DIAGONAL PLANK PANELING
STEP 1

To mark the wall for the position of the first plank, begin with a vertical line 1 foot out from an inside corner and a horizontal line intersecting it about 2 feet above the floor. Mark points on these lines 3 feet (or any other distance as long as it is exactly the same on both lines), connect these points with a line, and extend the diagonal to the corner and floor. Mark a second starting line from the first if you turn an inside corner.

STEP 2

Repeated miter cuts on planks are best made with a circular saw and the easy-to-make jig shown. To fit, measure along the diagonal and transfer the distance to the grooved edge of the first plank. Mark the miter cuts in the proper orientation, cut and attach to furring, tongued edge up. For subsequent planks, measure the edge the plank will fit against, and transfer to the appropriate edge.

STEP 3

Where the end of a plank meets a right angle such as the corner of the wall and the ceiling, or the corner of the wall and the floor, make the required miter cut, then measure from the last board to the ceiling or floor and mark this along the miter from the appropriate edge of the plank. Draw the second cutting line at right angles to the miter as shown.

STEP 4

Check the angle of the planks as you work by marking the same distance along both legs of a carpenter's square, putting these on the edge of the top plank and checking with the level as shown.

STEP 5

To turn an inside corner, use the second starting line and match boards if using random widths. For an outside corner, draw a starting line as shown, and cut the first plank only at the ceiling end. For the second cut, mark against the board the plank meets at the corner.

INSTALLING PLANKS DIAGONALLY

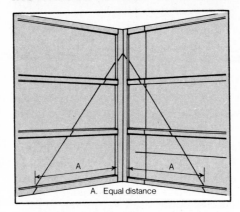

1. Marking starting lines. If you need a second starting line, mark the same distance from the corner as the first, and connect.

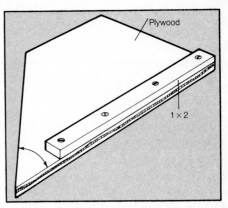

2. Making a jig. Miter a piece of plywood long enough to extend diagonally along plank, attach 1 × 2, and use to guide saw.

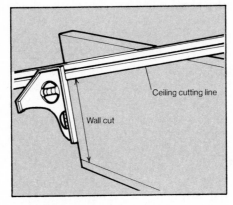

3. Fitting a corner. Mark a second cut from the grooved edge the distance from the last plank to the ceiling.

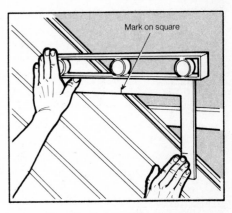

4. Checking the diagonal. Check each panel. The square can be used the same way to mark cutouts for windows and doors.

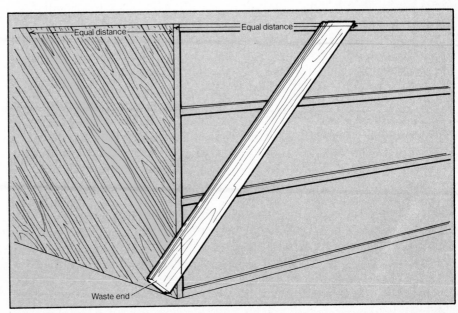

5. Turning an outside corner. Choose one board you will meet and measure from its outside edge to the corner; mark the same distance from the corner on the unpaneled wall. Snap a line from that mark to the bottom edge of the board you will meet, at the corner, for the starting line.

Working with Molding

Molding unites floors, ceilings, and walls and gives doorways and windows a decorative highlight. Molding also hides the ragged junctions of a wall with the floor and the ceiling. Installing molding to finish a room can be a simple job if you master the art of making various kinds of simple miter cuts to assure a tight fit.

For general use, you will find softwood molding in a great variety of shapes, as well as oak baseboard molding to match oak floors. To trim paneling, you can purchase molding with a finish that matches the paneling. Molding is designed for specific locations and uses: *Baseboard molding* and *base shoe molding* are used in conjunction to trim a wall at the floor; *cove* molding is used along the wall at the ceiling; *casing* is used around doors and windows; *cap molding* is used to cap wainscoting; and *corner molding* for both inside and outside corners hides seams and softens corners.

Molding is available in standard lengths from 6 to 14 feet in 2-foot increments. Try to get lengths that will span walls from corner to corner, but if a wall is too long, you can splice pieces together. When measuring for a job remember to take into account the extra few inches you may need for mitering to meet an adjoining piece at a corner. To cut miters in molding you need a good miter box and a saw with enough teeth per inch to make fine cuts without splintering the molding.

Putting on the molding is usually the last job in building or renovating a room. It is ordinarily painted, or finished in some other way, with a different color than the walls. This should be done and the walls should be painted before the molding is attached. A common exception to this rule occurs when baseboard molding is painted the same color as the room and the base shoe is stained a different color. Then the baseboard is painted with the wall.

TYPES OF MOLDING

Molding is milled in dozens of different shapes, so check a lumber dealer with a large supply when you plan your job. Because techniques for milling molding are not perfectly standardized, it is better to buy all pieces from the same milling lot if you can, to avoid fractional differences in size. Best of all, check the molding piece by piece when you can buy it from stock.

CUTTING MITERS
STEP 1

Using a miter box is quite simple, but you must take care to make the cuts in the right direction or you may be left with a piece too short to recut. For baseboard molding, mark the point at which it is to be cut at the top and put the molding in the miter box right side up with its back against the back of the box. When cutting an inside corner, set the saw guide so that the back of the molding (the wall side) will be longer than the front side; when cutting an outside corner, the saw should be set so that the front side will be longer than the back. Double check the orientation of the molding in the miter box and the position of the saw before cutting. To protect the face of the molding from splintering, you can apply a piece of masking tape down the cut. Test fit the molding before attaching it. You can adjust the angle by shaving down any face that causes a gap in the joint—but do this cautiously because it shortens the molding.

STEP 2

The procedure for cutting cove molding (for ceilings) is essentially the same as that for baseboard, except that the molding should be set in the box upside down, as shown, so it can be seated firmly against the bottom and the back. As with baseboard, the wall side is the long side for inside corners, the short side for outside corners.

TYPES OF MOLDING

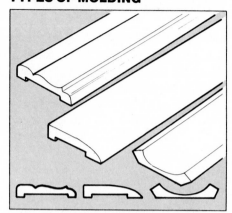

Casing (left) for doors and windows, baseboard (center) for floors, and cove (right) for ceilings are the most familiar moldings.

CUTTING

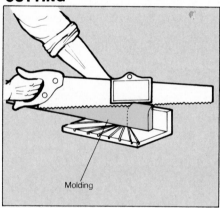

1. Cutting baseboard. The cut shown here is for an inside corner; the front face will be shorter than the back, or wall, side.

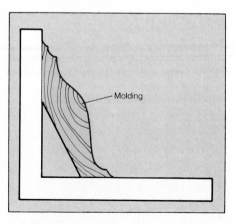

2. Cutting cove molding. Mark the bottom edge of cove molding and set it in the miter box upside down to make the cut.

BUTTING MOLDING AT RIGHT ANGLES
STEP 1
When butting molding with a figured face, at a right angle to other molding already in place, you must shape one piece to fit the contours of the other by making two cuts. First measure, mark, and cut the piece as if you were mitering it to fit into the corner.

STEP 2
Mark a second cutting line along the edge of the cut on the face and cut this, following the curves, with a coping saw held vertically. The second cut shapes the piece to fit over the face of the molding it abuts.

NAILING MOLDING
Depending on the size of the molding, use 6- or 8-penny finishing nails to attach baseboard, ceiling molding and casing; use 4-penny finishing nails for base shoe molding and drive them into the flooring. Nail into studs and top and bottom plates to assure that the molding won't pull away from the wall. Sink nail heads with a nail set and cover. Tighten corners with two 4-penny nails into the wall on either side as shown, one nail for base shoe molding.

LAPPED JOINT FOR MOLDING
If you must join pieces of molding along a wall, miter both pieces to make a smooth joint that can be tied together with a single nail as shown.

TRIMMING A WINDOW
Windows without sills can be framed like pictures with four pieces of casing, mitered at all corners. Windows with sills are trimmed on the sides and top with casing and on the bottom with a piece of window stool (the technical name for the sill) and an apron. Window jambs must be built out before molding can be attached, when a new surface has been put on a wall.

BASE MOLDING AT DOORS
At doors, where a baseboard butts against the door jamb but the base shoe protrudes, set it in position and mark it for beveling the end.

BUTTING TO MOLDING

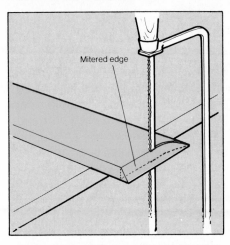

1. Cutting the molding. After mitering, make a perfectly vertical cut along the face edge of the miter cut.

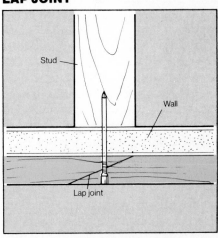

2. The fit. The two cuts should produce a face that fits the contours of the piece to which it is butted. Carve it where the fit isn't smooth.

NAILING MOLDING

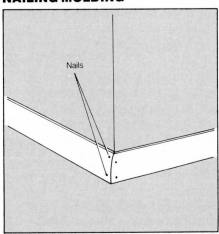

Use two 4-penny nails driven into the wall on each side of any mitered corner to keep the corner from spreading as the house settles.

LAP JOINT

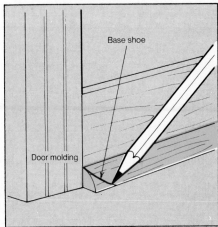

Before making miter cuts for this lap joint, check that it will fall over a nailing surface. It must be nailed to a stud or plate to hold tight.

WINDOW TRIM

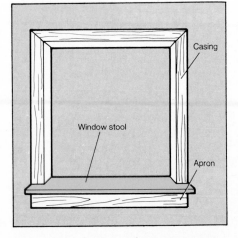

The window stool is traditional on double hung windows; standard sizes fit most windows. The stool should be installed first.

BASE MOLDING AT DOORS

Mark the base shoe before installation and bevel the end with a block plane to make a smooth junction with the doorjamb.

Setting Mirror Tile

Mirror tiles offer a quick and relatively inexpensive way to change the character of a room. A mirrored wall will greatly increase the apparent size of a room as well as its brightness from reflected light. There are several varieties of mirror tile to be found, the three most common being lightweight 1-foot-square tiles that are attached to the wall with double-sided tape; heavier tiles of various sizes, usually with beveled edges, that are attached to a wall with special mastic and with hardware to hold them in place; and longer strips of mirrored glass attached with clips.

The two main challenges in installing mirror tiles is to get them firmly fixed to the wall so they won't shift and crack or fall off, and to get them installed evenly so that reflection will not be distorted. Install mirror tile only on walls that are flat and even. Lightweight tiles that can be attached with tape are thin enough to cut at home, but heavier tiles and strips are too thick to cut yourself. With the thicker tiles, plan to leave an un-tiled border. Heavier tiles must be glued with a mastic made especially for mirrors so that the silvering on the back is not damaged. Check with your lumber or hardware dealer for a selection of adhesives for this job.

INSTALLING LIGHTWEIGHT MIRROR TILE
STEP 1

Measure the length of the wall and mark the midpoint at about eye level. If the wall is an even number of feet long (or closer to even than to odd), use a carpenter's level and straightedge to draw a horizontal line, and a plumb bob and chalk line to snap a vertical line, both through the midpoint. If the wall is an odd number of feet long, draw these lines to intersect 1 foot to the right or left of the midpoint. Be sure that the lines are true horizontal and vertical—they are the reference from which all tiles will be installed.

STEP 2

Peel back the protective cover from one side of squares of double-sided tape and stick one in each corner of the mirror as shown. Be careful not to touch the exposed adhesive because oils from your fingers can impair its bonding ability; also be sure that the wall surface to which the tiles will be stuck is completely clean and dust-free. Remove the other protective cover from the tape squares and stick the first tile onto the wall at one of the four corners of the intersecting reference lines. Install additional tiles, quadrant by quadrant, taking care that they are butted perfectly.

STEP 3

When you must cut a tile to fit along the edge of a wall or around an obstruction like a light switch, mark the cut on the mirror's surface, then score the mark with a glass cutter pulled along a straightedge and snap the cut.

INSTALLING HEAVIER TILE

Paneling a wall with heavy mirror tile requires either clips or special screws as well as mastic to hold the sections to the wall. Different products require different hardware so plan the job with your dealer.

LIGHTWEIGHT MIRROR TILES

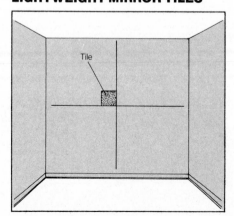

1. Marking reference lines. Accurate vertical and horizontal lines are necessary to get the tiles properly aligned on a wall.

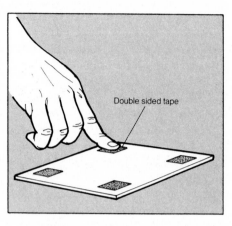

2. Applying tape. Don't uncover the side of the tape that will stick to the wall until you are ready to position the tile.

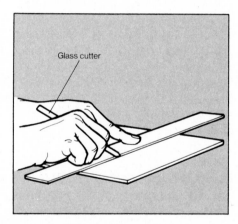

3. Cutting the tile. Score the tile with a glass cutter, using steady pressure in one swift motion. The glass will break along that line.

HEAVY MIRROR TILE

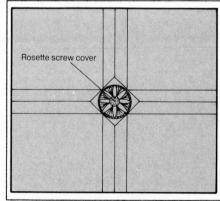

One way heavier tiles are held to a wall is with a screw capped by a decorative rosette that conceals the screw and holds the tiles.

Lining Walls with Cork

Cork is a wall covering that appeals to the eye with its wide variety of textures and patterns. It can also be used to satisfy more practical needs when it is installed to function as a large bulletin board. Cork walls are essentially maintenance-free and they absorb sound well.

There are two forms of cork wall covering available: flexible sheets (or rolls for bulk purchases) usually 1/4 inch thick, and stiffer tiles ranging from 1/8 inch to 3/4 inch in thickness. There are many colors and different surface textures in cork tile. If you are covering a large area, let the cork season for a few days in the room where it will be mounted.

Cork is applied either with adhesive spread on the wall or with an adhesive backing that is available on some tiles. These are more expensive than regular tiles so for large areas you will probably want to apply your own bonding agent. Use a V-grooved trowel to spread the adhesive. On walls that you are sure are dry, use a latex-based adhesive or follow the instructions that come with the tile. On walls that may be damp, use an alcohol-based adhesive. Where you need to cut tiles or sheets to fit, use a utility knife.

INSTALLING CORK TILES
STEP 1
Plan your installation as you would for ceramic tile (see page 64). Mark reference lines on the wall and apply adhesive according to the manufacturer's instructions. Before mounting a tile, check with a carpenter's square that its edges are in fact square; they can be trimmed with a utility knife to assure a good fit. Tiles should be attached to the wall with a slight space between them to leave room for expansion. To cut the tile to fit, mark it by notching with the utility knife at the point of the cut and using one leg of a carpenter's square as a cutting guide. An irregular surface can be difficult to mark for a cutting

line. If the tile tends to crumble when cut, cover the cutting line with masking tape and cut through that. If any tiles break while you are putting them up, just reunite the pieces and glue them down together.

STEP 2
Once the tiles are all in place, they should be pressed into the adhesive again to work out any gaps in the bond. The best device for smoothing out a cork wall is a rolling pin. Roll diagonally across several tiles at once, with firm pressure, and work your way over the entire wall. If thick tiles refuse to stay down (they may

INSTALLING CORK TILE

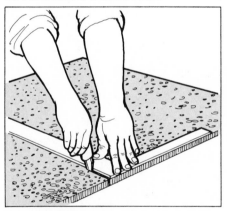

1. Cutting the tiles. Cut cork with a utility knife and straightedge; use a paper template to mark irregular shapes.

INSTALLING SHEET CORK

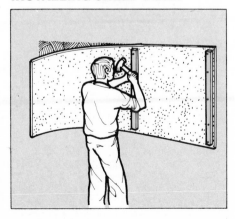

1. Tacking down the sheet. Use strips of wood tacked to the wall to hold the sheet flat against the adhesive.

rock under the rolling pin), tack them to the wall with finishing nails.

INSTALLING SHEET CORK
STEP 1
Apply adhesive as for cork tiles, align the sheet with reference marks, and press it into the adhesive. Tack strips of wood across the sheet as shown to hold it to the wall while the adhesive sets.

STEP 2
If you will be covering a switch or outlet, remove the face plate, attach the sheet over the open box or switch, then cut the opening.

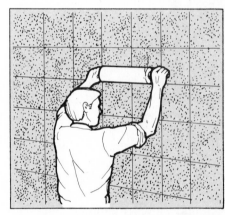

2. Setting the cork. A heavy rolling pin is the best tool for pressing tiles into the adhesive. Be sure that all tile edges are firmly bonded.

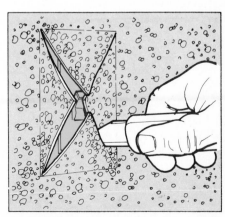

2. Cutting openings. There is no need to cut openings in sheets before installation; cut after mounting to insure accuracy.

Hanging Things on Walls to Stay

The right way to hang anything on a wall depends on two things: the construction of the wall and the weight and size of the object.

For general purposes, walls can be divided into two categories— They are either hollow (wallboard, plaster, or other surfaces over a stud frame) or solid (concrete block, brick, or plaster over masonry). Attachments to hollow walls are usually made with (a) nails into the wall surface or through it into a stud behind, (b) an expansion anchor or toggle bolt, both of which are mounted through holes in the surface and grip the wall surface from behind, or (c) a plastic anchor that is a sleeve fitted snugly into a drilled hole to hold the wall with friction when it is expanded by a screw driven into it.

Attachments to solid walls are made either by driving a masonry nail into the wall or by inserting a plug or wall anchor of some kind into a drilled hole. The plug or anchor in turn accepts a screw. The drawings below and right show the most common wall attachments. There are a great variety of different fasteners suitable for different jobs—from hanging a small picture to installing heavy kitchen cabinets—and different wall conditions from the basement to the attic.

LIGHT WEIGHT

Picture hooks can be attached to the surface of a hollow wall between studs to hold lightweight items, up to about 20 pounds.

MODERATE WEIGHT

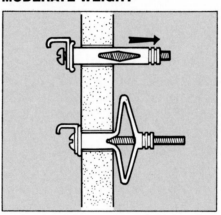

A hollow wall expansion anchor opens when the bolt is fully tight. It must be seated in a hole the diameter of the anchor.

MODERATE WEIGHT

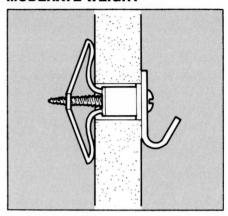

Plastic wing anchors work like expansion anchors. The wings are held closed to insert; they open as the screw is driven.

HEAVY WEIGHT

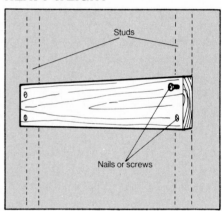

Such heavy objects as cabinets should be attached to a brace that has been securely screwed or nailed between two studs.

VERY LIGHT WEIGHT

Adhesive picture hooks have adhesive on the back. Before applying, be sure the wall is completely clean so adhesive will stick.

MODERATE WEIGHT

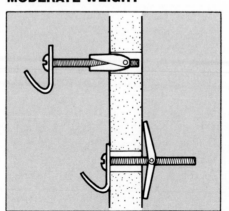

Toggle bolts have wings under spring tension that are held closed as the bolt is inserted in the hole in the wall, then pop open.

SOLID WALL, HEAVY WEIGHT

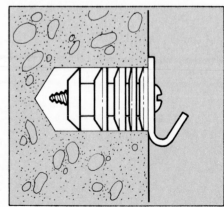

Anchors and plugs should be seated in holes drilled to their diameter so the fit is snug. A screw then jams the plug into the wall.

Painting Basics

Painting is the quickest, least expensive way to renew a room; it is probably the most common of all do-it-yourself projects.

The single most important factor in any painting job has nothing to do with paint, but rather with how well you prepare the surfaces to be painted. For paint to adhere properly, it must be applied to a clean, dry surface—free of dirt, dust, grease, and flaking paint or other wall covering. Also, paint only covers a surface, it doesn't fill in defects. Cracks, dents, popped nails, and any other surface defects will show as clearly after painting as before. The care you invest in cleaning, scraping, and patching will make the rest of your efforts worthwhile.

The two most common kinds of paint for interior use are *latex* paints and *alkyd* paints, both available in premixed colors. Latex paints are water-based which makes them easy to work with, odorless, quick to dry, easy to clean up after, and relatively inexpensive; their chief disadvantage is less durability than alkyd paints. Alkyd paints are often inaccurately referred to as "oil-based"—another type now used very little. They are synthetic-based, adhere to a variety of surfaces better than latex and provide a richer, more durable finish; their disadvantages include the need for chemical solvents for thinning the paint and cleaning tools, slow drying, an odor that necessitates ventilation of the work area, and relatively greater expense. There are a great number of different paints available and you should discuss your needs with a dealer.

In addition to the two basic tools discussed below, you will need a painting guide or edger for making neat lines at the edges of painted areas, paddles to stir paint, plenty of drop cloths to protect floors and furniture, a step ladder, and a good supply of rags or paper towels for cleaning up.

BRUSHES

Brushes are made with either natural or synthetic bristles. Natural bristles should never be used with a latex water-based paint, because the bristles absorb water and become clogged. Otherwise you can use synthetic or natural bristle brushes interchangeably. When shopping for brushes of any size, check the following points. The handle should be comfortable in your hand and easy to clean. The brush should feel full of bristles when it is gripped around them; the bristles should fan out slightly and not clump when pressed against your palm, and they should spring back to position afterward. The tips of the bristles should be flagged (see below). Spin the brush between your palms to shake out loose bristles, then tug the bristles a few times to see whether more come loose. If some do, the brush is inferior and will not last.

A prime rule of good painting is that the brush should fit the work. Most interior painting jobs can be handled with three sizes: a 1- or 1½-inch trim brush, a 2- or 2½-inch sash brush, and a 3- or 4-inch brush for large areas. Don't buy larger brushes to make the job go faster. You will find them unwieldy and too heavy after a very few minutes.

A GOOD BRUSH

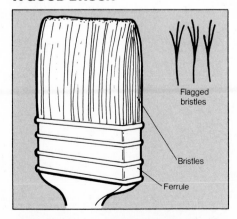

The ends of the bristles should be flagged or split to hold paint. The ferrule should be solidly attached, the handle comfortable.

ROLLERS

A roller consists of two parts, the frame and the cover, usually purchased separately. Roller frames and covers are a standard size, but the covers vary as to the thickness and composition of the nap. The nap will be specified on the package as short, medium, or long. Short nap, about ¼ inch thick, is used to apply a thin layer of paint smoothly and should be used for glossy paints. Medium nap, about ¾ inch thick, holds more paint and applies it with a slight stipple, making it the choice for most ordinary interior work. Long nap, about 1 inch thick, carries and deposits a large amount of paint and is designed for working on porous surfaces and surfaces with irregularities that the nap can push into. Covers used for most interior work are made of nylon.

Most roller frames are threaded inside the end of the handle to accept an extension handle for working higher than an easy reach. You can buy an extension or use a standard-size screw-on mop handle.

You will also need a roller pan for loading the roller with paint. Be sure to buy one that has a ribbed bottom so the cover will roll across it and pick up paint evenly, otherwise the paint will go on unevenly.

ROLLER FRAME AND COVER

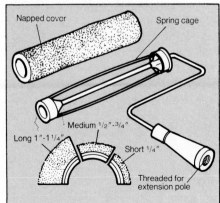

Use only roller frames that support the cover all along its full length. Support only at the ends allows the cover to sag.

STRIPPING WALLPAPER

Wallpaper can be painted over if there is only one layer on the wall, it is in good condition, and is not vinyl. If there are several layers on the wall, or if it is bubbled, peeling, or loose, it must be removed. You can do this in one of two ways: with a rented wallpaper steamer, shown at right, or with chemical agents.

FLAKING AND STRIPPING PAINT

Old paint that is peeling, blistered, or "alligatored," must be scraped or stripped entirely. Loose paint should be scraped with a paint scraper—if the flakes leave depressions, fill with joint compound and smooth them. Badly deteriorated paint, common on woodwork, can be stripped by melting it with a heat gun or by applying a chemical paint remover.

GETTING READY TO PAINT

A room ready to paint will look something like the one shown here—use the picture as a visual checklist of basic preparations. The walls have been cleaned, slick spots roughened with sandpaper and old paint has been scraped and patched. The floor and any contents of the room that cannot be removed are completely covered. Switch and outlet face plates are removed from the wall, but are left in the room. Wall and ceiling lighting fixtures are either removed or loosened from wall or ceiling to permit enclosing them in plastic bags. Other hardware such as door knobs, picture hooks, and thermostat covers have been removed.

The order in which you should paint an entire room is as follows: 1) ceiling, 2) walls, 3) trim, 4) doors, and 5) windows.

If you are painting a surface that has never been painted before, you must first prime it. There are both latex and alkyd primers, but new wallboard (and wallboard patches) must be primed with latex.

HANDLING PAINT

The two techniques illustrated at right will make handling paint easy and help avoid drips and a mess around the paint can.

STRIPPING WALLPAPER

Wallpaper is first loosened with moisture, then peeled from the wall with a broad scraper. A wallpaper steamer speeds the job.

STRIPPING PAINT

Chemical paint removers soften deteriorated paint so that it can be easily removed. Be sure to observe manufacturer's cautions.

GETTING READY TO PAINT

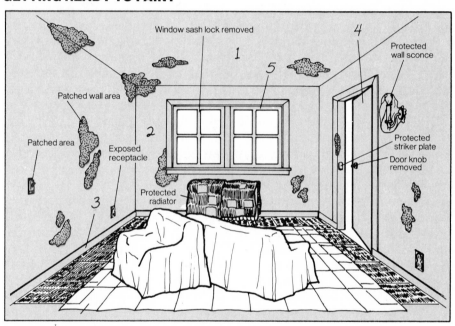

Half the work of painting a room is finished before you start to paint. Floors, furniture, and permanently installed appliances should be protected, hardware and fixtures removed, damaged areas repaired and primed. Numbers indicate the order in which to paint the surfaces.

HANDLING PAINT

1. Preparing the can. Use a hammer and nail to tap holes through the rim of the paint can to prevent paint from accumulating.

2. Loading paint. Don't dip the brush more than half way up the bristles. Tap it lightly on the rim to shed the excess.

USING A ROLLER
STEP 1
Roll the roller through the bottom of the paint pan, where the paint should not be more than 1/2 inch thick, distributing paint over the entire roller evenly. Start laying paint on the wall in a zigzag. Go back over the zigzag with parallel strokes at a 90° angle to the original zigzag.

STEP 2
Without reloading the roller, finish this area by carefully rolling up and down, overlapping the strokes slightly, or side to side, if you have decided to do your finish strokes that way. Start and stop your strokes gently so as not to leave roller marks on the wall.

CUTTING IN AND TRIMMING
Making a clean edge where a ceiling meets a wall of another color or along an edge where paint stops is called "cutting in." When painting a wall and ceiling different colors, the standard approach is to let the lighter of the two colors overlap this edge, cutting in the darker of the colors over it.

PAINTING TRIM
If you have a steady hand you can use the method described above for cutting in along trim. A quicker method is to use a painting guide, as shown.

PAINTING DOUBLE HUNG WINDOWS
STEP 1
You can mask glass in windows with tape laid up to the edge of the strips that divide the panes or you can paint the strips freehand. The method for painting a double hung window is to lower the top sash and raise the bottom sash as shown. Paint the outside sash first as far as you can reach, then paint the inner sash.

STEP 2
Reverse the position of the windows, but do not close either sash all the way. After the windows are painted, paint the sill and casing around them.

USING A ROLLER

1. Spreading the paint. Roll paint onto the wall in a zigzag, then cover the area by repeating the zigzag in the opposite direction.

2. Finishing the paint. Without reloading the roller, go over the painted area with parallel up and down strokes to smooth the paint.

CUTTING IN

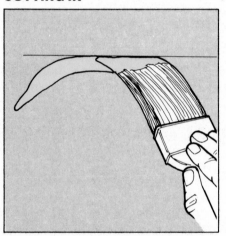

To paint a straight line between two surfaces, use a trimming brush, start the paint below the line, and pull the brush just along the line.

PAINTING TRIM

A paint trimmer or edger is useful for painting clean edges along trim. Trimmers of various kinds can be found in paint stores.

PAINTING DOUBLE HUNG WINDOWS

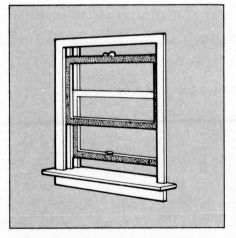
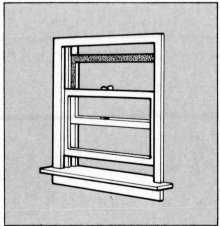

1. Starting the job. Raise the lower sash and lower the upper sash to within a few inches of the top and bottom; paint exposed areas.

2. Finishing the job. Reverse the positions of the sash and finish painting. Raise and lower sash after painting to preventing sticking.

Tiling Walls

Ceramic tile is an attractive wall surface anywhere and a practical one in bathrooms and kitchen because it is waterproof (and fireproof), durable, and easy to clean. It also works well on floors (see page 114). The variety of tiles available make it a decorating favorite.

Tile is clay that has been fired; it is produced in a variety of surfaces. The most important distinction between types of tile is whether it is *glazed* or *unglazed*. Glazed tile, available in matte or shiny finish, is impervious to stains but it can be scratched; it is the standard tile around sinks and tubs. Unglazed tile, made only in matte finish, picks up stains from grease and oil but resists scratching; it is the choice for floors. Both kinds can be used on walls.

Flat tiles are called field tiles and those shaped to fit around corners and edges are called trim tiles. Tiles larger than a few square inches are sold loose; smaller tiles can be purchased in sheet form with a few square feet of tile bonded to a thin webbing on the back.

To install ceramic tile, you need a clean surface that is sound and flat. Wallpaper and other flexible coverings should be stripped before tiling an old wall; unsound areas should be repaired. Both water-resistant wallboard and plywood make good surfaces for tiling in high moisture areas. The wall surface is marked with guidelines to position the tile, then covered with adhesive into which the tiles are pressed. The joints between tiles are then sealed with grout as described in *Installing a Ceramic Tile Floor* at page 114.

Tiling requires only a few special tools: a tile cutter for cutting straight lines in tile and tile nippers to cut odd shapes (both can usually be rented), a notched trowel for spreading adhesive (check with your dealer to match the trowel with the job), and a rubber float for applying grout. You will also need measuring tools and a level.

PATTERNS FOR LAYING TILE
There are two basic ways to lay tile on a wall: build the tiles up from the center of the wall in a pyramid shape (upper right), or start by laying the length of the bottom row, then work from one corner at the bottom diagonally up the wall (center right).

PLANNING THE JOB
If you are tiling to the top of a wall, and the ceiling is level, measure the height of the wall at both corners; if you are ending the tile part way up a wall, mark a horizontal line across the wall at the desired height and measure from the corners to that line. If you are tiling down to a floor and ending the tile with trim pieces, you should mark the horizontal guideline for tile position (see below) at the height of a trim tile plus a field tile, above the floor. If you are tiling from the edge of a tub, establish the horizontal guideline at the height of a single tile above the tub. If you are tiling around three sides of a tub, measure up the wall at each corner to the height you want tiled (a minimum of one tile above the shower head), then extend horizontal lines from those points to the center of each wall and note the distance of any gap where the lines meet. This will tell you how far out of level your tub is.

MARKING GUIDELINES
STEP 1
Tiling from the middle of a wall is the easiest way to do it, and your first measurement should be to determine the center of the wall. Lay out a run of tiles as a measuring stick, with the desired spacing for grout for tiles with straight edges, but no additional space for tiles with lugs on the edges that set the spacing when butted or, as shown, mark directly on the wall. Check whether the last tile on either side of the midpoint is more or less than half a tile wide. If it is less, mark half the width of a tile to

LAYING TILE

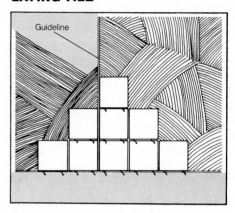

1. Pyramid arrangement. The easiest way to lay tile is to build it up in a pyramid starting at the intersection of the guidelines.

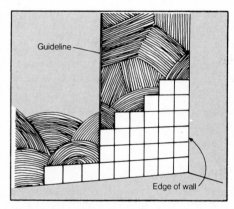

2. Jack-on-jack arrangement. A modification of the pyramid arrangement, this method works from one corner out.

ESTABLISHING A LINE

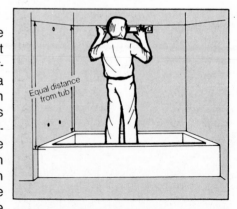

If horizontal lines established by measurements from the corners of a tub do not meet, the tub is out of level.

the right or left of the midpoint and use this as the position of the vertical guideline.

STEP 2
Use a carpenter's level to mark the vertical guideline at the proper point.

STEP 3
Check whether the floor or tub is level, as described above. If it is less than 1/8 inch off from one end to the other, mark the horizontal guideline from the highest point. If it is more than 1/8 inch off, mark the horizontal from the low end. If you are meeting a floor or counter with trim tile, put a piece of trim in position and a field tile on top, either held at the proper grout spacing or butted on lugs, and then put a level on the lugs or the grout space above. Mark along the bottom of the level and extend the line the length of the wall. If you are meeting a tub with field tile, measure from the top of a single piece of tile set on the lowest point. If you need to fit tiles against a ceiling, measure down from the top and use the measuring stick method, described above, to establish the height to which the first row of tiles must be trimmed, trim a few tiles to that height, and use one to establish the horizontal above the tub rim.

STEP 4
If you are mounting the kind of soap dish that sits flush to the wall, or other similar ceramic accessory, find the position where the piece is to be located and mark off the dimension of the part that will sit against the wall. Most pieces have flanges that fit over surrounding tile.

INSTALLING TILE
STEP 1
Tile can be bonded to the wall with a mix-it-yourself cement-based adhesive or, with greater ease, a premixed mastic adhesive. There are many products on the market and their use and instructions for use vary, so read the label information and determine the proper adhesive with your dealer if you are unsure. The basic method of applying a mastic adhesive is to

MARKING GUIDELINES

1. Locating the vertical guideline. Measure across the wall in tile widths, including grout space, to position vertical guide.

2. Marking the vertical guideline. After locating its position, use a carpenter's level to mark a vertical guideline.

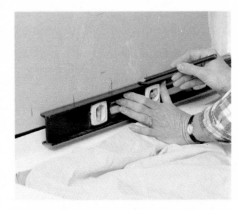

3. Establishing a horizontal guideline. Use the tub as a guide if it is level; if not, use a carpenter's level to mark the horizontal guide.

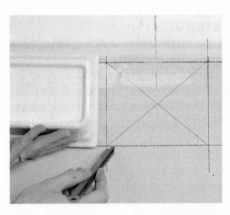

4. Marking for accessories. Any accessories like a soap dish or towel bar should be accounted for in the layout before tiling.

LAYING TILE

1. Applying adhesive. Adhesives vary, so follow manufacturer's instructions for application. You will need a trowel with V-shaped grooves on the surface that leave ridges of adhesive between valleys close to the wall surface. Work out from the guidelines, leaving them visible.

Wallpapering Basics

Wallpaper is a somewhat old fashioned term that actually covers a host of different products, from traditional paper to fabric-backed vinyl, paper-backed grass cloths, and even more exotic variations.

Several factors go into the choice of a wall covering. Does the area to be covered get a lot of traffic? If it does, you should look for a covering that can withstand scuffs and can be cleaned easily—a solid vinyl paper for the highest hazard areas like kitchens and bathrooms, vinyl-coated papers for bedrooms and halls. A low traffic area can take more delicate standard wallpapers. For extra elegance, you can choose flocked wallpaper with its surface slightly raised in patterns of velvet-like synthetic fibers; paper-backed foils with a metallic surface create a dramatic effect, as do murals; grass papers provide a soft, neutral surface.

Some wallpaper is available pre-pasted; most must be pasted at home, sheet by sheet as it goes up. However it is pasted, wallpaper must be applied to a clean, smooth surface. No matter how attractive the paper, any blemish in the wall beneath will show through clearly and spoil the effect. It is best to strip walls of old wallpaper before applying new. In cases where the wall is not sufficiently smooth, wallpaper liner—a thicker, blank wall covering —should be pasted on the wall as a foundation for a smooth surface.

To paper a room you will need a bucket of water, a bucket for mixing paste, a wallpaper smoothing brush —long and narrow with moderately stiff but pliable bristles—a long table, a long straightedge, scissors, a seam roller, a mat knife, a level, and measuring tools.

PLANNING THE JOB
Wallpaper is sold in rolls of various widths. Because patterned wallpapers must be matched side to side

along the edge of the strips, there is a fair amount of waste in trimming to keep the pattern repeating properly. To estimate material needs, as a general rule, determine the number of square feet in the area to be covered, less openings like windows, doors and fireplaces, then divide this by 30, a number derived by subtracting the likely wastage from the standard 36

square feet in a roll. Round up to the nearest whole number for ordering standard rolls. If you are buying other than standard 36-square-foot rolls, consult your dealer about how many you need.

The repeating pattern in wallpaper also requires careful planning of where the papering job should start and end.

PLANNING WHERE TO START

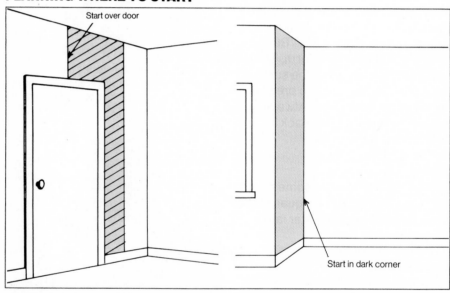

Start over door

Start in dark corner

If you are papering all the way around a room, the pattern of the paper is unlikely to line up perfectly where you hang the last sheet to finish the job. Plan the papering so that this meeting place is in the least conspicuous part of the room such as over a door or in a corner.

STARTING BETWEEN WINDOWS

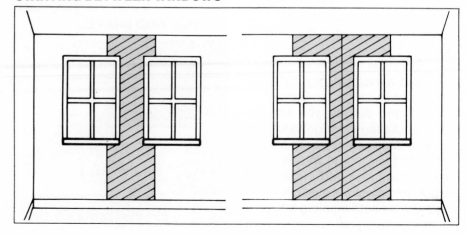

Use a roll of wallpaper as a measuring stick to divide the wall into increments as wide as the paper. If the strips at either corner will be less than half a roll wide, start with a strip centered on the middle of the room as shown at left; otherwise start as shown at right.

CUTTING WALLPAPER TO FIT
STEP 1
Because wallpaper comes in rolls, it must always be cut to fit the height of the wall, and because full widths do not always fit exactly across a wall, it often has to be cut narrower along its length. To cut a piece to length, allow about 2 inches of overlap at the top and bottom to be trimmed off after the paper is on the wall. This lets you adjust a sheet up and down a little to meet the pattern properly.

STEP 2
Long cuts on wallpaper should be marked at both ends, measuring in from the edge that will meet the piece already on the wall. Long cuts are usually made to fit the paper into corners and should be measured from the top and bottom of the wall because corners are rarely plumb.

PASTING WALLPAPER
STEP 1
Wallpaper paste is available both premixed in liquid form and dry for mixing with water at home. If you are mixing your own, make it up about 30 minutes before you start.

STEP 2
Lay a piece of the paper that has been cut to length on your pasting table with one edge flush with a long edge. Paste the paper with a paste brush from the table edge to the middle and about half its length. Shift the paper across the table so that the other edge lines up along the other edge of the table and paste the rest of that side. Lining the paper up with the table edges prevents paste from getting on the table top.

STEP 3
Fold the paper over on itself as shown and pull the remainder up on the table to paste.

STEP 4
When the entire sheet is pasted, fold it into a manageable package that will be easy to carry to the wall. These packets can be set aside a few minutes to allow the paste to soften the paper.

CUTTING TO FIT

1. Cutting for height. Allow about 2 inches of overlap at top and bottom of each strip. Unroll the paper, mark, and cut with scissors.

2. Cutting for width. Measure the width needed to fill an odd space and mark the strip. Make the cut with a utility knife.

PASTING WALLPAPER

1. Mixing paste. If you mix your own paste, work the powder into the water until it has a smooth, somewhat viscous consistency.

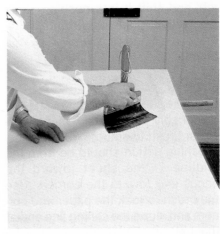

2. Applying the paste. Spread paste evenly with a wallpaper pasting brush. Align the strip with the edge of the table to keep paste off.

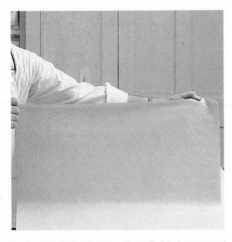

3. Completing the pasting. Fold the pasted section of a strip over on itself (paste to paste) and paste the remaining section.

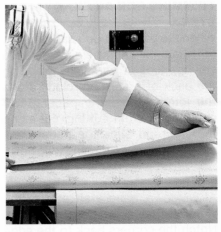

4. Folding the strip. When the strip is completely pasted it should be folded as shown, so it will be easy to carry to the wall.

A strong color and simple molding can make a plain room dramatic. Adding molding is one of the easiest ways to dress up a room.

You don't have to wallpaper from floor to ceiling—molding and wallpaper transform this room from plain to elegant.

Plank paneling and the simulated planks in sheet paneling come in a variety of widths; use uniform pieces or mix random widths.

Surround yourself with wood—an especially effective treatment if you are converting an attic into an extra bedroom or study.

Wood paneling is available in a variety of colors for different decorating needs.

You can have the advantages of paneling—to cover a deteriorated wall, for instance—and the effect of wallpaper with figured panels.

Molding and wallpaper with a decorative border combine to give this bath a feeling of luxury and frilly detail.

Long ceramic tile on both the wall and floor provides a background as streamlined and modern as the round, freestanding shower.

Wallpaper can do wonders for a bathroom, but it must be able to withstand a moist environment. Check with your dealer for the right paper.

(Left) Ceramic tile on the wall and floor offer handsome fire protection around a wood stove.

(Below) Small ceramic tiles, available in sheets for easy installation, enhance the high-tech elegance of this spacious bath.

(Opposite top) Long mirror panels are both functional and a device for enlarging a room.

(Opposite below) An entire wall of mirror panels doubles the apparent size of a room and doubles the effect of the decorating scheme.

FLOORS

Anatomy of Floors

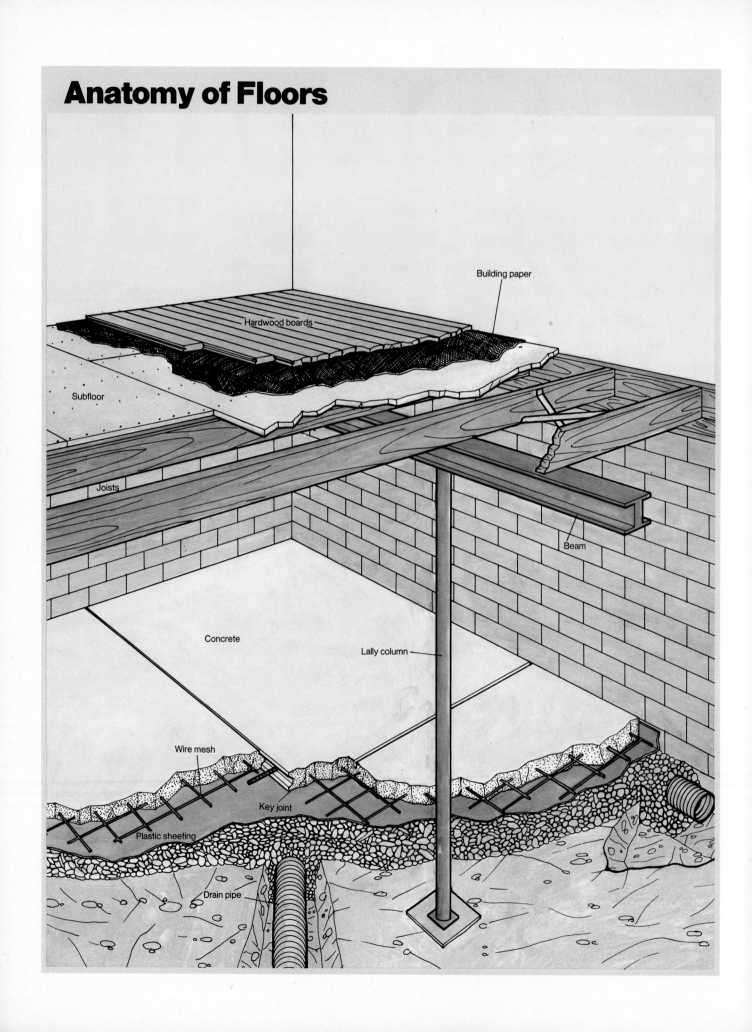

Building paper

Hardwood boards

Subfloor

Joists

Beam

Concrete

Lally column

Wire mesh

Key joint

Plastic sheeting

Drain pipe

This book concerns three kinds of floors: concrete floors, floors of various surfaces on subflooring laid over joists (the kind of floors on the ground and upper stories of most houses), and masonry floors. This section includes instructions for pouring new concrete floors and repairing old ones, rehabilitating the structure of floors on joists, repairing the surface of hardwood floors, and installing a variety of new floor surfaces from stone to carpet.

Structure

A concrete floor is essentially just a slab of concrete, but it hides some structural elements. A plastic barrier separates the slab from the ground, wire mesh reinforces the concrete and drain pipes carry wetness to a sump. Concrete floors are poured in sections separated by key joints that allow the sections to expand without cracking. **Pouring Concrete Floors** (pages 84-85) shows you how to build and set up forms for the sections of the floor, how to level the floor, and give it a smooth finish. **Repairing Concrete** (pages 86-87) ranges from sealing cracks to breaking out and replacing large damaged areas. **Installing Wood Floors Over Concrete** (pages 88-89) can be accomplished by laying boards called sleepers in adhesive on the concrete and laying a subfloor over them, or by building a framework then covering it with subflooring.

A framed floor on the ground level of a house sits on joists. They in turn sit on the sills on the top of the foundation at one end of the joists and (in all but very narrow houses) on a girder running the length of the house at the other end. The girder may be of two parts, supported by a Lally column or post where they join. For extra stability, the joists are often tied together with cross bridging which keeps them from moving side to side. The joists are covered with some kind of subflooring—sheets of

plywood, or particle board, or planks—on which the finished floor is installed.

Leveling Wood Floors (pages 90-91) is a fairly slow, somewhat demanding process made necessary by the failure of a post holding the splice of a two-piece girder. Temporary posts on either side of the splice take the weight of the floor above and a telescoping house jack is used to raise the sagging girder and with it the joists and floor above, over a period of several days. When the floor is level, the post and the concrete footing are replaced.

If a joist breaks or fails for some other reason, the floor will deform. If it is a hardwood board floor, the boards above the failed joist may ride together and make a noise when stepped on. **Silencing Squeaky Floors** (pages 92-93) shows how to replace a joist and how to solve several other problems and **Silencing Squeaky Stairs** (page 94) solves the same problems for noisy stairs.

Surface

In an older house, you may have hardwood floors in bad repair—they could be hidden treasures. First, **Replacing Damaged Floorboards** (pages 95-96) tells how to make hardwood floors whole again by cutting out damaged areas and filling with new boards. Then **Restoring and Refinishing Wood Floors** (pages 97-99) completes work on old floors.

You fill any cracks, sink any loose nails (silence any squeaky boards at the same time) and sand the surface with a rented floor sander, a noisy, dusty but rewarding job. The sanded floor is then sealed and finished to bring out its original beauty. To start fresh, **Installing Hardwood Floors** (pages 117-119) shows how to lay a new floor from scratch.

Where you wish to recondition an old floor by installing an entirely new surface, you will need the instructions in **Preparing Floors for New**

Surfaces (pages 100-101), if the old surface is not sufficiently sound or smooth to take adhesive for resilient sheet flooring, or for resilient, ceramic, or parquet tiles. Underlayment, as sheets of plywood or particle board for this purpose are called, is nailed over the old floor and the seams between the sheets are filled to make a uniformly flat surface.

There is a wide choice of floor coverings in addition to hardwood. One of the most versatile is resilient tile, appropriate almost anywhere in the house and practical because it is easy to clean. **Laying Resilient Tile** (pages 102-103) is an easy job, if you plan carefully. No matter what pattern you want to lay, a clean surface, straight work lines, and patience are all you need to lay a perfect floor. Resilient sheet flooring has the same practical advantages as resilient tile, but it requires the different installation procedures that are covered in **Installing Resilient Sheet Floor** (pages 104-105). Parquet tile—blocks of hardwood strips available in different designs—are installed much like resilient tiles. Using the directions in **Laying Parquet Tiles** (pages 106-107) and your own imagination, you can achieve the elegant effect of a handcrafted floor. For a solid country look, indoors or out, **Laying Masonry and Stone Floors** (pages 108-109) shows you how to pave your floor.

Wall-to-wall carpet softens and warms a floor, and has the additional advantage of making rooms below it quieter. **Installing Wall-to-Wall Carpet** (pages 110-112) explains the equipment and techniques necessary to do the job like a professional. If you have damaged carpeting, consult **Repairing Carpets** (page 113).

Where you need tough, waterproof, easy-to-clean floor surfaces, especially in bathrooms and kitchens **Laying Ceramic Tile Floors** (pages 114-116) may provide the answer. Beyond its practical value, tile offers endless possibilities.

Tools

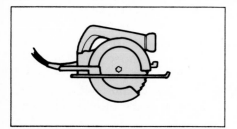

Circular Saw. This portable power saw makes quick work of most cutting jobs on which you would use a crosscut or rip saw. The base plate (which rides on the work) can be adjusted for cutting different angles. The saw takes different blades for different jobs—from cutting paneling to cutting bricks.

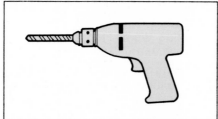

Electric Drill. With various accessories, the power drill can be used as a sander, to cut circular holes, to drive screws, and several other tasks besides drilling. Drills are available in different sizes—given as the size of the largest bit they can take—and with various power features, such as variable speed.

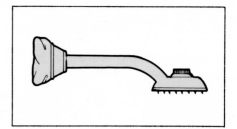

Knee Kicker. Essential for laying a wall-to-wall carpet tightly, the knee kicker grips the carpet with teeth so you can stretch it toward the walls with a push from your knee on the padded end. A larger device, called a power stretcher, performs the same function without the knee power.

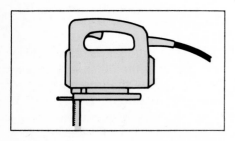

Saber Saw. Extremely useful for cutting irregular shapes and making interior cuts, the narrow blade of the saber saw makes it possible to guide it through fairly tight curves and to start cuts through a hole drilled inside an area to be cut out. There are many blades available for cutting different materials.

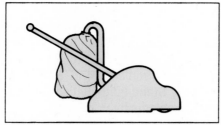

Floor Sander. Unless you restore floors professionally, you won't need to invest in a floor sander. They can be rented from most home centers which also supply the sandpaper inserts. There are both belt sanders and circular sanders for floors and the circular sander can be used for buffing.

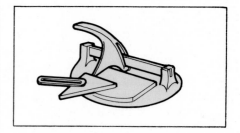

Tile Cutter. The cutter holds a piece of tile in place so that it can be scored by a cutting wheel attached to the handle of the cutter. When the tile is scored, it is broken neatly along that line by a pull on the handle. Unless you do a lot of tiling, it is more economical to rent the cutter.

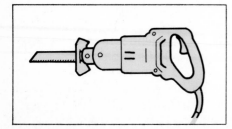

Reciprocating Saw. Like a heavy-duty saber saw, this power saw is handy for cutting out sections of walls or floors, or cutting through a roof for a skylight. These saws are available in one, two, or variable speed models with a variety of blades for different jobs. This is not a tool to buy to do just one project.

Floor Nailer. A device for making the tedious, tricky job of nailing hardwood flooring go more quickly and accurately. The floor nailer is loaded with a clip of nails, which it drives by spring action when hit smartly on the top knob with a mallet. You can rent one for laying a hardwood floor.

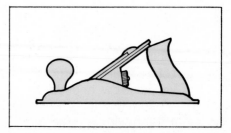

Plane. There are many kinds of planes for different work: the two kinds you may need for these projects are the small block plane, a one-handed tool for rounding corners and removing small amounts of wood, and the jack plane, a two-handed model for larger general planing jobs.

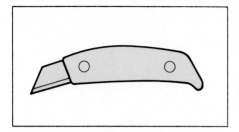

Utility Knife. Best for cutting building paper, wallboard, and many other relatively soft materials, the utility knife has razor-sharp replaceable blades.

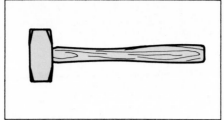

Sledgehammer. Available in various weights up to 20 pounds, the sledge hammer is used for demolition and for driving heavy objects, like posts, into place.

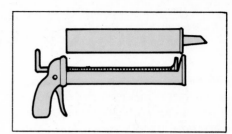

Caulking Gun. A standard-size holder for tubes of caulking or adhesive, this spring-loaded device dispenses an even bead that is easy to apply and manipulate.

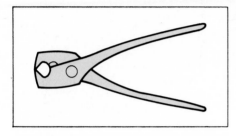

Tile Nippers. A tile cutter will cut only straight lines, so tile nippers are used for irregular cuts which are made by nipping small pieces of tile.

Notched Trowel. Used for spreading adhesive for setting ceramic and other tile. Different adhesives call for different sized notches so check your product.

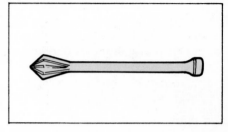

Star Drill. The star drill, for making holes in masonry, takes a lot of effort. It is hit with a five pound hammer and rotated slightly after each blow.

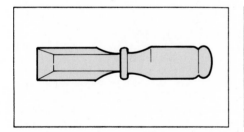

Chisels. Available in a great variety of types and sizes, chisels are used for gouging and trimming. Your hardware dealer can match a chisel to your specific need.

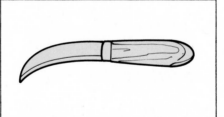

Linoleum Knife. The hooked blade, stronger than that on a utility knife, makes it easier and more accurate to cut tough resilient sheet flooring than with any other blade.

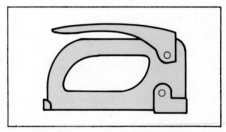

Staple Gun. A heavy-duty staple gun will make many projects go quickly. It is essential for installing ceiling tile and for stapling insulation between boards.

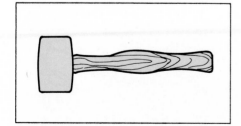

Mallet. A heavy hammer with a soft head of rubber, plastic, or leather used when weight is required and a metal head would do damage (as when operating a floor nailer, for instance).

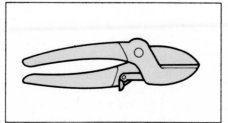

Shears. Heavy shears are necessary to cut various metal home improvement materials like aluminum studs and tracks, wire lath, and corner bead.

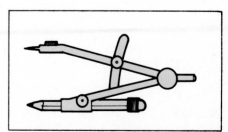

Compass. You can use a compass for tracing an irregular edge onto a piece of board or sheet of paneling that must be cut to fit the irregularity exactly.

Pouring Concrete Floors

A concrete floor instead of an old dirt floor can turn a basement or garage into more usable space and at the same time eliminate dampness. Before you begin, however, you should research the local building codes to see that the height of the ceiling is the legal distance from the floor. Also, you may be required to have an on-the-scene inspection of your grading job before you begin to pour the concrete.

Pouring goes rather quickly, but preliminary preparations should be planned and executed with care. You will have to grade the subsurface and add a layer of gravel, plastic liners, and steel reinforcements. A slanted drainage grade must be built to lead water to one corner of the room where, if need be, you may install a sump pump. In addition, you should dredge channels around the perimeter, and diagonally across the room, for installing drain tiles made of plastic tubing perforated to disseminate water through the gravel.

The truck that brings the ready-mix concrete may have to drive up onto your property to within ten feet of the basement window for the chute to reach. Prepare the ground around the area with 2 × 10 planks and polyethylene sheeting to catch any spills.

Have the concrete poured and spread it rapidly. For best results, fill one section of the floor at a time before going on to the next. Then use a screed and a darby as shown to remove excess concrete and smooth down aggregate that may rise to the surface. Allow "bleed water" to bubble up and disappear before you cut control joints and trowel the surface to a smooth finish.

When all is completed, the concrete slab must cure; the chemicals must interact with water to render the floor strong and durable. You can purchase a curing compound from a building supplier or keep the floor damp for a week or longer.

PREPARING THE GRADE
STEP 1
Remove surface of the old dirt floor so that it is 8 inches below the level where the surface of the concrete floor will be. The floor should slope 1 inch every 8 feet to the lowest corner where the sump pump will be located. Snap chalklines on the walls 8 inches above the dirt surface and tie string across the room to nails located every 4 feet along the chalkline.

STEP 2
Dig a hole 2½ feet deep and 2 feet wide in the lowest corner of the room for the sump pump. If you are not using a sump pump, fill the hole with clean gravel. Then dig a trench 4 inches deep and 6 inches wide about 5 inches from the walls around the room, and a similar trench diagonally across the room. Pour a 2-inch layer of gravel into the trenches, and on it lay lengths of drain tile to form a conduit around and across the room, so that the ends drain into the hole or are attached to the sump pump.

PREPARING TO POUR
STEP 1
Make key-jointed form boards by nailing 1 × 2s (with a ¼-inch bevel on the edges of one face) to the middle of as many 2 × 4s as you will need to span the length of the room (and to span half its width if the floor is to be poured in smaller sections). Then drill three ¾-inch holes in each board, one in the center, and two a foot from both ends. Nail three stakes (16-inch 1 × 2s) on the back of each form board so that the top of each stake is flush with the upper edge of the form board. Drive the forms into the dirt floor along the guideline that divides the basement in two. The key-joint molds should face the side of the room you intend to pour first. Align the top of the form with the guideline string and, using a level, check the grade of the form.

PREPARING THE GRADE

1. Leveling the old floor. Dig out the old floor 8 inches below the level wanted for the new; use string guides to keep depth even.

2. Digging out for a sump. Dig a 2½-foot-deep sump in the low corner; dig drainage channels around and diagonally across the room.

PREPARING TO POUR

1. Putting in the forms. Have a helper hold the key-jointed form. Drive the stakes down to the level indicated by the string.

STEP 2

Pour a 4-inch layer of gravel over the dirt floor. Then remove the guidelines. Insert steel reinforcing bars into gravel as shown. Spread polyethylene sheets over the gravel overlapping about 18 inches and extending up the walls to the chalk lines. Lay reinforcing wire mesh.

STEP 3

Insert 18-inch steel dowels ½ inch in diameter through the holes in the form boards so that half the dowel is on each side. Use wooden wedges in the back of the form to hold them in place. Pack gravel up tightly behind the form boards. Lastly, rub grease on the forms and dowels so the concrete will not bond to them.

SPREADING THE CONCRETE
STEP 1

Use a hoe and a shovel to spread the concrete. When a section is filled, use a rake to pull the reinforcing wire halfway up through the wet concrete.

STEP 2

Using a screed, level a section of the wet slab up to the reinforcing bars and pound them beneath the concrete surface with a sledge hammer. Then work the area level to the top of the form boards and nails in the wall.

STEP 3

Smooth the leveled surface with a rented darby. "Bleed water" will appear on the top of the slab, making it shiny. When completely dry, the surface will be dull.

STEP 4

When the concrete can withstand the toss of a 1-inch stone so that it bounces, leaving only a slight indentation, cut 1-inch-deep control joints every 10 feet. Then smooth the surface between the joints with an aluminum float and a steel trowel, moving backwards. If the concrete is too hard, dampen it a bit. In five to six hours wet the surface again and cover with polyethylene sheets for twenty-four hours. Then remove the forms and gravel packing, and pour the companion slab.

2. Laying reinforcing mesh. After the floor is filled with 4 inches of gravel covered with a plastic sheet, lay mesh and attach pieces.

3. Shoring up the form. After placing steel dowels in the form, bank up gravel behind it to hold it in place and hold back the concrete.

SPREADING CONCRETE

1. Initial spreading. Distribute concrete with a shovel from where it is dumped, then roughly level the surface with a rake.

2. Leveling the slab. Make a screed from pieces of 2 × 4 like the one shown above and level the surface to the top of the form.

3. Smoothing the surface. Use a large rented float called a darby to smooth the surface; then wait until the surface becomes dull.

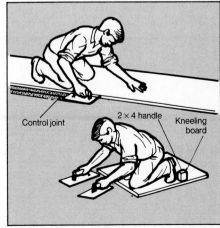

Control joint   2 × 4 handle   Kneeling board

4. Finishing. Smooth the surface in wide arcs with a float; follow immediately with a trowel to smooth away the marks left by the float.

Repairing Concrete

There are two kinds of damaged concrete floors: those that are merely cracked or pitted, with a structurally sound subfloor, and those that have buckled or heaved because of poor drainage or an unevenly compacted subsoil. The former can be easily patched and mended; the latter should be broken up and completely replaced with a new concrete slab after the structural problems underneath have been repaired. For example, a sagging wood subfloor should be rebuilt before the new slab of concrete is poured.

A 1/2-inch layer of new concrete can be poured directly over a flawed cement slab, if the subfloor is sound. On a large floor it is easier to pour the new surface in sections, using form boards to divide the room. Align the forms directly over the expansion joints of the old floor. They should be the thickness of the intended surface and may be applied with paneling adhesive which will hold them in place but will let them be removed after the concrete is poured. Cut new control joints over the old ones.

Very small holes in a reasonably sound floor can be patched very simply with epoxy. Small holes and cracks should be scraped clean and patched with any of several cement patching compounds. More serious cracks and large holes need more extensive preparation, including breaking up the damaged area and removing the debris. Always use goggles and gloves for such work to protect your eyes and hands. When patching large holes, pour the concrete in a cone on a piece of plywood so that it does not drip onto the good surface and harden there or mar it in some other way.

FILLING LARGE HOLES
STEP 1

To prepare the damaged area, break up the cracked concrete with a sledgehammer or an electric jackhammer until the pieces are small enough to remove easily. Angle the edges of the hole toward the center with a chisel and hammer. With a strong wire brush, roughen the edges of the hole and remove any loose chips or particles. Enlarge the hole by digging 4 inches deeper than the concrete slab and then tamp the dirt on the floor of the hole with the head of a sledgehammer or the end of a 2×4. Fill the hole with clean 3/4-inch gravel up to the bottom of the concrete slab.

STEP 2

Cut a piece of reinforcing wire mesh to fit inside the hole so that the ends of the wire rest against the sloped edges of the hole in the slab. A few bricks or pieces of debris placed under the wire will keep it at the right level while the concrete is poured. Then add water to premixed concrete until it is workable. Treat the edges of the hole with an epoxy bonding agent and, before it dries, pour the concrete into the hole, pushing it forcefully against the sides of the hole and under the wire mesh. When the hole is filled to the level of the slab, add a few more shovelfuls of concrete to counter any setting or shrinking. Pull the wire mesh about halfway up through the wet concrete with a rake.

STEP 3

With an assistant, work a 2×4 across the patch, sweeping it back and forth to smooth the new concrete. Any depressions that occur can be filled with more concrete and troweled smooth with the 2×4. When the "bleed water" evaporates and the surface looks dull, use a trowel to smooth the final finish. If the patch is too large to reach the center, lay boards across it and kneel on them, moving them back as you go along. The patch should cure for three to seven days. Sprinkle it with water and cover with a sheet of polyethylene to prevent the moisture

FILLING LARGE HOLES

1. Breaking out the damage. Break up damaged concrete back to the solid slab with a sledge or a jackhammer. Clear out the debris.

2. Getting ready to fill. Put reinforcing mesh, cut to fit, up to the edges of the hole on a few bricks or pieces of debris to hold it up.

3. Smoothing the patch. Level the patch roughly with a piece of 2×4 and finish with a trowel after the "bleed water" evaporates.

from evaporating. Check it every day and add more water if the surface becomes dry.

FILLING CRACKS
STEP 1
Some cracks in concrete are not worth the trouble of opening and filling. If a crack is a hairline or slightly larger, patch it with epoxy cement. If a crack is wide enough to get the blade of a chisel into it comfortably, open it up and cut under the sides as shown so the patching material can anchor itself under the beveled edges. Use a cold chisel and a baby sledgehammer. Sweep out debris and dust. Concrete patching material with a latex binder that substitutes for water is usually considered too expensive for large patches, but it is excellent for patching cracks. Follow mixing instructions on the product label.

STEP 2
When you are ready to fill the break, flush it out with plenty of water. This cleans the hole and conditions it for the patch so that the old concrete won't soak up water from the new.

STEP 3
Mix up the material for patching and pack it into the crack with the sharp edge of the trowel, forcing it into all the crevices and undercutting you have cleared out. Don't stint on the patching material; pack in as much as you can. When the crack is filled, level and smooth the patch with the flat surface of the trowel.

CAMOUFLAGING A FLOOR
Raw concrete holds stains amazingly; painted concrete is somewhat less tenacious. If you want to clean a badly stained floor you should consult your home center dealer for the right chemicals to use on your particular problem—there are as many solutions as there are stains. On painted floors, you can mask stains by splattering the surface with paint of contrasting color. If you try this, mask walls with newspaper and be prepared to splatter yourself.

PATCHING CRACKS

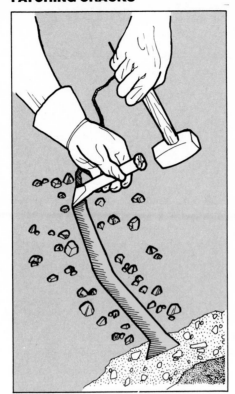

1. Clearing the crack. Enlarge a crack with a cold chisel, cutting under the edges to widen it at the bottom so the patch won't pop out.

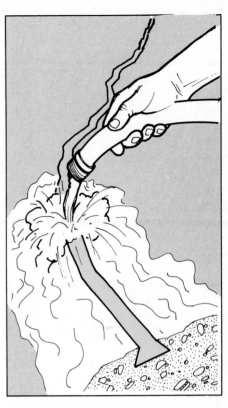

2. Flushing the crack. Water clears out small pieces of debris and also seasons the existing concrete to better accept the patch.

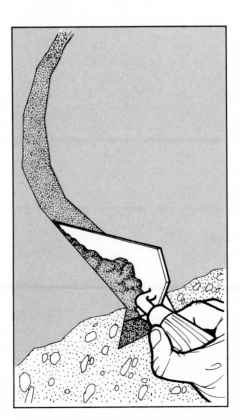

3. Filling the crack. Cut the patching material under the beveled edges of the crack with the edge of a trowel to fill every crevice.

CAMOUFLAGING A FLOOR

Whacking a loaded paint brush on a stick creates a splatter pattern on painted concrete that will disguise small stains.

Installing Wood Floors Over Concrete

If you plan to cover concrete with a wood floor, you have two options: build directly onto it or build a new subfloor over it. If the concrete is level, lay sleepers down and nail the new floor onto them as you would on floor beams. If the concrete is too uneven, it's best to build another subfloor suspended over the concrete base. If you are building directly onto a cement floor that is not level, you will have to resurface the concrete to make it level. A new floor cannot be built onto one that is uneven.

In deciding how to utilize a concrete floor, take the following factors into consideration. Concrete floors sweat, and unless they are properly lined with damp-proof polyethylene sheets, moisture will rot the wood. If you build directly onto the concrete by means of sleepers, you should sandwich sheets of polyethylene between two sets of sleepers, thus creating a thin film that is moisture-resistant. If heating the room will be problematical, do not build directly onto the concrete. Instead, raise the floor by adding a new subfloor and install insulation beneath the subfloor to prevent heat loss.

SUSPENDING A SUBFLOOR OVER CONCRETE
STEP 1
Locate a level line on each stud by use of a Hydrolevel. Measure the distance from the level line to where you want the subfloor by using a template of wood sawed down to the exact distance. Mark this spot on each stud with a chalkline.

STEP 2
Attach 2×6 boards for box beams along the two longest walls. Make sure that the box beams butt in the middle of a stud. Use three 10-penny common nails at each end of the beam to anchor it to a stud. The edge of the beams should touch the chalkline and be level, regardless of any variation in distance from the floor.

STEP 3
If the room is wider than 12 feet, you will need to install a girder of some kind for more strength than the box beams alone can supply. You can construct a girder beam by spiking two 2×8 boards together in four sections. In a 20-foot room, lay a 16-foot board so that it butts a 4-foot board and spike a second 16-foot board to both. Add another 4-foot board to the top of the two bottom boards and you'll have a girder beam of double thickness. Turn the beam on its side, crown side up, and toe nail it into the studs at the chalk mark. Shore up the center of the girder beam with blocks of wood. The girder and box beams should all be level. Check with a carpenter's level as you work.

SUSPENDING A SUBFLOOR OVER CONCRETE

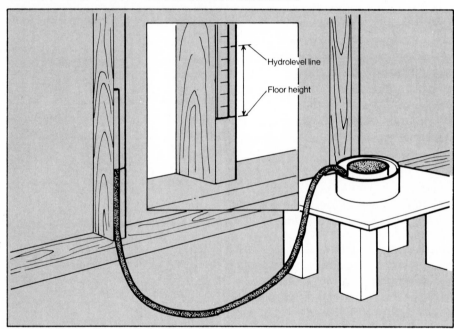

1. Finding the level line. The easiest way to find a level line around the room is to use a Hydrolevel, a simple reservoir and long plastic tube. Fill the reservoir with water colored with food coloring. Hold up the end of the tube and mark at the waterline in several places on the walls.

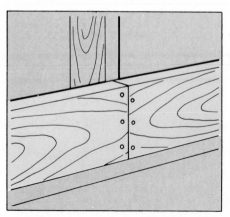

2. Attaching box beams. Cut 2×6s to fit along the longest walls; butt pieces if necessary. Nail along the walls below the chalkline.

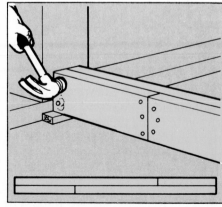

3. Installing a girder beam. If the floor spans a distance of more than 12 feet, install a lumber girder beam across the floor.

STEP 4
The first floor beam is nailed to the end wall, perpendicular to the box beams. Use three 10-penny nails to attach it to every stud it touches, and toe nail it into the box and girder beams using two 8-penny nails in each side and one in the top. Measure 15 ¼ inches along the box beams for the second floor beam, and every 16 inches thereafter to the opposite wall. Attach floor beams every 16 inches. As you proceed, unroll a sheet of polyethylene to serve as a moisture barrier. Staple the edges securely to the walls and box beams.

STEP 5
To each floor beam nail three legs of scrap lumber, one at each end and one in the middle, so that one end of the leg touches the floor and the other is lower than the top edge of the beam. When you have finished nailing all the floor beams and their legs, staple insulation over the beam, fiber glass down.

STEP 6
If your floor beams are exactly 16 inches apart, 4 × 8 plywood can be laid naturally upon them, the seams of the subfloor meeting in the center of a beam. Use 8-penny coated nails every 8 inches along a beam to anchor the floor securely. Use a half sheet to begin every other row so that the seams are staggered.

LAYING HARDWOOD DIRECTLY ON A CONCRETE FLOOR
Apply a coat of sealer to the concrete floor and allow it to dry. Then apply a rubber-based adhesive (or an asphalt mastic made for bonding wood to concrete) in ribbons about ⅛ inch thick and 4 inches wide along the border of the room. Lay the first 2 × 4 sleepers along the border, the 4-inch side into the adhesive. Next, lay rows of sleepers 18 inches to 48 inches long, allowing 10 inches between rows. The first piece should touch the border on one wall. Continue laying each sleeper alongside the previous one, letting their ends overlap 4-6 inches. Secure each sleeper with at least two concrete nails.

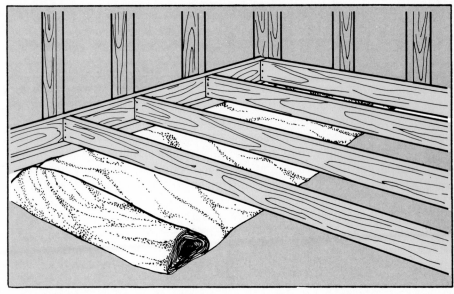

4. Installing floor beams. The floor beams should be placed 16 inches apart (on center). The first and last beams are nailed to the walls.

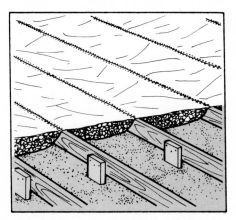

5. Attaching legs. Nail scrap lumber legs onto the floor a little below the tops of the beams. The legs should just touch the floor.

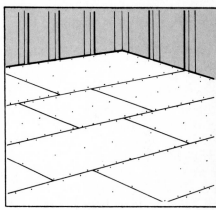

6. Installing the floor. Insulate the beams as shown left and cover with 4 × 8 sheets of plywood in a staggered pattern.

INSTALLING HARDWOOD FLOORING OVER CONCRETE

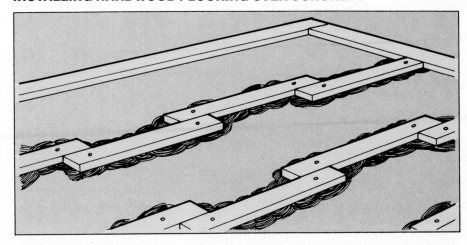

If your concrete floor is dry, level, and insulation is not a concern, you can dispense with subflooring and install a floor directly on sleepers that have been set in adhesive on the concrete. After concrete is sealed, hardwood is nailed directely onto the sleepers.

Leveling Wood Floors

The structure that holds up a house must bear tremendous weight, adjust to seasonal changes of weather, and withstand the constant traffic of those who live there. A sagging floor is not uncommon and is more often a nuisance than a portent of something disastrous. A small ³/₄-inch dip less than 30 inches long is a minor problem. Anything larger may be an indication of more serious structural damage such as rotten girders or a termite-ridden post. In older homes where the posts, girders, joists, and bridges are made from the original wood, shifting occurs. The wood absorbs moisture, especially if the posts are not set on footings, and termites can weaken major supports.

Most sags occur on the first floor where the heaviest furniture and appliances are located and where the major traffic occurs. These can be repaired quite easily from the basement or crawl space. Repairs to second-story floors are more difficult because of cosmetic considerations; the ceiling on the first floor must be removed and replaced, for instance, and a simple jack cannot be left up as a permanent solution. Consult a professional before undertaking any work above the basement level.

For first-floor sags, a telescoping house jack can be installed in the basement to bolster the drooping area, to function much like an additional post. If there is no basement, a smaller, bell-shaped contractor's jack can be rigged up in the crawl space. Use a steel post to replace an old one that is rotten or sinking so that the same problems won't occur later on. When replacing a joist, match the height and length of the old joist and be sure the new one is made of straight structural-grade lumber free of large knots and cracks, both of which are potential weak spots. Lumber that has been scientifically treated with preserva-

tives will withstand pressure better and weather other environmental influences. Replacing joists can be speeded up with a handy tool called a carpenter's nipper, used for clipping protruding nails that cannot be driven up into the finished floor.

JACKING UP A FLOOR FROM THE BASEMENT

Measure for the deepest point of a sag by laying an 8-foot straightedge across the sagging area of the floor. Locate this point in the basement by driving a nail through the floor. Lock the tubes of a telescoping house jack. Set the bottom plate on a 4 × 8 pad located beneath the sag point. Have a helper hold a 4 × 6 beam that will span the joists involved in the sag. Screw the jack so that it presses the beam firmly against the joists. Check the jack for plumb, then nail the jack's plates to the pad and beam. Raise the jack only ¹/₁₆ inch each day until the floor is level—any more may cause structural damage.

JACKING UP A FLOOR FROM A CRAWL SPACE

In the crawl space, build a pyramidal framework out of 6 × 6s until the pad for the contractor's jack lies close enough to the joists to be extended to press a beam against the joists involved in the sag. Raise the jack about ¹/₁₆ inch each day until the sag is corrected.

STRENGTHENING A WEAK JOIST
STEP 1
Plane one side of both ends of a new joist, making indentations ¹/₄ inch deep and 18 inches long. Extract the nails and remove any blocks holding the weak joist to the foundation and the girder.

STEP 2
Rest the indentations of the new joist on the girder and sill and position it 1¹/₂ inch from the old joist on the sill

and against the overlapping joist on the beam. The joist from the other side of the room should be firmly sandwiched between the old and new joists. Drive wooden shims under the indentations of the new joist so they force it up firmly against the subfloor.

STEP 3
Remove the old joist by cutting it with a saber saw near the girder and foundation sill. Pry it loose from the subfloor with a crowbar and cut the protruding nails flush with the floor. Split the ends of the old joist with a hammer and chisel. Pry the pieces out of the spaces between the subfloor and the girder and sill. Remove or cut the nails flush with the subfloor. Then install a second joist cut like the first. Shim it into place.

STEP 4
With 16-penny nails, nail the new joists to the joist sandwiched between them. Then, every 3 feet, nail a 2 × 4 wooden spacer between the joists. Toe nail the joists at the girder and foundation sill. Install new bridging where needed. Lastly, go upstairs and drive 8-penny finishing nails through the floor into the new joist to tie the floor to it and further anchor the joist.

PUTTING IN A NEW JOIST

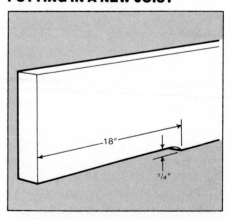

1. Fitting the new joist. The new joist should be of the same dimensions and length as the old. Plane both ends as shown.

REPLACING A POST
STEP 1

If the girder above the post is spliced, cut away the straps over the splice and replace them with two 3-foot pieces of ½ inch plywood. Use 25 to 30 8-penny nails on each piece. Erect 2 telescoping jacks 3 feet on either side of the old post and nail the top plates to the girder. Raise the girder ¹/₁₆ inch a day until it is completely supported by the jacks and the post is free of any weight. Remove the bolts that attach the post to the girder. With an assistant, tilt the top of the post away from the girder so that it can be lifted off the vertical steel dowel on which it is skewered.

STEP 2

On the floor, mark a footing the size required by your building code. Use a jackhammer to cut through the concrete floor. Remove all chunks of slab and dig a hole in the subsoil the depth required by the building code. When all the dirt is removed, dampen the hole and pour the concrete footing while the hole is still wet. The concrete filling should come to a point 4 inches below the floor slab. Release air bubbles by repeatedly thrusting a shovel into the wet concrete. With a straight piece of lumber, level the surface. Cure the concrete for 2 weeks by keeping the surface wet and covered with polyethylene.

STEP 3

Place the new steel column on the footing and adjust the screw so the top of the column reaches up snugly against the girder. Use the marks from the old post to center the plate. With the holes in the plate as a guide, drill pilot holes into the girder for the ³/₈-inch lag bolts that will attach the plate to it. Tighten the bolts just enough so that you can still move the column at its base. Tap it with a hammer and check with a level on all sides to be sure it is plumb. Tighten the adjusting screw so the post assumes the weight of the girder. Then tighten the lag bolts. Release the jack ¹/₁₆ inch a day until it can be taken down. Finish the floor by filling the hole with concrete.

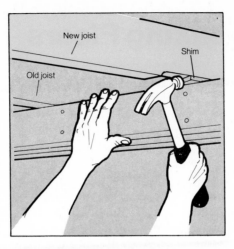

2. Placing the first joist. Set the joist on the far side of the overlapping joist at the girder and shim to force it against the floor.

3. Breaking out the old joist. Cut the joist at either end and remove it. Split the ends at the girder and sill, and remove the pieces.

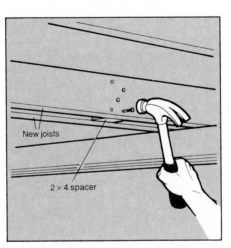

4. Installing the second joist. Replace the old joist with the second new one and nail the two joists together with 2 × 4 spacers between.

REPLACING A POST

1. Removing the old post. Use jacks on either side of the post to raise the girder so the post no longer supports it, then remove the post.

2. Making a new footing. Break through the concrete floor to lay a new footing; level the footing 4 inches below the level of the floor.

3. Setting the new post. Fasten the post to the girder above with lag bolts and tighten the post at the bottom. Fill in the floor.

Silencing Squeaking Floors

Squeaky floors are fairly common and there aren't many homes that don't have at least one. Although they are aggravating, they don't necessarily indicate anything seriously wrong with the floor or its structure. Usually the squeak is produced by two boards that rub against each other and can be easily silenced either by lubricating the boards that rub or reattaching them.

Frequent causes of squeaks are two boards that have warped and now rock when they are stepped on or cheaply manufactured floor strips with tongues and grooves that don't fit tightly. Sometimes the squeak is produced by a subfloor that has separated from the joists due to settling or because the joists have dried out. Weak or rotten joists can also separate as can those with faulty bridging between them. Occasionally, inadequate nailing of the subfloor to the joists causes squeaks.

Locate the squeak by having someone walk over the noisy area of the floor while you listen and watch from below. Look for springy boards, movement between joists, and bridging that gives when a weight is brought to bear. Just to be on the safe side, inspect the area around the squeak for structural damage needing more extensive repair such as replacement of girders, posts, or bridges.

SHIMMING THE SUBFLOOR

You can use simple wood shims to silence squeaks that are caused by movement between a joist and loose boards in the subfloor. Locate the squeak and gently tap shims into the space between the joists and the subfloor to prevent movement. Do not drive them too forcefully or they will cause the gap to widen even more by separating the boards from the joist. Wedge them in just firmly enough to fill up the space to eliminate the movement that causes the squeak.

CLEATING THE SUBFLOOR

If the squeak is caused by several boards in the subfloor, ones that are laid diagonally, you can eliminate movement by using a cleat—a length of 1×4 or 1×6. Locate the squeaky boards, and place the cleat along the joist that supports the loose boards. Prop it in place with a piece of 2×4 so it will lie snugly against the joist and the subfloor. Then use 8-penny nails to nail the cleat to the joist. Drive the nails in while the cleat is firmly wedged into

SHIMMING THE SUBFLOOR

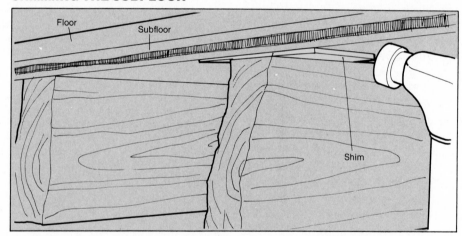

If floor joists are not tight against the subfloor in the area that is squeaking, shimming may solve the problem. Wedge shims between the joist and subfloor and tap them into place. Do not pound the shims into place because this will lift the floor and cause more squeaking.

CLEATING THE SUBFLOOR

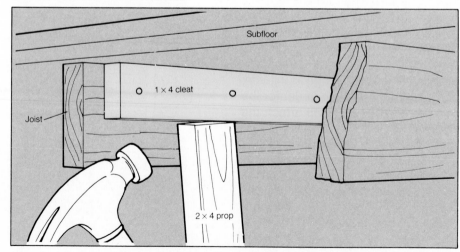

Where several boards in the subfloor above a joist are moving, a cleat to hold them is more effective than shimming the boards individually. A piece of 1×4, wedged against the subfloor and nailed to the joist and the flooring, will keep the subfloor from moving.

the right angle formed by the floor and the joist. When it is solidly attached, remove the 2×4 prop.

BRIDGING THE JOISTS

Locate the squeak and examine the joists that support the loose boards. If the troublesome area is rather large, involving boards that span several joists, install steel bridging between them. First, hammer the straight-pronged end into one joist near the top. Then drive the L-shaped flange on the other end into the opposite joist at the bottom, so that the steel bridge creates tension between the two joists. Install the companion bridge in a criss-cross fashion and proceed to the other joists. The result should be a series of joists more firmly braced and less liable to give beneath the weight of the floor.

INSTALLING SCREWS FROM BELOW

When individual boards are loose or bulging, the resulting squeak can be fixed by pulling the loose boards tight with screws inserted from below. Use wood screws of a length that will reach to no more than 1/4 inch below the surface of the finish floor. First, drill a pilot hole into the subfloor the size of the screw shank. Do not let this pilot hole penetrate into the finish floor. Then drill a pilot hole in the finish floor with a bit slightly smaller than that used for the subfloor. Be sure you stop drilling within 1/4 inch of the finish surface. Insert the screw through a large-diameter washer, and begin to turn it into the hole. As you tighten the screw, it will bite into the finish floorboards and pull them down.

SURFACE NAILING

If you can't gain access to the sub-floor, straight nails can be driven through the finish floor to anchor loose boards. Angle 8-penny nails through the floor so they penetrate a joist if possible. Position the nails in a criss-crossing series. On hardwood floors, drill a pilot hole narrower than the nail, to reduce the chance of splitting the wood. When the nails are in place, set them and fill the hole with wood putty the same color as the floor.

GLAZIER POINTS BETWEEN LOOSE BOARDS

When a simple squeak caused by two floorboards rubbing together cannot be silenced by lubricants, drive glazier points coated with graphite into the space between the boards. Set the points well below the surface, using a putty knife and a hammer. Space the glazier points 6 inches apart.

REINFORCING JOISTS

Squeaking over a large area may indicate that the joists beneath the floor are shifting slightly and giving inadequate support to the subfloor. Steel bridging, attached between joists as shown, holds the joists from moving side to side and stabilizes the subfloor.

SCREWS FROM BELOW

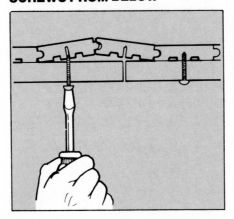

Drill a pilot hole through only the subfloor, then a smaller pilot hole into the finish floor. Pull the loose boards down with screws.

SURFACE NAILING

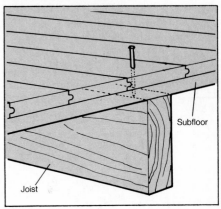

Subfloor

Joist

Nail down from the top with 8-penny nails when you can't get access to the floor from below. Try to locate joists and nail into them.

SETTING GLAZIER POINTS BETWEEN LOOSE BOARDS

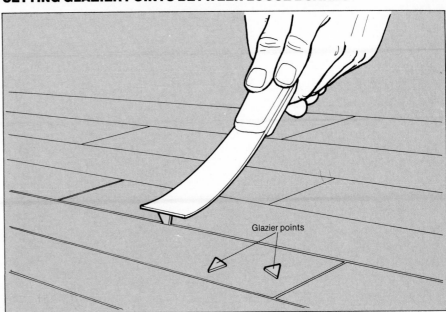

Glazier points

Where a squeak is caused by finish floorboards rubbing against one another, you can stop this movement by wedging glazier points between the boards. Lubricate the points with graphite and press them into place with a putty knife as shown; tap in any that stick, with a hammer.

Silencing Squeaky Stairs

The most common cause of squeaky stairs is a loose tread that rubs against other parts of the stairway. If the tread is separated from the riser (the vertical back board of each step), squeaking will result. Silencing it is a relatively simple matter of determining how the tread and riser are assembled and then closing the gap where the two separate. Techniques for this include: nailing them down, gluing them together, inserting wedges between the gaps, and reinforcing the tread and riser with wooden blocks. Occasionally a tread may be rubbing on the carriage (the diagonal, terraced structure that supports the risers and treads).

To locate the exact spot that causes the squeak, have someone step on each tread and rock back and forth. Watch closely both the middle of the tread and the ends to determine where the greatest movement occurs. Most squeaks can be eliminated from either above or below. If you can work from underneath the stairs because they rise over a closet or they parallel the basement stairs, fixing them is easier because you don't have to be concerned with the cosmetic effect.

NAILING/GLUING A SQUEAKY TREAD

Have someone stand on the loose tread while you drill $3/32$-inch pilot holes at opposing angles through the tread and into the riser at the point of the squeak. If the squeak is near the end of the tread, drill the holes into the carriage. Have the helper step off and apply a line of white wood glue between the tread and riser. Then insert two 8-penny finishing nails and set them while the helper stands on the tread. If nails will not hold the tread, drill an $11/64$-inch pilot hole into the tread and a $3/32$-inch hole into the riser. Then insert a No. 8 wood screw $2^{1}/_{2}$ inches, countersink it, and plug the hole with a piece of dowel.

WEDGING A LOOSE TREAD

Remove quarter round molding if you have it. Determine the kind of tread joints by inserting a knife between the tread and riser. Whittle sharply pointed wedges an inch or two long and drive them into the gap between the tread and riser at the points shown. Insert them just enough to silence the squeak. To conceal the wedges, cut off the ends with a utility knife and replace or add quarter round molding in the joint.

INSTALLING WOOD BLOCKS

Coat two sides of a 2×2 wood block

NAILING AND GLUING A SQUEAKY TREAD

Drill pilot holes through the tread into the riser with a helper standing on the tread, run glue under the tread, and drive in the nails.

INSTALLING WOOD BLOCKS

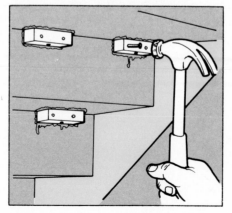

Cut several blocks from 2×2 scrap, coat the sides that will meet the riser and tread with glue, and attach with nails as shown.

with glue and press it into the joint between the tread and riser. Drive two nails into the riser and one up into the tread. Add as many blocks as are necessary.

REPLACING LOOSE WEDGES IN PREFAB STAIRS

Prefabricated stairs are built with wedges. If they come loose they can create squeaks. Simply split out the old wedge with a chisel and clean out the dried glue. Cut a new wedge to fit, coat the notch with glue, hammer the new wedge firmly into place, but not so hard that it lifts the tread.

REPLACING WEDGES IN PREFABRICATED STAIRS

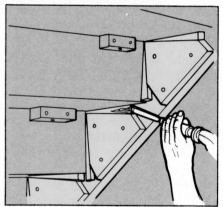

Where the wedges in prefabricated stairs no longer provide sufficient support, break them out and glue in new wedges.

WEDGING A LOOSE TREAD

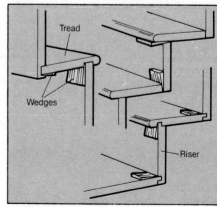

Tread

Wedges

Riser

The three examples above show the placement of wedges for different kinds of joints. Cut off wedges in place.

Replacing Damaged Floorboards

The causes of damaged floorboards are usually obvious. Furniture and heavy appliances can mar, crack, and tear wood fibers. Burns and stains are also common causes. If the cause is not immediately obvious, check out the entire floor, not just the damaged area. Also inspect the substructure for sagging girders, settling posts, or moisture and rotting due to plumbing leaks.

When buying replacement boards, take a sample of the old floor to your lumber dealer to make as close a match as possible. Be prepared to discover that nothing matches your floor completely and that you may, therefore, have to refinish the floor when the new boards are in place. A floor made of prefinished boards is not difficult to match although every floor changes with wear and tear over time and takes on its own unique characteristics.

The tools you'll need for replacing boards are: a hammer, a 1-inch chisel, a combination square, a pry bar, a portable power saw, 8-penny nails, and wood putty.

There are two methods for replacing floorboards. The easier way requires the removal of a rectangular area that encompasses the damaged boards, but it leaves a rather noticeable patch; this is no problem if the floor will be carpeted or the patched area will be under furniture. The second method is to remove individual boards in a staggered pattern. It is a little more difficult but the result is less noticeable.

RECTANGULAR PATTERN REPLACEMENT
STEP 1
With a square and pencil, measure a rectangle encompassing the boards to be removed, marking the lines 1/4 inch from the cracks to prevent sawing through nails. Adjust the blade of a portable power saw so that it nearly cuts through the boards. Lower the blade to the wood and work from the

center of a line outward. With a hammer and chisel, finish the cut, keeping the beveled side of the chisel facing into the damaged area. Then beginning at the midpoint of a cut side, lift the board out with a pry bar. You should use a small block of wood for leverage, being careful not to mar good boards in the area.

STEP 2
Use hammer and chisel to cut away the 1/4 inch remaining behind the saw cuts. Cut carefully and slowly so as not to ruin the edge of the adjacent boards. When the 1/4 inch is removed, set any exposed nail heads in the boards that border the cut area. Next measure the new boards to be cut; score pencil marks with a saw blade on the waste side of the marks so the kerf won't shorten the board. Lay one end of a scored board tightly into the area where it is to go and double check the scored mark to make sure it will be the right fit. Then saw it.

STEP 3
Lay the new board into place, sliding the grooves over the tongue of the old board. Blind nail the new board with 8-penny finishing nails driven in at a 45° angle through the tongue of the new board. It is not necessary to drill pilot holes first, but it may be helpful to do so to prevent the tongue from splitting. Then proceed to lay new boards one at a time in the same manner until you have reached the last board in the rectangular patch.

STEP 4
To lay the final board, first remove the tongue with a saw and sand the cut edge smooth so the board will fit snugly. Lay the board over its space and tap it into place, using a hammer and a block of wood. Face nail the last board with 8-penny finishing nails spaced every 12 inches and driven into pilot holes drilled 1/2 inch from the edges of the face. Set these nails and fill the holes with wood

RECTANGULAR PATTERN REPLACEMENT

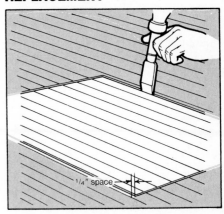

1. Making the cut. Cut around area with a saw set to slightly less than the depth of the finish flooring; finish cut with chisel.

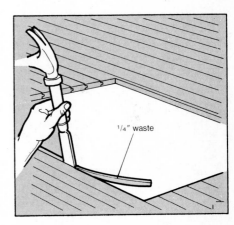

2. Finishing the cut. Use a chisel to cut away the 1/4 inch of board remaining along two sides of the cut and set any exposed nails.

3. Nailing new boards. Cut new boards to fit the space and fit them one by one by blind nailing at a 45° angle through the tongue.

putty. Lastly, sand and seal the new boards and stain them to match the finish of the surrounding boards.

STAGGERED PATTERN REPLACEMENT
STEP 1
With a hammer and chisel make vertical cuts across the boards to be removed with the beveled side of the chisel facing the damaged area. Then angle the chisel toward the vertical cut at 30° and begin to chisel through the board, cutting completely through. The edge of the section not to be removed should be sharp and clean.

STEP 2
Split the damaged area by making two rows of incisions with a chisel along the face of the board that has been prepared as above. Be careful when pounding that you don't damage good boards. Pry up as you move along so that the boards are split through. Then insert a pry bar into the incisions and pry out the middle strip. When it is completely out, pry loose the strip on the groove side of the board, and lastly, the strip on the tongue side. Begin the removal of each strip in the center of the section and work out to the ends. Set any exposed nails you come across.

STEP 3
Use a scrap of flooring as a hammering block and tap a cut-to-size replacement board into place sideways so that the groove side goes over the tongue of the old board. Then through the tongue of the new board, drive 8-penny finishing nails and set them. You may want to drill pilot holes first to avoid splitting the wood.

STEP 4
You cannot slide the last few boards into place. Instead remove the lower lips of their grooves with a chisel and tap the pieces into place from above, securing them with 8-penny finishing nails driven into pre-drilled holes. Set the nails and fill the holes with matching wood putty.

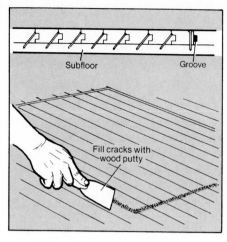

4. Installing the last board. Cut off the tongue of the last board and nail it in place as shown. Seal the edges of the patch with wood putty.

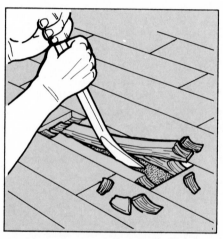

2. Finishing the cut. Break the damaged boards with lengthwise cuts and pry out the pieces starting with the grooved side.

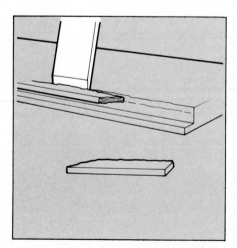

4. Placing the last boards. Strip the under half of the groove strip on the last board(s) so that they will fit down over the tongues of the old flooring. Fit the boards in place and attach with 8-penny finishing nails driven down into the subflooring.

STAGGERED PLACEMENT

1. Starting the cut. Mark off the damaged area with vertical cuts of a chisel; then cut toward these marks at a 30° angle as shown.

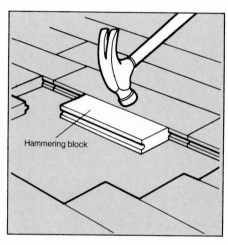

3. Replacing the boards. Slip a new board, cut to fit, against the tongue edge of the old floor and tap it into place.

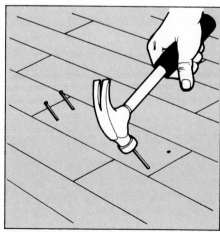

Restoring and Refinishing Wood Floors

When wood floors become so marred and scuffed that new coats of wax do little to improve them, it may be time to give them a major refinishing. Although refinishing wood floors is a major project that is both time-consuming and tedious, you can save quite a bit of money by doing them yourself instead of hiring a professional floor service.

You will, however, need to rent professional equipment from a reliable dealer. You'll need a drum sander, a smaller disk sander called an edger, and a polisher. Rent the sanders first and hold off on the polisher until you are ready for it. You can sand and seal about 200 to 250 square feet a day in an average room. Be sure to have the dealer show you how to load the drum and run the equipment. This will also let you know that they are in working order before you get them home. Ask if you need special wrenches for loading the drum. You'll need a three-prong plug for the electrical outlet, a respirator face mask, and rubber gloves.

Since most floors are not refinished until they are already in rather bad shape, you will need fine, medium, and coarse sandpaper. You should have ten to twelve sheets and the same number of disks for each room. After you have sanded the floor to your satisfaction, bleach out stains using full strength household bleach on the discolored areas. Wear gloves and goggles. When the area is bleached to the matching tone of the floor, wash it in warm water, vacuum, then go over it with a tack cloth (a special dust cloth) dampened with turpentine and varnish.

There are several types of oil-based penetrating sealers, all of which are used to bring out the natural grains of wood rather than conceal them. Some sealers match the natural hues of wood, others are clear and colorless. A third type, called pickling stains, are tinted various colors, such as green, blue,

PREPARING THE FLOOR

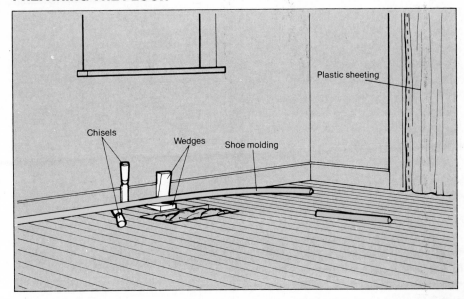

All the surface of the floor must be cleared before sanding. Remove duct grates and any other hardware on the floor. Seal the room from the rest of the house so sawdust won't escape. Furnishings not on the floor, like drapery, should be removed or bagged.

amber. They color the wood without covering the grain. All oil-based sealers penetrate the wood below the surface and do not scuff or show scratches, unless the wood fibers themselves are damaged.

The final protection for a refinished floor is a polyurethane coating that doesn't yellow and provides an extremely hard protective glaze when dry. A thin coat of paste wax over the polyurethane finish will prolong its life. Varnish and shellacs yellow, wear through easily, and must be stripped completely off when the floor needs refinishing.

PREPARING THE ROOM

Before you begin to refinish the floor, strip the room of furniture and pictures. Take down drapes or pin them up from the floor and wrap them in plastic bags. Dust will coat anything left in the room that is not covered. Remove floor registers (and cover the vent), radiator caps, and the quarter round moldings at the baseboards. Seal off doorways into other rooms, and open the windows wide

for ventilation. Sanding will create extremely flammable dust, so turn off any pilot lights in the area.

PREPARING THE FLOOR

When the room has been stripped of furniture and wall hangings, remove the quarter round molding at the baseboard. Begin at the doorway and carefully pry the molding away from the baseboard. Use two chisels, one to separate the molding from the baseboard itself and the other to pry the strips up from the floor. As you proceed, place small blocks of wood behind and under the molding to prevent it from snapping back into place. As you move along, move the wedges with you. Number the sections as they are removed so that you remember in what order to replace them when the job is over. When all the molding is off, pull out any finishing nails that remain in the baseboard or floor. Replace any boards that are very badly damaged. Set all nails that protrude from the floor, or they will tear the sandpaper when you are stripping.

SANDING THE FLOOR
STEP 1

Load the drum with the sander unplugged. Thread a sheet of 20-grit coarse sandpaper into the loading slot of the drum. Turn the drum one complete revolution and thread the other end of the sandpaper into the slot. Secure the paper by tightening the nuts on both ends of the drum. The sander should come with wrenches for this purpose. On the third sanding with the 100-grit fine paper, you may have to fold an extra piece of it as a wedge.

STEP 2

Tilt the drum up off the floor and turn it on. When the motor reaches top speed, lower it slowly and let the sander pull you forward steadily. The drum should never be allowed to stand in one spot while it is running, or it will gouge the wood. Move slowly forward with the grain. When you reach the wall, tilt the sander up, walk it back to where you began, and move it to the side so that the second pass will overlap the first by two or three inches. Each pass should be in the same direction and with the grain of the wood. On parquet or herringbone patterns, the first sanding pass should be at a 45° angle to the boards, the second at 45° in the cross direction, the third pass can go straight across the floor. When you finish the floor with the coarse sanding, load the edger and sand close to the walls. Then repeat both the drum and edger sandings with medium paper and lastly with fine.

STEP 3

In tight areas where neither the sander nor the edger can reach, such as around radiators and in corners, remove the old finish with a paint scraper. Pull the scraper toward you with both hands bearing down on it with a firm steady pressure. Scrape with the grain as much as possible and be careful not to splinter the wood. When the blade grows dull, sharpen it with a file. When you have removed the finish in these areas, sand them by hand using all three grades of paper.

PUTTING IN SANDPAPER

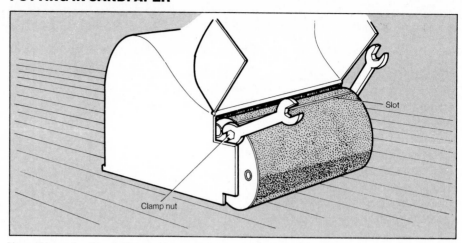

You will have to change the sandpaper in the drum sander as it wears down and as you need finer grits to finish the floor. Most models operate like the one shown above, with both ends of a length of sandpaper gripped by a slot on the drum that is tightened from both sides.

OPERATING THE SANDER

The sander must be turned on, maneuvered, and stopped with the drum tilted up, so the sandpaper is not in contact with the floor. When the sander is running, slowly lower the drum to the floor and let the action of the drum pull the sander along. Sand with the grain of the wood.

TREATING HARD-TO-REACH AREAS

In corners and around pipes and other obstructions that can't be removed, you must use hand labor instead of the power sander. Scrape the floor with a paint scraper, pulling it toward you and working with the grain. Sharpen the scraper often.

SEALING AND FINISHING
STEP 1

Wearing rubber gloves, apply the sealer with a rag in broad strokes along the wood grain. Have a helper wipe up any excess quickly before it dries. Begin against the wall opposite the door, so you don't seal yourself into a corner. Work in strips about 3 inches wide and apply the sealer generously. After about twenty minutes, most of the sealer will have penetrated the wood. Any puddles forming should be mopped up by your helper while you begin the next strip. If you both work at the same pace, you should be able to keep kneeling on dry floor until the last strip when your helper will have to back out of the room over wet sealer. When you have completed the floor, allow it to dry for eight hours.

STEP 2

Make a batch of putty with dust from the final sanding and enough sealer to produce a thick paste. This mix will match your floor better than commercial hues. Force it into cracks and nail holes with a putty knife. Scrape the excess off to make a smooth surface. Sand the putty areas by hand when they are dry, using fine 100-grit paper.

STEP 3

Load the polisher with a pad of fine steel wool (obtained from the rental service) by fitting the polisher with the heavy-duty brush and pressing the steel wool into the bristles. Polishing the floor after the sealer has dried will buff out any bubbles that form in the sealer coating. You'll have to do the corners, edges, and hard-to-reach areas by hand with pads of fine steel wool. When finished, vacuum and wipe with a tack cloth.

STEP 4

With a long-handled roller, apply a coat of polyurethane. Do the edges and corners with a brush. Roll with the grain. After eight hours smooth the surface with fine steel wool as above. Vacuum and wipe with a tack cloth. Apply a second coat and let it dry twenty-four hours.

SEALING THE FLOOR

Applying a penetrating sealer is a two-person job. One spreads the sealer with a rag, the other wipes up any excess left on the surface.

BUFFING THE SEALER

A power floor polisher loaded with steel wool over a heavy brush scours irregularities from the surface of the dry sealer.

FILLING BLEMISHES

Homemade putty, composed of dust from the last sanding and sealer mixed to a thick paste, should be used to fill cracks.

FINAL FINISH

Finish with two coats of polyurethane, buffing between coats. Let the first coat dry eight hours, the second twenty-four hours.

Preparing Floors for New Surfaces

An underlayment is necessary to eliminate irregularities in a subfloor over which resilient flooring will be laid. Underlayment is either 1/4-inch plywood or hardboard or up to 1/3-inch particle board. When installed correctly, underlayment strengthens the floor, creates a more secure and stable surface, and provides the smooth base needed for laying tiles or any resilient sheet flooring materials. It also allows the slight raising of a floor to meet the floor in an adjoining room.

Always store hardboard panels flat and avoid breaking the smooth face surface. You should, however, let them stand against the wall for some time before laying them, with air space between each panel, so they can adjust to the temperature and humidity conditions in the room where they are to be put down. Similarly, it is not wise to install underlayment in exceedingly moist or humid weather or at times when the atmosphere is unusually dry. Underlayment should be in harmony with normal room conditions where it is to be laid or it may shrink or swell later.

There are four methods of fastening underlayment. *Coated box nails* have a sheath of resin which melts with the heat of the friction of being driven into wood. The resin rehardens when the nails are in place, holding securely. *Screws* also make excellent fasteners to hold underlayment in place but the number of screws and screw holes needed in a single sheet makes this method quite time-consuming. Many professional home builders use *staples* driven in by a power nailer which you can rent from a tool renter. This method is fast and leaves no bulges but staples don't hold the underlayment sheets as securely as coated nails or screws. *Adhesive* is often used by contractors and works well if you score the downward side of the hardboard to create a rough surface to stick to.

UNDERLAYMENT ON PANELED SUBFLOOR

Remove the quarter round molding at the baseboard. If you are building a new home, slip the underlayment into the space between the wallboard and the subfloor before the walls are finished and the baseboard attached. If the underlayment is hardboard, lay the rough surface up. With grade A-C plywood, lay the grade A side up. Be sure that the panels of underlayment always span the seams of the subfloor. If the edge of the first panel of underlayment falls directly over a seam, cut it so that it and subsequent panels do not.

UNDERLAYMENT ON BOARD-BY-BOARD SUBFLOOR

Lay the first panel of underlayment across the direction of the boards in the subfloor. If the end of the panel falls directly over a seam in the floor, cut it so that it falls in the middle of a board. Locate the floor beams in the subfloor by the nail heads and extend their lines onto the underlayment. Drive 8-penny coated box nails (or staples or screws) every 4-6 inches along the floor beams, 3/8 inch from the edges of the underlayment. Leave about 1/16 inch between sheets of underlayment for minor expansion and contraction.

UNDERLAYMENT ON A PANELED SUBFLOOR

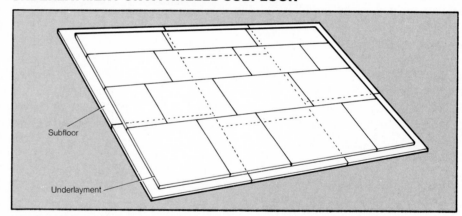

Subfloor

Underlayment

In order to make a floor sound, underlayment over paneled subflooring must be arranged so that its seams never fall directly over seams in the subflooring. In order to achieve this where uncut sheets fall directly over seams, cut the first sheet so subsequent ones are offset.

UNDERLAYMENT ON BOARD-BY-BOARD SUBFLOOR

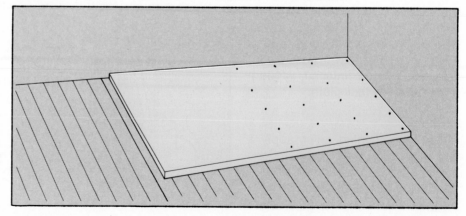

As overpaneled subflooring, underlayment on a board subfloor should be arranged so that its ends do not fall directly over seams in the subfloor. Locate joists by finding nails in the subfloor and nail the underlayment to the joists at 4- to 6-inch intervals.

NAILING TECHNIQUES

Coated box nails are very difficult to drive into any surface, especially the hard materials used in particle board and hardboard. When you hit them slightly off center, they bend and fold up. To compound the difficulty, the hammer tends to slide on the slippery surface of the nail head. One way to minimize this problem is to hold the hammer loosely rather than tightly. Doing so allows the head of the hammer to find the true surface of the nail head, resulting in a cleaner, more straightforward strike. Don't hammer hard on the assumption that forceful strokes will make the nail and the hammer blows press the underlayment firmly to the subfloor. Instead, hammer with an easy stroke and apply pressure to the underlayment with your free hand, kneeling close to the spot you are nailing, or have a helper exert pressure. Plan your last blow to drive the nail head flush with the surface. Try to eliminate dimpling the underlayment with hammerhead indentations. Dimples can become visible in the flooring above, after a time appearing as slight depressions.

REMOVING A BENT NAIL

If you try to remove a bent nail by grabbing the nail head with the claw of the hammer, you will probably pull its head from the shank. Instead, drive the claw of the hammer into the shank with a second hammer; the soft metal in the nail can be forced into the claw rather easily. Then lean the hammer sideways to pull the bent nail out.

FINISHING THE SURFACE

The purpose of underlayment is to provide a perfectly smooth surface on which to place resilient flooring. After you have put down the underlayment, patch any cracks or indentations. Add wood putty to any space between panels that is greater than 1/4 inch. If you have dimpled the surface badly, fill the pockets with putty, smoothing the patches so that they are flush with the good surface. Lastly, sand down the putty after it has dried.

NAILING TECHNIQUES

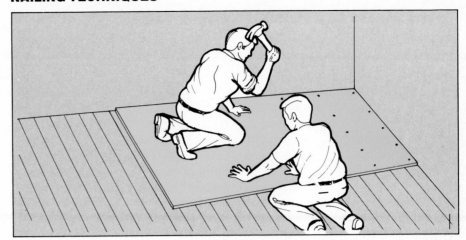

Nailing down underlayment is tricky because the underlayment is hard and the nails are relatively weak. The work can be greatly eased by a helper pressing down on the sheet near the point where you are driving a nail. If you are working without help, apply the pressure yourself.

REMOVING A BENT NAIL

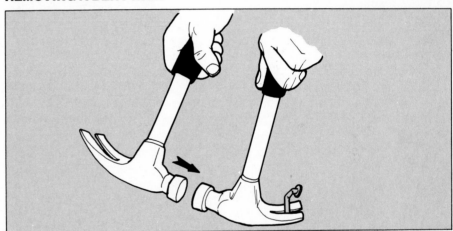

Bent nails, a common occurrence in putting down underlayment, are most easily removed by driving the hammer claw into the shank of the nail. If you pull on the head, it may pop off.

FINISHING THE SURFACE

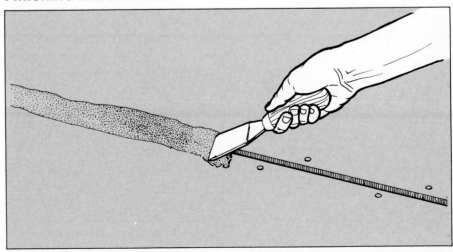

To make a smooth surface suitable for the application of adhesive to hold tile, fill with wood putty the gaps between sheets of underlayment, and any dents, and smooth off.

Laying Resilient Tile

Homeowners with a creative bent often enjoy installing resilient tile because it is relatively easy and fun. For a successful job, however, you've got to plan ahead, make proper preparations, design your pattern and color combinations, measure accurately, and work on a day when you won't be interrupted. You must also have a proper subfloor for the tile and follow the instructions that come with the product you have bought.

A wood floor makes a suitable base for tile only if there is at least 2 feet of ventilation between it and the ground. If it doesn't have this space, you should consult a professional contractor to learn how it can be made suitable. Wooden flooring laid over a durable subfloor will suffice, if the boards are at least 4 inches wide and they are smooth and sound. If there are any damaged boards, replace them. Nail any loose boards down tight, sand them smooth, and fill cracks and splits with wood putty. Before you lay the tile, cover the wood floor with 15-pound asphalt-saturated felt flooring paper. If the entire floor is in poor condition or if it is only a single layer of wood subfloor, install an underlayment.

Concrete can serve as a base for tile only if it is smooth and dry. If it is not perfectly dry throughout the year it will harm the tiles. Be sure the slab is never subject to moisture penetration; test it during the rainy and humid seasons of the year. If you think it is safe, fill the cracks and dimples with a latex underlayment compound as directed by the manufacturer.

The tile and all the materials should be kept at a room temperature of at least 70° for twenty-four hours before and after it is laid.

PLOTTING A DESIGN

Plot your design on graph paper, letting each square represent one tile. If you use 12-inch tiles, you'll need one graph square for each tile. A 16-foot room will require sixteen tiles per side. If you use 9-inch tiles, multiply the dimensions of the room by 1.33 to determine how many tiles to a side. A 16-foot room will need 21.3 or twenty-two graph squares per side. The number of square feet in the room equals the number of 12-inch tiles you'll need. For 9-inch tiles, multiply the number of square feet by 1.78.

PREPARING TO LAY THE TILE
STEP 1

Measure and mark the center points of two opposite walls and stretch a chalkline between nails driven into them. Do the same on the other walls. Do not snap the lines yet. Use a carpenter's square to determine that they intersect at a true 90° angle.

If the pattern is to be laid on a diagonal, measure the shorter chalkline from the intersection to the wall. Then measure that distance on either side of the nail. Do the same on the opposite wall and drive nails into the four new points. Stretch chalklines between these nails so that they intersect in the middle.

STEP 2

Lay dry tiles in one quadrant. Begin at the intersection and extend them out at 90° along the strings all the way to the two walls as shown. Duplicate the color combination on the graph paper. If you discover the last tiles are less then one half tile width from the wall, move the chalk string to make a wider border at the wall. If the last tile is more than one half tile width from the wall, leave the chalk string where you have it. In either case, now snap the string and mark your line on the floor.

For a diagonal pattern, lay dry tiles along two perpendicular lines point to point and a row of tiles along the intersecting diagonal line. If the places where the border tiles butt the walls are not aesthetically pleasing to you, adjust the chalk strings; then snap them.

PLANNING A DESIGN

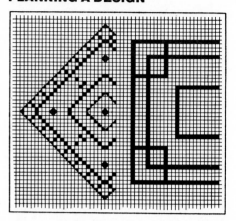

If you are using different colors, plot out the design you want on graph paper, using one square for each tile.

PREPARING TO LAY THE TILE

1. Marking guidelines. Measure the walls to find their midpoints and stretch strings or chalklines between them; add diagonals as described for diagonal designs.

2. Adjusting the guidelines. Lay out tiles along two of the guidelines and check the fit at the walls; adjust the lines as necessary.

SETTING TILES

Spread adhesive along one chalkline with a notched trowel angled 45° to the floor. Begin at the intersection and work toward the wall, leaving part of the chalkline exposed for guidance. Adhesive should be laid half as thick as a tile. Set a row of tiles along the line, letting each tile butt the preceding one. Drop tiles into place; do not slide them. Set a row perpendicular to the first, and fill in the tiles between them.

For a diagonal pattern, begin at the intersection of diagonal lines and lay a row along one diagonal. Use this as a base line on which to build your pattern. After finishing a section, roll it with a rented roller or a rolling pin.

TRIMMING A BORDER

Align a dry tile over the last set tile from the wall. Then place a third tile over these two and push it to ⅛ inch from the wall. Using this top tile as a guide, score a line with a utility knife on the tile immediately under it. Snap the tile on the scored line, and fit into the border the piece that was not covered by the top tile. For a diagonal pattern, score the border tiles from corner to corner with a straightedge and a knife. Snap them to make triangular halves to complete the sawtooth border pattern.

CUTTING AROUND A CORNER

Align a tile over the last set tile on the left side of the corner. Place a third tile over these two and push it to ⅛ inch from the wall as above. Mark the edge with a pencil. Then, without turning the marked tile, align it on the last set tile to the right of the corner. Mark it in a similar fashion. Cut the marked tile with a knife so as to remove the corner section. Fit the remaining part around the corner.

MAKING IRREGULAR CUTS

To cut an irregular shape, use the procedure for borders and corners, but move the top tile along the irregular shape to locate its surfaces on the tile to be cut. At curved surfaces, bend a piece of solder wire and transfer the curve to the tile being marked.

SETTING TILE

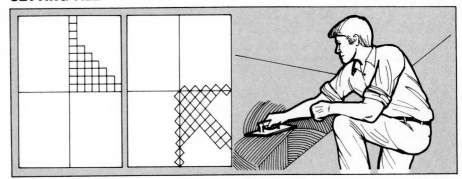

Apply adhesive with a notched trowel in one quadrant, leaving the guidelines visible. Set the first tile at the intersection of the guidelines, dropping—not sliding—it into place.

TRIMMING THE BORDER

Set two tiles atop the one closest to the wall, slide the top tile against the wall, and mark the one beneath. Score the marked tile with a utility knife and break it along the line.

CUTTING AROUND A CORNER

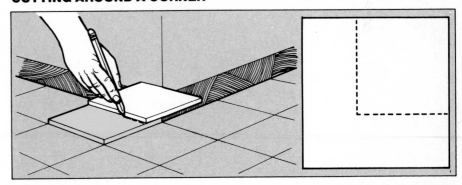

Set two tiles atop the tile closest to one side of the corner to be cut out, mark that dimension, then shift the two tiles to the other side of the corner to mark the other dimension.

MAKING IRREGULAR CUTS

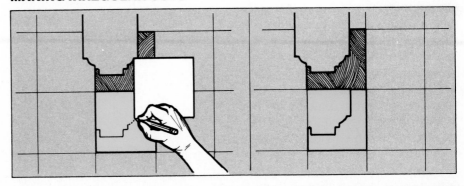

Mark an irregular cut with the tile-over-loose-tile method, moving the guide tile along the irregular surface and marking at each point; connect the marks to outline the cut.

Installing Resilient Sheet Floor

Manufacturers have developed many new types of resilient sheet flooring (often simply called linoleum) in recent years, including new materials, innovative design, and a wide range of colors and color combinations. Many of the new floorings are durable, attractive, and long-lasting. After deciding on the type you want, order it to arrive at least three days before you intend to lay it, so it can adjust to the temperature conditions in your home.

Resilient sheet flooring can be installed over several types of old flooring but in all cases the floor must be in good condition. You can lay resilient flooring over old if it is completely smooth and still tightly adhered to the subfloor. Concrete must be dry, level, and clean. A wooden floor is suitable if the boards are not rotten or warped, and only if they are firmly nailed down. If these conditions cannot be met, then it's best to install an underlayer of plywood or hardboard.

Prepare the room by removing all the furnishings, including the covers on the floor registers and the shoe molding along the baseboard. The baseboard does not have to be removed if you cannot do it without damaging walls or doorjambs. When you remove shoe moldings and baseboards, number the pieces so you can replace them in the same order.

Design the floor by using a piece of graph paper to map out the shape and dimensions as accurately as possible. Make a scale drawing to include all such irregularities as closets, alcoves, fireplaces, and doorways. If your floor is very irregular, you may want to make a full-size felt template to guide you when cutting the sheets. Your drawing should be meticulously done if the room will require more than one 12-foot sheet of flooring. Determine where the seam will go in regard to design, pattern, and traffic flow. It's best not to put a seam where traffic is heaviest.

INSTALLING FLOORING WITHOUT A SEAM

Unroll the flooring in a large open space to make a rough cut. Transfer the floor plan onto it with a water soluble felt-tipped pen and cut the flooring so that it's about 3 inches oversize all around. You will cut the excess away after the flooring has been positioned in place. Apply adhesive according to the manufacturer's instructions, taking care to note the "open time" you will have before it dries.

Some flooring does not require adhesive. Some brands require that you spread only a 6-inch wide smear of mastic along the edges. Some flooring has to be stapled down or fixed with double-sided tape.

Take the flooring to the room and lay the longest edge against the longest wall first. Position the entire piece making sure it curls up 3 inches on every wall.

Follow the instructions given below for trimming the floor to make it fit the room leaving a 1/8-inch gap at the walls to allow for expansion.

INSTALLING FLOORING WITH A SEAM

Take your floor plan to your dealer and have him make the rough cuts. If you do it yourself, ask whether to reverse the sheets at the seam so the design falls into place. Use a linoleum knife and heavy scissors to cut the most intricate piece first, making it 3 inches oversize on all sides, including the seam. If you are using adhesive, spread it on the floor for this piece, stopping about 10 inches from the seam. Position the flooring. Then cut the second sheet so it overlaps at the seam at least 2 inches. Spread the adhesive over the rest of the floor, stopping 2 inches from the edge of the first sheet. Position and align the second piece carefully. Then cut half-moon shapes at the end of each seam so the ends butt the walls. With a straightedge and utility knife, cut through both sheets at the point where the seam will be. Lift up both halves and apply adhesive. Clean the seam and use the seam sealer recommended for your flooring.

INSTALLING FLOORING WITH A SEAM

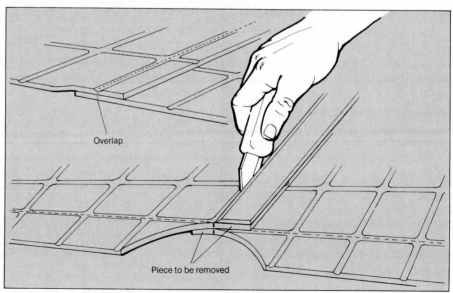

Overlap.

Piece to be removed

To make a perfect seam, install the two parts of the flooring with adhesive, overlapped as shown. Cut away the untrimmed edge that meets the wall at the seam so the seam will butt against the wall, then cut through the overlap to make the seam.

TRIMMING
STEP 1
Trim for an outside corner by cutting straight down the curled up flooring. Begin at the top edge and cut to where the wall and floor meet.

STEP 2
Trim for an inside corner by cutting the excess flooring away with increasingly lower diagonal cuts on each side of the corner. Gradually these cuts should produce a wide enough split for the corner to wedge through and the flooring to lie flat around it.

STEP 3
Remove the curled up flooring at the walls by pressing it down with a long 20- to 24-inch piece of 2×4. Press the flooring into the right angle where the wall and floor meet until it begins to develop a crease at the joint. Then position a heavy metal straightedge into this crease and cut along the wall with a utility knife, leaving a 1/8-inch gap between the edge of the flooring and the wall. This is necessary for the material to expand without buckling.

STEP 4
The best way to have the flooring meet a doorjamb is to cut away a portion of the jamb at the bottom so that the flooring will slide under it. Trim the flooring to match the angles and corners of the doorjamb, overcutting about 1/2 inch for the edge to slip under the jamb.

FINISHING THE JOB
Clean the flooring only with a solvent recommended by the manufacturer to avoid damaging the finish. It is important to clean up any adhesive that may have spilled or oozed up onto the surface. Then roll the flooring so that it sets firmly and flatly in the adhesive. You can use a rented linoleum roller or lean heavily on a rolling pin and work your way across the floor. Start at the center of the room and roll firmly to remove air bubbles. After the floor has been cleaned and rolled, replace the baseboard and the shoe molding.

TRIMMING SHEET FLOORING

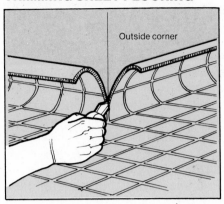

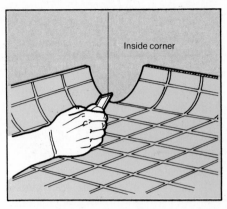

1. Trimming an outside corner. Start at the top of the flooring where it overlaps the corner; cut down to floor.

2. Trimming an inside corner. At an inside corner, cut the flooring in V-shaped sections down the corner until the flooring can lie flat.

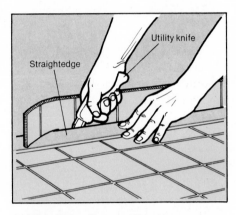

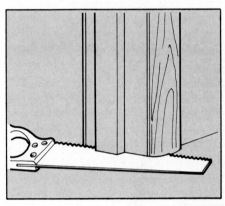

3. Trimming along walls. Use a heavy straightedge like a 2×4 to crease the flooring against the wall, then cut away excess.

4. Cutting under a doorjamb. Cut under a doorjamb as shown, resting the saw on a piece of new flooring.

FINISHING THE JOB

Use a linoleum roller or rolling pin to flatten the floor and force out any air bubbles. When replacing the molding, do not nail it to flooring so the flooring will be free to shrink and expand slightly without buckling.

Laying Parquet Tile

In general, parquet is arranged and laid very much like resilient vinyl tiles with some differences, particularly its two adjacent tongued edges and two grooved edges. It will have to be sawed, not snapped, when you need smaller pieces for borders.

It is very important to have a smooth level undersurface on which to lay parquet tiles. Unlike resilient tiles that follow slight bumps and indentations in the underlayment, parquet is hard and inflexible and tends to rock on uneven surfaces, making for a very unsteady floor condition.

Parquet can be set on old wood floors if they are smooth and even. Remove old paint, lacquer, wax, and shellac by sanding with a rented sander. Nail down any loose boards and set all nails. If any boards are badly damaged or rotten, you should put an underlayment down before laying new parquet flooring.

It is not wise to lay parquet tiles directly on a concrete subfloor since concrete is prone to sweat. An underlayment over the concrete is advised unless you know from experience that your concrete slab remains completely dry throughout the year.

Parquet should not be installed over old resilient flooring. Either remove it or cover it with an underlayment.

PREPARING TO LAY THE TILES
STEP 1
Mark the working lines by measuring the center points on two opposite walls. Drive a nail into each and stretch a chalkline between them, and do the same on the other walls, but do not snap the chalklines yet. With a carpenter's square, determine that they form a true 90° angle. If this is done accurately, the tiles form a grid perfectly centered in the room. If the room is irregularly shaped, or the walls are curved or bowed, or the room has various entrances, you may want to adjust the working lines

to minimize whatever visual effects the shape of the room will have on the grid pattern. If one wall is usually hidden by furniture, make the adjustment there.

STEP 2
Practice laying out several tiles along two work lines that form a quadrant. Get used to the tongue-and-

groove construction of the tiles. There will be two adjacent edges with tongues, and two adjacent edges with grooves. If you place them correctly, tongue into groove, you will create the basket weave pattern of the parquet floor. Alternate the grains from wood tile to wood tile, placing the tongues into the grooves and vice versa.

PREPARING TO LAY THE TILES

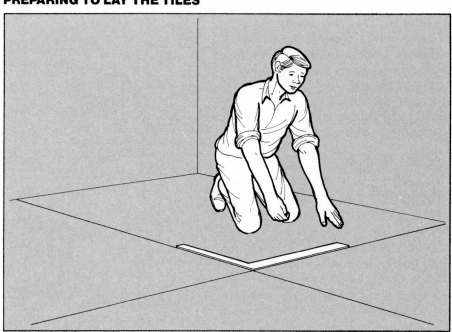

1. Establishing working lines. Measure to find the centers of all four walls of the room. Stretch strings or chalklines between these points and check that they meet in the center at right angles. If they do not, adjust them until they do.

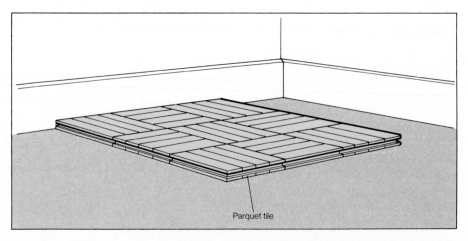

Parquet tile

2. Making a trial run. Fit several tiles together to form the pattern you want and observe how the tongues and grooves are oriented, then lay tiles along two work lines and note how wide the tiles against the wall will be. Adjust the lines if the filler tiles will be too narrow.

LAYING AND SETTING THE BLOCKS
STEP 1

Before you begin to spread the adhesive read the instructions and note how much time you will have to work before it dries. Apply the adhesive along one chalkline with a notched trowel angled at 45° to the floor. Begin at the intersection and work toward the wall, leaving part of the chalkline exposed for guidance. Lay the first tile into a corner of the intersection. Align the edges of the tiles, not the tongues, with the lines. Place the second tile against the first one, engaging the tongue and groove. Avoid sliding the tiles any more than is necessary. After you've laid four or five tiles, strike them with a rubber mallet to bed them. The first ten or twelve tiles determine the alignment for the rest of the floor.

STEP 2

To make a border, align a tile over the last one and place a third tile over those two, pushing it to ½ to ¾ inch away from the wall. It helps to place a wood spacer of that width between the top tile and the wall. This gap is needed for the cork expansion strip that comes with the tiles. Mark the middle tile using the top one as a guide. Then saw along the mark. The top tile will be the piece to place in the border.

STEP 3

Using a tile for a guide, mark how much of the doorjamb must be removed to allow the tile to fit under it. Then trim the bottom of the jamb with a saw.

FINISHING THE JOB

Allow the adhesive to dry overnight and then replace the baseboard and shoe molding. Insert the cork expansion strip before replacing these; be sure to drive nails into the baseboard, not down into the tile. If an inward swinging door will not clear the raised floor, remove it and shave off part of the bottom edge. Finish the floor with a reliable paste wax and buff it twice a year. Wet-mopping or scrubbing will ruin the finish.

LAYING AND SETTING THE TILE

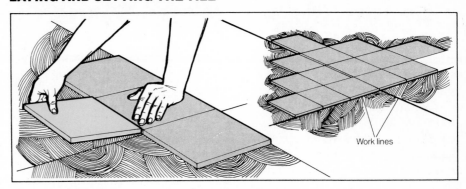

1. Setting the first tiles. Spread adhesive with a notched trowel. Seat an edge of a tile in place and drop the tile into the adhesive. Don't slide tiles into position.

2. Creating the border. Measure for the trim tile by putting a tile atop the one seated closest to the wall and a third tile atop those two pushed against the spacer at the wall.

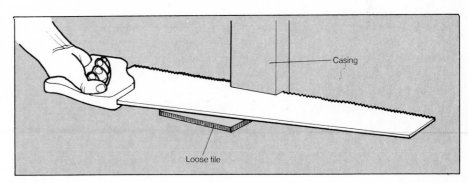

3. Cutting under doorjambs. The easiest way to get a tight fit under the casing around doors is to cut it with a saw resting on a tile to gauge the correct depth.

FINISHING THE JOB

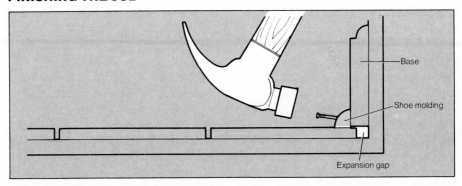

Replace the molding around the floor, nailing first the base molding and then the base shoe. The shoe, as shown, is nailed into the base molding, not the tile.

Laying Masonry and Stone Floors

Masonry comes in two types: man-made bricks and finished or rough-hewn stones. Bricks that are made especially for floors are known as "pavers." They come in full size, or in splits for lighter weight where structural problems would be created by the weight of full size. If you are not going to lay masonry on a concrete slab at ground level, you should consult a building expert for advice on how to reinforce the substructure that is to hold the weight of the floor.

Brick may be laid either with mortar or without. Mortarless brick can be laid on a subfloor of either wood (covered with felt paper) or concrete. Bricks laid on wood should not exceed $1^5/_8$ inch in thickness, but any thickness may be laid on concrete. Since splits are not as heavy or solid as full size bricks, they should be laid in mortar to secure them. When laying bricks on concrete, the slab must be clean and dry but irregularities can be eliminated by mortar.

Rough-hewn masonry exerts a tremendous weight and should be laid over concrete. Make sure the slab is clean so that the mortar will bond to it. In laying stone masonry, creative decisions must be made as you go along to achieve a pleasing arrangement of stones, since they must be pieced together puzzle-fashion. You will also have to vary the thickness of the mortar to keep the tops of the stones level. In addition, some stones will have to be trimmed to fit, and you must also keep the joints between stones approximately equal in width.

Most masonry flooring has a porous surface that must be sealed with a sealer recommended by your building supplier. When the surface is tightly sealed, your floor can be maintained by sweeping and occasionally damp mopping with a mild detergent. Stone floors are hard and durable in themselves but a light coat of wax heightens the texture of particular stones and deepens their character. Not all wax is "friendly" to masonry, so check the instructions on the label.

LAYING WORK LINES

Determine whether your room has square corners by placing tile or square masonry flush up into the corner. Stretch a chalkline along the outside edge of each tile and snap it. If the wall is crooked you will find variations in the distance between the chalkline and the wall. A variation less than the width of a mortar or grout joint will not matter. If the corner of the chalklines is a true 90° angle, snap a second chalkline parallel to the first and two joint widths from it. Do the same on an adjoining wall.

LAYING MORTARLESS BRICK

On a wood floor, first lay two layers of 15-pound felt paper. If your wall is straight you will not need to lay work lines. You can use the baseboard along the wall as your guide. If the wall is not straight, lay work lines a little less than one brick length or width (depending on how you are laying them) from the wall. Lay the first run of bricks on this line. When the floor is completely laid, you can go back and cut bricks to fit this border. Lay each brick butted tightly to the adjoining bricks. You can walk on the bricks as they are laid. To make each run of bricks as straight as possible, reset the work lines every course or two. To keep the runs straight, you may adjust the joints between bricks now and then, but remember that the best floor will have very tight butt joints.

When you have finished the border, spread fine sand over the entire surface and sweep it diagonally into the joints between the bricks. Repeat this twice, allowing two or three days between sandings. When the floor has dried completely, apply several coats of masonry sealer to lock the sand in place.

LAYING WORK LINES

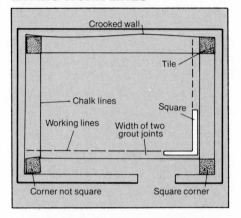

Snap a chalkline between the outer edges of two square tiles or pieces of masonry set in the corners; use square to find adjacent lines.

LAYING MORTARLESS BRICK

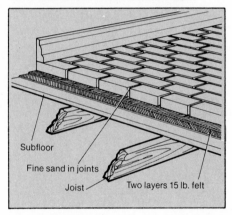

Over either concrete or wood, lay two thicknesses of 15-pound felt building paper to provide a bed for the brick.

SPLITTING A BRICK

You will need a kind of chisel called a brickset to cut bricks to fit along the edges of a floor. Score the brick, then break.

LAYING MORTARED BRICKS

After you have laid your work lines, lay a course of bricks dry for a trial run. Then soak the bricks in water for three or four minutes. Apply a spread of mortar over a workable section of slab along the work line. Lay the first brick in the center and work out. Place a wood spacer between bricks to assure equal mortar joints. Make sure the surface is level.

MORTARING THE JOINTS

Mortar the joints after the brick has set for twenty-four hours. Use a small trowel and pack the mortar in tightly. When it is hard enough to hold an impression, carve each joint with a convex tool such as a jointer or a dowel. After several hours wipe up mortar tags with a burlap sack.

LAYING ROUGH-HEWN MASONRY

Begin in a corner opposite your supply of masonry and mortar and an exit. Lay a couple of pieces dry to determine how they will sit. Then sprinkle the slab so it is damp, and apply mortar evenly for two or three stones. Tap each stone in place with a rubber mallet and check to see if it is level with neighboring stones.

TRIMMING STONES

Trim stones to fit along walls and other obstructions. Trimming is done by laying a stone over its neighbor and marking lines where it will be trimmed. Score it with a brickset or stonemason's chisel. Prop the stone and strike the scored line with brick-set and hammer.

GROUTING THE JOINTS

After the stones have set for twenty-four hours, prepare grout (three parts sand and one part cement) and mix it to a soupy consistency, not as stiff as mortar. Pour it from a coffee can or trowel it into the joints between the stones. With a wet sponge, wipe up grout that spills onto the stone surface. Before the grout sets hard, smooth it with a trowel. When the floor is completely dried, finish with a sealer recommended by your building supplier.

LAYING MORTARED BRICK

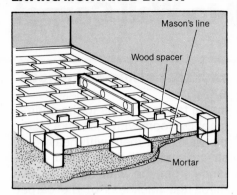

Spread mortar over a manageable area, then set bricks, using wood spacers to keep a correct distance apart.

MORTARING THE JOINTS

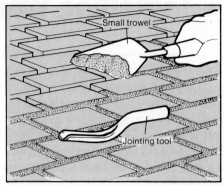

Fill between the bricks, packing the mortar tightly with a trowel. When the mortar has dried sufficiently, shape with a jointing tool.

LAYING ROUGH-HEWN MASONRY

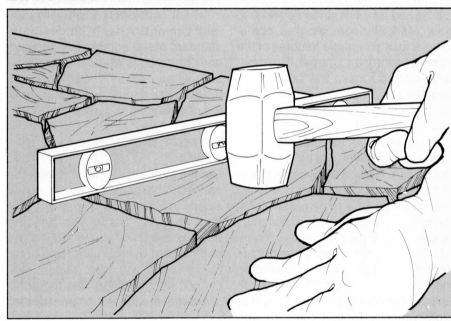

Spread only enough mortar to cover an area that will hold two pieces of stone. Set the pieces in the mortar and tap gently with a mallet as needed to seat them. Check the work with a level frequently and adjust the stone for level by further tapping.

TRIMMING STONES

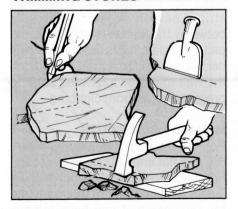

Score a stone along the line where it must be trimmed, using a brickset. Put the stone on a piece of board and knock off the excess.

GROUTING THE JOINTS

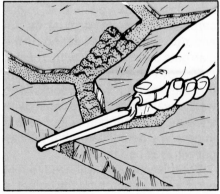

Fill between stones with mortar mixed to a soupy consistency so that it can be poured into the joints; smooth it with a trowel.

STEP 3

The drawing on the right shows the sequence of stretching and hooking the carpet onto the tackless strip. Follow it as you work to find the correct placements for the knee-kicker and power stretcher. You will use three techniques: "hooking" (with the knee-kicker), "stretching" (with the power stretcher), and "rolling" (pressing the edge of the carpet by hand and hammer onto the back row of nails on the strip.

1) Hook corner A. 2) Stretch toward B. 3) Roll edge A-B. 4) Stretch toward C and hook. 5) Roll edge A-C. 6) Stretch toward D and hook. 7) Hook edge C-D. 8) Stretch toward edge B-D and hook.

Check the carpet to make sure it is evenly stretched. If the seams or the pattern are distorted, unhook the carpet and restretch it.

FINISHING THE JOB
STEP 1

The last step is to trim the carpeting between the wall and the tackless strip. Use a rented wall trimmer to make the job easy. If you can't get one, a utility knife will do. First adjust the trimmer to the thickness of the carpet. Slice downward into the carpeting at a 45° angle, leveling it out when you reach the floor, leaving just enough edging to tuck down into the gap between the strip and the wall. Make cuts in corners and around obstacles with a utility knife.

STEP 2

Use a putty knife, trowel, or screwdriver to push the edge of the carpet into the gully between the tackless strip and the wall. If the carpet edge bunches up and creates an unsightly bulge, trim it a bit to make it shorter.

STEP 3

The final step is to clamp the carpet to the binder bars at the doorways and any place you have installed them. Trim the carpet with a utility knife so it will fit under the binder bar. Tuck it in under the metal lip. Then, with a block of wood and a hammer, gently tap the lip down over the carpet edge so that it holds firmly.

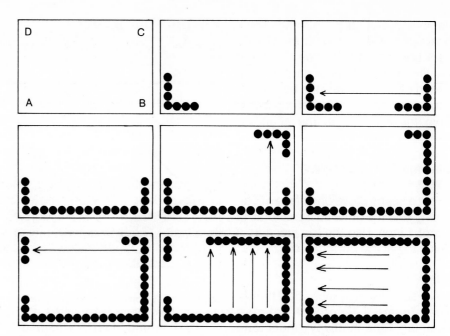

3. Stretching sequence. Carpeting should be stretched in the sequence shown above. The circles indicate points of attachment and the arrows indicate the direction of stretching.

FINISHING THE JOB

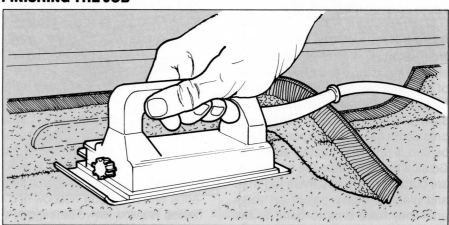

1. Trimming the carpet. Cut the carpet at the wall with a rented wall trimmer, or a utility knife if a trimmer is not available. Leave enough carpet to be tucked against the wall.

2. Tucking in the carpet. Push the carpet down with a screwdriver or putty knife between the tackless strip and the wall.

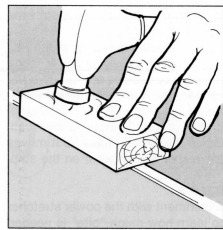

3. Clamping with binder bars. Slip the carpet into binder bars at doorways and close bars with gentle taps on a wood block.

Repairing Carpets

There are two secrets to making carpet repairs: work slowly and patiently and have saved extra scraps of carpet from any installation. If you have no scraps, take patches for holes from unseen areas like the back of closets or under furniture you never move.

Small areas can often be repaired by setting in new tufts with a tuft-setter as shown below. Tuft-setters are available from carpet dealers.

To patch a rip that has not damaged the backing, fold back the torn section and apply latex seam adhesive to the backing. Tuck the torn part back into the carpet and press it with a smooth rolling action using a large bottle. If adhesive oozes up, clean it with water and detergent. When the adhesive has dried, replace any loose or missing pile as explained below.

If the rip goes through the backing, release the tension, using a knee-kicker in the corner nearest the rip. Lift the corner off the tacks and roll it back. With thread to match the color of the pile, mend the rip with 1-inch-long stitches spaced ¼ inch apart. Depending on the direction of the rip, run the stitches either parallel to rows of pile or perpendicular to them. Check frequently to make sure you are not stitching the pile down on the face of the carpet. Then work in a thin, wavy strip of adhesive and cover the wet backing with a paper towel. Roll the carpet back to the wall and rehook it on the tacks.

Always keep an eye out for matching the pattern of any carpeting and for keeping patches and tufts of pile tilted in the same direction as the rest of the carpet.

PATCHING A SMALL AREA
Cut the damaged pile down to the backing with a cuticle scissors. Pick out pile stubs with tweezers. Apply a little latex cement to the backing. Set replacement tufts, cut from the edge of a piece of scrap carpet, into the

cement. For loop pile, poke one end of a long piece of yarn into backing and make successive loops, adjusting the length accordingly.

PATCHING A LARGE AREA
STEP 1
Reduce the tension slightly with a knee-kicker and tack down a strip of carpet into the floor. Do this on all four sides of the damaged area.

STEP 2
Cut a patch slightly larger than the damaged area, and cut a hole in the carpet around the damage ½ inch smaller than the patch. Match the pattern, if any, and pile and tack tem-

porarily one edge of patch into hole, letting the other sides overlap. Then cut the carpet so the patch will fit snugly. Remove the tacks and the patch.

STEP 3
Cut four strips of seam tape 1 inch longer than the sides. Coat with seam adhesive and place under the hole as shown. Insert an awl through the center of the patch; cup your other hand over the patch. Push the patch down and into the hole and off the awl. Press edges into seam tape and fluff up pile with your fingers. Do not remove the four scrap pieces for 5 hours.

PATCHING A SMALL AREA

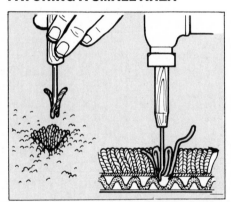

Remove pile down to the backing in the damaged area and use a tuft setter, and tufts cut from scraps of the same carpet, for repair.

2. **Cutting out the damage.** Cut around the damage so the hole is slightly smaller than the patch; trim using patch as a guide.

PATCHING A LARGE AREA

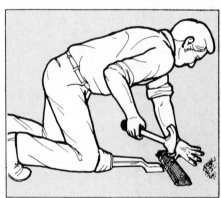

1. **Preparing the area.** Use a knee-kicker and strips of scrap carpet tacked upside down to slacken tension and isolate the damage.

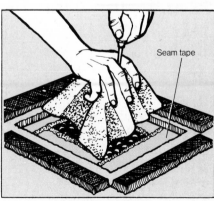

3. **Seating the patch.** Apply seam adhesive to strips of seam tape and slip them under the edges of the damaged area to hold the patch.

Laying Ceramic Tile Floors

Manufacturers have introduced many new kinds and styles of ceramic tile that make it easier for the average homeowner to tile a floor successfully. Make a scale drawing on graph paper including all the idiosyncracies of your floor plan so that a dealer can suggest the best materials and the right quantities. Be sure to order extra tiles for mistakes, cracked or chipped pieces, and for trimming. You'll also want to have a few on hand for repairs.

In deciding color and design, remember that floors with busy patterns or several colors tend to look smaller. Small tiles give the illusion that the floor is larger; large tiles make the floor look smaller. Similarly, dark colors shrink the floor visually, while light colors expand it.

There are several different types of adhesives, but manufacturers recommend specific kinds for their tiles. Most do-it-yourselfers use a "thin-set" rather than a heavy mortar base. Thin-set adhesives come with organic, cement, and epoxy bases. Organic bases, called mastics, are water-resistant and tend to irritate the lungs and skin while being used. Cement bases are excellent for applying tiles to concrete or masonry subfloors. Epoxy is the strongest base, having high bonding power, but it hardens quickly and is therefore trickier to work with; it, too, can be irritating to the skin.

Ceramic tiles should be installed only over very sound subfloors. Concrete is the best subfloor for them but it must be dry, clean, and free of holes. Some adhesives require that a sealer be laid on concrete before they can be spread. A wood base is suitable if the boards or panels are securely fastened to the joists. Remove old finishes and sand rough areas smooth. Sound resilient floors will take ceramic tiles, but resilient flooring that is cushioned is too soft and springy and should be removed.

WORK LINES AND BATTENS

Ceramic tile may be laid from the center of the room or, more traditionally, from one corner. Measure the room for work lines (see page 108). In addition to accurate work lines, it will help in laying individual ceramic tiles to install battens made from 1 × 2s or 1 × 3s. Nail them (or glue them in the case of a concrete subfloor) at right angles to each other along the two adjacent work lines. Be sure they form a perfect right angle.

SPACERS

Inserting spacers between individual tiles, as you lay them, makes it easier to maintain equal spacing of grout joints, imparting a more professional look to the finished room. Spacers can be made from splits of wood the size of the grout joints. These must be removed before grouting. If you buy molded spacers, you can leave them in and grout over them. The traditional method of spacing between tiles, used by professional tile setters for centuries, employs a spacing cord the thickness of the grout joint. Soak the cord or rope in water and lay it damp between the tiles as you set them. Lift off after adhesive sets.

BEDDING TILES

After you have laid several rows of adjoining tiles, it becomes important to bed them correctly so that they are level with each other. An easy way to do this is to make a beating block. Use a block of wood large enough to cover several tiles at once and cover it with a padding of felt or thin carpet. Then beat in the tiles by laying the block over several rows and tapping it firmly with a hammer. Slide the beating block along and beat in the others to achieve a smooth, even surface. Every so often use a carpenter's square to check positioning and a level to check the bedding. Make adjustments as necessary.

USING BATTENS AS GUIDES

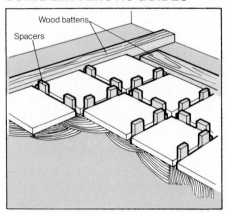

Find the perimeter work lines and nail straight pieces of batten (1 × 2s or 1 × 3s) along the lines; butt tiles against them.

SPACING WITH CORD

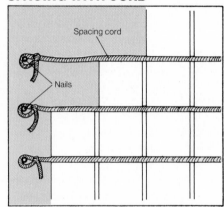

One way to space tiles is to use pieces of wood or molded spacers (top picture); another is to use dampened cord or rope of the desired thickness.

BEDDING TILES

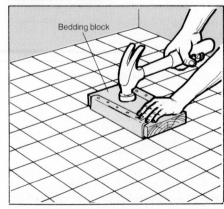

When laying individual tiles, seat them firmly into the adhesive by tapping on a bedding block covered with padding like old carpet.

DRY RUN

After you have snapped your chalklines along the intersection at the center of the room to be tiled, it's best to lay out the tiles or sheets of tile in a dry run. Sometimes, by adjusting the grout joint slightly between each tile, you can avoid having to cut tiles to border the wall.

SPREADING ADHESIVE

Use a notched trowel to spread the adhesive. The manufacturer's suggestion on the label will tell you what size trowel to use. Note carefully the open time you have to work with the adhesive before it has dried. Spread about a square yard to start. Always spread the adhesive just up to the chalklines with enough left exposed to guide you in laying tiles.

LAYING TILES

When laying tiles individually, place each one where it is to go and wiggle it with a gentle twisting motion to get it into place. Butt it up against the battens, insert a spacer, and lay the next tile. If you discover that they are running out of line with each other, wiggle them into position rather than lifting them off the adhesive.

MAKING CUTS
STEP 1

In the photo right, the sheet tile was laid over the toilet hole in a bathroom floor. While the adhesive was still wet, the required cut was made with a utility knife and the unnecessary portion removed.

STEP 2

To patch the areas around the toilet hole use nippers; for more intricate cuts, make a cardboard template and trace the shape onto the tile.

LAYING THE SADDLE

Cut off the bottom of the door if necessary. Apply adhesive to the floor and the bottom of the saddle. Allow for equal spaces on each side to let the wood door frame expand and a space for a grout joint between the saddle and the tile floor.

DRY RUN

Avoid messy problems by placing tile (sheet tile here) on the dry floor to check for fit and spacing—before applying the adhesive.

LAYING TILES

Small tiles are available bonded to a webbing so they can be laid as sheets. Larger tiles must be laid individually.

2. Finishing the cut. Use tile nippers to cut tiles separated from the sheet for fitting around the edges of the opening.

SPREADING ADHESIVE

Spread adhesive evenly—leaving work lines visible—with a notched trowel that meets the adhesive manufacturer's specifications.

MAKING CUTS

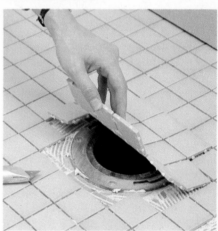

1. Roughing out a cut. This sheet was laid over a drain pipe, then the backing cut with a utility knife to rough out the opening.

LAYING A SADDLE

If you are finishing a doorway with a saddle, put it in place with adhesive before cutting tiles to fill the border.

SEALING UNGLAZED TILE

Remove the spacers used to position the tiles and be sure there is no dried adhesive on their surface. Remove any adhesive between tiles that would make the joint too shallow for grouting. Let the tiles set for the length of time recommended by the manufacturer of the adhesive you have used. Tiles can break very easily if they are walked upon at this stage. When they have completely set, apply a sealer.

CAULKING

Joints that are larger than your established grout joint should be caulked, especially around the walls in a bathroom or any areas that will be subject to prolonged wetness.

GROUTING
STEP 1

Apply grout with a rubber-faced float or a squeegee by spreading the grout over the face of the tiles and forcing it down into the joints between them. Be sure the joints are filled.

STEP 2

When the surface is well covered with grout, scrape off the excess with a squeegee or float. Work diagonally across the tiles and as you remove the excess check to make sure the joints are filled and there are no air pockets.

STEP 3

Remove the remaining grout with a sponge soaked in clean water. Wipe the tiles and rinse the sponge frequently, changing the water when it gets dirty. Get the tiles as clean as possible. Then wait about thirty minutes for a thin haze to appear and wipe it off with a soft cloth.

TOOLING

The grout is slightly rough when it dries. For a smoother look, tool it with a jointer or the end of a toothbrush. Some grouts take two weeks to cure; check the length of time suggested by the manufacturer. Put plywood over the floor to keep from stepping on new grout. When cured, the grout should be sealed.

SEALING UNGLAZED TILE

Unglazed tile absorbs stains and should be sealed with a sealant manufactured for that purpose, applied with a polyurethane roller.

GROUTING

1. Applying the grout. Spread grout across the tiles with a rubber float, pressing the grout into the spaces between tiles.

3. Cleaning the tiles. After the bulk of the excess grout is removed, clean the floor with a sponge, rinsing it frequently.

CAULKING

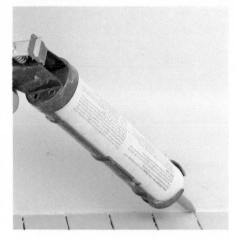

Use silicone caulking compound in a caulking gun to fill gaps between walls and floor and especially between a tub and the floor.

2. Removing the excess. Work diagonally across the floor, removing the grout from the surface with the float.

TOOLING

Smooth the grout between tiles with any rounded tool—the handle of a toothbrush works well—leaving a slight depression.

Installing Hardwood Flooring

Putting in a hardwood floor is a job that requires thorough knowledge of the process and a certain expertise in handling wood. If you are doing this project for the first time, study the procedure in detail, and discuss it with your lumber dealer.

Assuming the substructures are sound and sturdy, the subfloor must be adequately prepared to receive the new flooring. A wooden floor will make a good subfloor if there are no seriously damaged boards. Drive down all nails flush, correct any bowed boards, replace badly warped or split boards. With a resilient tile floor, be sure the tiles are all fixed tightly; replace or re-cement any loose ones. If a wooden or tile floor is badly damaged, lay a new subfloor.

Concrete makes a good subfloor if it is dry. A moisture barrier—a thin sheet of polyethylene sandwiched between sleepers made of 2×4s— will keep out dampness that could rot the floor.

When ordering boards judge the quality by standards set by the National Oak Flooring Manufacturers Association. In order of decreasing quality they are: clear, select, No. 1 common, No. 2 common. The standards are determined by color, grain, and imperfections, such as streaks and knots. When ordering 3/4-$\times$ 2¼-inch boards, multiply the number of square feet in the room by 1.383 to determine the amount of board feet you will need including wastage. For other size boards, ask your dealer how to compute the quantity.

To prepare the room, remove the shoe moldings, the baseboards (numbering them so you can replace them in the same sequence), radiator grates, and floor vents. Also lay a piece of new floor on top of the old near the door, to see how much of the door may need to be shaved off to permit an unobstructed swing. Allow for the height of the threshold, if there will be one.

LAYING WORK LINES

After you have laid asphalt-felt building paper (see below), it is important to lay work lines based on either a wall that is square or on the center of the room. First mark the joist lines on the building paper with chalk. Next find the midpoints of the two walls that are parallel to the joists and snap a chalkline between them. From this line, measure equal distances to within about ½ inch of the end wall where you will begin laying boards. Snap a chalkline between these two points and let this be your work line for the first course of boards regardless of how uneven the wall behind it may be. Any gap between the first course and the wall can be filled with boards trimmed to fit or the baseboard and shoe molding will cover it. If the room is square, expansion stripping made of cork can be added before you replace the baseboards, or the boards can be started against the wall.

REVERSING DIRECTION

If you intend to lay boards in hallways or closets that open off the room, you will have to butt two boards, groove end to groove end, at the transition point. To reverse tongue direction, place a slip tongue, available from flooring dealers, into the grooves of the last course of boards nailed down and slip over it the grooves of the boards that will reverse the tongue direction. Then nail the reversed boards into place, driving the nails through the tongues, and proceed as usual.

FRAMING BORDERS

Obstacles such as fireplace corners should have a professionally finished look. This can be done with a miter box to saw boards at 45° angles to make the corners of the frame. You'll have to remove the tongues from any boards that will run perpendicular to the flooring or that must butt against hearth stones.

LAYING WORK LINES

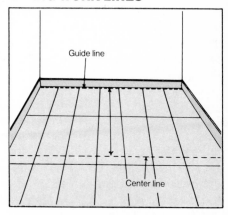

Establish a work line, about ½ inch from one wall, parallel to the center line by measuring from both sides of the center line.

REVERSING DIRECTION

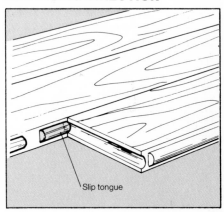

Where you must change the direction of the tongue-and-groove pattern, butt boards groove to groove with a slip tongue between.

FRAMING BORDERS

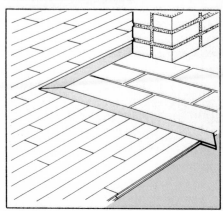

Treat flooring as you would molding to border such areas as a hearth. Miter the boards and rip off the tongue where necessary to fit.

LAYING BUILDING PAPER

Remove the baseboard and shoe moldings and tack down any loose boards in the subfloor, setting all exposed nail heads. Over the sub-floor lay a covering of 15-pound asphalt-saturated felt building paper. Butt the seams tightly and cut the edges flush with the walls. Nail around the edges of each sheet. When it is in place, mark the position of the joists on it with chalk.

ALIGN A STARTER COURSE

Along the work line drawn ½ inch from the wall, lay out the starter course (the first row of boards) the full length of the wall. Drill holes along the back edges of the boards and over the joists, slightly smaller than the nails. Then face nail.

NAILING THROUGH A TONGUE

Pre-drill holes through the tongue of the first course of boards into the joists. Then drive in finishing nails and set them. The first few rows of boards will be too close to the wall to use a power nailer.

LAYING A FIELD

Lay out several courses of boards in the way you intend to install them. Plan six or seven rows ahead in an attractive layout. Stagger the end joints so that each joint is more than 6 inches from the joints in the adjoining rows. If you can't find pieces the right length, you may have to cut pieces to fit at the end of each row. Try to fit your pattern so that no end piece is shorter than 8 inches. Leave ½ inch between the end of each row and the wall. When you have laid out a field of rows, begin to fit and nail.

FITTING AND NAILING

As you lay each row, use a scrap of board as a tapping block. Don't hit the block too hard or you may damage the tongue. To keep from marring the board with the hammer when you nail, do not hammer nails flush into the tongue. Instead leave the nail head exposed, place the nailset sideways over it, and drive the nail home by hammering the nailset. Then use the tip of the nailset to hammer the nail flush into the board.

LAYING BUILDING PAPER

Cut building paper to fit closely around obstructions, tack down sheets, then mark joist locations on the paper.

NAILING THROUGH THE TONGUE

1. Pre-drilling. The tongue is fairly delicate so pre-drilling is advisable. Drill nail holes at the places marked for joists.

LAYING A FIELD

Plan the pattern of the boards by laying out several courses. Seat boards against one another by angling them into position.

ALIGNING THE FIRST BOARDS

Using the work lines as a guide, position the first course of boards and pre-drill, then face nail them in position and set the nails.

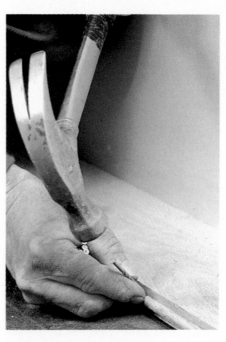

2. Driving the nails. Put the nail into the drill hole and drive it most of the way home; then finish with a nailset.

FITTING AND NAILING

Fit boards together tightly by using a scrap piece of flooring as a tapping block to protect the tongue of the board being fitted.

USING A POWER NAILER

When you reach the fourth row or so of boards, you will have enough room to use a rented power nailer. Begin about 2 inches from the wall and slip the power nailer onto the tongue of the last board laid. Hold·the new board in position by placing your heel over it. Strike the plunger with a rubber-headed mallet, hard enough to drive a nail through the tongue and into the floor. Drive a nail into each joist and into the subfloor halfway between joists. Place a scrap of board under the nailer to keep it from marring the board.

CUTTING AROUND OBSTACLES

When you come to an obstacle such as a radiator or a corner, trial-fit the boards, measure carefully, making a cardboard template if necessary to transfer the cut onto the board. Decide whether you should save the tongue or groove. Clamp the board to a workbench and cut to fit with a hand power saw.

DOORWAYS

To finish a doorway where the new floor will meet a floor that is lower, install a clamshell reducer strip by face nailing it. (The name comes from its rounded top that resembles half a clamshell.) The reducer strip is made so that one side will fit over the tongue of the adjoining board. The strip can also be butted to meet boards that run perpendicular to the doorway. The photo right shows a doorway between two floors of equal height where a board has been installed perpendicular to the floorboards by removing the tongue.

THE FINAL BOARD

For gaps of more than ½ inch between the final board and the wall, remove the tongue sides of as many boards as you need, cut them to width, and wedge them into place with a pry bar. Hold them tightly with the pry bar by placing your foot on the bar while its hooked end pulls the filler board up tightly against the last board. Face nail these last boards and then replace the baseboards and shoe moldings.

USING A POWER NAILER

A power nailer which can be rented from most home centers makes laying a floor go much faster than hand nailing every board. When clear of the wall (a few courses of boards), seat the nailer over the edge of the board at a joist and strike the head sharply with a rubber mallet.

CUTTING AROUND OBSTACLES

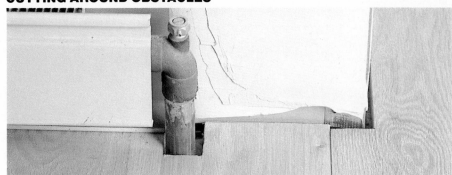

Corners, radiator pipes, and other obstacles require that boards be cut to fill in or fit around. Lay flooring up to the obstacle so that you can measure where the board to be shaped will actually lie. Slip the board to be cut alongside the adjacent board and measure for the cut.

DOORWAYS

To end this floor at a doorway, a board was cut to the width of the entrance and its tongue shaved off. The board was placed with the grooved edge facing in and screwed down through counterbored holes that were then filled with wood plugs cut from the same wood.

THE FINAL BOARDS

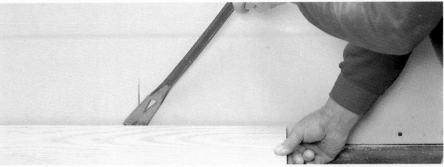

The last course of boards to be installed in a floor must be stripped of their tongues and face nailed. To get this last course tight against the rest of the floor, use a pry bar between the wall and the last course to wedge it into position.

Flooring is milled in great variety to meet your decorating needs—these relatively short boards draw attention to the floor.

Wood floors can be laid with seams tight as a drum for an unbroken surface or more loosely for a less formal look.

Short, uniform strips laid diagonally transform a floor into a showpiece. Skilled woodworkers can add fancy borders around the edges.

Parquet tiles appear fancy, but are easy to lay. Laid more like ceramic tile than plank flooring, they offer the elegance and durability of wood.

Ceramic tile is ideal for a kitchen floor. Take time to plan a pattern—this pattern was no more complicated to lay than one with no design.

(Above) If you're an artist, you can paint with bits of tile. Your work will be on display for a lifetime.

(Right) Tile is the flooring of choice for bathrooms because it is easy to keep germ-free and is waterproof.

(Below) Kitchen and bath are not the only places for tile—here a simple pattern of large tiles can make a room formal.

Sheet flooring need not be relegated to purely functional uses. The variety of patterns available makes it appropriate for any room.

Not all sheet flooring has a slick surface. This pattern imitates the appearance of a sisal mat without the cleaning problems.

Kitchens with sheet flooring are easy to clean and slightly more forgiving to objects dropped on them than tile or stone.

Wall-to-wall carpeting softens a room (and softens the sound of footfalls). Coordinate the color with your overall decorating scheme.

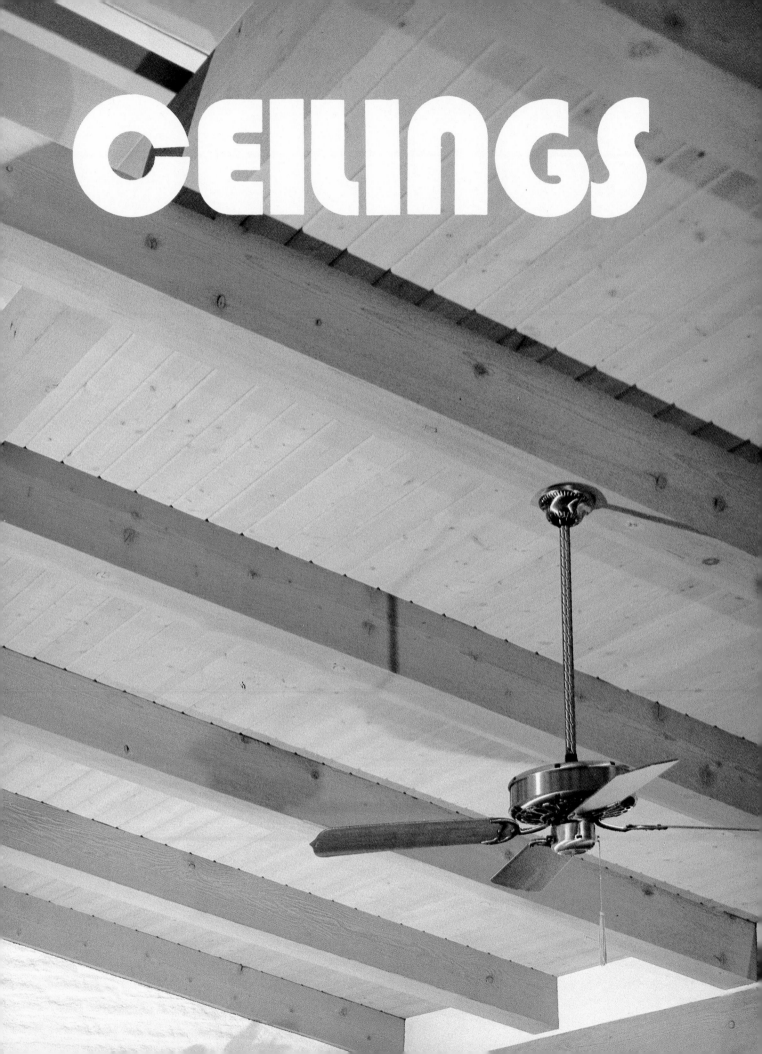

CEILINGS

Anatomy of Ceilings

Wallboard

Lath

Metal reinforcing lath

Tape

Plaster

Joists

Suspended ceiling system

Ceilings are probably the most neglected of the three surfaces that define a room. Because they are out of reach, they tend to be out of mind during consideration of a rehabilitation—but they are never out of sight. Sometimes a new coat of paint is all that is needed to make a ceiling a bright contribution to the overall impression of a room; but sometimes an entirely new ceiling is needed. Ceiling-mounted light fixtures often require opening the ceiling, working inside, then closing it up. The most extensive intrusion into the ceiling you can make is to open it right through to daylight. Skylight installations involve a lot of work, but the effect of natural light overhead in a room makes the effort really worthwhile.

Structure

In a sense, an ordinary plaster or wallboard ceiling has no structure—it is merely a surface attached to the bottom of the floor above. Another way to consider the structure of a ceiling is that it is the same as the structure of a floor. Either lath and plaster or wallboard is attached to the undersides of the joists that tie the walls of the house together. As a house settles, these joists may slip slightly out of line causing an uneven ceiling. This problem is most easily corrected by installing a new surface onto furring strips that have been shimmed level, or by suspending a ceiling on a grid system hanging from the original ceiling. Both procedures are discussed below.

The inside of a ceiling is most important in any lighting installations because joist location often determines where you can install a fixture; bringing power to the fixture usually requires running wiring between joists. The job is easiest when you can work in an attic or crawl space that has no flooring at all or only rough flooring that can be removed and put back without harm.

If you are working on a ceiling below a finished floor, the damage to be caused by going in from above makes that approach impractical, and so you must cut into the ceiling and work from below. **Installing Ceiling Light Fixtures** (pages 149-153) gives directions for both situations as well as instructions for running wiring through finished ceilings and down walls to outlet boxes or switches. The procedures for **Installing Ceiling Fans** (page 154) is essentially the same as for light fixtures, differing mainly in the kind of support the fan requires.

The most involved ceiling project, **Installing Skylights** (pages 142-146), requires altering the structure of the ceiling by cutting joists to make an opening for a light well. The joists you cut are tied to other joists with headers that frame the opening. Adding a skylight also means, of course, cutting through the roof as well as cutting rafters and framing them off with headers.

Surface

You will be concerned with ceiling surfaces in new construction, or when a ceiling is in bad shape, or when the ceiling has never been finished, as in an unfinished basement or attic.

Finishing a Ceiling with Wallboard (pages 130-131) is the way to construct a plain ceiling suitable for painting or wallpapering. On an unfinished ceiling, wallboard is simply attached to the underside of the joists with adhesive and nails, then the seams are taped and plastered like seams on a wall. The only difference between covering a ceiling and a wall with wallboard is that working above your head is a good deal harder. If you are covering a finished ceiling with wallboard to conceal defects, you may need to level the existing ceiling with shimmed furring strips first. Again this work is essentially the same as preparing

walls for new surfaces.

Ceiling tile, often referred to as acoustic tile, now comes in a wide variety of colors and finishes. The tiles are far easier to manage than sheets of wallboard. **Covering Ceilings with Tile** (pages 132-133) is a two-step operation: attaching furring strips to the ceiling, then stapling the tiles to the furring. Unfinished ceilings are easier to cover with tile, but finished ceilings can be tiled either on furring strips or, if the surface is flat and clean, attached directly to the ceiling with adhesive.

The panels in a suspended ceiling sit in a grid system that hangs from wires attached to the joists or ceiling above. **Installing a Suspended Ceiling** (pages 134-137) is a straightforward task, once you have established the work lines that determine the location of the grid elements. If you like, you can include illuminated panels in the ceiling.

If you are finishing a ceiling, you should consider whether soundproofing is necessary. The easiest way to soundproof a ceiling is to quiet the floor above with a carpet, but that will take care of impact noise only—itself no small matter. **Soundproofing Ceilings** (pages 138-139) deals with both unfinished and finished ceilings.

Finishing Attic Ceilings (pages 140-141) confronts a set of problems different from finishing basement ceilings. In an attic you have the choice of following the roof line for an open cathedral ceiling, or of putting up collar beams from which to hang a flat ceiling.

If you have removed a bearing wall and have added a beam, you can disguise it by adding other beams with **Making and Installing False Beams** (page 147). To repair breaks in a ceiling inside which you have had to work, and to repair other damage, **Repairing Ceiling Damage** (page 148) gives you instructions for both plaster and wallboard.

STEP 5

Starting with the joists at either end of the ceiling, put a screw eye into every fourth joist at each chalk mark. Twist a piece of suspension wire through each screw eye so that it hangs down 6 inches below the ceiling line. Cut runners so that they cross the strings exactly at a notch that will accept a cross T (these notches are 3 inches apart along the length of the runner) and hang from the wires as shown so that they just touch the strings. Check that the strings are taut and level as you work. Runners are to be butted, or attached, to span long distances, depending on the product.

STEP 6

Using the strings as guides, attach the cross Ts between the runners. Along the wall, cut the cross Ts to fit between the inside of the wall angle and the runner. Attach the cross Ts to the runner and sit the other ends on the lower lip of the wall angle.

STEP 7

When the grid system is complete, simply slide the panels through the grid at a diagonal and let them flop down into position, adjusting them as necessary. At the walls, cut panels to fit with a utility knife. If you are installing illuminating panels (see next page), first bring power cables to the panels from a junction box in the ceiling. *Make sure power is off before attaching the cables at the junction box.* Get an extra pair of hands to raise the illuminating panel into position in the grid and wire the panel to the power cable. Then set the rest of the panels in place.

BOXING IN PIPES
STEP 1

If a pipe or duct intrudes below the level of the ceiling, you can box it in with members of the grid system or with framing (see below). To box pipes with the grid system, you will need U-shaped channel molding and extra wall angle, both twice the length of the box. Figure the box, or break as it is called, into your original layout plans and leave the ceiling

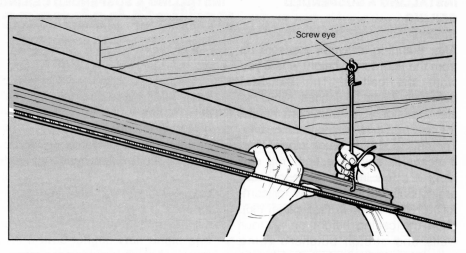

5. Hanging the runners. Attach screw eyes to every fourth joist at the point where the chalkline crosses it and twist wire through the eyes so that about 6 inches of wire hangs below the height of the wall angle. Attach the runners with the bottom edge at string level.

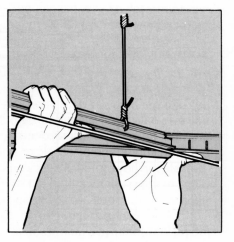

6. Setting the cross Ts. Install cross Ts in the notches of the runners, using the strings as guides for placement.

7. Installing the panels. Angle panels through the grid and set them in place, but install and wire any lighting panels first.

BOXING PIPES AND DUCTS

1. Hanging runners below the obstruction. Hang runners below the obstruction from wires attached above the edges of the main ceiling; use strings (as above) to mark the level. Attach the runners to wall angle with pop rivets through pre-drilled holes, where they meet the wall.

open at that point. Attach suspension wires to the ceiling along both edges of the gap and hang runners from them at least 3 inches lower than the pipe. Attach wall angle to hold runners where they meet the walls and fasten the runners to the wall angle at both ends with pop rivets (a pop riveter is an inexpensive tool available at any hardware store). Drill the pieces one at a time. Mark the wall angle and drill it, then mark through the holes onto the runners and drill them. Install cross Ts in the slots at the required intervals between the runners.

STEP 2
To keep the side panels in position, you must pop-rivet U-shaped channel molding to the runner at the edge of the break, and wall angle to the runner hanging directly below, as shown. Drill as described above. Cut panels to fit the sides of the break and install them separated by pieces of crossT cut to fit the channels.

INSTALLING ILLUMINATED CEILINGS
There are several ways to bring light through a suspended ceiling: you can buy pre-wired luminous panels that sit in the grid the way regular panels do; you can put fluorescent fixtures on the ceiling in one or more spots, with translucent plastic panels in the grid below; or you can run fluorescent tubing over the entire ceiling and suspend a ceiling composed entirely of translucent panels below. For long runs of fluorescent tubing, you can connect the fixtures end-to-end with special lock nuts and connectors available where you buy the fixtures.

The best size of fluorescent fixture to use in a luminous ceiling is a 4-foot length of 40-watt rapid-start lamp. To determine the number of lamps you need, sketch out the dimensions of the ceiling planning for the lamps to lie in parallel lines between 18 and 24 inches apart. (The narrower spacing gives a more even light, but is more expensive.) On both ends allow about 8 inches between the ends of the lines and the wall.

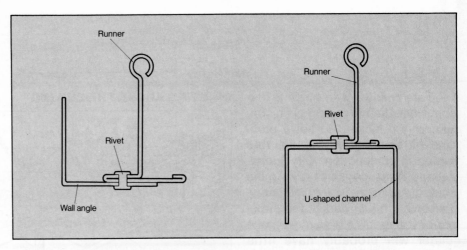

2. Attaching channels for vertical panels. Pop-rivet U-shaped channels to the runners, on either side of the gap in the main ceiling, and wall-angle to the runners hanging below in the configuration shown here. Panels cut to fit sit in these holders held in place by cut-down cross Ts.

MASKING WITH PANELING

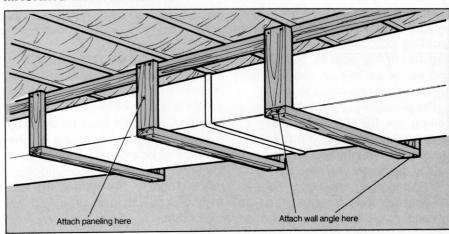

A break can also be masked with framing and paneling on the vertical surfaces. Frame around the obstruction as shown. Attach paneling to vertical faces and the wall angle to one edge. Slip a panel into the wall angle and attach on the other edge with wall angle.

FLUORESCENT LIGHTING FOR A LUMINOUS CEILING

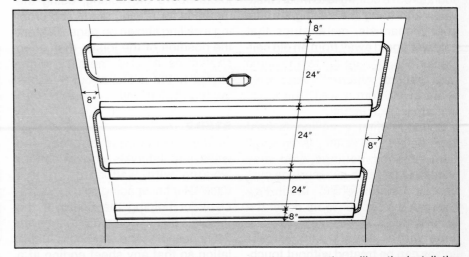

When you are putting up fluorescent tubes to illuminate an entire ceiling, the installation shown above is more efficient than individual rows of lights each connected to a junction box. The rows are connected with jumper cables.

Finishing Attic Ceilings

Finishing an attic is a relatively inexpensive way to add living space to a home. An attic offers attractions many basements can't—including access to natural light and natural ventilation. The walls and floors in an attic are essentially the same as in the rooms below (see *Framing in an Attic*, page 29) but ceilings are somewhat different. Before anything else, you must check the usable headroom in an attic. Seven feet is the minimum for a ceiling. Is the space large enough to convert?

Ceilings in attic conversions require measures different from those in the rooms below. Because all or some of a ceiling is attached to the inside of the roof, it must have provisions for stopping heat in all but perfect climates. If you don't insulate, you may wind up with an attic office or bedroom that is stifling on summer days and hard to keep warm in the winter.

There are variations in attic ceiling treatments in two basic types, a flat ceiling or a cathedral ceiling. The flat ceiling is built on collar beams that serve the same function in the ceiling as joists do in the rooms below. It follows the roof line to a knee wall and this creates odd angles to deal with where the ceiling meets the roof and the wall (see opposite page). You can use strings hung from nails to simulate such a ceiling to get a sense of what the space will look like, as you plan the conversion. The ceiling is to be insulated along the roof and between the collar beams.

A cathedral ceiling gives a sense of greater space and eliminates the need for ceiling framing. It is also looks good with sheet or plank paneling that goes on the same way as on walls, but with special provisions for insulation.

If your attic already has collar beams supporting the roof, you can still leave the ceiling open to the top of the roof. The beams can be used to support a storage platform.

PLANNING THE CONVERSION

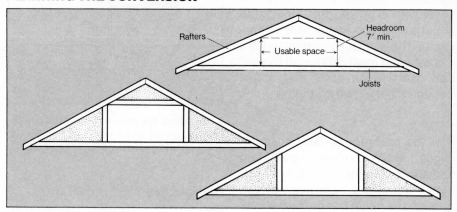

Measure the amount of floor space in an attic that falls under portions of the roof that are at least 7 feet high—this is the amount of livable space you have to work with. You can set the walls farther under the roof and use the lower space for storage or sleeping.

BUILDING A FLAT CEILING
STEP 1

Measure the height of the ceiling and mark it on the inside edge of opposing rafters, then measure between the outside edges of these rafters at the ceiling height to obtain the collar beam length. Cut 2 × 6s to that length less ½ inch, then measure the angle of the roof slope and cut the ends of each beam to fit. Attach the beams to the same side of each air of rafters by driving two 16-penny nails through the beam into the rafter, then two from the other side of the rafter. Toe nail blocking between the rafters to provide nailing surfaces for the flat ceiling and for the part of the ceiling that follows the roof line.

STEP 2

Check the insulation requirements for your area and buy batt or blanket insulation with the appropriate R-value and appropriate width. Fill the part of the floor under the eaves that will be walled off, taking care not to block the ventilation that is necessary to keep the attic dry. Staple blankets (vapor barrier facing in) or stuff batts between studs, between rafters, and between collar beams, making a snug fit where the ends of batts or blankets meet.

INSTALLING A FLAT CEILING

1. Installing collar beams. Mark opposing rafters for the height of the ceiling, measure the angle, and cut collar beams to fit.

2. Insulating the attic. If you build a flat ceiling, tack insulating batts between the beams before putting up wallboard.

PLASTERING OBTUSE ANGLES
STEP 1
If you have a reasonably steady hand and like handwork, you can hide the seams where a flat wall meets the roof line by sculpting it with joint compound (see *Taping and Plastering Wallboard*, pages 37-40). Spread on a fairly thick first coat with strokes perpendicular to the seam. Try to keep as regular a line as possible, feathering the edges and smoothing ridges between strokes. Let the first application dry and smooth it with sandpaper and a damp sponge.

STEP 2
Fill the angle with a second layer of compound, feathering the edges and smoothing the angle further. Allow to dry and sand as above. Finish with a few more coats.

WALLBOARD CATHEDRAL CEILINGS
If you are finishing an attic, insulate between the rafters as described above and cover with wallboard. Tape the seams and tape the peak of the ceiling as you would an inside corner.

PANELED CATHEDRAL CEILINGS
If you want to finish a ceiling with plank panels, especially effective in attic conversions, nail planks across rafters, fitting them as you would on a wall (see pages 53-55). At the peak, measure the angle at which the sides of the ceiling meet and bevel a plank to fit between the converging surfaces.

CATHEDRAL CEILING WITH EXPOSED COLLAR BEAMS
If the structure of your house requires the retention of existing collar beams for roof support, fit the ceiling surface around the beams. Collar beams below a cathedral ceiling can provide support for a sleeping loft, if the roof is high enough, or for storage.

PLASTERING OBTUSE ANGLES

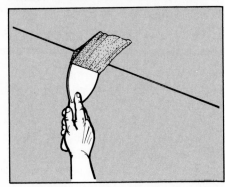

1. Covering the seam. Use compound without tape. Apply a fairly large amount to fill the seam and smooth it between panels.

2. Finishing the seam. Let the first application dry, then apply additional layers, smoothing and sanding until the seam is regular.

WALLBOARD CATHEDRAL CEILING

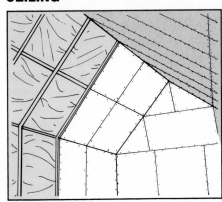

Insulate between the rafters and install the wallboard horizontally. You can install sheet paneling over the wallboard.

PLANK PANELED CATHEDRAL CEILING

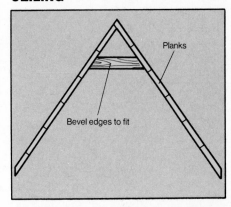

Planks

Bevel edges to fit

Panel the ceiling to within a few inches of the peak and bevel a filler strip to close the gap. Nail the strip to planks on either side.

CATHEDRAL CEILING WITH COLLAR BEAMS

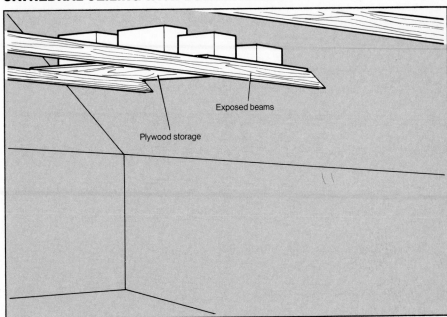

Exposed beams

Plywood storage

Existing collar beams must sometimes be left in place for structural reasons; check with a builder if you are not sure. Cut ceiling surface material to fit around beams for a cathedral ceiling. For storage, use ½-inch plywood for flooring between beams.

Installing Skylights

Bringing daylight in all its variations through a ceiling is an attractive way to light a room. A skylight can serve as a window to look through or as a light source at the top of a well that opens into the ceiling a few feet below. You can buy or build skylights that open for ventilation or units that are sealed. The job of installing a skylight is somewhat more complicated than other projects in this book, and you may want to get professional help. Whether you do it yourself or have the job done for you, read all the directions below to inform your planning and purchasing.

Skylights can be constructed from scratch and glazed at home, purchased as plastic domes, or other kinds of plexiglass and glass fittings, to be mounted on a curb you build and seal yourself, or purchased as prefabricated units that are installed directly on or through the roof. This section gives instructions for installing a purchased skylight on a curb. They can also be used together with the manufacturer's instructions for installing a prefabricated unit. Glazing your own skylight is outside the scope of this book; ask your glass dealer for the best sources of information.

Whether you build your own or buy a ready-made skylight, you will have to cut through the roof and the rafters below and frame around the opening, to keep the roof structurally sound. If there is a crawl space or an attic between the roof and the ceiling below, you must open the ceiling and frame and finish a light well up to the roof. In most cases, a skylight is set on the roof if it sits over a light well; where it opens through the roof directly into a room, it may sit in the opening or not, depending on the kind of unit. Prefabricated skylights usually come with instructions for specific models and dimensions that make planning easier.

To install a skylight you must work on the roof and in attic or crawl spaces below and that can be awkward (less difficult in the case of a flat roof or cathedral ceiling). Don't attempt the project if you aren't comfortable working on the roof; use ladder brackets (they hold a ladder along a roof from the peak) or toe board jacks (they hold planks along the roof) to ensure good footing. The nature of the space under the roof will dictate whether you should cut through the roof and work your way down, or cut up through the ceiling first.

When you plan the location of a skylight, try to determine the structure between the ceiling and roof at that point—you may want to change your plans to avoid a complicated framing problem. Also, put a piece of cardboard on the roof where the skylight will lie to check whether it looks all right from the outside. Check again later, with the actual skylight in place, but not attached, to be sure it looks straight.

Framing the walls of a light well is much like framing walls for rooms, except that the work may involve surfaces meeting at angles other than 90 degrees. Careful measuring and cutting of angles on framing members is the only extra work required.

Besides the skylight itself, you will need lumber to frame openings, finishing materials for a light well (if there is one), and roofing cement, metal flashing, and perhaps some extra shingles, for sealing the skylight at the roof. The work can be accomplished with ordinary carpentry tools: a circular saw (a reciprocating saw will make the job go faster), a stout chisel, and measuring tools including a level, plumb bob, and a sliding T-bevel (an adjustable straightedge for measuring angles).

BUILDING THE CURB

Curb-mounted skylights require the construction of a curb, a simple open box of lumber. The purpose of the curb is to elevate the skylight above the roof to permit sealing the roof around it. Use 2×6 lumber, unless otherwise specified in the manufac-

ANATOMY OF A SKYLIGHT

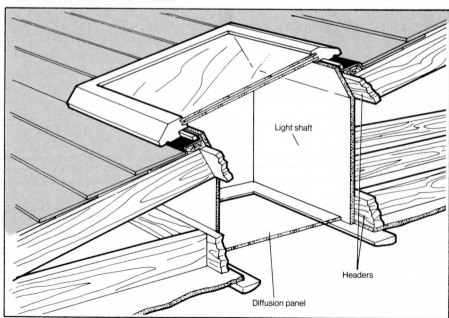

Light shaft

Headers

Diffusion panel

A skylight opening through a roof above an attic lets light into the room below through a light well. Installing the skylight and constructing the light well require cutting through the roof and ceiling below and framing and covering short walls between the openings.

turer's directions. Measure and cut the lumber, making sure it is not warped, so that the box will have the inside dimensions specified for the skylight. Pre-drill for nails at the butt joints and attach the pieces. To be sure that the curb is square, measure between opposite corners (diagonally across the curb); the two diagonals should be the same length. Keep the curb from getting out of square by tacking pieces of strapping across opposite corners, as shown.

ADDING FLASHING

Flashing consists of pieces of aluminum bent to fit against the curb and the roof to keep out water. You can bend flashing to fit all four sides of the curb, as shown here, or only the top and bottom, with the sides covered by step flashing (see page 145). The aluminum can be purchased from hardware stores or lumberyards and cut to fit with shears. Bend continuous flashing so that the piece at the bottom will fit onto the curb first, the sides will overlap the bottom piece, and the top will overlap the side pieces. To facilitate the bending process, make full size paper templates to be sure your bends will work; then use a straight 2×4 for the actual bending—working against the curb itself can be awkward. The flashing will be attached to the curb when the curb is mounted on the roof.

SITING THE SKYLIGHT

If you can work above the ceiling in an attic or crawl space, mark the center of the place where you want the skylight and drill a locater hole that can be found from above. Make adjustments as necessary to minimize framing around openings. Try to butt at least one side of the skylight to a rafter (see lower right). Outline the area to be cut from the roof (the inside dimensions of the curb) and, for a straight light well, locate the ceiling cut directly below with the plumb bob as shown. Mark through the roof with a drill at the corners of the opening. For other light wells (page 146), use a T-bevel and strings

BUILDING THE CURB

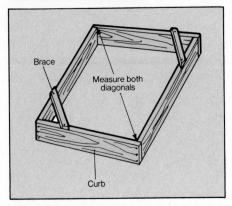

Lightly tack the curb together; check that it is square by measuring to see that both diagonals are the same and finish nailing.

SITING THE SKYLIGHT

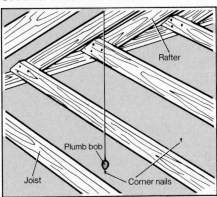

For light wells with straight walls, mark the position you want from below, then use a plumb bob to locate points on roof.

ADDING FLASHING

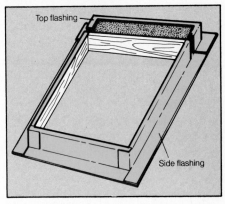

Bend the flashing to fit the curb according to the pattern shown here, then double check the fit on the roof before attaching.

MARKING THE ROOF

Drill up through the roof from the points marked and push 16-penny nails through the drill holes to indicate the skylight position.

HEADER PLANS

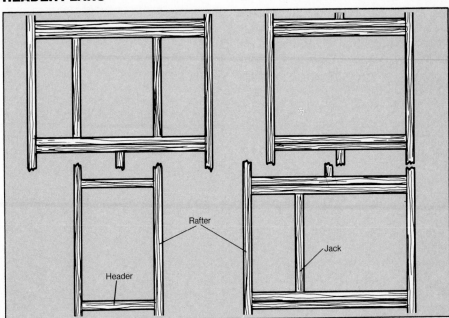

Rafters that are cut to make the opening for the skylight must be secured with headers. If the skylight does not fit between existing rafters, jack rafters must be installed to create framing of the required width. Double the headers when bridging more than two rafters.

to mark off the angles and the locations of the corners, running strings from the corners of the roof opening to the floor. If you can't work above the ceiling, probe through it to find joist locations and cut a section of the ceiling away between joists inside the area you will eventually remove. Measure and mark the cut in the roof, working through the hole in the ceiling. If this is not practical, cut an entry hole in the roof.

INSTALLING THE SKYLIGHT
STEP 1
Cutting the typical roof covered with shingles or shakes is a two-step process—first the roof covering is cut, then the roof sheathing beneath. The illustration at top left shows a cross section of the cuts required for mounting a skylight curb. The curb sits on the roof sheathing, supported by rafters and headers beneath. The inside dimension of the curb is the dimension of the actual hole through the roof; the material that covers the roof is cut back to the outside dimension of the curb. Put the curb in position on the four nails that indicate its proper location and mark its *outside* outline on the roof with chalk.

STEP 2
Use a circular saw with a combination blade to cut wood shingles, a chisel or utility knife to cut asphalt, shears to cut a tin roof. If using a circular saw, set the blade depth to the thickness of the shingles so as not to cut the sheathing beneath. Cut around the marked outline and pry up the roofing material. Save asphalt shingles for any patching necessary around the curb.

STEP 3
Snap chalklines between the nails marking the inside dimensions of the curb and cut the sheathing with a circular saw set to the depth of the sheathing. Pry the piece of sheathing off the rafters.

STEP 4
Measure 1½ inches in from the hole (3 inches for double headers) along the rafter or rafters that cross the

CUTTING THE ROOF

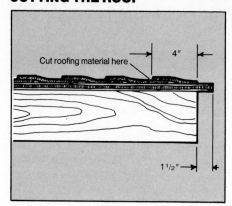

Roofing material and the rafters below are cut back to leave 1½ inches of roof sheathing for mounting the curb and for attaching headers.

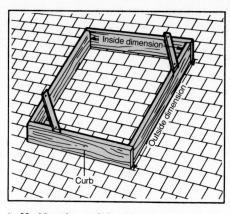

1. Marking the roof. Position the curb on the nails marking the location for the skylight and mark the inside and outside dimensions.

2. Cutting the roofing material. Cut all the way through shingles so the pieces outside the outline don't pull up with those inside it.

3. Cutting the sheathing. Pry out any nails along the line of the cut so the circular saw blade won't be damaged when cutting.

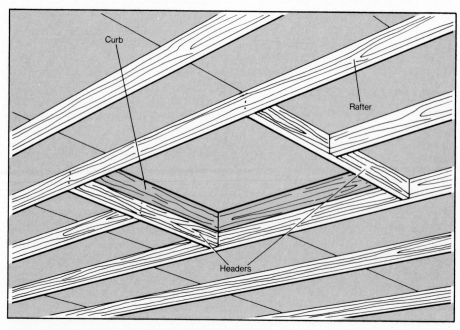

4. Framing the opening. After the curb is installed, support for the interrupted rafters is added below. The headers should be of lumber the same dimension as the rafters, attached with nails through rafters into header ends and into the ends of the cut rafters.

hole you've cut in the roof; mark them at right angles to the roof line with a square. Support the rafter you will cut, with props of 2×4s nailed to the side of the rafter on either side of the section to be removed, and make the cuts. The top flashing, then the curb, are installed before the headers so that the curb can be attached from below, through the sheathing where the headers will sit.

STEP 5
Pull the roofing material back about 4 inches from the hole in the roof, cover the sheathing beneath with roofing cement—spread it with a spatula—and slip the top flashing under it. Cover the flashing with a layer of roofing cement and lay the roofing material back down. Be generous with the roofing cement. Too much is no problem—too little is.

STEP 6
Set the curb in place. Use 12-penny nails to attach the curb from below, nailing up through the sheathing. Where the curb sits atop rafters, toe nail down through the curb into the rafters. If you are installing jack rafters, nail up through the sheathing where the jack rafters will sit. When the curb is secured, finish the framing between rafters below.

STEP 7
Attach the side flashing pieces, then the bottom piece, as described above. Nail the flashing to the top of the curb with 1-inch galvanized nails coated with caulking compound. Nail the roofing material back down on the roof outside the edge of the flashing, with roofing nails dipped in roofing cement, and cover the nail heads with more cement. You can also use small pieces of flashing material overlapped along the sides, shown right.

STEP 8
Apply sealant to the top of the curb and put the skylight in position on the curb. Attach it through the holes around the edge of the skylight with the size nails or screws specified by the manufacturer.

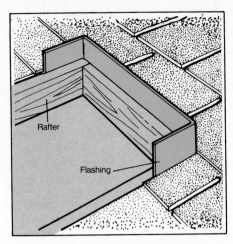

5. Installing the top flashing. Peel back the roofing material and cement the top flashing in place for the curb to fit into.

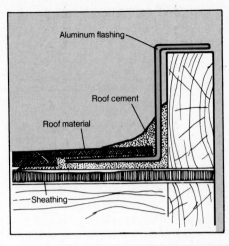

6. Seating the curb. The cement around the flashing and curb should seal the two to each other and to the roof to prevent leaks.

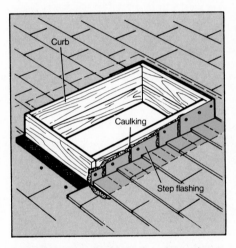

7. Adding step flashing. An alternative to bending long pieces of side flashing, step flashing pieces must overlap by 2 inches.

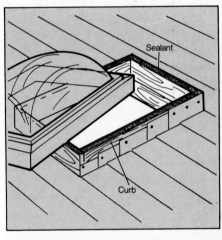

8. Seating the skylight. The skylight is set into a waterproof silicone sealant spread in a wavy bead along the top of the curb.

SETTING A SELF-FLASHING SKYLIGHT

Installation of a self-flashing skylight with a built-in curb is the same as for a skylight curb. Roofing material is cut back to the outside dimension of the skylight, then roofing cement is spread around the hole in the roof and the skylight set into it and nailed down. Roofing cement is applied over the flashing and shingles nailed over it.

FRAMING THE LIGHT WELL
STEP 1

Building the walls for a light well is a straightforward framing job but the angles involved are usually different from those in ordinary wall construction. The easiest situation is a light well descending straight down from a flat roof—here you have all right angles to work with. In the other situations shown at right, some studs are cut to fit the slope of the roof line or the flare of the light well. Cut away the ceiling surface at the points you marked (see page 143) to expose the joists above. Tack lengths of 2×4 across several joists, about a foot back from each side of the cuts you must make in them, to keep them from bowing down. Measure back from the edge of the hole in the ceiling a distance equal to the width of the headers you will install on either side of the hole. Use lumber the same dimension as the joists for the headers. If the light well is flared, cut the joists at the angle of the flare; stretch strings from the corners at the top of the well to mark these angles. Frame in the hole in the ceiling as you did the hole in the roof.

STEP 2

Sketch plans for the walls of the light well. They have top and bottom plates as in an ordinary stud wall. In the example shown here, the walls perpendicular to the roof joists are constructed square and are secured to the roof joists by nailing through a wedge as long as the top plate made by ripping a 2×4 to fit the angled gap. Construct these end walls first, then nail them in place.

STEP 3

The side walls shown here are built with studs angled at the top to conform to the angle of the roof line. The angle at the top of the studs is the same for all and it is most easily cut in an adjustable miter box. Set the box for the correct angle (double check it) and cut all the pieces at the same time. Measure the height of each stud carefully for a tight fit. Corners are built as for any stud wall (see page 27).

TYPES OF LIGHT WELLS

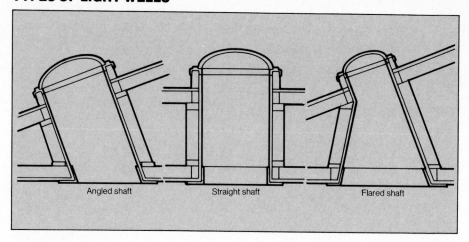

Angled shaft   Straight shaft   Flared shaft

Straight-walled light wells are the easiest to construct; angled walls are demanding and require skill. If you want a flared well, you may wish to work with a professional, doing the skylight installation yourself and leaving the difficult framing job to the expert.

ATTACHING STRAIGHT END WALLS

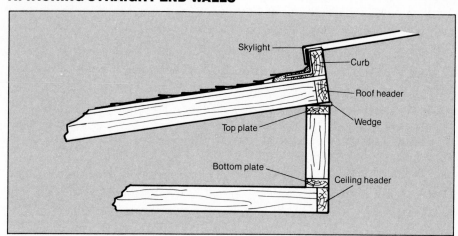

A straight end wall is simply a short stud wall with a wedge between the top plate and the rafters. To cut the wedge, measure the angle of the roof line and set the blade of a table saw, or the shoe of a circular saw, to that angle and rip a piece of 2×4. Tack this to the top plate.

COMPLETING THE LIGHT WELL

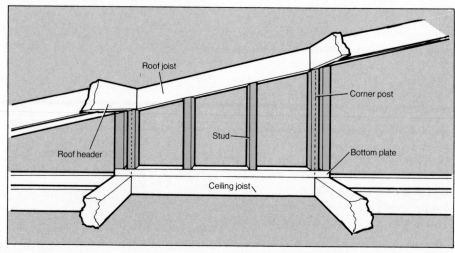

Finish the inside of the light well with wallboard as described on pages 33-40. Trim the opening with molding. If you wish to add a plastic diffusion panel at the bottom of the well, set the molding ½ inch inside the well as a support or use hardware specially designed for the panel.

Making and Installing False Beams

You can change the appearance of a room completely by adding simulated beams across a plain ceiling. If you have added a structural beam when removing a bearing wall to make a room larger, you can disguise its presence by flanking it with simulated beams.

False beams can be purchased, prefabricated in molded plastic that attaches to the ceiling with adhesive, or in wood that has been milled into a U-shaped track with gouges on the outside that look like hand adze marks—and they can be constructed of wood at home. Anyone comfortable with a hammer and saw can fashion false beams with a professional look. Wood false beams can be shaped and stained or painted for different visual effects. They can be scarred and stained for a rough-hewn look, or sanded and painted, or sanded to soften the edges and stained to resemble a time-worn piece of lumber. For the more expert woodworker, a ceiling is a challenge; for instance, a grid of beams crossing at right angles can add elegance to a high ceiling.

Decorative wood beams are attached to tracks mounted on the ceiling surface. Installing wood false beams requires locating the joists in the ceiling, but molded beams can be attached to wallboard or plaster between joists.

BUILDING AND INSTALLING FALSE BEAMS
STEP 1
Measure the ceiling and decide on a plan, spacing the beams evenly. Mark guidelines on facing walls. If you are installing milled wood beams, go to the next step. If you are installing molded beams, run a wavy line of adhesive along the ceiling and set the beams in place—they are light and easy to handle. If you are building beams, use 1 × 4s or 1 × 6s to make the beam itself, gluing and nailing the sides flush with the bottom, either butted or mitered. Set the nails.

STEP 2
There are a great variety of ways to finish a false beam. You can paint it, stain it to look like any of several woods or to look aged, or give it a modern look with a clear finish. If you want a rough-hewn look on a homemade beam, roughen the surface with a rasp before staining. Smooth the corners with sandpaper, a plane, or a rasp, depending on the effect you want. If you are painting, fill cracks and nail holes with wood putty before painting; if you are staining, fill afterward with putty matching the stain.

STEP 3
Find the joists and use 16-penny nails to attach lengths of 2 × 4 or 2 × 6 (the same width as the false beam) on the ceiling as a track across the joists, or along the joists, depending on your plan.

STEP 4
Slip the milled or homemade beam onto the track and attach with nails through the side of the false beam. Set and fill these nails and touch up as necessary.

MAKING AND INSTALLING FALSE BEAMS

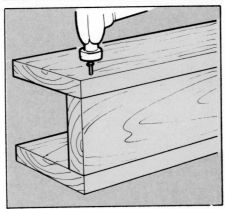

1. Building the beam. Cut three pieces of 1-inch lumber to the desired length and build a long box as shown. Make the joints tight.

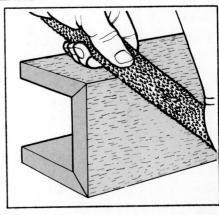

2. Finishing the beam. Roughen the beam with a rasp to give it a rustic appearance; fill cracks and sand it for a modern room.

3. Attaching the tracks. Attach tracks to the ceiling by nailing to the joists above. Have a helper support the tracks while nailing.

4. Attaching the beam. Lift the beams into position on the tracks and nail through the sides of beams into the track.

Repairing Ceiling Damage

Ceiling repairs are similar to wall repairs, but they are easier to accomplish if you have access to the ceiling through a crawl space or an unfinished (or roughly finished) attic. If a ceiling is stained by leaks but is otherwise undamaged, let the ceiling dry, then prime it to hide the stain before repainting.

SMALL HOLES IN WALLBOARD

From above, set a piece of wire mesh or lath overlapping the hole and fix the corners to the wallboard with the same compound you will use to fill the hole. With the mesh secured, fill the hole from below with plaster, building up layers, and finish with joint compound smoothed with a taping knife.

LARGE HOLES IN WALLBOARD

If you have access from above, cut the damaged wallboard back to the edge of the joists on either side of the damage and frame the opening with 1 × 2 as shown. Secure the wallboard patch and tape and plaster the seams.

SMALL HOLES IN PLASTER
STEP 1

From below, either tack metal lath to the existing lath or stuff the hole with newspaper soaked in plaster.

STEP 2

Fill the hole with plaster to within ¼ inch of the surface and allow to dry.

STEP 3

Wet the patch and apply a last coat of finish plaster, smoothing the surface with a straightedge.

FIXING BULGING PLASTER

If you have access from above, prop up the ceiling as shown, carefully pull and scrape out plaster protruding between the laths, wet the old plaster, and fill between laths—forming new ridges over them—with quick-setting plaster.

REPAIRING HOLES IN WALLBOARD

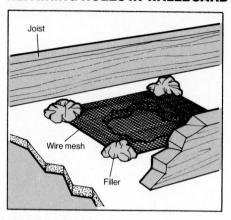

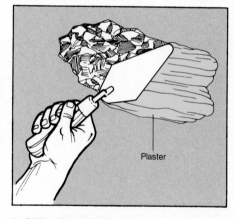

From above, secure mesh with plaster, then fill. If you can't work from above, use method shown on page 44.

Nail the batten frame to the joists so the bottom of the frame is flush with the bottom of the joists.

REPAIRING HOLES IN PLASTER

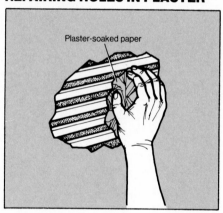

1. Providing a backing. Soak newspaper in plaster, crumple, and stuff between pieces of lath as a foundation for plaster.

2. Filling the hole. Fill hole to just below surface and let it set and recede before applying the finish.

FIXING A BULGE

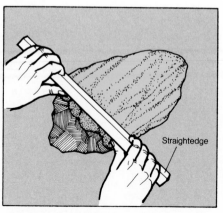

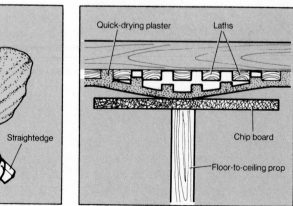

3. Finishing the patch. Apply a finish coat, smooth with a taping knife or straightedge, and feather the edges.

Prop up the bulge with a flat surface larger than the bulge and attach with new plaster from above.

Installing Ceiling Light Fixtures

Interior artificial lighting is categorized as either *general*, which illuminates a room as a whole, or *local*, which lights specific areas. Much general lighting in homes is supplied by ceiling fixtures, as is some local lighting that may be directed at dining room tables or pictures on a wall. Ceiling lights are hung on the ceiling, recessed into it, or hung above it in the case of a suspended ceiling (see page 137).

With the great diversity of bulbs and fixtures available for different purposes—from casting a diffuse light to spotlighting with a focussed beam—the range of possible lighting schemes is endless. On this page there are four fairly simple projects that offer dramatic lighting effects. The next two pages give directions for installing fixtures in ceilings under the various circumstances you are likely to encounter in the average home, followed by directions for running power cable to these installations. Finally there are directions for installing track lighting.

Adding ceiling lights usually involves the two operations of bringing power to the location of the light and installing the fixture. In most situations you must break into existing ceilings, then patch the area after the installation is done. Unfinished ceilings are the easiest to work in; lighting should be carefully planned to take advantage of this before finishing basement or garage ceilings. Ceilings below crawl spaces and unfinished attics are easier than those below finished rooms because joists are exposed. If the attic has rough flooring, it is still easier to open the floor and work from above than to open the ceiling from below. Ceilings under finished rooms must be cut open to give access to a joist, or two joists, depending on the type of ceiling. Running wire to the fixture may also require cutting the ceiling and the wall in a few places to reach a power source.

VALANCES

A valance is a baffle attached to a wall, cabinet, or ceiling to deflect and concentrate light upward or downward and to conceal the light source, which is usually a fluorescent tube. When it directs the light down, as in the example shown at right, it accents the wall and furniture below; when used to deflect light upward, it bounces it off the ceiling for a soft, general lighting effect. A valance can be attached along a wall with nothing to stop the light shining out from the top or bottom to combine these effects. The best results are obtained using distances in the installation that approximate those given in the drawing here.

COVES

A cove baffle to direct light creates indirect, general lighting. The base of the cove is installed not less than 12 inches from the ceiling, parallel to the ceiling and perpendicular to the wall, with the lighting fixture attached to the wall just above the cove base. A second board at least 5 inches wide is attached to the cove base at a 45° angle to deflect the light upward and out, away from the wall and into the room. Two other arrangements for homemade ceiling lighting are shown below.

COVE LIGHTING

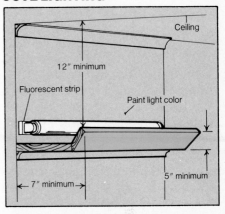

Like a valance on its side, the cove directs light upward and across the ceiling. Build the unit before installing it with angle irons.

LIGHT BOX BETWEEN BEAMS

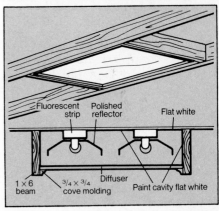

Use 1×6s and a diffuser panel to create a light box in a beamed ceiling. Paint the inside white and install polished reflectors.

VALANCE LIGHTING

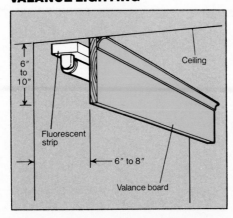

A board hung from the ceiling with angle irons directs light downward. Paint the inside surface white for maximum reflectivity.

LIGHT IN A FALSE BEAM

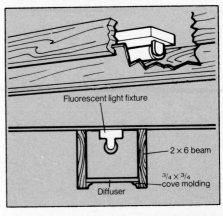

A fluorescent tube hidden in a false beam uses cove moldings to hold a diffuser panel in place. The beams will throw light downward.

INSTALLING A JUNCTION BOX FROM INSIDE AN ATTIC OR CRAWL SPACE
STEP 1

Installing ceiling fixtures is relatively easy when there is no finished floor above the ceiling. If there is no floor at all, lay planks across joists so you can get to the work area. Determine the location on the ceiling where you wish to install the fixture; drill through the ceiling with a 1/8-inch bit to check whether that point is directly below a joist. If you hit a joist, move 2 or 3 inches to either side of the hole and drill again. When you find a point where nothing blocks the way, drill a locator hole with a 3/4-inch bit. If the attic or crawl space has rough flooring, use a 1/8-inch bit on an 18-inch extension to drill an additional hole, up through the floor above as well, and use a piece of wire to mark the spot.

STEP 2

If the space has rough flooring, cut the floorboard 1 inch in from the nails that hold it to the joists on either side. Use a junction box with a flange, if the fixture is to be located within 4 inches of a joist, or a junction box on a bar hanger, if the location is farther from a joist.

STEP 3

Position the box over the locator hole (or as close to it as you can in the case of a flanged box) and trace around it. Mark the corners with drill holes down through the ceiling. Use the same procedures with a bar hanger box, positioning the box over the locator hole.

STEP 4

Connect the drill holes below to outline the box, then cut out the ceiling inside the outline with a keyhole saw. Back upstairs, fit the box through the hole in the ceiling and attach it to the joist (if flanged) or between the joists (if a hanger bar) with screws, marking and then pre-drilling the screw holes.

STEP 5

If you have opened the attic floor, repair it as shown at right.

INSTALLING A JUNCTION BOX FROM ABOVE

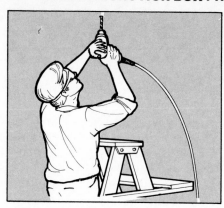

1. Locating the fixture. Drill up through the ceiling to determine that there is no joist in the way, then to mark the location of the box.

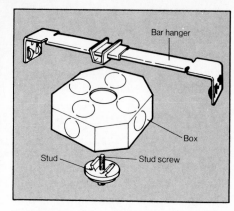

2. Choosing a box. Use a flanged box where the box is close to a joist. Use an adjustable bar hanger for installations between joists.

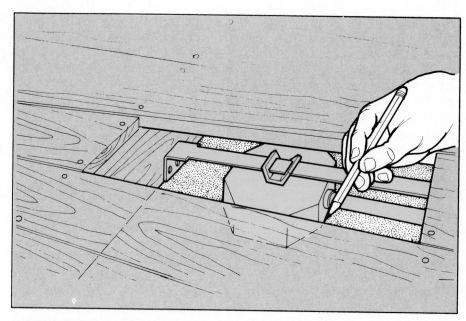

3. Marking for the cut in the ceiling. Outline the box in position and drill holes through the ceiling to mark this outline below. To cut a plaster ceiling, use masking tape along the outside of the outline to keep the plaster from crumbling when you cut.

4. Cutting the ceiling. The box will be seated through the ceiling; make the cut clean to reduce ceiling repair work afterward.

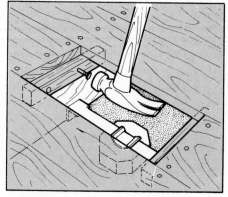

5. Repairing flooring. Use 2 × 3 cleats nailed to joists as shown to support the cut floorboard; nail the floor piece to the cleats.

INSTALLING A JUNCTION BOX FROM BELOW

Where there are finished rooms above a ceiling you must install fixtures from below. Directions for both wallboard and plaster ceilings are given here.

OPENING A WALLBOARD CEILING

Drill a ½-inch hole into the ceiling where you want the fixture; if you hit a joist at this spot, move it a few inches and drill again. Probe through the joists on either side and mark the ceiling along the centers of the joists so that you will be able to nail a patch to the joists. Mark a cut at least 16 inches wide.

OPENING A PLASTER CEILING

Use a hammer and cold chisel to open the ceiling enough to expose a strip of lath running perpendicular to the joists. If you see nails in the lath, you are directly under a joist; no nails indicates that you are between joists. Cut a narrow opening along the piece of lath until it extends slightly beyond the outside edges of a pair of joists. Use a keyhole saw to remove the strip of lath directly above the opening.

INSTALLING AN OFFSET HANGER BAR

Clear away any nails or plaster from the bottom of the joists and use wood screws to attach an offset hanger bar as shown at right.

INSTALLING A JUNCTION BOX IN A WALLBOARD CEILING

Cut a patch for the ceiling. Position the junction box (use either of the boxes shown on the previous page), measure the location, and transfer the outline of the box to the wallboard patch; cut an opening in the patch for the box. Install the box as described on the previous page and nail the patch in place. Finish with tape and joint compound.

CLOSING A PLASTER CEILING

Follow the directions given on page 148 to repair the gap cut in the lath and plaster ceiling.

OPENING A WALLBOARD CEILING

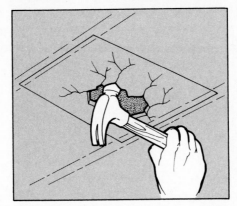

Find an unobstructed point at which to install the box and mark the ceiling for cutting wallboard between joists.

OPENING A PLASTER CEILING

Break into the ceiling to find a strip of lath and follow it to the two joists on either side. Protect ceiling along cut by masking with tape.

INSTALLING BOX WITH AN OFFSET HANGER

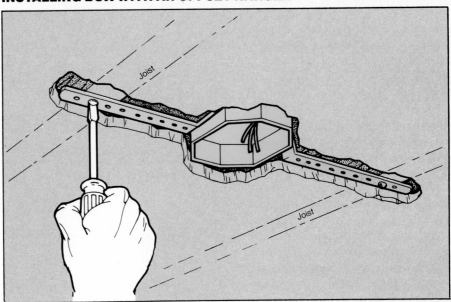

Plaster ceilings do not allow working space between joists; in this kind of ceiling the junction box is attached with an offset hanger bar screwed to the bottoms of the joists. The cut must expose enough of the joists on either side to permit attachment of the bar.

PATCHING WITH WALLBOARD

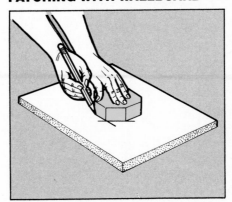

Cut a wallboard patch to fit and cut an opening in it for the junction box. Attach the box and repair the ceiling with the patch.

PATCHING PLASTER

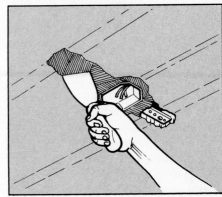

Use wire mesh or crumpled, plaster-soaked newspaper to fill the gap; plaster to within 1/16 inch of surface, then finish.

RUNNING WIRE THROUGH FINISHED WALLS AND CEILINGS

In finished rooms you must cut into the ceiling and wall in a few places and pull power cable through from a switch or power source with fish tape, an item readily available at hardware and electric supply stores.

FISHING WIRE TO AN UNFINISHED ATTIC OR CRAWL SPACE

From above, drill a ³/₄-inch hole through the top plate of the wall (between studs) where the switch or outlet box from which you will run the cable is located. Drop a length of narrow chain through the hole down to the switch or junction box, connect fish tape to the chain, and draw it into the attic. In the attic, attach power cable to the tape and draw it back down to the switch or junction box. Wire to the ceiling box and to the switch or box below.

FISHING WIRE THROUGH FINISHED WALLS AND CEILINGS STEP 1

Cut the wall and ceiling as shown at top right and drill through the studs between the wall outlet and the point where the cable will run across the ceiling. Protect these studs with metal plates (see page 32). Notch the top plate at the point where the cable will pass, so the ceiling can be closed over it. Push the fish tape up the wall toward the cut at the junction of the ceiling and catch the end with another piece of tape to draw it through. Attach the bottom of the tape to cable and pull it up the wall and out through the ceiling cut.

STEP 2

Repeat the operation from the junction box to the ceiling cut, pushing tape along the ceiling until you can catch it at the ceiling cut. Attach the tape to the cable and pull it across the ceiling to the junction box. Pull enough cable into the box to do the necessary wiring; attach the cable to the junction box. Wait until all other work is finished before wiring into house circuit.

FISHING WIRE TO AN UNFINISHED ATTIC

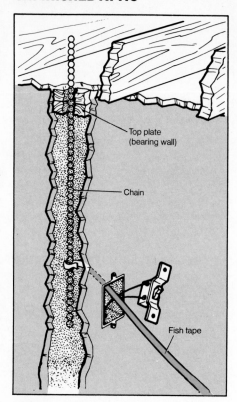

Drill a ³/₄-inch hole through the top plate of the wall through which the cable will run and drop a chain to pull up fish tape.

FISHING WIRE THROUGH A FINISHED WALL AND CEILING

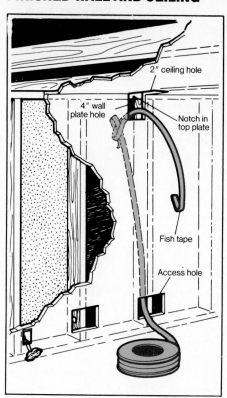

1. Cutting the wall and ceiling. At the junction of the wall and ceiling you must notch the top plate to make room for the cable.

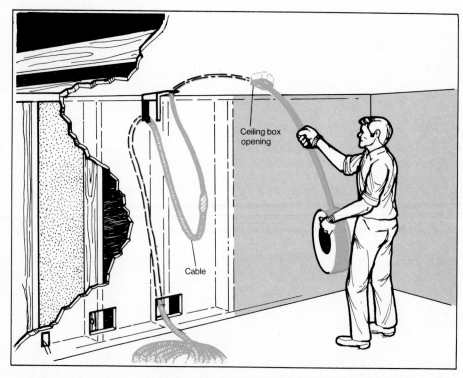

2. Fishing the cable. First catch and pull fish tape up through the wall, then pull cable through the wall with the fish tape. Push the tape through the ceiling box to the opening at the wall, attach to the end of the cable, and pull it through to the ceiling box.

INSTALLING TRACK LIGHTING

There are two basic types of track lighting: one has a line cord that plugs into an outlet, the other is wired directly into a power source installed in the ceiling. The first type is the easier to install because it does not require bringing power to the track. For the best appearance, plan the installation so that only a minimum amount of line cord runs across the ceiling. Follow manufacturer's instructions for installation.

For the type wired directly into a power source in the ceiling, first locate the desired position of the track and follow the procedures given above for installing a junction box in the ceiling. Install the track itself using the procedure given below. *Do all the work with the power in the junction box circuit turned off.*

STEP 1

The track will come with an adapter plate to cover the junction box and hold the track connector and electrical housing in place. Assemble these pieces and then splice like-colored wires together from the track's electrical connector to the wiring in the junction box. Attach the adapter assembly to the junction box with the screws provided in the track kit. With the adapter in place, use a straightedge to draw a line from the center of the mounting slot to the end of the track as a guide for installing the clips that will hold the track to the ceiling.

STEP 2

Drill holes on the line for anchors into which you will drive the screws that hold the clips to the ceiling. Install the anchors and screw the clips to the ceiling.

STEP 3

Connect the track channel to the electrical connector at the junction box. Make sure that the connection is tight. Slip the track onto the track connector and snap the track into the clips. Tighten the screws on the sides of the clips to fix the track in place. Attach the fixtures according to manufacturer's instructions.

INSTALLING TRACK LIGHTING

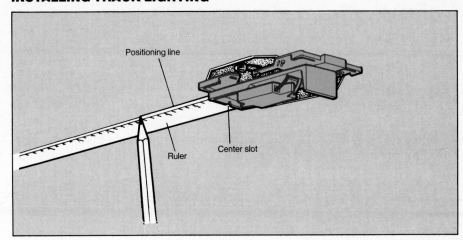

1. Siting the track. Align a straightedge with the center slot on the track connector and draw a line across the ceiling the length of the track. Use a chalkline if the track is long.

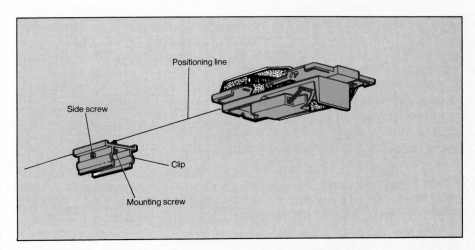

2. Installing the clips. Mark locations for the number of clips called for by the manufacturer's instructions, spaced evenly to the end of the track. Install with anchors.

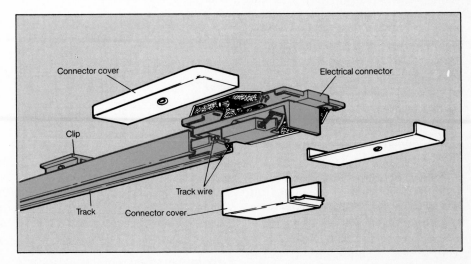

3. Installing the track. The wiring that powers the track light fixtures is built into the track. Push the track firmly into the electrical connector and attach cover plates.

Installing Ceiling Fans

Although it consumes electric power, a ceiling fan can serve as an energy saver. In air-conditioned rooms, the cool air pools on the floor. With the paddles of a slow-turning ceiling fan stirring the air, cool air is distributed throughout the room. Also, moving air seems to make a room cooler. The relatively small amount of power used by the fan achieves the same effect as the much greater amount of power the air conditioner would use if you turned it up in order to cool the room further.

The same is true in heating situations. A room may be comfortable at floor level, but uncomfortably warm near the ceiling—in a sleeping loft or the upper berth of a bunk bed, for instance. A ceiling fan corrects this situation by circulating the rising warm air throughout the room. You need not then burn as much energy to heat the lower part of the room. If you heat with a wood stove, moving the hot air away from the stove with a ceiling fan increases the stove's efficiency by distributing the warmth around the room. It alleviates the problems of a room with an unpleasantly hot zone near the stove and cold air in the rest of the space.

There are a number of features to consider when choosing a ceiling fan: single or variable speed, fixed or moveable paddles, built-in light, one-direction or reversible motor (the latter more expensive but very convenient). Installing a ceiling fan is essentially the same as installing a ceiling light fixture, except that the fan must be more securely anchored on the ceiling. Ceilings must be at least 7 feet high.

Wiring for fans is just like that for light fixtures. A fan can be hung from a box where a light fixture was previously hung, to avoid having to install a new box and to fish-wire to it, so long as the junction box is secure (reinforced, if necessary). If it is a variable-speed fan you will have to change the switch that controls that box to one with multiple positions.

FLUSH MOUNTING

Manufacturer's instructions are specific to each model. The illustrations here show common situations. If you are installing a fan on an unfinished ceiling, or want to take the trouble to cut into a finished ceiling, you can anchor a fan to a joist or header by notching the joist to a depth that brings the edge of the box just flush with the ceiling surface. You can also mount the fan on a block fixed between joists. Follow product instructions—fans of different sizes have different bracing requirements.

FLUSH MOUNTING

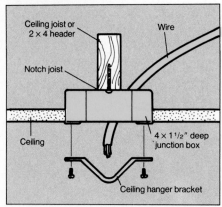

The junction box for a ceiling fan must be attached through the ceiling with wood screws to a joist that has been notched.

SURFACE MOUNTING

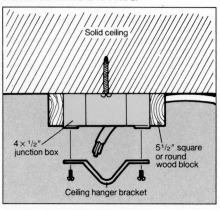

You may also frame around a box mounted directly on the surface, attached to a ceiling joist above. Drill through trim for cable.

SURFACE MOUNTING

To mount a fan flush with the surface, find a joist and attach the box to the joist with 2-inch wood screws through the ceiling. Frame around the box to mask it. Run wire across the ceiling to the box according to applicable building code standards.

HANGING FROM AN ISOLATION MOUNT

The fan will communicate less vibration to the ceiling and run more quietly, if you use an isolation mount in the junction box. Install the mount in the ceiling.

CHECK THE LOCAL CODES

No matter what kind of fan you install, check to be sure that the installation conforms to local electrical codes. When purchasing a fan, verify that it has been tested and approved according to current electrical standards by a recognized laboratory. Call your local electrical inspector if you have any questions.

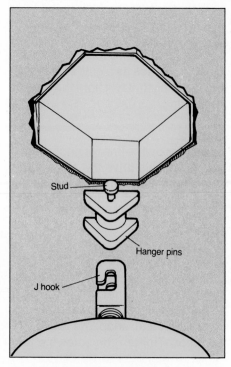

In an isolation mount, the hanger hook fastens over the pins attached to the ceiling.

Glossary

Apron The piece of trim around the interior side of a window that sits below the window stool and supports it.

Baseboard A piece of trim, either plain or milled, installed around a room at the base of the walls to conceal the joints of walls and adjoining floor covering.

Baseboard shoe A narrow piece of trim, usually quarter round, attached to the baseboard at the floor to hide any gaps.

Batten Any small strips of lumber used for bracing, for a rigid guideline, for furring, and for some plank panel walls, among many small jobs.

Batts Short lengths of insulation usually about 4 feet long, sold flat instead of in rolls. Batts are also available with and without paper foil backing.

Beam A horizontal structural member that sits on posts or walls and supports the platform or roof above it.

Bearing wall A wall that supports the floors or roof above it. Where there are floors above, the bearing wall often supports the ends of the joists overlapped to span the width of the structure. If a bearing wall is removed, its load-carrying function must be replaced by a beam.

Building code The rules and regulations governing the acceptable specifications and building types allowed in a city or town. Local building permits are almost always required for new construction or major renovation.

Building paper Also called *felt paper* or *tar paper,* used as a cushion or a moisture barrier between layers in a house, such as between a hardwood floor and the subfloor, or between exterior siding and sheathing.

Carpet stretcher A device that grips the carpet and stretches it either with force applied by the knee (to a knee kicker, a small carpet stretcher) or mechanical force (in a larger power stretcher).

Casing The boards lining the inside of a doorway or window frame, or more broadly, the flat trim nailed around such openings.

Caulking A soft compound for sealing joints against leaks (of water, or air, or noise). It may be silicone, neoprene, or one of a variety of other synthetic compounds.

Ceramic tile Fired clay tile that is hard and may be glazed or unglazed, 1 square inch or smaller to 1 square foot to larger in size, available in a profusion of colors, shapes, patterns, and textures.

Chair rail A piece of molding that runs around a room about 3½ feet above the floor (approximately the height of a chair back). It evolved from wainscoting.

Cleats Structural members that hold larger parts in place.

Collar beam Beams between rafters that tie them together and support the roof; also beams hung between rafters to support a ceiling.

Concrete A mixture of sand or gravel, Portland cement, and water that sets hard. Usually reinforced with wire mesh when poured for basement floors.

Corner bead A rigid metal corner attached to an outside wallboard or plaster corner to strengthen it and to provide a foundation for joint compound in finishing the corner.

Countersink Used with a countersink bit, to bore a beveled opening in a pilot hole that is wide enough to accommodate the head of a flathead screw slightly below the surface when fully driven.

Crawl space An unusable low space, above or below the house, just tall enought to permit such work as jacking up a sagging ground floor from below or installing ceiling fixtures from above.

Cripple stud The shortened stud above a doorway or window. It maintains the structural integrity of the wall and provides a nailing surface for wall coverings.

Cross bridging Diagonal braces between joists that keep them from bending out of line. Single diagonal braces are called *bridging;* they may be wood or metal.

Darby A flat, wide board with a handle used for the first smoothing of concrete just after it has been poured. These can be rented.

Diffusion panel A translucent piece of plastic under a light fixture or skylight that admits light, but masks what is above.

Double header A header double the thickness of the rafters or joists it is attached to. Used for long spans.

Filter mask A device to cover the nose and mouth to prevent the inhalation of dust and dangerous particles in the air.

Fish tape Flat, flexible metal tape used for pulling wiring through walls where there is no easy access behind the wall surface.

Flashing Strips of thin metal attached to a roof or at the junction of a roof with such structures as a chimney or a skylight, to prevent leaks.

Floorboard A board in a wood floor. Floorboards may be milled or not and are various lengths and widths.

Footing The concrete base supporting foundations, chimneys, and such structural members as posts.

Framing The process of building a house, or walls within a house, from wood in the form of a framework to support wall, floor, and ceiling.

Furring The process of leveling parts of a ceiling, wall, or floor by means of wood strips called *furring strips,* before adding the finish surface.

Glazier's points Small wedges of metal most commonly used to hold a pane of glass in a window frame; also used for various other small repairs.

Girder A main beam, usually running the length of a structure, that supports the floor joists and is itself supported by a post (or posts) in mid-span and at either end by the foundation.

Hardboard Sheet material composed of wood fibers compressed at high heat. The resulting material is quite hard.

Header A structural member, running at right angles to joists and rafters and connecting to the rest of the framework, at such openings as those for skylights, doorways, or stairways.

I-beam A steel beam that in cross section looks like a capital I. Used to span distances greater than wood beams can support.

Jack rafter A rafter shorter than full length, cut for the installation of a skylight, for example.

Jack stud A stud in a doorway or below a window, that does not reach the top plate.

Jamb The vertical inside face of a door or window opening.

Joint compound A thick, spreadable substance that dries hard and can be finished like plaster. It is used to fill the seams between sheets of wallboard and for small repairs to damaged plaster or wallboard walls.

Joist A horizontal structural member that supports a floor and a ceiling in the case of middle floors, and a ceiling alone in the case of a top floor. Joists are often tied together with cross bridging for extra rigidity.

Knee wall A wall built under a sloping roof that does not reach to the height of the ceiling.

Lath A strip of wood used as a foundation for plaster walls and ceilings. Laths are nailed close together but not touching. Plaster oozes through the cracks between laths to anchor the surface.

Masonry Any construction of bricks, concrete, or stone.

Molding Various types of wood used for decorative or practical trim. Molding styles range from flat lath to ornately carved, grooved, or stamped picture-frame moldings. It is usually applied to conceal joints of dissimilar surfaces.

Nailer An extra piece of wood added to a framework to provide a nailing surface for all edges of something (usually a sheet of wallboard or paneling) to be attached.

On center A phrase designating the distance between the centers of regularly-spaced holes, or such parts as studs in a wall.

Particle board Inexpensive sheet material composed of wood chips, or particles, and adhesive pressed into sheets. Fairly brittle and not as easy to nail through as wood.

Partition A wall that divides space but plays no part in the structural integrity of a building.

Pilot hole A hole drilled to make it easier to drive screws into wood. Pilot holes are drilled slightly narrower than the diameter of the screw to be used.

Plaster A mixture of sand, lime, and water of a consistency that can be applied to a wall or ceiling with a trowel. Various plasters have different uses, such as for patching holes, or for finishing a smooth surface.

Plate A horizontal member, at the top or bottom of a wall, to which the studs are fixed; either top plate or bottom plate may be doubled.

Prehung door A door that is delivered from the factory already hung in its casing so that it need only be attached to the doorway.

Rafter A structural member that supports a pitched roof, serving for the roof sheathing the same purpose as joists for floors.

Riser The vertical facing of a step in a staircase where the steps have been closed in.

Roof sheathing The material, usually boards or sheets of plywood, attached to the top surface of the rafters as a foundation for such roofing material as shingles.

Roofing cement A synthetic or tar-based waterproof substance used to seal joints, cracks, or holes in a roof.

Row running cutter A knife for cutting carpeting that follows the rows of pile.

Saddle The strip under a door that joins the floors of two rooms by concealing the seam between them.

Sash The frame which holds the glass in a window. In either a casement window or one that slides up and down, the sash is the part that moves.

Screed Forms on stakes driven into the ground that serve as a guide for leveling a concrete floor.

Shims Thin wood wedges used for tightening the fit between pieces, as when they fill the gap between the top plate and joists in new wall construction, or for leveling strips of furring over an uneven surface.

Shiplap A milling treatment for the edges of boards that results in one board overlapping the next along one edge when they are joined. Used often in plank paneling.

Sleepers Boards laid over a concrete floor as a foundation for the subflooring of a new floor.

Spacer block A piece of lumber used between larger attached members to maintain a uniform separation (for instance, between two studs at the outside corner of a frame wall). Also called a *filler block.*

Stain Any of various forms of water-, latex-, or oil-based coloring agents, transparent or opaque, designed to penetrate the surface of wood.

Starter hole A hole drilled inside the outline of a shape to be cut out of a sheet of material (such as wallboard, to accommodate an electrical outlet) to permit inserting a saber saw, coping saw, or keyhole saw blade to make the cut.

Stud Vertical member of a frame wall, usually placed at either end and one every 16 inches on center to facilitate covering with standard-width wallboard or paneling. May be 2×3, 2×4, 2×6 depending on the structural requirements of the wall.

Subfloor The floor surface below a finished floor. Usually made of sheet material like plywood, in older houses it is likely to consist of diagonally attached boards.

Sump A hold dug in the lowest corner of a basement to collect water from the floor so that it can be pumped away.

Tack cloth A piece of cheese cloth or other lint-free cloth treated with turpentine and a small amount of varnish to produce a tacky surface that picks up and holds dust and lint.

Tackless strip A thin strip of wood or metal in which many small, sharp teeth are imbedded to grip the edges of a wall-to-wall carpet when they are hooked over the teeth. The strip is nailed down; it takes its name from the amount of tacking it eliminates from carpet installation.

Tongue and groove The milling treatment of the edges of a board resulting in a protruding tongue on one side and groove the same size on the other. For the purpose of joining several boards.

Underlayment A smooth surface laid down to receive another surface, such as sheets of plywood under a ceramic tile floor.

Vapor barrier Either plastic sheeting or the sealed side of fiberglass insulation installed beneath a wall's surface as a waterproof barrier to keep moisture from within a room from condensing and causing rot inside walls or under the roof.

Wainscot Paneling that reaches from the floor to about one third the height of a wall, capped with molding.

Wallboard Also known as gypsum board, drywall, and plasterboard, a paper covered sandwich of gypsum plaster used as the primary wall covering in almost all homes. It can be finished to look like a plaster wall, or used to support other wall coverings.

Window stool Molding that connects the window sill with the interior of a room, often referred to erroneously as the window sill.

Wood rasp A hand tool used to shape rough edges or curves in wood.

Index

Picture Credits

We wish to extend our thanks to the individuals, associations, and manufacturers who graciously provided photographs for this book.

American Olean Tile Co. 1000 Cannon Ave., PO Box 271, Lansdale, PA 19446-0271. 12 top left, 75 top left, 76 top, 122, 123 top left, 123 bottom

David Arky 57 W. 19 St., New York, NY 10011. 69, 70, 71

Armstrong World Industries, Inc. PO Box 3001, Lancaser, PA 17604. 9, 10, 13, 125 top left

Bristol Fiberlite Industries 401 E. Goetz Ave., PO Box 2515, Santa Ana, CA 92707. 8 top and bottom left and right, 11 bottom left, 126-127

Congoleum Corp. 195 Belgrove Dr., Kearny, NJ 07032. 124, 125 top right

Crane Co. 300 Park Ave., New York, NY 10022. 75 bottom, 123 top right

DG Shelter Products Box 610, Marion, VA 24354. 73 top left and right

Theodore Drum, Sharon, CT 06069. 69, 70, 71

Georgia-Pacific Corp. 133 Peachtree St. N.E., Atlanta, GA 30303. 12 bottom left, 73 bottom.

Hoyne Mirrors/Hoyne Industries, Inc. 840 Highway 155 S., PO Box 697, McDonough, GA 30253. 77 top and bottom

Levelor Lorentzen, Inc. 1280 Wall St. W., Lyndhurst, NJ 07071. 11 bottom right, 125 bottom

Masonite Corp., Eastern Hardboard Division PO Box 311, Towanda, PA 18848. 78-79, 120 top, 120 bottom left, 121

Stratford Co. c/o Hayes-Williams, 475 Park Ave. S., New York, NY 10016. Title page, 14-15

Ulrich Inc. c/o David Ulrich, 100 Chestnut St., Ridgewood, NJ 07450. 11 top

Wall-Tex, Columbus Coated Fabrics 1280 N. Grant Ave., Columbus, OH 43126. 69, 70, 71

Warwick Photo Bank Street, Warwick, NY 10990. 65, 66, 67, 115, 116

Russell T. Welchman Warwick, NY 10990. 118,119

Weyerhauser Co. Paneling Division Headquarters, PO Box 1188, Chesapeake, VA 23320. 74 top, 74 bottom left and right

Tom Yee, 114 East 25th Street, New York, NY 10010

LUMBER

Sizes: Metric cross-sections are so close to their nearest Imperial sizes, as noted below, that for most purposes they may be considered equivalents.

Lengths: Metric lengths are based on a 300mm module which is slightly shorter in length than an Imperial foot. It will therefore be important to check your requirements accurately to the nearest inch and consult the table below to find the metric length required.

Areas: The metric area is a square metre. Use the following conversion factors when converting from Imperial data: 100 sq. feet = 9.290 sq. metres.

METRIC SIZES SHOWN BESIDE NEAREST IMPERIAL EQUIVALENT

mm	Inches	mm	Inches
16 x 75	⅝ x 3	44 x 150	1¾ x 6
16 x 100	⅝ x 4	44 x 175	1¾ x 7
16 x 125	⅝ x 5	44 x 200	1¾ x 8
16 x 150	⅝ x 6	44 x 225	1¾ x 9
19 x 75	¾ x 3	44 x 250	1¾ x 10
19 x 100	¾ x 4	44 x 300	1¾ x 12
19 x 125	¾ x 5	50 x 75	2 x 3
19 x 150	¾ x 6	50 x 100	2 x 4
22 x 75	⅞ x 3	50 x 125	2 x 5
22 x 100	⅞ x 4	50 x 150	2 x 6
22 x 125	⅞ x 5	50 x 175	2 x 7
22 x 150	⅞ x 6	50 x 200	2 x 8
25 x 75	1 x 3	50 x 225	2 x 9
25 x 100	1 x 4	50 x 250	2 x 10
25 x 125	1 x 5	50 x 300	2 x 12
25 x 150	1 x 6	63 x 100	2½ x 4
25 x 175	1 x 7	63 x 125	2½ x 5
25 x 200	1 x 8	63 x 150	2½ x 6
25 x 225	1 x 9	63 x 175	2½ x 7
25 x 250	1 x 10	63 x 200	2½ x 8
25 x 300	1 x 12	63 x 225	2½ x 9
32 x 75	1¼ x 3	75 x 100	3 x 4
32 x 100	1¼ x 4	75 x 125	3 x 5
32 x 125	1¼ x 5	75 x 150	3 x 6
32 x 150	1¼ x 6	75 x 175	3 x 7
32 x 175	1¼ x 7	75 x 200	3 x 8
32 x 200	1¼ x 8	75 x 225	3 x 9
32 x 225	1¼ x 9	75 x 250	3 x 10
32 x 250	1¼ x 10	75 x 300	3 x 12
32 x 300	1¼ x 12	100 x 100	4 x 4
38 x 75	1½ x 3	100 x 150	4 x 6
38 x 100	1½ x 4	100 x 200	4 x 8
38 x 125	1½ x 5	100 x 250	4 x 10
38 x 150	1½ x 6	100 x 300	4 x 12
38 x 175	1½ x 7	150 x 150	6 x 6
38 x 200	1½ x 8	150 x 200	6 x 8
38 x 225	1½ x 9	150 x 300	6 x 12
44 x 75	1¾ x 3	200 x 200	8 x 8
44 x 100	1¾ x 4	250 x 250	10 x 10
44 x 125	1¾ x 5	300 x 300	12 x 12

METRIC LENGTHS

Lengths Metres	Equiv. Ft. & Inches
1.8m	5' 10⅞"
2.1m	6' 10⅝"
2.4m	7' 10½"
2.7m	8' 10¼"
3.0m	9' 10⅛"
3.3m	10' 9⅞"
3.6m	11' 9¾"
3.9m	12' 9½"
4.2m	13' 9⅜"
4.5m	14' 9⅓"
4.8m	15' 9"
5.1m	16' 8¾"
5.4m	17' 8⅝"
5.7m	18' 8⅜"
6.0m	19' 8¼"
6.3m	20' 8"
6.6m	21' 7⅞"
6.9m	22' 7⅝"
7.2m	23' 7½"
7.5m	24' 7¼"
7.8m	25' 7⅛"

All the dimensions are based on 1 inch = 25 mm.

NOMINAL SIZE (This is what you order.)	ACTUAL SIZE (This is what you get.)
Inches	Inches
1 x 1	¾ x ¾
1 x 2	¾ x 1½
1 x 3	¾ x 2½
1 x 4	¾ x 3½
1 x 6	¾ x 5½
1 x 8	¾ x 7¼
1 x 10	¾ x 9¼
1 x 12	¾ x 11¼
2 x 2	1¾ x 1¾
2 x 3	1½ x 2½
2 x 4	1½ x 3½
2 x 6	1½ x 5½
2 x 8	1½ x 7¼
2 x 10	1½ x 9¼
2 x 12	1½ x 11¼

WOOD SCREWS

SCREW GAUGE NO.	NOMINAL DIAMETER		LENGTH	
	Inch	mm	Inch	mm
0	0.060	1.52	³/₁₆	4.8
1	0.070	1.78	¼	6.4
2	0.082	2.08	⁵/₁₆	7.9
3	0.094	2.39	⅜	9.5
4	0.0108	2.74	⁷/₁₆	11.1
5	0.122	3.10	½	12.7
6	0.136	3.45	⅝	15.9
7	0.150	3.81	¾	19.1
8	0.164	4.17	⅞	22.2
9	0.178	4.52	1	25.4
10	0.192	4.88	1¼	31.8
12	0.220	5.59	1½	38.1
14	0.248	6.30	1¾	44.5
16	0.276	7.01	2	50.8
18	0.304	7.72	2¼	57.2
20	0.332	8.43	2½	63.5
24	0.388	9.86	2¾	69.9
28	0.444	11.28	3	76.2
32	0.5	12.7	3¼	82.6
			3½	88.9
			4	101.6
			4½	114.3
			5	127.0
			6	152.4

Dimensions taken from BS1210; metric conversions are approximate.

BRICKS AND BLOCKS

Bricks

Standard metric brick measures 215 mm x 65 mm x 112.5. Metric brick can be used with older, standard brick by increasing the mortaring in the joints. The sizes are substantially the same, the metric brick being slightly smaller (3.6 mm less in length, 1.8 mm in width, and 1.2 mm in depth).

Concrete Block

Standard sizes

390 x 90 mm
390 x 190 mm
440 x 190 mm
440 x 215 mm
440 x 290 mm

Repair block for replacement of block in old installations is available in these sizes:
448 x 219 (including mortar joints)
397 x 194 (including mortar joints)

NAILS

NUMBER PER POUND OR KILO

Size	Weight Unit	Common	Casing	Box	Finishing
2d	Pound	876	1010	1010	1351
	Kilo	1927	2222	2222	2972
3d	Pound	586	635	635	807
	Kilo	1289	1397	1397	1775
4d	Pound	316	473	473	548
	Kilo	695	1041	1041	1206
5d	Pound	271	406	406	500
	Kilo	596	893	893	1100
6d	Pound	181	236	236	309
	Kilo	398	591	519	680
7d	Pound	161	210	210	238
	Kilo	354	462	462	524
8d	Pound	106	145	145	189
	Kilo	233	319	319	416
9d	Pound	96	132	132	172
	Kilo	211	290	290	398
10d	Pound	69	94	94	121
	Kilo	152	207	207	266
12d	Pound	64	88	88	113
	Kilo	141	194	194	249
16d	Pound	49	71	71	90
	Kilo	108	156	156	198
20d	Pound	31	52	52	62
	Kilo	68	114	114	136
30d	Pound	24	46	46	
	Kilo	53	101	101	
40d	Pound	18	35	35	
	Kilo	37	77	77	
50d	Pound	14			
	Kilo	31			
60d	Pound	11			
	Kilo	24			

LENGTH AND DIAMETER IN INCHES AND CENTIMETERS

Size	Inches	Length Centimeters	Diameter Inches	Centimeters*
2d	1	2.5	.068	.17
3d	1/2	3.2	.102	.26
4d	1/4	3.8	.102	.26
5d	1/6	4.4	.102	.26
6d	2	5.1	.115	.29
7d	2/2	5.7	.115	.29
8d	2/4	6.4	.131	.33
9d	2/6	7.0	.131	.33
10d	3	7.6	.148	.38
12d	3/2	8.3	.148	.38
16d	3/4	8.9	.148	.38
20d	4	10.2	.203	.51
30d	4/4	11.4	.220	.58
40d	5	12.7	.238	.60
50d	5/4	14.0	.257	.66
60d	6	15.2	.277	.70

*Exact conversion

PIPE FITTINGS

Only fittings for use with copper pipe are affected by metrication: metric compression fittings are interchangeable with Imperial in some sizes, but require adaptors in others.

INTERCHANGEABLE SIZES		SIZES REQUIRING ADAPTORS	
mm	Inches	mm	Inches
12	⅜	22	¾
15	½	35	1¼
28	1	42	1½
54	2		

Metric capillary (soldered) fittings are not directly interchangeable with imperial sizes but adaptors are available. Pipe fittings which use screwed threads to make the joint remain unchanged. The British Standard Pipe (BSP) thread form has now been accepted internationally and its dimensions will not physically change. These screwed fittings are commonly used for joining iron or steel pipes, for connections on taps, basin and bath waste outlets and on boilers, radiators, pumps etc. Fittings for use with lead pipe are joined by soldering and for this purpose the metric and inch sizes are interchangeable.
(Information courtesy Metrication Board, Millbank Tower, Millbank, London SW1P 4QU)